Konrad H. Jarausch, Christian F. Ostermann, Andreas Etges (Eds.)

The Cold War

The Cold War

Historiography, Memory, Representation

Edited by
Konrad H. Jarausch, Christian F. Ostermann,
and Andreas Etges

ISBN 978-3-11-049522-5
e-ISBN (PDF) 978-3-11-049617-8
e-ISBN (EPUB) 978-3-11-049267-5

Library of Congress Cataloging-in-Publication Data
A CIP catalog record for this book has been applied for at the Library of Congress.

Bibliografische Information der Deutschen Nationalbibliothek
The Deutsche Nationalbibliothek lists this publication in the Deutsche Nationalbibliographie; detailed bibliographic data are available in the Internet at http://dnb.dnb.de.

Cover Image: BlackBox Cold War – Exhibition at Checkpoint Charlie, Berlin.
Typesetting: Dr. Rainer Ostermann, München
Printing: CPI books GmbH, Leck
♾ Printed on acid free paper
Printed in Germany

www.degruyter.com

Acknowledgements

This volume grew out of an international conference on the history, memory and representation of the Cold War in Berlin. The editors would like to thank the following co-sponsors: the Berlin city government, the European Academy Berlin, the German Historical Institutes in Moscow, London, and Washington, the Centre for Contemporary History in Potsdam, the Military History Research Institute in Potsdam, the Allied Museum in Berlin, the German-Russian Museum Berlin-Karlshorst, the Berlin Wall Foundation, the Airlift Gratitude Foundation (Stiftung Luftbrückendank) in Berlin, and the John F. Kennedy Institute for North American Studies of the Freie Universität Berlin. The Woodrow Wilson Center's Cold War International History Project in Washington also co-sponsored the conference and, through an additional grant, made this publication possible. In addition, we would like to thank Andrea Despot from the European Academy as well as the student assistants, secretaries, and interns who helped make the conference a success, Pieter Biersteker and others for their invaluable help during the proofreading and, finally, Elise Wintz and her colleagues at de Gruyter for their assistance in finally bringing this work to publication.

DOI 10.1515/783110496178-202

Contents

Konrad H. Jarausch, Christian F. Ostermann and Andreas Etges

Rethinking, Representing, and Remembering the Cold War: Some Cultural Perspectives

A quarter century ago, the fall of the Berlin Wall, heralded the definite end of the Cold War, confronting the United States and the Soviet Union and their respective camps. Most Red Army installations in East Germany are defunct, grass is growing over former parade grounds, and fences around areas with buried ammunition are rusting away. The Eastern military alliance of the Warsaw Pact has been dissolved and most of its former Central European member states have now joined the North Atlantic Treaty Organization. Though embers of the conflict still smolder, particularly in Asia where the Cold War intersected with decolonization and turned violently hot, the arms race has stopped and concern has shifted to preventing nuclear proliferation to Iran or North Korea. Not only has the Soviet empire crumbled, but the Communist regime that controlled Russia since the Bolshevik revolution in 1917 no longer exists, eliminating one side of the East-West conflict. The other protagonist, the U.S., has found out in wars in Iraq and Afghanistan that the transition to a multipolar world is no less complicated. While tensions between Washington and Moscow have reemerged in recent years as a central dynamic of international relations (especially after Russia's seizure of Crimea), leading commentators occasionally proclaim the beginning of a "new Cold War," the new confrontation lacks the Cold War's ideological and potentially globally destructive underpinnings.[1]

It is astounding how rapidly the ideological and political-military confrontation that dominated world politics in the second half of the twentieth century has faded into oblivion, especially in Western Europe. The personal fear, engendered by civil defense drills and exhortations to build fall-out shelters, has completely disappeared. Soviet and East German Army uniforms that once struck terror into the hearts of travelers crossing the Iron Curtain in Berlin are now on sale by street hawkers, offering shiny medals to tourists. While memories of crises fade among the eyewitnesses, an entire generation has grown up in the meantime for whom Berlin or Cuba are but geographical expressions, lacking the sense of danger that pushed the world to the brink of nuclear annihilation. Since 9/11 the threat of international terrorism and the confrontation with Islamic radicalism have replaced

1 David Martin on the "New Cold War" on CBS Sixty Minutes, September 26, 2016 and Scott Wilson, "Obama Will Make Public Case for Unity with Europe as Russia Revives Cold War Memories," *Washington Post*, March 26, 2014.

DOI 10.1515/9783110496178-001

Communism as chief adversary in Western minds.[2] The transition to a "new world (dis-)order" has dimmed the joy over the peaceful revolution in Eastern Europe but created a sense of closure which places the Cold War clearly into the past.

Echoes of the Cold War, referring to the Crisis over Ukraine and to China's rise within the global system, reveal rather conflicted and simplistic memories of the East-West struggle, depending upon personal experience and political agenda. Some observers recall the Cold War as a period of frightful and perpetual crises between the rivaling superpowers, endangering the survival of mankind, while other commentators recollect the period as an era of extraordinary stability due to superpower hegemony. Similarly, anti-Communists emphasize the repressive nature of the Eastern bloc, though post-Socialist defenders of the prior regimes stress their predictability and order. While former dissidents tell stories of heroic protest within, erstwhile members of the security apparatus still claim that the Soviet system was toppled by subversion from without. Once excited about leading the grand social experiment of Communism, some intellectuals tend to portray the Cold War as a time of ideological commitment, while ordinary citizens rather remember the shortages of consumer goods and the lack of international travel. Often unexamined, such partial memories stand next to each other without yet coalescing into a convincing understanding of the Cold War as a whole, or worse, may lead to dangerous assumptions underlying political perceptions and policy decisions.[3]

As a result of such mixed associations, narratives of the ending of the Cold War also continue to differ between Western triumphalism and Eastern defensiveness. In the West, hardliners tend to emphasize the effect of the costly arms race and attribute their victory to President Ronald Reagan's staunch anti-Communism as well as his "Star Wars" (Strategic Defense Initiative) initiative. Liberals instead prefer to attribute the peaceful revolution to the attractiveness of capitalist consumer goods as well as to its support of human rights that helped undermine the dictatorships.[4] In the East, post-Communist defenders of the prior regime blame the mistaken policies of Mikhail Gorbachev for leading to the dissolution of the Soviet Union, while erstwhile dissidents rather stress their own contribution to the civic contestations that overthrew the party rule. Such one-

2 Samuel P. Huntington, *The Clash of Civilizations and the Remaking of World Order* (New York: Simon & Schuster 1996).

3 See Geir Lundestad, ed., *International Relations since the End of the Cold War: New and Old Dimensions* (Oxford: Oxford University Press 2013).

4 See the controversial volume, edited by Ellen Schrecker, *Cold War Triumphalism: The Misuse of History after the Fall of Communism* (New York: New Press, 2004).

sided understandings, repeated in the popular media during relevant anniversaries, fail to do justice to the enormous complexity, multidimensional nature, and interactive character of the East-West conflict.

Coming to grips with the Cold War requires its historicization not just among scholars but also the general public.[5] While key participants have written lengthy memoirs, much of the archival documentation has also become available on the Eastern side, thanks in part to the Cold War International History Project at the Woodrow Wilson International Center for Scholars in Washington. The realization that the Soviet-American confrontation is finally over makes it possible to step outside the mind-set of the two combatants and treat the period truly as having become part of the past. Such a process of distancing can surely be observed in Western film productions. In the much acclaimed TV series "The Americans" (2013–) which is set in Washington in the 1980s, during the Second Cold War, a Soviet KGB couple lives with their two "American" kids under false identities in the US, fighting a literally deadly war against the attempts of the Reagan administration to destroy the "evil empire." In "Deutschland 83" (2015), an internationally successful eight-episode German TV production, an East German spy living in West Germany informs about Western military planning and "Able Archer 83," a major NATO exercise that some in the East believed was the cover for a first strike on the Soviet Union. Steven Spielberg's movie "Bridge of Spies" (2015), set during another major time of confrontation between the superpowers in 1960, tells the story of the most famous prisoner exchange on Glienecker Brücke between West Berlin and Potsdam in East Germany, where the Soviet spy Rudolf Abel was exchanged for U-2 pilot Francis Gary Powers. In those three cases Cold War America and its Western Allies are not shown as the by definition superior places, and the main Soviet and East German characters are portrayed with a lot of sympathy. That might also be due in part to a certain nostalgia regarding the good old (bad) days of the Cold War, when the lines were clearly drawn, but when the enemy was also acting according to certain rules.

Finally, the recent methodological shifts of the historical discipline towards constructivism and cultural analysis make it possible to probe a wide range of public representations and to engage individual as well as collective memories. David Lowe and Tony Joel have made a first and highly readable attempt to highlight main features of how the Cold War has been remembered internationally, in North America, Europe, Asia and Australia. They discuss "the bomb," atomic culture and bunkers, cities like Vilnius, Prague, Budapest and Warsaw, and Hanoi,

---

5 For the concept of historicization see Konrad H. Jarausch and Michael Geyer, *Shattered Past: Reconstructing German Histories* (Princeton: Princeton University Press, 2003), 1–33.

museums and memorials, spies, textbooks and other things. What the authors sometimes lack in depth, they surely make up in breadth.[6] Our volume intends to further this ongoing process of critical reflection on the history, memory, and representation of the Cold War. In contrast to Lowe and Joel, it presents a set of international essays, written by experts in their respective fields.

Historiography

Writing about the Cold War after its end has liberated historical scholarship from the politicization it had endured – not just in the East, where it had been in the service of the Communist party, but also in the United States where Cold War history was all too often the academic extension of a debate over American foreign policy. With the hindsight of two-and-a-half decades after the end of the confrontation, the twists and turns of Cold War historiography in the United States, from the orthodox school in the 1950s that defended US containment strategy, to the Vietnam era revisionist critique that saw often economically motivated machinations, to the 1970s post-revisionist synthesis, seem less dramatic: They all shared a singular obsession with finding fault for the ongoing conflict, often focusing on America's role in it. The "new" Cold War history since 1989/91 has started to shed this focus on the "blame game" by exploring other issues, such as the impact of ideology and ideas, the vagaries of alliance politics and the idiosyncrasies of junior partners, and more broadly the significance of individual actors, the international system structure, and the role of sheer contingency.[7]

Increasing temporal distance has initiated a shift from arguing *within* to reflecting *about* the Cold War that is revealing the underlying interactive pattern. Instead of focusing either on "Communist aggression" or "capitalist imperialism," post-Cold War historiography approaches the struggle between the superpowers as a process of mutual escalation. Rather than repeating moral condemnations, the new scholarship analyzes the clashing aims and competing interests of the two blocs which led to conflicting strategies: Incompatible ideologies tended to foster misperceptions which encouraged the demonization of the respective enemy. These fears of subversion prompted the suppression of dissi-

6 David Lowe and Tony Joel, *Remembering the Cold War: Global Contest and National Stories* (New York: Routledge, 2013).

7 Melvyn P. Leffler and Odd Arne Westad, eds., *The Cambridge History of the Cold War* (Cambridge: Cambridge University Press, 2010), 3 vols.; Petra Goedde and Richard Immerman, eds., *The Oxford Handbook of the Cold War* (Oxford: Oxford University Press, 2013).

dence at home and hostile actions abroad that reinforced a sense of danger which required undertaking enormous armaments. Fortunately, Europe escaped large-scale bloodshed, but Asia, Africa and Latin America paid a terrible price in proxy wars, civil strife and insurgencies. Without relativizing the difference between dictatorship and democracy, this emerging research is redefining the conflict as an interaction, promoted by both sides.[8]

An important impulse for historicizing the Cold War has been the unprecedented release of archival documentation of the main actors in the conflict. While the United States accelerated its declassification of Cold War era documents in the 1990s, the demise of the communist regimes and the democratic transitions in Eastern Europe and Russia threw open archival doors that had been firmly closed by party-state control in the former Warsaw Pact. This archival revolution was uneven and witnessed setbacks with renewed narrowing due to the authoritarianism in Russia, highly charged political controversies over the communist legacies in Eastern Europe, and security concerns in post-September 11 America. Yet the new documentation was essential for overcoming Cold War era historiography's limitation, characterized by "one hand clapping" due to an almost exclusive reliance on American and West European sources which often reduced Soviet and Communist actors to superficial caricature.[9] Now the story could be told from both or rather many sides, making it international in perspective and interactive in its dynamic.

Since the mid-2000s, the opening of access to documents from the PRC Foreign Ministry has also brought China's role in the rise and fall of the Cold War system into sharper relief. This fresh evidence broadened the Cold War lens to the global south, where local and regional players and tensions influenced the East-West struggle as much as they were affected by it. In this global Cold War, American and Soviet policies appear as rival versions of European modernity that struggled with each other to often violent effect in Third World countries. Recent trends in Cold War research focus on South-South relations, manifested most concretely in the Non-Aligned movement, and, in the direction of transnational approaches, on the role of non-state (sometimes domestic) actors that transcended, undermined and fortified the Cold War "system."[10] In terms of periodization, the 1970s, marked by detente and economic shifts, are emerging as the crucial decade in the

---

8 Cf. Melvyn P. Leffler, *For the Soul of Mankind: The United States, the Soviet Union, and the Cold War* (New York: Hill and Wang, 2007).

9 See the stream of documentary disclosures in the Cold War International History Project Digital Archive at www.cwihp.org.

10 Odd Arne Westad, ed., *Reviewing the Cold War: Approaches, Interpretations, and Theory* (London: Frank Cass, 2000); see also idem, *The Global Cold War: Third World Interventions and the Making of Our Times* (Cambridge: Cambridge University Press, 2005).

transformation of the polarized structure and its legacies for today. Nonetheless, entire swaths of the globe, from the Middle East to parts of Latin American and South and Southeast Asia remain largely underdeveloped in terms of historical coverage, due in no small measure to the continued lack of archival access. Even a quarter century after the Cold War's end, its historicization as a global conflict still remains a work in progress.

The globalization of approaches to the Cold War has, ironically, also raised new questions about the role of Europe in the East-West conflict. Much of the traditional literature treated the confrontation as a "grand game" between Washington and Moscow, in which the rival superpowers were the only relevant actors globally while their allies were reduced to the role of simple pawns.[11] No doubt, many contemporaries shared this conviction, and confrontations such as the Cuban Missile Crisis reinforced the notion that the Europeans had little impact on crucial decisions. But such a top down view misses the repeated and complex efforts of European countries to reassert some degree of input, agency, in some cases even independence within and between the conformity of the blocs, from Tito's break with Moscow and his later nonaligned initiatives to de Gaulle's withdrawal from the NATO command structure. Not surprisingly the Washington-Moscow perspective also had and continues to have difficulties in dealing with German *Ostpolitik*, the reconciliation between Bonn and its Eastern neighbors which helped lay the foundation for the Helsinki Conference on Security and Cooperation in Europe.[12] Much of the recent European scholarship therefore seeks to bring the efforts of the old continent to overcome the confrontation back into the picture.

The new emphasis on social and cultural questions has opened the Cold War lens methodologically as well, profoundly transforming interpretations of its history. Already before 1989/91 some sociologists had probed the domestic impact of the East-West confrontation, exploring the potential convergence of the rival blocs as advanced industrial societies. After the peaceful revolution some scholars also started to analyze the survival and return of civil society in the East, while others turned towards examining the impact of human rights on containing the Second Cold War and on subverting the Cold War divide.[13] At the same time

---

11 Alexander von Plato, *Die Vereinigung Deutschlands – ein weltpolitisches Machtspiel: Bush, Kohl, Gorbatschow und die geheimen Moskauer Protokolle* (Berlin: Links, 2002).

12 Frederic Bozo et al., eds., *Europe and the End of the Cold War: A Reappraisal* (New York: Routledge, 2008); Andreas Wenger et.al., eds., *Origins of the European Security System: The Helsinki Process Revisited, 1965–75* (Milton Park: Routledge, 2008).

13 Jürgen Kocka, *Civil Society and Dictatorship in Modern German History* (Hanover: University Press of New England, 2010) and Samuel Moyn, *The Last Utopia: Human Rights in History* (Cambridge, MA: Belknap Press of Harvard University, 2010).

historians approached the conflict as an ideological struggle between the Congress of Cultural Freedom and other Western cultural agents and the Communist "peace movement," shifting attention from the arms race to the competition for "hearts and minds." More recently a veritable explosion of "Cold War culture" studies has begun to treat virtually all cultural manifestations of the second half of the twentieth century as somehow related to the Cold War.[14] Going beyond military hardware and diplomatic crises, the focus on culture has initiated a reconceptualization Cold War history.

The cultural turn in historical writing can, as Siegfried Weichlein shows, open up new subjects for investigation and suggest novel arguments for interpretation. Considering the very conception of a Cold War as a product of representations in high and popular culture shifts attention to differences in ideas, values and lifestyles between East and West. It raises questions about how an entire way of thinking, speaking and writing was refocused into an increasingly polarized outlook not just by politicians like Stalin or Truman but also by intellectuals like Jean-Paul Sartre or Raymond Aron. Such a perspective also suggests that the antagonism between the totalitarian view of Communism and the neo-fascist understanding of capitalism was inculcated by textbooks, novels, and films. Seen in this light, culture was not a passive reflection of Cold War politics but an active contributor to the East-West confrontation by coloring ways of thinking and behaving that left a deep imprint, even after the conflict was resolved. The essays in this volume demonstrate that representation and memory offer important new insights into the dynamics of the Cold War.[15]

Representation

A constructivist perspective inspired by Stuart Hall suggests that the Cold War did not just "happen," but that it was the product of a transformation of cultural representation.[16] While it built upon a traditional cleavage between Eastern and

---

14 Volker Berghahn, *America and the Intellectual Cold Wars in Europe: Shepard Stone between Philanthropy, Academy and Diplomacy* (Princeton: Princeton University Press, 2001). Cf. Annette Vowinckel, Markus Payk and Thomas Lindenberger, eds., *Cold War Cultures: Perspectives on Eastern and Western European Societies* (New York: Berghahn Books, 2012).

15 See the contribution by Siegfried Weichlein in the volume. He is directing an interdisciplinary project on Cold War culture at the Université de Fribourg in Switzerland.

16 Stuart Hall, ed., *Representation: Cultural Representation and Signifying Practices* (London: Sage Publications & Open University, 1997).

Western Europe, the confrontation between socialism and capitalism resulted from a profound intellectual realignment. Resuming the conflict between Lenin and Wilson, a new "othering" between Communism and Democracy took the place of the joint effort to vanquish Hitler, Mussolini and Tojo.[17] Inspired by conflicting interests in shaping the post-war world, the emergence of this new clash involved a changed classification of "us versus them," transforming former allies into antagonistic camps of peace versus freedom. Within three years Berlin's reputation changed from the murderous Nazi capital into the valiant "outpost of freedom."[18] In 1946 Winston Churchill's famous "Iron Curtain" speech in Fulton suggested an apt metaphor of division that thereafter symbolized the polarization of Europe. By extolling the moral superiority of the central values of equality versus liberty in their respective blocs, scholars and educators collaborated in the justification of the conflict, while popular culture productions such as spy-novels and movie thrillers reinforced the confrontation.

Though the concept of the Cold War was an American invention, David Reynolds argues that West European scholars were complicit in spreading the narrative of a struggle between Communism and democracy to their national audiences. Preoccupied with the loss of empire, British historians accepted the notion of bipolarity and attempted to carve out a special role as sophisticated advisors to the crude but powerful Americans. While French scholars tended to blame Yalta for the Cold War and tried to reassert an independent great power role, they could not resist the pull of bloc confrontation in siding with the West. In Germany historians wrestled with Nazi responsibility for World War Two and the Holocaust, but often blamed the division of the country as well as of the entire continent on the Cold War. More directly affected than their neighbors, they sought security in the Western alliance, while hoping at the same time for a magic policy to supersede the East-West conflict. Ultimately European academics sought ways to escape from superpower domination and contributed to overcoming the conflict.[19]

Not surprisingly, Vladimir Pechatnov states that Soviet and Russian scholars have tended to blame the Western camp for waging a Cold War against Russia. In Marxist terms, historians denounced the tendency of monopoly capitalism

---

17 Arnold Mayer, *Wilson vs. Lenin: Political Origins of the New Diplomacy, 1917–1918* (Cleveland: World Publishing Company, 1959).

18 Scott Krause, "Outpost of Freedom: A German-American Network's Campaign to Bring Cold War Democracy to West Berlin, 1941–1963" (PhD diss., University of North Carolina – Chapel Hill, 2015).

19 See David Reynolds' contribution to this volume. Cf. idem, *From World War to Cold War: Churchill, Roosevelt, and the International History of the 1940s* (Oxford: Oxford University Press, 2006).

to stabilize itself through imperialist expansion, seeking not only to control Western Europe, but also to retain the former colonial possessions. Understandably Soviet-bloc academics tried to defend the fruits of the victory in the "Great Patriotic War" over Nazi Germany which liberated their own country and gave it control over the entire Eastern half of the European continent. In many ways the orthodox Soviet version saw the Cold War as a heroic struggle against Western subversion and encirclement, led by the all-powerful United States. As a matter of pride and profound geopolitical anxiety, Moscow wanted to be recognized as equal superpower with world-wide influence and their possessions ratified through international agreements like the Helsinki Conference, establishing a form of co-existence that reduced the danger of nuclear war.[20] Only dissidents in samizdat publications dared challenge this defensive aggressiveness. The loss of empire and the break-down of socio-economic support systems have confronted Russian historians with new challenges in the period after 1991.

Regarding the United States, Christopher Moran reveals that the Central Intelligence Agency sought to uphold the moralizing narrative of the Cold War by suppressing the critical memoirs of whistleblowers. During the 1970s former employees who had become disaffected with the cloak-and-dagger operations of the CIA decided to divulge some of the dirty secrets of American intelligence operations. When Victor Marchetti, Philipp Agee and Frank Snepp tried to publish their indictments of illegal actions and mistaken policies, the intelligence community was aghast, since these disclosures threatened to rob Washington of its political righteousness. Hence the CIA directors asked the courts to suppress the texts, which created successive scandals, since the left-wing public was eager for details which supported its critical views. Shamefully, conservative judges restricted the freedom of speech by upholding the contracts which had sworn CIA employees to secrecy. But the whistleblowers' evidence of massive wrong-doing ultimately buttressed the case of revisionist historians who blamed U.S. imperialism for the Cold War.[21]

Falk Pingel's textbook analysis demonstrates how the concept of a Cold War gradually came to dominate the European curriculum in recent history. In the initial post-war years school books in East and West still referred to the hopes

---

20 See Vladimir Pechatnov's contribution to this volume. Cf. idem, *Ot so͡iuza – k kholodnoĭ voĭne: sovetsko-amerikanskie otnoshenii͡a v 1945–1947 gg.: Monografii͡a* (Moscow: MGIMO, 2006).

21 See Christopher Moran's contribution to this volume. Cf. idem and Christopher J. Murphy, eds., *Intelligence Studies in Britain and the US: Historiography since 1945* (Edinburgh: Edinburgh University Press, 2013).

for peaceful cooperation in the future. But during the 1950s the contest between the superpowers and the division of Germany started to permeate the texts with each side blaming the other. A decade later the bi-polar paradigm of the capitalist versus the communist countries was firmly established as cause of successive crises, although the concept of the Cold War remained largely a Western invention. During the 1970s most West European books and their East German counterparts started to refer to coexistence between the blocs and even voice some hope for convergence of advanced industrial societies so as to avoid further confrontation. But during the second Cold War, various attempts at East-West reconciliation through textbook consultations remained fruitless. Nonetheless towards the late 1980s mutual portrayals became less hostile, thereby facilitating a peaceful end of the conflict.[22]

According to Paul Bleton, spy fiction was also a central instrument for anchoring the Cold War in popular culture since it masqueraded as entertainment while spreading a political message. In the early years of the East-West conflict authors like John le Carré or titles like the James Bond series reinforced the ideological hostility by portraying the other side as dangerous subversion which had to be stopped at all costs. Not only in the Anglo-American countries, but also in France a whole "culture industry" sought to satisfy the ravenous appetite of the public by producing cheap paperbacks. The spy genre apparently owed its attraction to a combination of adventure story and crime thriller, in which a usually male hero overcame all sorts of dangers due to his quick wit, physical stamina or technological gadgets, only to be rewarded by exciting sex. During the 1970s, however, the spread of détente undercut the Manichaeanism of the plots, sowing doubt about the morality of a particular side.[23] As a result of this gradual loss of certainty, espionage novels lost their glamour and even contributed to overcoming Cold War hostilities.

Christoph Classen shows that film and television played perhaps an even more important role in creating Cold War mentalities due to their pretended realism. Direct propaganda documentaries were less effective than regular action thrillers, since a didactic tone and crude stereotyping could not compete with the excitement of an attention-grabbing plot. Especially after the building of the Wall, numerous tunnel or escape films presented riveting accounts of Commu-

22 See Falk Pingel's contribution to this volume. Cf. idem, *The European Home: Representations of 20th Century Europe in History Textbooks* (Strasbourg: Council of Europe Publishing, 2000).
23 See Paul Bleton's contribution to this volume. Cf, idem, *Les anges de Machiavel: Essai sur le roman d'espionnage: Froide fin et funestes moyens, les espions de papier dans la paralittérature française, du Rideau de fer à la chute du Mur* (Quebec: Nuit Blanche, 1994).

nist repression and heroic flights to freedom. In Eastern Europe, movies showed evil and decadent capitalists whose sinister designs had to be foiled by upstanding socialist counter-spies. Even more effective were, however, the indirect dramatizations of dictatorship in Westerns where an outsider defeated villains and reestablished law and order or in "sandal-epics" like the Ten Commandments where freedom loving Jews outwitted dictatorial Egyptians. On television several long-running series like "I Spy" also followed similar plot-lines. But with détente, movies and TV gradually became more complex and abandoned cliché-ridden oversimplifications.[24]

Cultural representations therefore contributed considerably to the rise of a Cold War mentality by justifying and dramatizing the East-West conflict. No doubt, political analysis and decision-making in Moscow and Washington initiated the struggle between Communism and democracy. But the reorientation from cooperation in the Grand Alliance to hostility between the rival blocs required intellectual support in order to convince the public. Western academics like Hannah Arendt or Zbigniew Brzeziński helped by elaborating a "totalitarianism theory" which equated the brown and red dictatorships, whereas Eastern intellectuals like Christa Wolf still claimed to be fighting Fascism, only in a new, more devious American guise.[25] While writers of textbooks gradually included the Cold War in their descriptions of the recent past, the mass media of both sides reinforced mutual stereotyping through their popular culture productions which dramatized the dangerous consequences of the conflict. Only the fear of nuclear annihilation in movies like Dr. Strangelove and the differentiation of plots in the later Len Deighton novels slowly undercut bipolarity and questioned the necessity of a continuation of the Cold War.

Memory

In spite of the physical ruins and mental aftereffects left behind by the East-West conflict, the memory boom in cultural studies has largely ignored the subject of the Cold War. Though Maurice Halbwachs' notion of collective memory would be open to being applied to the East-West conflict, Pierre Nora's nostalgic evocation

---

24 See Christoph Classen's contribution to this volume. Cf. idem, *Bilder der Vergangenheit: Die Zeit des Nationalsozialismus im Fernsehen der Bundesrepublik Deutschland 1955–1965* (Cologne: Böhlau Verlag, 1999).

25 Eckart Jesse, ed., *Totalitarismus im 20. Jahrhundert: Eine Bilanz der internationalen Forschung*, 2nd rev. ed, (Bonn: Bundeszentrale für Politische Bildung, 1999).

of the French heritage in its *lieux de mêmoire* seems inappropriate for that topic. Moreover, the normative power of the moral imperative to remember the Holocaust has overshadowed concerns with recollections of other historical events like the First World War, even if the media seeks to revive different legacies during anniversaries. The conceptualization developed by Jan and Aleida Assmann might, however, be useful, since it distinguishes a deeper cultural memory from a more current communicative memory.[26] The related differentiation between individual remembrances, group recollections and public commemorations also offers a useful method to engage the impact of the East-West conflict.[27] While generally ignoring the topic itself, the discussion of memory provides some conceptual tools for addressing the legacy of the Cold War.

Jay Winter's reflections on the changing European attitudes towards war suggest some of the difficulties which accepted rituals of commemoration face in dealing with the Cold War. In spite of its all-encompassing nature and ideological hostility, the East-West conflict has not left behind as many military or civilian cemeteries as the two World Wars. Since the huge conventional and nuclear armaments were never actually used on the continent, the character of the Cold War is less tangible, making it difficult to recapture.[28] To be true, confrontation between the blocs did leave behind plenty of physical remains such as the Berlin Wall, military bases and former missile sites, which are now abandoned. It also created a sizable group of victims of Communist repression, clamoring for monetary compensation as well as public acknowledgement of their suffering. On some sites like the border crossing point Checkpoint Charlie a tourism industry has even developed that attracts thousands of visitors. But somehow the Cold War, nonetheless, appears more difficult to remember, because it was largely a contested state of mind.

In contrast, Vietnam was a place where hundreds of thousands of American soldiers did fight the Vietcong in one of the deadliest proxy wars of the Cold War. This part civil war and part post-colonial struggle has left plenty of physical remains. While much has been written about the American remembrance of the

---

26 Jan Assmann, "Communicative and Cultural Memory," in *Cultural Memory Studies: An International and Interdisciplinary Handbook*, eds. Astrid Erll and Ansgar Nünning, (Berlin: Walter De Gruyter, 2008), 109–118; Aleida Assmann, *Cultural Memory and Western Civilization: Functions, Media, Archives* (New York: Cambridge University Press, 2011). Cf. also Konrad H. Jarausch and Martin Sabrow, eds., *Verletztes Gedächtnis: Erinnerungskultur und Zeitgeschichte im Konflikt* (Frankfurt: Campus, 2002).

27 Jarausch, "Survival in Catastrophe: Mending Broken Memories," in *Shattered Past*, 317–341.

28 Cf. Jay Winter, *Remembering War: The Great War between Memory and History in the Twentieth Century* (New Haven: Yale University Press, 2006).

Vietnam War, Jennifer Dickey's contribution takes a critical look at how the war has been presented in museums and historic sites in Vietnam. The official Vietnamese master narrative of the "War of National Salvation against the Americans," or the "American War," as it is called here, more or less excludes references to the larger context of the Cold War. Instead it is celebrated as the victory of "national unity achieved through heroic sacrifice," in a narrative that does not engage the local population, but is mainly aimed at international tourists.[29]

Muriel Blaive shows in her essay that the recovery of Cold War memory through every-day history might even destabilize the very concept. In Western recollections the confrontation is, indeed, conceptualized as Cold War due to the media repetition of political rhetoric. But on the Eastern side of the border, references to the second half of the twentieth century are generally framed as "life under Communism," accentuating the dictatorial regime rather than the international conflict. In oral interviews many Czech citizens admit their own cooperation in upholding a repressive regime without any pangs of conscience, since there seemed to be no alternative to it. Their justification for maintaining the border to Austria revolved around arguments of self-protection as reason for policing their own behavior and intercepting others trying to flee to the West. This collaboration perspective is rather antithetical to anti-Communist celebrations of heroic attempts to escape from dictatorship to freedom.[30] Ironically, the post-Communist media are now supplanting that local memory with an imported Western version of the Cold War while citizens struggle to sort out their personal recollections of the fallen dictatorship.[31]

Even where the notion of the Cold War has been accepted, dealing with the physical remains of military sites has proven rather complicated as Wayne Cocroft's article shows. Since many installations were abandoned once the East-West conflict had subsided, communities faced the unenviable task of deciding what to do with old bunkers, airfields or missile silos. It generally took local initiatives, supported by former service personnel, in order to gather the funds necessary for conserving the sites. Many of the installations were physically large, contained complicated equipment, and needed to be cleared of explosives that were left behind. On a broader national level, politicians and academics had to

29 See Jennifer Dickey's contribution to this volume. Cf. idem, Samir El Azhar and Catherin Lewis, eds., *Museums in a Global Context: National Identity, International Understanding*, (Washington, DC: AAM Press, 2013).

30 See Muriel Blaive's contribution to this volume. Cf. idem, ed., *Clashes in European Memory: The Case of Communist Repression and the Holocaust* (Innsbruck: Studienverlag, 2011).

31 Marci Shore, *A Taste of Ashes: The Afterlife of Totalitarianism in Eastern Europe* (New York: Crown Publishers, 2013).

be convinced of the importance of historic preservation for objects from a recent past that many were only too happy to forget. As a result, the degree of musealization remains rather fragmentary, with some command posts preserved and made accessible to the public, but the vast majority decaying for lack of interest and financing.[32] Though the Cold War is included in some larger museums, the preservation of its sites still remains in its infancy.

The political difficulties of remembrance are particularly evident in Berlin, one of the flash-points of the Cold War. In her contribution, Hope Harrison demonstrates how determined the citizens of the city were to eradicate all traces of the divisive Wall in order to resume their previous lives. Only a small minority of intellectuals and SED-victims pushed for the preservation of some remnants and the establishment of a memorial at the Bernauer Strasse, where the most dramatic flights had taken place. The development of a Master Plan was complicated by the politics of the SPD-PDS coalition government in the city, because the post-Communist junior partner did not want to be reminded of its previous misdeeds. In the debate between dramatizing the experience of fear by reassembling pieces of the barrier from different sites and using only authentic remnants in their actual places the advocates of historic preservation ultimately won out over proponents of more dramatic staging. The resulting concept supported a decentralized approach, including all extant remnants, but at the same time it also upgraded the Bernauer Strasse memorial with a new museum, a virtual recreation of the Wall and a park hinting at its extent.[33]

Sybille Frank's essay suggests that a lack of public provision encourages private initiatives which commercialize the past. In order to exemplify the rise of a Cold War heritage industry in Berlin it analyzes a dispute over the international crossing-point of the Berlin Wall at Checkpoint Charlie. In 2004, the private Wall Museum at Berlin's former Allied border control point inaugurated a temporary Wall victims' memorial on the site. It comprised a replica of the Berlin Wall and more than 1,065 crosses, each displaying the name of one Wall dead – none of whom, however, had actually died at the border crossing. While the Berlin Senate scandalized the private Wall memorial as inauthentic, market-led trivialization of a serious period of German and world history, the Wall Museum promoted its memorial as a pilot project for a new public culture of remembrance that offered international Cold War tourists emotional Wall stories at a place of international

32 See Wayne Cocroft's contribution to this volume. Cf. idem and John Schofield, eds., *A Fearsome Heritage: Diverse Legacies of the Cold War* (Walnut Creek, CA: Left Coast Press, 2007).

33 See Hope Harrison's contribution to this volume. Cf. idem, *Driving the Soviets up the Wall: Soviet-East German Relations, 1953–1961* (Princeton: Princeton University Press, 2003).

attention. With news coverage gradually changing sides to the museum's viewpoint, the Senate eventually had to adopt new concepts of heritage display to retain authorship.[34]

Finally, Hanno Hochmuth illustrates the difficulty of doing justice to the multiple legacies of the Cold War in Berlin, since traces of both sides compete with each other. The city is full of remnants of the East-West conflict such as the American monitoring station on top of the Teufelsberg or the Soviet military memorial in the Treptower Park. One such institution is the German-Russian museum in Karlshorst, the site of the surrender of the Wehrmacht in World War Two. Intended to explain to Russian soldiers the reasons for being stationed in Germany, its revised exhibit continues to focus on the Second World War. Its counterpart is the Allied Museum, created after the fall of the Wall as a nostalgic gesture of thanks to the Western forces stationed in Berlin, and located on the premises of the American movie-theater and library in Dahlem.[35] Since both institutions tell only part of the story and the commercial Wall Museum is too triumphalist, a group of scholars, politicians and museum curators including the editors of this volume has advocated the construction of a more comprehensive Cold War Museum. The establishment of a picture gallery and a "black box" already anticipates some of its future content.[36] The challenge will be to find an innovative and balanced method for its implementation.

The Cold War as Culture

As illustrated by the contributions to this volume, a cultural approach to the Cold War provides a chance to escape its polarizing logic by questioning the very construction of the concept. Without in any way displacing traditional documentary accounts of the arms race or international crises, the inclusion of a cultural perspective can illuminate a whole new set of aspects of the East-West conflict. On

34 Cf. Sybille Frank, *Wall Memorials and Heritage: The Heritage Industry of Berlin's Checkpoint Charlie* (New York: Routledge, 2016).
35 Cf. Hanno Hochmuth, "HisTourismus; Public History und Berlin-Tourismus," in: *Vergangenheitsbewirtschaftung: Public History zwischen Wirtschaft und Wissenschaft*, Christoph Kühberger ed. (Innsbruck: Studienverlag, 2012), 173–182.
36 See Konrad H. Jarausch and Christian Ostermann, "A Proposal for a 'Cold War Center: Exhibition at Checkpoint Charlie'" (MS, June 8, 2010). Cf. Jürgen Reiche and Dieter Vorsteher, "Zentrum Kalter Krieg. Ausstellung am Checkpoint Charlie" (Berlin, February 1, 2011); Jula Danylow and Andreas Etges, "A Hot Debate over the Cold War: The Plan for a 'Cold War Center' at Checkpoint Charlie, Berlin," in: Jennifer Dickey et al., eds., *Museums in a Global Context*, 144–161.

the one hand, it makes it possible to "link changing lifestyles, mass consumption and mass culture as well as educational systems with the overarching systemic conflict between the US and the USSR." It thereby illuminates the deep and distorting imprint of the confrontation on popular culture and daily life.[37] On the other hand, a cultural approach also raises the question how the notion of a "Cold War" was itself created among the political leaders of the superpowers and then transmitted to their populations as a way of thinking about the rivalry of Communism and Democracy. Going beyond the conventional analysis of clashing ideologies, such a perspective addresses the creation as well as dissemination of the core concept in order to explain how such a metaphor could dominate international discourse for half a century. It therefore frees scholars to reflect on their own role in the conflict.

A cultural view suggests that representation played a key role in the construction of the competing camps by transforming the former Allies into enemies and the erstwhile foe Germany, or rather its now two separate parts, into an ally or enemy, depending on which successor state belonged to one or the other camp. Confronting each other in journals and conferences, intellectuals strove to prove the superiority of the ideas of their own side, by extolling freedom or peace respectively. Cultural productions such as novels and films made ideology tangible, by creating human figures whose struggles illustrated the implications of a belief system. The labors of propagandists attached certain styles such as socialist realism to the East or abstract expressionism to the West, even if the connection was tenuous at best. Different social groups responded to such messages, with feminists admiring the various reforms of Communism while youths instead flocked to American life-styles, symbolized by rock music and jeans.[38] The cultural struggle also involved a polarization that forced contemporaries to choose sides and a policing of boundaries that treated dissidents as heretics. "Othering" was therefore central to the ideological competition of the Cold War.

A cultural approach also makes it possible to reflect on the paradoxical ubiquity as well as disappearance of Cold War memories. The older generation which lived through the East-West conflict still retains many recollections of the fear of nuclear bombs or international crises and the relief of détente that inspire stories of the "duck and cover" exercises in school. Not just victim groups, but

37 Vowinckel, *Cold War Cultures*, 347. Cf. Peter J. Kuznick and James Gilbert, eds., *Rethinking Cold War Culture* (Washington: Smithsonian Institution Press, 2001).

38 Uta Poiger, *Jazz, Rock and Rebels: Cold War Politics and American Culture in Divided Germany* (Berkeley: University of California Press, 2000). Cf. Michael Lemke, *Vor der Mauer: Berlin in der Ost-West Konkurrenz* (Cologne: Böhlau Verlag, 2011).

also former soldiers stationed on both sides of the Iron Curtain talk about having to participate in maneuvers that were designed to obliterate the ideological enemy at the risk of their own annihilation. Nonetheless, public memory culture is curiously silent on the topic, except for occasional triumphal references in the West about "winning the Cold War" and apologetic disclaimers in the East about having prevented World War Three by deterring a NATO attack. In contrast to the World Wars, there is no Europe-wide holiday, no central memorial location, no systematic reflection on its legacy.[39] It is almost as if the Cold War that held the entire globe in suspense during the second half of the twentieth century had never happened.

The essays in this volume therefore underline the importance of rethinking Cold War historiography in terms of representation and memory. Lowe and Joel have argued that "the Cold War not only persists but grows in its remembering," though this "global contest" is being told in many different "national stories."[40] The military sites that are being preserved in various locations are a step in the right direction by recalling the danger of nuclear annihilation. The commercialization of other places through a "heritage industry" shows considerable interest but does not adequately fulfill the public desire for information. The Cold War sections in the big national museums of history like the Smithsonian, the Deutsches Historisches Museum etc. are too brief to do the job, while the East European efforts to remember the Communist dictatorship or Soviet control in places like the "House of Terror" in Budapest are too ideologically one-sided. Instead a new institution is necessary that connects the global conflict with its local implications, treats the confrontation as an interactive process and pays attention to its cultural construction. Berlin would be the perfect place to do it. Lowe and Joel agree that the city "is universally recognized as the quintessential Cold War city both 'then and now'." No other place on the globe "comes close to symbolizing the contracted struggle between East and West on the same level as Germany's capital."[41] The realization of a new Cold War museum at Checkpoint Charlie – one of the most famous "sites of memory" of the conflict – would make a huge contribution towards a more sophisticated understanding of the Cold War.[42]

39 Klaus-Dietmar Henke, ed., *Die Mauer: Errichtung, Überwindung, Erinnerung* (Munich: Deutscher Taschenbuch Verlag, 2011). Cf. Vojtech Mastny and Zhu Liqun, eds., *The Legacy of the Cold War: Perspectives on Security, Cooperation, and Conflict* (Lanham, MD: Lexington Books, 2014).
40 Lowe and Joel, *Remembering the Cold War*, 245.
41 Ibid., 210.
42 Sven Felix Kellerhoff, "Den Grusel am Checkpoint erlebbar machen," *Die Welt*, September 20, 2012. Cf. Claus Leggewie, *Der Kampf um die europäische Erinnerung: Ein Schlachtfeld wird besichtigt* (Munich: Beck, 2011).

The international initiative to create a museum of the Cold War in Berlin is especially important because it could convey a positive message. Although the world repeatedly teetered on the brink of self-destruction, reason ultimately prevailed and the hostile blocs found a way to de-escalate tensions so as to preserve peace. The reality of the danger of the nuclear arms race and of successive international crises should not be forgotten although they passed without incinerating the globe. The pervasive fear of Communist repression also needs to be recalled in order to honor the freedom drive of the suppressed populations, though the Western transgressions in supporting military dictators and ideological witch-hunts should be admitted as well. But more importantly, the non-violent ending of the Cold War through international understanding from above and the peaceful revolution from below needs to be emphasized. In order to guard against a relapse into military confrontation and ideological hostility, the fact that it was possible to overcome decades of deadly conflict sends a signal of hope that surely has universal significance.[43]

43 Konrad H. Jarausch, "Die Teilung Europas und ihre Überwindung. Überlegungen zu einem Ausstellungskonzept für Berlin," *Zeithistorische Forschungen*, online-edition, 5 (2008) Nr. 2, http://www.zeithistorische-forschungen.de/16126041-Jarausch-2-2008 (page last visited on October 29, 2017); and Wolfgang Thierse, "Das Haus für die weltgeschichtliche Dimension," *Der Tagesspiegel*, September 19, 2012.

Siegfried Weichlein

Representation and Recoding: Interdisciplinary Perspectives on Cold War Cultures

"When the legend becomes fact, print the legend."[1]

The most prestigious prize in the early years of the Cold War was the West European left. Socialists, communists and the Soviet Union had suffered tremendously under Nazi occupation, repression and genocide. The communist left in France, Belgium and Italy looked favorably to the Soviet Union. In the unfolding political antagonism between the United States and the Soviet Union both sides were fighting to win over this group. Would the West European left turn to their ideological neighbors on the left and their interpretation of history and society or would they follow the American example of a modern liberal consumer society, of consensus capitalism and a modern welfare state? Whoever succeeded in this competition for loyalty would be able to determine politics in Western Europe for a long time.[2]

Culture and cultural patterns were crucial in generating loyalty to one system or another. The Cold War was a cultural as much as a military conflict, whose "full arsenal" included literature, cinema, music, and art, and whose foot soldiers were "ballerinas, violinists, poets, actors, playwrights, painters, composers, comedians, and chess players."[3] Movies were essential for the entertainment of the middle and the underclasses, particularly for the young. The Lorraine Communist youth watched movies showcasing comrade Joseph Stalin, but also

1 Maxwell Scott, *The Man Who Shot Liberty Valance*, Carleton Young, (John Ford; 1962; Hollywood, California: Paramount Pictures).

2 See Julia Angster, "Konsenskapitalismus und Sozialdemokratie: die Westernisierung von SPD und DGB" (Zugl. Tübingen, University, Diss., 2000, Oldenbourg, 2003); Abraham Boxhoorn, *The Cold War and the rift in the governments of national unity. Belgium, France, and Italy in the spring of 1947, a comparison*, Amsterdamse historische reeks (Amsterdam: Historisch Seminarium van de Universiteit van Amsterdam, 1993); Alessandro Brogi, *Confronting America. The Cold War between the United States and the Communists in France and Italy* (Chapel Hill: Univ of North Carolina Press, 2011).

3 David Caute, *The dancer defects. The struggle for cultural supremacy during the Cold War* (Oxford [u.a.]: Oxford University Press, 2005).

DOI 10.1515/9783110496178-002

icons of the Hollywood entertainment industry like Humphrey Bogart.[4] The Lorraine miner's youth followed culturally not one consistent model, but rather two opposing models, those of comrade Stalin and of Humphrey Bogart's coolness.

This paradox leads to some general observations: First, the social and political background did not determine the cultural role models that young communist workers followed in a free society. The concept of culture is not identical with political attitudes. Stalin himself loved Hollywood movies, especially Western. Seen from the vantage point of cultural history, the readers and the viewers did not have one cultural imaginary but several. Culture and politics are not related directly, but rather in indirect and subtle ways of coding and displacement. There are limits to the impact of the Cold War political antagonism on culture. They seem to follow different logics and can only partly and temporarily be identified. Clearly there are limits to the cultural representation of the Cold War. Consequently, the cultural history of the Cold War does not simply have the task to explain success and failure in the political-cultural enterprise of seducing certain social groups into political loyalty. It rather deals – at least in the 1950s and 1960s – with hybridity and ambiguity of conflicting preferences. Historical actors did not neatly fit into the bipolar schemes of the Cold War. They could oppose the United States in Vietnam and embrace Hollywood movies and music from New York. One could adore Stalin and Bogart. Cold War culture was not a container of cultural attitudes and political preferences, which were being constantly synchronized by Cold War cultural institutions. Therefore, Cold War culture varied also from country to country. It meant something different for Germans, French and Britains. Accordingly, we can speak of many Cold War cultures in plural. "The Cold War," "la guerre froide" and "Kalter Krieg" is not the same, but denote different Cold War cultures.[5]

Secondly, Cold War culture cannot be found alone in those cultural artifacts that represent the Cold War, but also in entertainment culture or in children's films. We can find Cold War culture and places where we wouldn't expect them to be. The film version of Rudyard Kipling's novel *Kim* from 1950 involved a clear Cold War ideology by propagating the narrative of the British Empire as the advance of "civilization" against the leftist de-colonizers.[6] The Cold War was in

4 See Fabrice Montebello, "Joseph Staline et Humphrey Bogart: l'hommage des ouvriers. Essai sur la construction sociale de la figure du 'heros' en milieu ouvrier," *Politix* 24 (1993).

5 Annette Vowinckel, Marcus M. Payk, and Thomas Lindenberger, *Cold War Cultures. Perspectives on Eastern and Western Societies* (New York: Berghahn Books, 2012).

6 Ian Wojcik-Andrews and Jerry Phillips, "Telling Tales to Children: The Pedagogy of Empire in MGM's Kim and Disney's Aladdin," *The Lion and the Unicorn* 20, no. 1 (1996).

this literary-political tradition seen as a new chapter in an old story, i.e. the "Great Game," the conflict between Britain and Russia in Central Asia in the late 19th century. The imagery of the British Empire inspired Cold War culture to such an extent that some even referred to the Cold War as "Great Game II."

Thirdly, there is a social dimension to this, since genres like children's books or movies attracted different audiences than political speeches. We look at least at two dynamics. Lowbrow was brought into the fold by Cold War mass culture such as movies, lowbrow literature or mass print culture. But that didn't mean that the more aspirational middlebrow classes were lost. Cold War culture came in different codes, styles and formats. Building on prewar experiences middlebrow institutions such as book clubs (Saturday Review of Literature, Book of the Month Club) and new magazine formats as *Life* and the *New Yorker* conveyed a sense of Western culture ex- or implicitly set against communism. Cold War culture thereby fed into the pursuit of greater cultural prestige through products and memberships within the middle classes.[7] Narratives of the West and the East, of freedom and egalitarianism were not restricted to high culture but also part of low- and middlebrow culture.[8]

A plethora of topics in the cultural Cold War has been studied, ranging from the arts and cultural institutions to gender aspects, vacation patterns and the postwar polio crisis.[9] Whoever refers to the fine arts, to highbrow or lowbrow culture, to intellectual history or political semantics, to iconography or gender roles in the context of Cold War culture uses dissimilar concepts of culture. The analytical approach and the questions in these cases are different, sometimes even incompatible. A cultural history of the Cold War that is focusing on the arts, literature, music, sculpture, painting etc. is obviously looking at a different Cold War from the studies that employ a concept of culture centered around institutions like publishing houses, universities or museums, worldviews, intellectual paradigms or aesthetic styles. What an exhibition in London has called the "conscription of the arts"[10] focuses on a Cold War that is different from an intellectual

---

7 Greg Barnhisel, *Cold War modernists: art, literature, and American cultural diplomacy, 1946–1959* (New York: Columbia University Press, 2015).
8 Cf. Sabina Mihelj, "Negotiating cold war culture at the crossroads of east and west: uplifting the working people, entertaining the masses, cultivating the nation," *Comparative Studies in Society and History* 53, no. 3: 509–31.
9 See Simon Willmetts, "Quiet Americans: The CIA and Early Cold War Hollywood Cinema," *Journal of American Studies* 47, no. 1 (2013); Christopher Endy, *Cold War holidays. American tourism in France*, The new Cold War history (Chapel Hill, NC [u.a.]: University of North Carolina Press, 2004).
10 Muriel Blaive, "Utopian Visions: The 'Cold War' and its Political Aesthetics," *Zeithistorische Forschungen* 5 (2008).

history of Herman Kahn and the RAND Corporation.[11] Others have found the cultural Cold War in science fiction, in Western movies and the changing role of cowboys.[12] Nearly every topic of cultural analysis has been used to narrate a cultural history of the Cold War. These studies give a sense of many different Cold Wars.

Cold War culture in the 1950s shared one characteristic: modernism. The Cold War was a conflict between different concepts of modernity, not only varying to block affinity, but to many of the variables. Cold War modernism is a concept first applied in the arts. It encompassed expressionism and abstract art, jazz, new ways of designing as well as architecture. But the point for Cold War culture was, that modernism always had political implications. Here lies the problem which this article wants to address. In the interwar years, modernist culture as well as artists had aligned themselves with the political left in rejecting tradition and bourgeois society. That had become especially clear in the Spanish campaign in the late 1930s. When modernism was to be a common denominator for a Western zone it had to be recoded and made compatible with a democratic, capitalist bourgeois system. Recoding modernism in the 1950s did not simply mean better distribution to fit new audiences. It also meant giving new meaning to modernism and modernity. That was of particular importance for Germany, Austria and Italy, the countries on the losing side in 1945. Modernism stood politically for the enemy in Nazi Germany as well as in Mussolini's Italy. Aesthetically Nazi industrial (not public!) architecture used modernism just the same way as Western societies.[13] Whereas both societies voluntarily embraced democracy, getting rid of one's cultural past was another matter. But bringing Germany, Austria and Italy into the Western fold essentially meant introducing a cultural style to these societies that stood for everything they had abhorred 20 years earlier. The problem was the link between democracy and modernism.

---

11 See Bernd Greiner, "Macht und Geist im Kalten Krieg. Bilanz und Ausblick," in: id. et al. eds, *Macht und Geist im Kalten Krieg*, Hamburg 2011, 7–27.

12 See David Seed, *American science fiction and the Cold War: literature and film* (Edinburgh: Edinburgh University Press, 1999); Andrea Weiss, "Cold War Femme: Lesbianism, National Identity, and Hollywood Cinema," *Journal of Cold War Studies* 14, no. 3 (2012); Stanley Corkin, "Cowboys and Free Markets: Post-World War II Westerns and U.S. Hegemony," *Cinema Journal* 39, no. 3 (2000); Nicholas J. Cull, "British Cinema and the Cold War: The State, Propaganda and Consensus," *Cold War History* 3, no. 1 (2002); Jacqueline Foertsch, *Enemies within: the Cold War and the AIDS crisis in literature, film, and culture* (Urbana [u.a.]: University of Illinois Press, 2001).

13 David Gartman, *From autos to architecture fordism and architectural aesthetics in the twentieth century* (New York, NY: Princeton Architectural Press, 2009), 132–35.

In the following remarks I try to sketch out a meta-perspective on Cold War culture. The central thesis of the following paragraphs is that the research on the Cold War heavily depends on the notion of culture it employs. From both notions of culture follow different perspectives on Cold War culture:

- Culture was about representation. Culture can be seen as being informed and to a certain degree steered by the Cold War, its antagonisms, its abundant quest for loyalty among different social groups. Culture in this sense is a way to foster loyalty, to make claims and to counter others.
- Culture was about producing new meanings of the Cold War instead of repeating and distributing preexisting ones. Culture refers to looking onto the Cold War, recoding its meaning and engaging in critique, parody and satire. Its dominant modes were distancing and reflexivity.

Cold War culture was both. It got a Cold War message out and it was self-reflexive in that it reflected on the Cold War and recoded its meaning in new ways. The coexistence of representation and recoding denote a time around 1960, where it was unclear whether literature, painting, music, and academic life would keep distributing Cold War messages or whether they would reflect on the Cold War in new ways. The following paragraphs are particularly interested in these years between 1955 and 1968 and their ambiguity in Cold War culture.

This distinction between representation and recoding is meant heuristically to look into the various functions of Cold War culture. In the topics under investigation these two notions are in many cases both present and at work. Culture was representing something else and at the same time recoding the Cold War. This is obvious in the notion of the Cold War itself, which not only represented a political antagonism between the US and the USSR but also recoded a few years after the end of World War II the hitherto dominating dichotomy of "fascism versus anti-fascism" into a new antagonism. At the center of Cold War culture stood memory, i.e. recoding the memory of the shared war against Nazi-Germany. Intellectual tools like totalitarianism reframed the discontinuity of the Cold War to World War II as continuity. There were others, most prominently modernism.

One caveat on Cold War culture must be made in advance. "Cold War" and "Cold War culture" are terms that are used in the sources mostly in the Western hemisphere. The common man in Eastern Europe rather described the era between 1947 and 1991 as "life under communism."[14] A cultural history should be aware of this structuring difference. "Culture" as well as "Cold War" are analytical con-

---

14 Blaive, 320; Muriel Blaive and Berthold Molden, *Grenzfälle österreichische und tschechische Erfahrungen am eisernen Vorhang* (Weitra: Verl. Bibliothek der Provinz, 2009).

cepts applied by historians, not expressions that are evident in the sources. The Cold War is no longer simply an *explanans*, but rather an *explanandum*, a concept that has to be made visible and reconstructed.

The Cold War itself was a metaphor and makes sense only in a certain vocabulary and perspective.[15] The effort to embed the Cold War in cultural history may be expressed by the term "Cold War culture."[16] Culture refers then to the patterns and worldviews that gave meaning to the term "Cold War" and made it possible. Since the patterns came from different national, social, political and religious backgrounds, there were many "Cold War cultures."[17]

1 Cold War Culture as Representation

The best-known form of the cultural Cold War is the representation of the political conflict in the arts. The notion of culture clearly implies representation. On the theoretical side it is just unclear what is being represented.[18] On the political side of Cold War culture we encounter many uses of culture to represent the Cold War antagonism from one side or the other. Cold War politics made use of culture to seek loyalty in Western societies, and to counter the claims of the other side. Culture was to represent something political, it had to transmit essentially political claims about the US, the West, Western society and Western culture. Within this Cold War usage of culture, we are dealing with at least two dimensions of culture: cultural practices and artifacts on the one hand and a political notion of what culture means on the other hand. This meaning of culture is administered by Cold War politics and only by them. The problem arises, that cultural practices run into a contradiction when they are not allowed to produce their own meaning.

An example in place is the *Congress for Cultural Freedom* trying "to nudge the intelligentsia of Western Europe away from its lingering fascination with Marxism and Communism towards a view more accommodating to 'the American way.'" The CCF had offices in 35 countries, employed dozens of personnel, published

---

15 Anders Stephanson, "Fourteen notes on the very concept of the Cold War," *H-Diplo Essays* (2007).

16 This differs from the use of the term "Cold War culture" in: Gordon Johnston, "Revisiting the cultural Cold War," *Social History* 35, no. 3 (2010).

17 As Annette Vowinckel's book rightly emphasizes. Vowinckel, Payk, and Lindenberger.

18 Stuart Hall and Open University, *Representation: cultural representations and signifying practices*, Culture, media, and identities (London; Thousand Oaks, Calif.: Sage in association with the Open University, 1997).

over twenty prestigious magazines, held art exhibitions, owned a news and features service, organized high-profile international conferences, and rewarded musicians and artists with prizes and public performances.[19] The left liberal members were of particular importance for the US, since the political left was to be gained for the cause of Western liberal democracy. Among the initial founding members were such luminaries of the literary world as François Bondy, Irving Brown, James Burnham, Sidney Hook, Michael Josselson, Arthur Koestler, Melvin Lasky, Nicolas Nabokov and Ignazio Silone. They all shared a leftist, in the case of Koestler and Silone even communist history. They all had distanced themselves from communism. Their strategic aim was to win the hearts and minds of their former peers. The meeting in Andlau near Strasbourg in September 1951 sought to counter communist claims in the intellectual field:

1. How do we reach the mind of the communist intellectual?
2. The Diamat (Dialectical Materialism) is a persistent challenge of the free world. What are the ways and means to respond to this challenge and what common anti-Diamat action can be devised for the intellectuals of the free world?[20]

The CIA financed periodicals of the CCF, which were designed to disseminate liberal values among the leftist intelligentsia. Among the journals were the German "*Der Monat*," edited by Melvin Lasky, the French periodical "*Preuves*," the Italian Journal "*Tempo presente*" and the British magazine *Encounter*. When the military-intellectual collaboration became publicly known in 1967, it met sharp criticism. The Ford Foundation took over the financial responsibilities from the CIA, but the public impact of the CCF declined from then on.[21]

Another way to win over the intellectuals was academic research of Eastern Europe and the Soviet Union. U.S. institutions were crucial in developing Centers

---

19 Frances Stonor Saunders, *Who paid the piper? The CIA and the cultural Cold War* (London: Granta Books, 1999); Michael Hochgeschwender, *Freiheit in der Offensive? Der Kongress für Kulturelle Freiheit und die Deutschen*, Ordnungssysteme (München: Oldenbourg, 1998).

20 Giles Scott-Smith, "The Congress for Cultural Freedom, the end of ideology and the 1955 Milan Conference: 'defining parameters of discourse'," *Journal of Contemporary History* 37, no. 3 (2002): 438.

21 See Christopher Lasch, *The agony of the American left*, 1. Vintage Books ed ed. (New York: Vintage Books, 1969), 64–111; Elena Aronova, "The Congress for Cultural Freedom, Minerva, and the Quest for Instituting "Science Studies" in the Age of Cold War," *Minerva* 50 (2012); Peter Coleman, *The liberal conspiracy. The Congress for Cultural Freedom and the struggle for the mind of postwar Europe* (New York [u.a.]: Free Press [u.a.], 1989); G. Scott-Smith, "'A radical Democratic political offensive': Melvin J. Lasky, Der Monat and the Congress for Cultural Freedom," *Journal of Contemporary History* 35, no. 2 (2000).

for Eastern European Studies, Ukrainian and Russian Centers, that were founded e.g. at Harvard University (1948), the Free University in West-Berlin (Osteuropa-Institut, 1951), in Amsterdam (Russland Instituut, 1948) or at the University of Fribourg in Switzerland (1957). Academic research went hand in hand with the distribution and dissemination of anticommunist politics. US institutions like the Ford Foundation or the Rockefeller Foundation relied on highly motivated actors like the Jesuit Gustav Wetter S.J, or the Dominican Professor of Philosophy Joseph Maria Bocheński, who not only founded the *Osteuropa-Institut* in 1957 in Fribourg, but also the periodical *Studies in Soviet Thought* and the book series *Sovietica*.[22]

The CCF as well as these centers and institutes represented the Cold War conflict as between freedom and repression. The 1953 conference of the CCF in Hamburg was on "Science and Freedom." In his opening remarks the social democratic mayor of Hamburg Max Brauer made it clear that science could only blossom in freedom, not under state authority. The Milan conference in 1955 similarly focused on "The Future of Freedom."[23]

For others the anticommunist message of freedom required depoliticization and the end of the age of ideologies. The historian H. Stuart Hughes argued in 1951 for "the end of political ideology," brought about by the threat of communism:

> In such a situation the ideological differences, the issues dividing capitalist and partly socialist states – that now characterize the Western coalition – may cease to be of much practical importance. Pressed by the same necessities, these states will doubtless begin to resemble each other.

Stuart wanted the old political divisions to be forgotten in the interest of defending basic freedoms.[24] But instead of depoliticizing the conflict, "the end of ideology" (Daniel Bell) reinforced the dominant Cold War polarities.[25]

The quest for cultural hegemony in the Cold War addressed primarily literary circles, since in the 1950s literature was still viewed as the leading art genre in Central Europe. One characteristic of Cold War culture in the 1950s was that it

---

22 See The Rockefeller Foundation Annual Report 1957, New York 1957, 235; Josef Maria Bocheński, *Die kommunistische Ideologie und die Würde, Freiheit und Gleichheit der Menschen im Sinne des Grundgesetzes für die Bundesrepublik Deutschland vom 23.5.1949* (Freiburg 1954).

23 See Scott-Smith, "A Radical Democratic Political Offensive," 438.

24 H. Stuart Hughes, 'The End of Political Ideology', *Measure*, 2 (Spring 1951): 153–4, 156.

25 See Thomas H. Schaub, *American fiction in the Cold War*, History of American thought and culture (Madison, Wis.: University of Wisconsin Press, 1991), 23; Daniel Bell, *The end of ideology. On the exhaustion of political ideas in the fifties* (Glencoe/Ill.: Free Press, 1960).

was largely set in the world of print culture. The war of ideas was fought out in the Gutenberg galaxy. This is why the material side of print culture, new editions in paperback, book clubs for the distribution of books and in Eastern Europe the allotment of paper quotas for publishing houses played such an important role. Print was the prime medium of propaganda and of dissent on both sides in the Cold War. The Reader's Digest made high quality literature of cultural and political content available to middle class consumers. For its editor David Reed Reader's Digest was one of the "three great international institutions," together with the Catholic Church and the Communist Party. The Cold War saw the "mightiest outpouring of mass market books of every kind." Whereas books had been sold in bookstores, paperbacks were on sale also in drug stores and newspaper dealers. The anti-Communist print culture of the 1950s in the United States relied heavily on networks; on small publishers offering quantity discounts often leading to prices of 20 cents per book. Reading groups, educational organizations, and periodicals provided the political guidance for their mass audience. Many of these books did not even rely on bookstores or drugstores but rather on mail-order catalogs. In addition, leading conservative anti-Communist authors provided their audience with comprehensive reading lists. Because of the impact of print culture, the anti-Communist movement survived the demise of Sen. Joseph McCarthy.

The political culture of Communism as well as of the Soviet Union also relied on print culture. Nikita Khrushchev and his allies ensured that the entry in the *Great Soviet Encyclopedia* on Lavrentiy Beria, a rival in the quest for power after Stalin's death in 1953, was replaced by a larger entry on the "Bering Sea" using a "small knife or razor blade." Print culture could produce both, loyalty and dissent, in the United States as well as abroad. The leftist students critique of United States politics rested entirely on the righteousness of print. The students believed in the transformative and democratic power of print. "Once a person had read the truth, that person would naturally become an active democratic citizen with the power to resist the injustice and intolerance of life the United States."[26]

The political orientation of leftist writers was of particular importance, since they were often aligned with political parties, in France with the communist party PCF. Intellectuals such as Jean-Paul Sartre, Albert Camus, René Char and André Breton were members of the communist party and consequently declined to take part in the CCF International Conference in Paris 1952, whereas W. H.

26 Greg Barnhisel and Catherine Turner, *Pressing the fight print, propaganda, and the Cold War*, Studies in print culture and the history of the book (Amherst, Mass. [u.a.]: University of Massachusetts Press, 2010), 4, 10, 12, 19.

Auden, Czesław Milosz, Ignazio Silone, André Malraux and William Faulkner did. For the members of the PCF among the French literary elite the Hungarian uprising in 1956 was a caesura. Many of them left the party. Khrushchev's speech at the Twentieth Congress of the Soviet Communist Party in 1956 further demotivated the communist intellectuals. Among those intellectuals leaving the PCF were François Furet, Albert Camus and many others later turning more and more liberal. German writers responded to the uprisings in 1953 and 1956 differently. Besides their vehement protest against the Russian troops, members of the "Group 47" – never in tune with Marxism – were more concerned with national unification and the Nazi crimes.[27]

Besides print culture visual culture with popular movies was on the rise. Films played a crucial role in the cultural Cold War, because they reached a broader audience.[28] Movies took up contemporary issues like the suppression of the Hungarian Catholic Church after February 1949, when Cardinal Mindszenty was sentenced in a show trial to lifelong prison.[29] At least three Cold War movies told his story: *Guilty of Treason* (Felix Feist 1950), *The Prisoner* (Peter Glenville 1955) starring Alec Guinness and in 1966 *Mission: Impossible*.[30] They all portrayed Cardinal Mindszenty through the cultural trope of a martyr. The movies appealed emotionally to an American and Western audience while denouncing the Soviet atheist policies and the suppression of the church. Thereby older Catholic anticommunism was enlisted for the US, not a natural ally of the Catholic Church.[31]

The movies on Mindszenty represented the enemy as something abstract: the communist system, atheism and dictatorship. The plot represented a bipolar

---

27 See Anita Krätzer, *Das Amerikabild im Prosawerk von Max Frisch. Studien zum Amerikabild in der neueren deutschen Literatur. Max Frisch – Uwe Johnson – Hans Magnus Enzensberger und das "Kursbuch"* (Bern, Frankfurt: University of Michigan, 1982).

28 See Tony Shaw, *British cinema and the Cold War. The state, propaganda and consensus* (London: Tauris, 2001); *Hollywood's cold war* (Edinburgh: Edinburgh University Press, 2007); David W. Ellwood, Rob Kroes, and Gian Piero Brunetta, *Hollywood in Europe: experiences of a cultural hegemony*, European contributions to American studies (Amsterdam: VU University Press, 1994).

29 See Tony Shaw, "Martyrs, Miracles, and Martians: Religion and Cold War Cinematic Propaganda in the 1950s," *Journal of Cold War Studies* 4, no. 2 (2002).

30 The Soviet-made "*Conspiracy of the Doomed*" (Michail Kalatozov 1950) also referred to Mindszentys story. See ibid., 15.

31 See ibid., 14–19; for cold war movies cf. Thomas Patrick Doherty, *Cold War, cool medium: television, McCarthyism, and American culture*, Film and culture (New York, N.Y. [u.a.]: Columbia University Press, 2003); Ronnie D. Lipschutz, *Cold War fantasies: film, fiction, and foreign policy* (Lanham, Md. [u.a.]: Rowman & Littlefield, 2001); Seed; John Pollard, "The Vatican, Italy and the Cold War," in *Religion and the Cold War*, ed. Dianne Kirby (Basingstoke: Palgrave Macmillan, 2003), 109.

structure of the conflict, with morality standing against immorality, Christian values against atheism. The message was clear: A devout Catholic could single-handedly resist Communist dictatorship and brainwashing. The particular evil quality of the enemy was essential. The communist interrogator did not resort to torture, but rather to psychological means when he tried to break the Cardinal's will. The political message suggested that totalitarian systems like the Third Reich and the Soviet Union all resorted to "robot like enslavement."[32]

Films were used to intervene politically in the Italian elections of April 1948. Immediately before the ballot, the movie *Ninotchka* (Ernst Lubitsch, 1939), an anti-Communist comedy about the Soviet communist nomenclatura starring Greta Garbo, was released in Italy to counter the slim lead of the Italian Communist Party (PCI) in the polls.[33] For the communist side winning the national elections was a lesson to be learned from fascism, the Second World War and the resistenza. Their learning the lesson of fascism and World War II primarily involved the intellectuals. The liberal-conservative parties drew another consequence from former dictatorships. That lesson was – in their idiom – to resist Soviet dictatorship and to affirm the values of liberal democracy. The PCI tried to win over the intellectuals; the Hollywood movie went for the common man. The PCI finally lost the elections.

The link between culture and politics seems particularly obvious in cultural diplomacy. It is an endeavor to "manage the international environment through making (one's) cultural resources and achievements known overseas and/or facilitating cultural transmissions abroad."[34] Examples came from the US and the USSR. The Bolshoi Theatre was sent as a cultural envoy to the West, repeating its tours many times in the 1950s and 1960s. The company's shows drew the masses and were a guaranteed success. Also, classical musicians and sportsmen represented the Soviet Union abroad. Countless initiatives showed the public diplomacy of the USSR.[35] Historical research on the cultural Cold War has come up with many examples for the "conscription of the arts" in the service of one side or the other.[36]

---

32 Shaw, "Martyrs, Miracles, and Martians: Religion and Cold War Cinematic Propaganda in the 1950s," 17.

33 See Brogi.

34 Jessica Gienow-Hecht and Mark C. Donfried, "The model of cultural diplomacy. Power, distance, and the promise of civil society," in *Searching for a cultural diplomacy*, ed. Jessica Gienow-Hecht and Mark C. Donfried (New York [u.a.]: Berghahn Books, 2010), 14.

35 See Tobias Rupprecht, "Socialist high modernity and global stagnation: a shared history of Brazil and the Soviet Union during the Cold War," *Journal of Global History* 6, no. 3 (2011): 519.

36 Claire F. Fox, *Making Art Panamerican cultural policy and the Cold War* (Minneapolis, Minn.:

Was culture just an extension of politics in the Cold War or were its dissimilarities from politics more important than its similarities? Frances Stonor Saunders and Scott Lucas argue that cultural involvement in Cold War issues was more or less directed by political interests.[37] Contemporaries like the American writer Paul Goodman observed similarly:

> The current disease is to make Cold War capital out of everything, no matter what. We cannot dedicate a building of Frank Lloyd Wright's in New York without our Ambassador to the United Nations pointing out that such an architect could not have flourished in Russia.[38]

Nearly everything in the cultural world has been explained via the influence of the Cold War, including dance, college football or the post war polio crisis, read as a manifestation of the body politic's own affliction.[39] This brings up the question, whether there was a cultural sphere in the 1950s and 60s that was independent from the Cold War. Not everything can be attributed to the influence of the Cold War. David Caute has taken issue with the "constant determination to find a Cold War 'smoking gun' behind all cultural activity. ... At a certain point 'culture' collapses under the weight of investigation into merely another term for 'propaganda'."[40] Others like Jessica Gienow-Hecht admit political machinations, but argue nevertheless for a (semi-)autonomous sphere of culture.[41]

University of Minnesota Press, 2013); Sarah Davies, "The Soft Power of Anglia: British Cold War Cultural Diplomacy in the USSR," *Contemporary British History* 27, no. 3 (2013); Yale Richmond, *Practicing public diplomacy: a Cold War odyssey*, vol. 5 (Berghahn Books, 2008); Jessica C. E. Gienow-Hecht, "'How Good Are We?' Culture and the Cold War," *Intelligence & National Security* 18, no. 2 (2003); Naima Prevots, *Dance for export: cultural diplomacy and the Cold War*, Studies in dance history (Hanover, NH [u.a.]: University Press of New England [u.a.], 1998).

37 See Saunders; Scott Lucas, *Freedom's war. The American crusade against the Soviet Union* (New York: New York University Press, 1999); Giles Scott-Smith and Hans Krabbendam, *The cultural Cold War in Western Europe 1945 – 1960*, Cass series Studies in intelligence (London [u.a.]: Cass, 2003), 4.

38 Barnhisel, 25.

39 Christina Ezrahi, "Dance as a Lens on American Cold War Culture," (2015); Benjamin Phillips, "College Football and American Culture in the Cold War Era," (Malden, USA2010); Foertsch; "'A Battle of Silence': Women's Magazines and the Polio Crisis in Post-war UK and USA," in *American Cold war culture*, ed. Douglas Field (Ediunburgh: Edinburgh UP, 2005).

40 Scott-Smith and Krabbendam, 4.

41 It constituted "the transmission of ideas, dreams, mores, traditions, and beliefs from one generation to the next, from one continent to another, one group of people to another in the form of schools, galleries, orchestra halls, shopping centers, department stores and information centers." Jessica Gienow-Hecht, "Culture and the Cold War in Europe," in *Cambridge History of the Cold War*, ed. Odd Arne Westad Melvyn P. Leffler (Cambridge: Cambridge UP, 2010), 398–99.

Indeed, Cold War culture did not invent its genres and formats, nor did it govern all aspects of cultural life. The cultural Cold War produced a lot, but hardly anything new. The genres of the cultural Cold War where established in the inter-war years with science fiction in place already in the 1920s. The media of the cultural Cold War including TV were technological innovations predating World War II. Anti-communism predated the Cold War so that the Cold War can be seen as one chapter of the history of the East-West antagonism since 1917.[42] Besides Cold War culture existed cultural, even countercultural movements as the youth movement or the student movement, the women's and ecological movements, that were largely independent of the Cold War. Not everything was part of the cultural Cold War. Cold War culture was in many ways part of bigger stories.

2 Cold War Modernities

Cold War culture tapped into broader and into older themes, most prominently into modernism and modernity. The Cold War has been explained more generally as a conflict between conflicting models of modernity. Modernism played a major role in the Soviet Union as well as in the West between the wars.[43] Its ubiquitous role was such that modernism and modernity served themselves as a meta-frame for capitalism and communism. Both claimed to be the better, if not the only way to modernity. Whereas in the 1920s and the 1930s modernism took on a rather leftist outlook, rejecting traditional and bourgeois society. Modernism was strong in the US as well as in the USSR. Modernity and modernism were older than the Cold War, they preceded and outlived it. Still: "the Cold War became the apotheosis of 20th century modernity, visually as well as socially."[44]

The autonomy of the arts stood at the center of the 1950s modernism. It was spelled out theoretically in aesthetical polemics and practically in the fine arts. In the theoretical debate art was seen as the opposite of politics. "Art is not political" was used in an anti-communist way to counter uses of art as propaganda: Art is not propaganda. Modernist aesthetics distanced itself from propaganda as it was observed in mass culture. Modernism should be high art. High art was serious

42 Jost Dülffer, *Europa im Ost-West-Konflikt 1945–1991* (München: Oldenbourg, 2004).

43 Susan Buck-Morss, *Dreamworld and catastrophe: the passing of mass utopia in East and West* (Cambridge, Mass.: MIT Press, 2000).

44 Odd Arne Westad, "The Cold War and the international history of the twentieth century," in *The Cambridge History of the Cold War*, ed. Odd Arbe Westad Melvyn P. Leffler (Cambridge: Cambridge UP, 2010), 10, 17.

and no propaganda at all, went the claim. This argument against propaganda ran against communist propaganda. Since communist politics was seen as pervading every aspect of society and culture, resisting communism meant resisting politics. Being anti-propaganda, anti-mass culture and apolitical or even anti-political went hand in hand. Politics was perceived as a threat to art. Anti-communist aesthetic ideology in the 1950s insisted, that freedom implied autonomy of the arts, a point the New Critics and New York intellectuals were making over and over. The social function of the arts was seen in their relative autonomy in relation to politics. Literature as all other fine arts was beyond politics, "but by moving beyond politics it fulfilled an essentially political task." This asserted the political impact of apoliticality.[45]

What modernism was in the realm of culture, modernity was in the political Cold War. The Cold War has been described as a conflict between opposing concepts of modernity, that of liberal capitalism and that of socialism. This is the basic line of Odd Arne Westad's and Melvyn Leffler's three volume "Cambridge History of the Cold War". The Cold War was essentially a "conflict between the two versions of western modernity that socialism and liberal capitalism seemed to offer." The intensity of the Cold War "was created by each side's conviction that they represented the last, best hope for the rescue of a rational, transcending modernity from the horrors of war and nationalist conflict." Both camps shared a rational vision of society, opposed to violence, nationalism, and war. That both stood for conflicting versions of the same modernist paradigm was made patently clear in the Third World. From the perspective of the new African states the Cold War was a

> conflict between the two versions of Western modernity that socialism and liberal capitalism seemed to offer. The globalization of the Cold War that these struggles led to both intensified the superpower conflict through international interventions and increased the cost of the competition, while destroying many of the societies in which the battles were carried out.[46]

What then was Cold War modernism? It was a contested cultural term shared by both sides.[47] "It is commonplace for the cultural Cold War to be viewed as an aesthetic combat zone between realism and modernism: differing rationales for the

45 Roland Végső, *The naked communist. Cold War modernism and the politics of popular culture* (New York, NY: Fordham University Press, 2013), 95.

46 Melvyn P. Leffler and Odd Arne Westad, *The Cambridge History of the Cold War Volume 1: Origins, 1945–1962* (Cambridge: Cambridge University Press, 2010), 10.

47 For modernization utopias within the Soviet Union cf. Buck-Morss.

production, consumption and judgment of art, music, literature and so forth."[48] But Cold War modernism could be found in the East as well as in the West, since both shared "early cinema, urban architecture, mass leaders, media manipulation, the mass-utopian myth of industrial 'modernization' itself."[49] Already in the interwar years the science fiction genre had favored the demonization of the enemy. "In the 1920s, the contrast of 'communist heaven' and 'capitalist hell' was a generic theme in Soviet science fiction, projecting onto the 'other' all of the negative aspects of industrial society." After the Second World War, US TV series on 'alien invaders' inscribed the fear of Communism into science fiction fantasies.[50] More broadly, modernism linked various fields together, that had formerly been seen as disconnected. It was a powerful tool to see architecture, politics, the military and city planning, defense needs and the mobilization of the labor resources through one lense. "Seen through this historical prism, the great Cold War enemies, while having been truly dangerous to each other, appear as in fact close relatives."[51]

The two sides shared central aspects of Cold War modernism. "Both the United States and the Soviet Union placed education at the center of their social systems in a way never before seen among great powers."[52] Education was no longer a privilege for the cultural and political elite, but a characteristic of the broader society. The United States as well as the Soviet Union educated young students from Third World countries and from their allies in Europe. "Against the traditions of privilege, heritage, family and locality, both Soviets and Americans offered a modern and revolutionary alternative." For Americans this meant the "globalization of the United States immigrant perspective, in which people could choose the communities to which they wished to belong," for the Soviets it meant the universalization of the "Bolshevik's hatred for 'old Russia', considered backward and underdeveloped."[53] The ideological focus on anti-privilege, modernity and innovation also facilitated the advancement of new social elites in East and West. "It made it easier for individuals to willingly seek inclusion. ... Entry into the elites was probably more open in social terms in these two countries than in most others" including their allies, particularly Britain and France.[54] Both sides

48 Johnston, 291.

49 Buck-Morss, 235.

50 See John Cheng, Astounding wonder. Imagining science and science fiction in interwar America, (Philadelphia: University of Pennsylvania Press, 2012).

51 Buck-Morss.

52 Ibid., 13.

53 Ibid., 14.

54 Ibid., 15.

were convinced that their vision of a modern and rational society would be successful. The future was surely theirs. The world would unavoidably move "in the direction of the aims they themselves had set."[55]

Modernism was one of the most prominent topics in the cultural politics within the Soviet sphere, being outlawed in 1948 as an outgrowth of Western politics and capitalist influence. Contrary to the official condemnation of formalism as bourgeois class aesthetics, modernism survived for instance in the GDR as a way to express social inclusion and egalitarianism. Modern design was popular in West as well as in East Germany. "Modern design was considered to be able to wipe out the national Socialist legacy which was regarded as either the apex of capitalism (East) or the combination of all reprehensible characteristics of Wilhelmine culture (West)."[56] Particularly the turn of the century furniture was now ridiculed as "Gelsenkirchener Barock."[57] Journals, discourses and practices in East and West Germany embraced instead a modern, Scandinavian style, since it was considered inclusive and egalitarian. Such modern design helped to communicate a new cultural identity after Nazi dictatorship.

In the art world many shared the strong belief, "that art should be autonomous from the practice of daily life, not subject to evaluation of social or political criteria."[58] This detachment from everyday life was aesthetically brought to the fore by formal elements of modernist art, particularly its techniques of representation. "Modernism was a set of formal techniques and attitudes unique to each art form but sharing some important commonalities across genres: allusiveness, abstraction, fragmentation and indirectness, the sense of being belated within a cultural tradition, the subsumption of emotion under formal technique, the retreat of the personality of the artist into the background behind different 'masks' or narrative voices, and, above all, high seriousness."[59] That high seriousness was expressed in formal art language, shying away from realism as well as from tradition.

Interwar modernism with its sympathies for the left had met fierce criticism from the political establishment in Europe. Politics in the United States as well is in Europe harbored well into the 1950s skepticism if not outright hostility toward

55 Ibid., 13.
56 See Natalie Scholz and Milena Veenis, "Cold War Modernism and Post-War German Homes. An East-West Comparison," in *Divided dreamworlds? The cultural cold war in East and West*, ed. Joes Segal and Peter Romijn (Amsterdam: Amsterdam UP, 2008), 160.
57 See 'Weg von Tante Frieda', Der Spiegel, 26 September 1951, 32–33, quoted in: Scholz, *Cold War Modernism and Post-War German Homes*, 164.
58 Barnhisel, 3.
59 Ibid.

modernist art. Besides its aesthetical traditionalism the political establishment saw modernists as unreliable precisely because they insisted on their autonomy. Proponents of this argument often pointed to the modernists' alignment with the republican and communist left in the Spanish civil war 1936–39. The communist air about modernism stemmed from that period and was signified by Picasso and his alignment with the Communist Party. When modernist artists like Picasso and others joined the Communist Party in 1945 this was seen as proof for the profound communist affiliations of modernist art.

Suspicions about the modernist art were widespread and reached beyond McCarthy's campaign against supposed communists in Hollywood and the art world. When in 1947 President Harry Truman looked at Yasuo Kuniyoshi's painting *Circus girl resting*, a part of the touring exhibition *Advancing American Art* organized by the U.S. State Department, he remarked: "If this is art, I'm a Hottentot." In a letter to Assistant Secretary of State William Benton of 2 April 1947 he referred to the exhibition as "the vaporings of half-naked lazy people." He saw himself in complete accordance with the American people at large:

> There are a great many American artists who still believe that the ability to make things look as they are is the first requirement of a great artist. They do not belong to the so-called modern school. There is no art at all in connection with the modernists, in my opinion.[60]

Two days after this letter, Secretary of State George Marshall ordered that the exhibition now in Czechoslovakia and Haiti stay in place and do not move on as Ambassador of US culture. Three weeks later, the Office of International Information and Cultural Affairs (OIC) funds for 1948 were eliminated. The OIC had organized the exhibition.[61] Marshall was deeply skeptical about spending "taxpayers' money on modern art."[62] The examples for anti-modernist resentment in the 1950s are legion. Harry Truman would have welcome Soviet realism after 1948 aesthetically, had he not been US President. Why then could modernism overcome the anti-modernist opposition (even in the White House)?

Convincing the public of modernism meant aligning modernism in some way with the United States. If modernism was to be brought into the Western cultural Cold War its more revolutionary political associations from the interwar years had to be replaced by "a celebration of the virtues of freedom and the assertion

---

60 Quoted in: New York Times, January 20 1986.

61 Michael L. Krenn, *Fall-out shelters for the human spirit: American art and the Cold War* (Chapel Hill: University of North Carolina Press, 2005).

62 Greg Barnhisel, "Perspectives USA and the cultural cold war: Modernism in service of the state," *Modernism-Modernity* 14, no. 4 (2007): 735.

that the individual is sovereign."[63] To align modernism to freedom would then mean reframing its political alliances. Modernism should serve as an argument about freedom as a characteristic of the US. In 1952 Alfred H. Barr Jr., New York's Museum of Modern Art's first president (1929–1944), had claimed in a *New York Times* article that realism was the preferred style of totalitarians, while abstract art symbolized political freedom.[64]

The more difficult task was to reconcile the autonomy of the arts with US mass culture. When Alfred Barr from the MoMA pointed to the proof of modernism for a free society that was easily countered by Soviet politics pointing to the self-declared aloofness and elitism of abstract expressionism. Modernism indeed shied away from any content as well as from the masses and embraced formalism. Reconciling modernism's quest for autonomy with conservative politics while at the same time reconciling it with mass culture proved to be the Achilles heel of the cultural Cold War. The tension between elitism and mass culture was tolerable only as long as the modernist autonomy of the arts was an argument against socialist realism in the 1950s. In the decade of détente that could no longer be sustained. The 1960s saw a loosening of the cultural antagonism between modernism and realism. The relationship between modernism and mass culture was finally redefined. The 1960s and the 70s saw several attempts to reconcile modernism with mass culture in pop art (Roy Lichtenstein, Andy Warhol, Tom Wesselmann), documentary literature and interior design on a mass basis. Artists increasingly drew on popular and mass cultural forms and genres and overlaid them with modernist and avant-gardist strategies. Still viewed skeptically by conservative cultural critics as non-art, supermarket-art, Kitsch-art, or as a coca-colonization of Western Europe, it was a huge success, which led others to expect that this was finally bridging the gap between high-brow and low-brow forms of art, between modernism and the marketplace. After the high spirited modernism of the 1950s countered the communist claim, that the US had no high culture, the 1960s modernism answered to the claim, that modernism was too much high-brow, elitist and implicitly denied the masses access to art.

63 *Cold War modernists: art, literature, and American cultural diplomacy, 1946–1959*, 3.

64 Russell H Bartley, "The Piper Played to Us All: Orchestrating the Cultural Cold War in the USA, Europe, and Latin America," *International Journal of Politics, Culture, and Society* (2001): 580; Eva Cockroft, "Abstract Expressionism: weapon of the Cold War, Artforum, June 1974," in *How New York Stole the Idea of Modern Art* ed. Eva Cockroft and Serge Guilbaut (Chicago: Chicago University Press, 1983).

While modernism had accused socialist realism of performing kitsch in the early 1950s, it was now modernism to take the same blame from conservative cultural critics. Reconciling modernism with mass culture, meant that

> it was possible to imagine that art could be found as much in the arrangement of merchandise in a department store window, in the graphics of a magazine advertisement, in the silhouette of the women's dress, or in a streamlined kitchen appliance as in the paintings hanging in a museum. Suddenly the curators of exhibitions at the Museum of Modern Art appeared to think that when it came to his stylistic ingenuity, there was not much difference between the Kandinsky canvas and a Kalvinator refrigerator.[65]

The clash between modernism and realism was fought differently in every country. Modernism lost the connotation of rebellion. Beginning in the 1940s and more broadly in the 1950s it became part of the American cultural establishment. In Europe that came later. One reason for this shift was the influence of Americanization in Europe, increasing after 1945 when Germany, Austria and Italy embraced US culture. The postwar economic boom and the rise of the welfare state in the 1950s reduced resentments against American consumer society. "Consensus capitalism" or "consensus liberalism" became a notion that even the Social democratic left could agree on. It integrated unions as well as socialist parties into Western political systems, from which they had been excluded by liberal elites in the interwar years. Even politicians like Willy Brandt adopted the cultural style of Kennedy with home stories and a public role of his wife.[66]

Still, modernism was not evenly distributed, was not the dominant art everywhere. Modernism reached the status of established art in the various European countries and the US at different times. In the United States that was already the case in the 1940s. In France with its culture of surrealism in the 1930s the culmination point of modernism was in the late 1940s. The latecomers where Britain and Germany, where only after protracted domestic cultural wars modernism was allowed into the cultural pantheon. In Britain, individualist modernism not only ran against lasting Victorian traditions of art and style, but also against imperial memories. Adopting modernism here was felt by many as losing the empire to the US again – and this time forever.

---

65 Richard H. Pells, *Modernist America art, music, movies, and the globalization of American culture* (New Haven [u.a.]: Yale University Press, 2011), 85–98, 85; Andreas Huyssen, *After the great divide. Modernism, mass culture, postmodernism*, Language, discourse, society (Basingstoke u.a.: Macmillan, 1988), 197.

66 See Daniela Münkel, "Als 'deutscher Kennedy' zum Sieg?" Willy Brandt, die USA und die Medien," *Zeithistorische Forschungen* 1, no. 2 (2004).

The arrival of modernism in official Western Germany establishment was signified by architecture. Chancellor Ludwig Erhard embraced Cold War modernism in the construction of the new chancellery in Bonn which embodied the Mies-van-der-Rohe style.[67] Architectural modernism became identified with democracy because of such characteristics as "newness, openness, abstraction, ambiguity, and technological innovation."[68]

Modernism was a decidedly Western aesthetic style of fine arts, design and urban planning after all. The Eastern European governments launched a "disinfection campaign" against American culture and influence, focusing on Jazz music, Hollywood films and on architecture. "Cosmopolitan" served as a code word for America, whereas "democratic" was a synonym for countries under communist rule. In 1954 the East German Guide for Architects made clear that architecture was divided between the "forces of reaction," embodied by the CIAM (Congrés international d'architecture moderne), and the democratic forces led by the Soviet Union:

> As in other capitalist countries, building is predominantly formalist and subordinated to the cosmopolitan ideology of American imperialism. This is why buildings look alike whatever their location, where they are in West Germany, Italy, France, or America. The housing, banks, administration buildings, hotels, and stores in the form of shapeless boxes are an expression of the profit hunger of monopoly capitalism under American dominance. The obliteration of all national character continues relentlessly. This is evident as well in the destruction of valuable historical complexes. Thus architecture is replaced by mere construction.[69]

The Soviets tried to counter modernism by emphasizing traditional high culture: Russian and Soviet history stood for classical culture, whereas American society merely offered materialism and popular culture, ran the argument. Only high culture embodies common humanistic values, whereas the American cosmopolitan formalism catered to individualism, the enemy of socialist democracy. Indeed, one of the key goals of communist cultural policies was to make high

67 Burkhard Körner, "Der Kanzlerbungalow von Sep Ruf in Bonn," *Bonner Geschichtsblätter* 49/50 (2001).

68 Jane C. Loeffler, *The architecture of diplomacy. Building America's embassies*, rev. 2. ed. (New York: Princeton Architectural, 2011), 7, 8.

69 Edwin Collein, *Handbuch für Architekten* (Berlin: Verl. Technik, 1954). quoted in: Anders Åman, *Architecture and ideology in Eastern Europe during the Stalin era: an aspect of Cold War history* (New York, Cambridge, Mass.: Architectural History Foundation, MIT Press, 1992), 251; David Crowley, "Europe Reconstructed, Europe Divided," in *Cold war modern design 1945 – 1970*, ed. David Crowley and Jane Pavitt (London: V&A Publishing, 2008), 45.

culture accessible to the masses. After their defeat of Nazi Germany, the Soviet cultural commissars saw themselves as the only remaining standard bearers of high culture.[70] In East Berlin the cultural commissars distinguished between the anti-Semitic and nationalist roots of Nazism and the legacy of Weimar or Viennese classicism, which they promoted from the beginning. Several cultural organizations, including VOKS, showed the Soviets interest in German high culture.[71]

"Winning the minds of men" referred particularly to West Germany.[72] Referring to high culture in many cases meant invoking the three "B"s: Bach, Beethoven and Brahms, as well as Schiller and Goethe, Kant and Hegel and others. Gaining the loyalty of the Western Germans looked promising to the Soviets, since they could rely on a long tradition of German anti-Americanism.[73] The Soviet approach wasn't completely implausible since high culture served as one of the few sources for German identity, supposedly left untainted by the Nazis and by anti-Semitism. Adopting a democratic system while clinging to the valued classicism around 1800 posed a problem in the 1950s since Westernization also involved a controversial Americanization of cultural styles. If the adoption of Western democratic values meant a reevaluation of Germany's cultural past, West Germans remained skeptical. They "clearly feared the adoption of democratic values at the expense of their cultural heritage."[74]

The American government understood the need to appear as culturally attractive to high-brow Europeans. President Truman had already demanded of US cultural diplomacy to present a "full and fair picture" of American life to Europe and to the Third World.[75] Moreover, Eisenhower feared that Europeans might see Americans as "a race of materialists. ... Spiritual and intellectual values are deemed to be almost nonexistent in our country."[76] In a series of exhibitions that went on tour, private US institutions promoted domestic design as a charac-

---

70 See Gienow-Hecht, 403.

71 See Bernd Bonwetsch, *Sowjetische Politik in der SBZ, 1945 – 1949 Dokumente zur Tätigkeit der Propagandaverwaltung (Informationsverwaltung) der SMAD unter Sergej Tjul'panov*, Archiv für Sozialgeschichte Beiheft (Bonn: Dietz, 1998); Dagmar Buchbinder, "Kunst-Administration nach sowjetischem Vorbild: Die Staatliche Kommission für Kunstangelegenheiten," in *Die DDR – Analysen eines aufgegebenen Staates*, ed. Heiner Timmermann (Berlin: Duncker & Humblot, 2001).

72 Gienow-Hecht and Donfried, 15.

73 See Jessica Gienow-Hecht, "Trumpeting down the walls of Jericho: The politics of art, music and emotion in German-American relations, 1870–1920," *Journal of social history* 36, no. 3 (2003). The New York Philharmonic did not hire a single long-term non-German conductor until 1906.

74 Ibid., 404.

75 Gienow-Hecht and Donfried, 15.

76 Quoted in Barnhisel, "Perspectives USA and the cultural cold war: Modernism in service of the state," 734.

teristic of the American way of life. "Design was not a marginal aspect of the Cold War but central – both materially and theoretically – to the competition over the future."[77] Between 1951 and 1955 the MoMA curated several exhibitions such as the "American Home 1953" dedicated to displaying design in US households, co-produced with a number of government agencies, most notably the State Department, the Mutual Security Agency and the United States Information Agency (USIA). The MoMA thereby assumed an unofficial role in the Foreign Service.[78]

Another cultural battleground was France. In 1955 the MoMA sent the exhibition "50 years of American Art" to Paris, later to Zurich, Barcelona, Frankfurt, London, The Hague, Vienna and Belgrade. It was designed to counter anxieties about American cultural homogenization and imperialism. Indeed, French intellectuals on the left and the right saw American consumerism and mass culture as threats to French culture. The exhibition formed part of a "Salute to France," an arts festival organized by the United States Information Service (USIS) to pay tribute to French civilization.[79] American art was presented for instance through designer chairs by Charles Eames, Henry Bertoia and Eero Saarinen. The exhibit "50 years of American art" focused on interior design household appliances and living rooms. The MoMA also featured expressionist paintings in a 1956 exhibition on "Modern Art in the United States," which included 12 painters such as Willem de Kooning, Franz Kline, Robert Motherwell, Jackson Pollock, and Mark Rothko. It could be seen in eight European cities, among them Vienna and Belgrade.[80]

---

77 David Crowley and Jane Pavitt, *Cold War modern: design 1945–1970* (London: V&A Pub., 2008), 14; Elizabeth Armstrong, *Birth of the cool: California art, design, and culture at midcentury*, ed. Michael Boyd, et al., California art, design, and culture at midcentury (Newport Beach, Munich, New York: Orange County Museum of Art Prestel Art, 2007); Robert H. Haddow, *Pavilions of plenty. Exhibiting American culture abroad in the 1950s* (Washington [u.a.]: Smithsonian Inst. Press, 1997).

78 See Helen M. Franc, "The Early Years of the International Program and Council," in *The Museum of Modern Art at Midcentury: At Home and* Abroad, ed. John Elderfield, vol. 4 of Studies in Modern Art (New York: The Museum of Modern Art, 1995), 112–114. This aspect has been particularly well researched. Cf. Alessandro Brogi, "A question of balance: How France and the United States created Cold War Europe," *International History Review* 30, no. 2 (2008); Giles Scott-Smith, *Networks of empire. The US State Department's Foreign Leader Program in the Netherlands, France, and Britain 1950 – 70*, European Policy (Bruxelles [u.a.]: Lang, 2008); Laura A. Belmonte, *Selling the American way. U.S. propaganda and the Cold War* (Philadelphia, Pa.: University of Pennsylvania Press, 2008); Martina Topić and Siniša Rodin, *Cultural diplomacy and cultural imperialism European perspective(s)* (Frankfurt am Main [u.a.]: Lang, 2012).

79 See Gay McDonald, "Selling the American Dream: MoMA, Industrial Design and Postwar France," in *Journal of Design History* 17 (2004), 397–412.

80 See Gerard Holden, *International relations during and after the cold war. A comparative approach to intellectual history and culture*, Sonderveröffentlichung des FKKS (Mannheim: FKKS,

The connection between culture and politics was even more obvious in the rise of Jazz as musical expression of America's commitment to 'freedom.'[81] Unlike abstract expressionist painting Jazz served as a reminder of the mass cultural roots of American Cold War modernism. Jazz critics like John Wilson (New York Times) and Marshall Stearns saw Jazz as an original product of American modernism. They were quick to point out that its roots did not lay in Wall Street, but in a segregated South, and that Jazz was an artistic expression of underclass African-American culture.

In 1958, Secretary of State John Foster Dulles sent musicians like Dave Brubeck to Poland for 12 concerts, and then to Turkey, to Pakistan, Afghanistan, India, Ceylon and finally to Iran and Iraq. Dizzy Gillespie went to Greece, Louis Armstrong to Africa. Duke Ellington, Thelonious Monk, Benny Goodman and Miles Davis also participated in this endeavor in Jazz diplomacy. Dave Brubeck's wife wrote an ironic song for Louis Armstrong:

> The State Department has discovered jazz
> It reaches folks like nothing ever has.
> When our neighbors called us vermin,
> We sent out Woody Herman.
> That's what they call cultural exchange.[82]

Jazz diplomacy was pretty successful by the standards of cultural diplomacy. One of the most popular Soviet orchestra leaders Leonid Osipovich Utyosov praised US Jazz in 1961 in an article for the *Sovietskaya Kultura* and countered thereby the communist wholesale critique of culture in the US. For him prohibiting Jazz as "a forbidden fruit" of capitalism was "dangerous and interfered with the education of youth in musical taste." Jazz was not a "Western imperialist weapon to sabotage the morals of young people." Quite to the contrary: Jazz transcended the contamination of the market:

1998); Richard Alan Schwartz, *Cold War culture: media and the arts, 1945 – 1990*, Cold War America (New York, NY: Facts on File, 1998); Serge Guilbaut, *How New York stole the idea of modern art. Abstract expressionism, freedom, and the Cold War*, Paperback ed. (Chicago [u.a.]: University of Chicago Press, 1995); Manfred J. Holler and Barbara Klose-Ullmann, "Abstract expressionism as a weapon of the Cold War," in *Culture and External Relations: Europe and Beyond*, ed. Jozef Bátora and Monika Mokre (Farnham [u.a.]: Ashgate, 2011); Belmonte.

81 For Cold War and Music cf. Danielle Fosler-Lussier, *Music in America's Cold War diplomacy* (University of California Press, 2015); Paul Devlin, "Jazz Autobiography and the Cold War," *Popular Music and Society* 38, no. 2 (2015); Shellie M Clark, "Soothing the Savage Beast: Music in the Cultural Cold War, 1945–1991," (2015).

82 Quoted in *The American Interest*, Spring 2006.

> We need Jazz. ... Good Jazz is art. ... I must say that Jazz is not a synonym for imperialism and that the saxophone was not born of colonialism. (It had its roots) "not in the bankers' safes but in the poor Negro quarters."[83]

Why did abstract art, Jazz, and expressionism, play such an important role as exponents of modernism in the cultural Cold War?[84] First, private and public institutions in the United States tried to prove thereby that the allegation, that the US had only low culture, was wrong. In the early 1950s a serious artist was a modernist. He shied away from the masses, from mass taste and avoided simplistic realist representations and mistrusted political messages. Instead he investigated the psychological complexities of an individual subject. The serious modernist artist did just that according to officials in the US cultural diplomacy circles. According to Arthur Schlesinger abstract art was proof of individualism as well as freedom. Both would find their place in US art, whereas according to the Soviet model freedom and individualism had no place in art. Soviet culture sought – according to Schlesinger – to undermine the individual, thinking, acting subject. Direct political control of the arts "either throttles the serious artist or makes him slick and false."[85] The apolitical nature of expressionist art could be seen as proof for the freedom of cultural production. "Its very apoliticality made 'modernism' ... a key component in an argument about the cultural superiority of the West."[86] Finally, modern art, particularly expressionist art, was attractive to

---

83 Quoted in Penny M. Von Eschen, *Satchmo Blows Up the World: Jazz Ambassadors Play the Cold War* (Cambridge, MA, USA: Harvard University Press, 2004). Cf. Stephen A Crist, "Jazz as Democracy? Dave Brubeck and Cold War Politics," *The Journal of Musicology* 26, no. 2 (2009); Lisa E. Davenport, *Jazz Diplomacy: Promoting America in the Cold War Era* (Jackson, MS, USA: University Press of Mississippi, 2009); Keith Hatschek, "The impact of American jazz diplomacy in Poland during the cold war era," 4, no. 3 (2010); Mark Carroll, *Music and ideology in Cold War Europe* (Cambridge [u.a.]: Cambridge University Press, 2003); Von Eschen. On Aaron Copland see Emily Abrams Ansari, "Aaron Copland and the Politics of Cultural Diplomacy," *Journal of the Society for American Music* 5, no. 3 (2011).

84 See Barnhisel, "Perspectives USA and the cultural cold war: Modernism in service of the state."; Mathews Jane de Hart, "Art and Politics in Cold War America," *The American Historical Review* 81, no. 4 (1976).

85 Barnhisel, *Cold War modernists: art, literature, and American cultural diplomacy, 1946–1959*; Arthur M. Schlesinger, *The vital center the politics of freedom* (Cambridge, Mass.: Riverside Press, 1949).

86 See Justyna Wierzchowska, *The absolute and the cold war: Discourses of Abstract Expresionism* (Peter Lang. Internationaler Verlag der Wissenschaften, 2011); Végső; Barnhisel, "Perspectives USA and the cultural cold war: Modernism in service of the state," 733–34.

left liberals, since its aesthetic style conveyed at once a modernist utopia and a distance from the past.[87]

Aesthetic modernism and political modernization

Modernism made claims about art in the age of the Cold War that was largely dominated by claims about modernity and modernization. The relation between modernism and modernization has therefore been a hotly debated issue in Cold War historiography. Were modernism and modernization opposites or could they be reconciled. Anticommunist liberalism as well as cultural critics wanted modernism to be the aesthetic expression of modernization, but modernism was itself in many cases a critique of modernization. This resulted more broadly in a modernist politics of anti-modernization, or even, in Jeffrey Herf's terms, "reactionary modernism." This ran into considerable resistance. Many anticommunists kept pointing to the critical stance of modernism toward modernization. They saw modernism neither as an ideological expression nor as a valid critique of modernization. Art should formulate ethically correct forms of modernization and certainly no scathing criticisms of it, ran the argument of anti-modernist modernization. Modernism could not easily be reconciled with the politics of modernization. Still they had to be related in some way, since "anti-Communist liberalism emerged at the meeting point of aesthetic modernism and political modernization."[88]

The Harvard historian Arthur Schlesinger Jr. tried to bridge the gap between modernism and modernity in one of the Cold War liberalism's most influential bestsellers. In 1949 he published *The Vital Center*, arguing that the Cold War antagonism was a "tension inherent in the very logic of modernity." Modernity was an "age of anxiety," since the industrial modernization failed to produce adequate forms of social organizations. Modernity had not been able to protect the individual from anxiety. He saw modern art or modernism as an authentic expression of that anxiety caused by modern freedom. For Schlesinger modernism was no critique of modernization, but rather the fullest expression of freedom whose material conditions were produced by modernization.[89]

Also: Modernization and modernism were no strict opposites, since modernization went along with its own version of modernism. Albert Wohlstetter, a defense intellectual, and Edward Shils, a Chicago sociologist, are good examples.

87 See Cockroft.
88 Végső, 176.
89 Schlesinger.

Wohlstetters relationship with the art historian Meyer Schapiro witnessed their shared interest in modernism and modernity. This could be called the modernism of modernization. According to Nils Gilman it came in at least three flavors:

> a technocosmopolitan flavor, which argued that modernity must be built on the foundations of tradition; a revolutionary flavor, which argued that modernization required a radical rupture with tradition; and an authoritarian flavor, which argued that this radical rupture could take place only through the force of a centralizing and omniscient state.

That also worked in the other direction. Modernist art had its own idea about the social and the political future. As Nils Gilman pointed out:

> Modernism was not just an aesthetic phenomenon but also a form of social and political practice in which history, society, economy, culture, and nature itself were all to be the object of technical transformation. Modernism was a polysemous code word for all that was good and desirable.[90]

Modernization theory and modernism shared two characteristics: both were essentially elitist and both were resolutely anti-populist. Both even shared a sense of authoritarianism.

Modernization theory stood at the center of the evolving Cold War social sciences. The social sciences as systems of knowledge claimed to understand successfully the other side. Western "defense intellectuals" like Frederick Osborn used social scientific approaches to analyze Communism, make capitalism compatible with the welfare state and to portray Modernism as the aesthetic consequence of that approach.[91] The social sciences seemed to hold "the key to understand the mysterious world behind the iron curtain."[92] Just as physics had shaped World War II, social science could shape the postwar period.[93]

---

90 Nils Gilman, *Mandarins of the future. Modernization theory in Cold War America*, New studies in American intellectual and cultural history (Baltimore [u.a.]: Johns Hopkins University Press, 2003), 7–9.

91 Wierzchowska; Pamela M. Lee, "Aesthetic Strategist: Albert Wohlstetter, the Cold War, and a Theory of Mid-Century Modernism," *October*, no. 138 (2011).

92 Lynne Viola, "The Cold War within the Cold War," *Kritika-Explorations in Russian and Eurasian History* 12, no. 3 (2011): 684.

93 David Engerman, "The Rise and Fall of Wartime Social Science: Harvard's Refugee Interview Project, 1950–54," in *Cold war social science*, ed. Mark Solovey (New York: Palgrave Macmillan, 2012). Cf. Lawrence Freedman, "Social Science and the Cold War," *Journal of Strategic Studies* 38. (2015); Mark Solovey, *Shaky foundations the politics-patronage-social science nexus in Cold War America* (New Brunswick, NJ [u.a.]: Rutgers University Press, 2013).

Claiming expert knowledge, social scientists advised political actors on how to deal with the challenges of a postwar world. Their influence peaked in the 1950s and early 1960s. Herman Kahn, director of the RAND Corporation, saw himself as a new Clausewitz in the era of nuclear war. As leading defense intellectual he published a treatise under the title "On Thermonuclear War" in 1959.[94] Just like Daniel Bell, Albert Wohlstetter came from the far left and embodied personally the inclusion of social science into respectable Cold War culture. Their compelling argument that secured them hegemony in the scientific discourse was modernization. Securing the best way to modernize society was tantamount to winning the Cold War. The modernization paradigm became so prominent, that after the "Sputnik Shock" of 1957 the perceived incompatibility of political, economic and social systems was overshadowed more and more by the shared utopia of technical and industrial modernization. The Cold War was thereby partly depoliticized or better de-systemized. This did not mean, that the war was less dangerous and brutal – quite to the contrary. Though the military confrontation moved to proxy wars in the Third World, the convergence theory shared by both sides claimed that the industrial-technical maximum would be the social and political optimum. Modernization theory moved both sides from confrontation to competition.

At the turn from the 1950s to the 1960s modernism lost its grip on Cold War culture. New forms arrived that were more prone to popular and mass culture. A new "erotics of the art" (Susan Sontag) replaced the formalism and high seriousness of modernism. The youth culture put other cultural dichotomies center stage than that of modernism versus realism. Why did the Cold War modernist project end in the US with the Eisenhower era and beyond the US around 1960?

First, the occupation with Europe's moderate left and its loyalty faded away. Modernism and consensus capitalism had succeeded as role models. The threat of a communist takeover of Western Europe was gone after the Hungarian uprising in 1956 and its appalling impact on Western leftist intellectuals. Modernism had been successful and was part of the establishment. A new generation trying to find new answers did not see modernism on the side of the solution but rather on the side of the problem. Modernism seemed to convey a sense of order, coherence and control and to evade the immediate experience that art was supposed to capture.[95]

---

94 See Herman Kahn, *On Thermonuclear War* (Princeton, NJ: Princeton University Press, 1960). On Kahn see Sharon Ghamari-Tabrizi, *The worlds of Herman Kahn. The intuitive science of thermonuclear war* (Cambridge, Mass. [u.a.]: Harvard University Press, 2005); Janet Farrell Brodie, "Learning Secrecy in the Early Cold War: The RAND Corporation," *Diplomatic History* 35, no. 4 (2011).

95 Barnhisel, *Cold War modernists: art, literature, and American cultural diplomacy, 1946–1959*; Lynn Keller, *Re-making it new contemporary American poetry and the modernist tradition*, Cambridge studies in American literature and culture (Cambridge [u.a.]: Cambridge University Press, 1987).

Secondly unidirectional informational programs gave way to cultural exchange programs. Modernisms high seriousness and aloofness was understood as part of that essentially educational and non-communicative culture, the youth culture as well as the students wanted to distance themselves from. Already the Eisenhower administration, but then particularly the Kennedy administration intensified and broadened these exchange programs. Finally culture itself changed. Cold War modernism had been essentially a print phenomenon. The audience had engaged with modernism in forms of print: posters, magazines, manifestoes, small-press books, broadsides, advertisements, gallery flyers, catalogs and programs for musical and theater performances. Even modernist painting was essentially two-dimensional. "Much of modernism in the visual and literary arts concerned itself with the problems of capturing dynamic motion in a static medium."[96] By the 1960s visual culture gained importance and with it TV. Movies had been central to culture all along, but the television brought a new quality to visual culture and to where people could get their information and their world views from. TV ownership in the US went up from 9 % in 1950 to almost 90 % in 1960. Already contemporaries saw that the rise of visual culture would not only alter the audiences but also the notion of culture itself. George F. Kennan voiced these concerns in West Berlin in 1961: Mass culture with a centralized influence of the new visual media could lead to a society under complete control, where nobody had any desire for more sophisticated forms of culture. An age illuminated by TV screens would in fact be a dark age, he told the audience.[97]

The rise of visual Cold War culture had a lasting impact on the notion of culture as well as on the Cold War. It changed the dynamics between culture and the Cold War that had been established in a print culture. Until the advent of the electronic age visual culture didn't change the communication at work in Cold War culture. What had formerly been distributed uni-directionally by print was now distributed by visual media. The Cold War on TV did not allow for any form of comment. Visuality allowed for more immediate emotional contact. This contact bridged social, cultural, as well as linguistic divides. Images, TV, and movies played a crucial role in the imaginative and affective construction of the Cold War, a conflict, that in the US and Western Europe at least, lacked material reality.

What visual culture did change in the cultural Cold War was the personal and emotional immersion of the audience as well as the range and accessibility

96 Barnhisel, *Cold War modernists: art, literature, and American cultural diplomacy, 1946–1959*, 257.
97 Ibid., 258.

of information. That did not only hold true for warfare as with the often cited Vietnam war, which was the first war on TV. It included new formats and genres that displaced the Cold War in Western or later in science fiction and began to exhibit new characters and plots.

Visualizing the Cold War enemy took on many forms. Mapping the blocks was common throughout the 1950s. It was probably the most common visual feature of the Cold War. Cold War maps offered a visual construction of the Soviet Union.[98] The 1951 version of the National Geographic Society's "World Map" had the US at the center. It used the Van der Grinten projection that made neighboring countries Canada and the USSR larger than they were. The projection was used between 1922 and 1988. The US was surrounded by a USSR in Eurasia and a USSR in Siberia, a dominant presence that called quite visually for resistance if not containment. The map presented a political message packaged as a self-evident map. As the editors explain, the US is in the center, "since it is the source of so much of the leadership and aid, so many of the men, machines, and raw materials needed for the preservation of freedom in older lands." The connection between space, nationhood and citizenship spelled out a clear Cold War message. The National Geographic Society's maps – just as this World map – were the basis for maps used by newspapers and TV. As the centerpiece of public cartography it visualized the Cold War for generations.[99]

3 Cold War culture as recoding

Culture means more than the extension of politics. The representational link between culture and politics can be replaced by a relational link.[100] Wars and conflicts do not only use culture for non-cultural ends. Culture is rather a way to produce meaning of wars and conflicts itself. Conflicts themselves are culturally constructed, framed and reframed. What are commonly referred to as the "Eastern and the Western blocs" did not just employ cultural means to political ends; they were themselves profoundly shaped by the repertoire of cultural forms which governed the antagonism of the Cold War. Methodologically it is therefore useful to go beyond a conception of representation and to focus on culture as

---

98 Timothy Barney, *Mapping the Cold War: cartography and the framing of America's international power* (University of North Carolina Press, 2015).

99 Ibid., 99; Jeremy Black, *Maps and Politics* (London, GBR: Reaktion Books, 2000), 31.

100 See Stuart Hall, "The work of Representation," in *Representation*: Cultural Representations and Signifying Practices, ed. Stuart Hall (London: SAGE Publications, 1997), 15–64.

re-imagination and re-coding. Cold War culture not only narrated or visualized political threats and the Cold War antagonism, but it eventually became a platform for criticism and re-imagination of the Cold War itself.

Modernism and modernity had modified the Cold War binary code of "West versus East" or "US versus USSR" into "modern versus traditional" or "progress versus tradition/reactionary." Again – as with the political binary codes – both sides could use them and link modernity to their own system. That reframed the Cold War dichotomy and allowed for partial consensus and coexistence. Deadly conflict was reframed as competition.

Giving new meaning to Cold War culture therefore meant not only opposing the political dichotomy "US – USSR" but also the dichotomy "modern – traditional." Historically this reframing can be traced in cultural texts, images, movies and artefacts, that distance themselves from politics and modernism and reframe the Cold War. From a moral or religious standpoint one could argue for the inherent immorality of the Cold War. From a more disillusioned or even nihilist background, pursuing a Cold War seemed anyway useless and self-gratulatory. As literary styles irony, parody and satire were at hand for plotting the Cold War. Spy novels and science fiction read the Cold War culture psychologically through anxieties[101] and literary introspections into the twisted self and looked at its antagonisms and schisms.[102]

Re-coding I: The spy novel

The Cold War's international and global threats were reenacted and recoded in literature.[103] The most prominent literary topics dealing with the Cold War critically

101 Eva Horn, *Der geheime Krieg. Verrat, Spionage und moderne Fiktion* (Frankfurt a.M.: Fischer Taschenbuch, 2007); Jessica Wang, *American science in an age of anxiety. Scientists, anticommunism, and the Cold War* (Chapel Hill, NC [u.a.]: University of North Carolina Press, 1999). Cf. Daniel Cordle, "Beyond the apocalypse of closure: nuclear anxiety in the postmodern literature of the United states," in *Cold war literature: writing the global conflict*, ed. Andrew Hammond (New York: Routledge, 2006).

102 See Ron Theodore Robin, *The making of the Cold War enemy: culture and politics in the military-intellectual complex* (Princeton, NJ [u.a.]: Princeton University Press, 2001); Tom Engelhardt, *The end of victory culture. Cold war America and the disillusioning of a generation* (New York, NY: BasicBooks, 1995).

103 See Marcus M. Payk, "Die Angst der Agenten. Der Kalte Krieg in der westdeutschen TV-Serie "John Klings Abenteuer," in *Angst im Kalten Krieg*, ed. Bernd Greiner, Christian Th. Müller, and Dierk Walter (Hamburg: HIS Verlag, 2009); "Globale Sicherheit und ironische Selbstkontrolle die James-Bond-Filme der 1960er Jahre," *Zeithistorische Forschungen* 7 (2010); Michael Kackman,

were 'destruction' and 'treason', as laid out in abundant espionage novels.[104] A particularly well known example of the literary critique of the Cold War is John le Carré's (non de plume for David Cornwell) *The Spy who Came in from the Cold*, first published in 1963 right after the Cuban Missile Crisis. Le Carré's protagonists in Britain and in East Germany are literally of the same kind. The tragic ending of this prize winning novel leaves no space for great heroes and bad villains, rather for an "ambiguous moralism."[105] The individual is "to seek his skeptical balance between ethical and political requirements through flexibility and reason, and learn to live with ambiguity."[106] The same can be said of Le Carré's later spy novels evolving around Smiley as the central character. Neither Graham Greene nor Ian McEwan followed a representational and moralizing view of the Cold War in their novels.[107]

The Cold War spy novel mostly did not reduplicate political narratives. It imagined the Cold War in ambiguous forms. That is even true of the James Bond saga. Whereas Ian Fleming's print novels from the 1950s employed a bipolar view of West and East, the James Bond movies, starting with *Dr. No* in 1962, not only had a Soviet counterintelligence organization SMERSH (acronym for Russian: Специальные Методы Разоблачения Шпионов = Special Methods of Spy Detection), but also an international syndicate of criminals under the acronym SPECTRE (acronym for SPecial Executive for Counter-intelligence, Terrorism, Revenge and Extortion). The Bond saga transfigured the Cold War into a plot with three antagonists: Bond, the Soviet Union and – the longer the more – global criminals – often with a Nazi background.[108]

Citizen spy: television, espionage, and Cold War culture, Commerce and mass culture series (Minneapolis, Minn. [u.a.]: University of Minnesota Press, 2005).

104 See Edward P. Comentale, Stephen Watt, and Skip Willman, *Ian Fleming & James Bond. The cultural politics of 007* (Bloomington, Ind. [u.a.]: Indiana University Press, 2005); James Chapman, *Licence to thrill. A cultural history of the James Bond films*, 2. ed., Cinema and society series (London [u.a.]: Tauris, 2007); Andrew Hammond, *Cold War literature. Writing the global conflict*, Routledge studies in twentieth-century literature 3 (London [u.a.]: Routledge, 2005); Adam Piette, *The literary Cold War: 1945 to Vietnam* (Edinburgh: Edinburgh University Press, 2009); Nicholas J Cull, "Reading, Viewing and Tuning into the Cold War," in *The Cambridge History of the Cold War. Volume II: Crises and Détente*, ed. Melvyn P. Leffler and Odd Arne Westad (Cambridge: Cambridge University Press, 2010).

105 Myron J. Aronoff, *The spy novels of John Le Carré. Balancing ethics and politics* (Basingstoke [u.a.]: Macmillan, 1999).

106 R. L. Garthoff, "The spy novels of John Le Carre: Balancing ethics and politics," *Political Science Quarterly* 115, no. 1 (2000): 150.

107 See Brian Diemert, "The Anti-American: Graham Greene and the Cold War in the 1950s," in *Cold War Literature. Writing the Global Conflict*, ed. Andrew Hammond (London: Routledge, 2006), 212–225.

108 Chapman; Comentale, Watt, and Willman.

Spy novels were popular well beyond Britain. In contrast, espionage as shown in Jean Bruce's popular French *OSS 117* novels – sold in more than 24 million copies – has to be seen against the background of the *Parti Communiste Français* (PCF). OSS 117 explicitly contested the model of Cold War modernity represented by the US. Instead it had a certain French modernity. At its center were elements of aristocratic tradition and of hypermodernity.[109]

French spy novels were obsessed with delivering a French version of Cold War modernity. The popular French spy novels *OSS 117* for instance played with the figure of an Anglo-American agent, but set center stage a vision of a French modernity different from the US model. Hubert Bonnisseur de la Bath not only handled his technical equipment with ease but was also of noble descent, thereby clearly distinguished from his American rivals.[110] But with de Gaulle's comeback in 1958, France's cultural dependence on Anglo-Saxon models ended due to a desire to reassert France's position in the world. French Cold War modernity had a quite positive relationship to tradition. It valued social cohesion more than the market model. The French spy novel represented a third way between the bloc modernities of the East and West.

Re-coding II: Science fiction dystopias

Dystopias of all kinds were on the rise in the 1960s, containing displaced imaginations of Cold War fears, anxieties, paranoia and hopes. "One of the most striking aspects of literature written during the Cold War is the prevalence of dystopian and/or anti-utopian works."[111] They referred to politics in at least two ways. Dystopias satirized both society as it existed and the utopian aspiration to transform it.[112] According to Keith Booker, dystopian societies in science fiction novels

---

109 Paul Bleton, *La cristallisation de l'ombre. Les origines oubliées du roman d'espionage sous la IIIe République*, Médiatextes (Limoges: Pulim, 2011); "Metamorphosis of the popular novel," *Quinzaine Litteraire*, no. 974 (2008).

110 *Les anges de Machiavel. Essai sur le roman d'espionnage: froide fin et funestes moyens, les espions de papier dans la paralittérature française, du Rideau de fer à la chute du Mur*, Collection "Etudes paralittéraires" (Québec: Nuit Blanche, 1994); *Western, France: la place de l'Ouest dans l'imaginaire français* (Paris: Belles Lettres [u.a.], 2002); "Reheating the planet for spies in from the cold?," *Quinzaine Litteraire*, no. 974 (2008); "Metamorphosis of the popular novel."

111 Derek Maus, "Series and systems: Russian and American dystopian satires of the Cold War," *Critical Survey* 17, no. 1 (2005): 72.

112 Chris Ferns, *Narrating utopia. Ideology, gender, form in utopian literature*, Liverpool science fiction texts and studies (Liverpool: Liverpool University Press, 1999).

were "generally more or less thinly veiled re-figurations of a situation that already exists in reality."[113] Their themes infection, invasion by stealth, and subversion were all related to Cold War anxieties and paranoia. They grew stronger after America's Vietnam debacle. Economically, science fiction became the dominant genre at the box office replacing the Western. The genre played on the fear that America's capacity would not suffice to resist invasion by communist enemies and that the country would not be able to maintain its way of life in a post-apocalyptic world. Lesser-known authors like Frederick Pohl, Poul Anderson and Philip Wylie contributed to this genre of Cold War science fiction as much as the better-known Isaac Asimov, Ursula K. LeGuin, Ray Bradbury and Harlan Ellison.

In an influential essay in 1965, Susan Sontag pointed to certain aesthetic characteristics of Cold War science fiction:

> Science fiction films are not about science. They are about disaster, which is one of the oldest subjects of art.

She went on:

> The science fiction film ... is concerned with the aesthetics of destruction, with the peculiar beauties to be found in wreaking havoc, making a mess. And it is in the imagery of destruction that the core of a good science fiction film lies.[114]

Cold War science fiction exploited an aesthetic attraction of destruction, which refers not to the death of the individual but to "collective incineration and extinction." The aesthetic of mass destruction points not to scientific, or even political utopias, but to inadequate responses to disaster, war, the Holocaust and nuclear annihilation. Susan Sontag relates the Cold War aesthetics to a more general 20th century experience of catastrophes. Science-fiction novels and films reveal human limitations in responding to "the most profound dilemmas of the contemporary situation." The need to cope with these extreme experiences leads to a desire to neutralize and even beautify terror and anxiety.[115]

Science fiction novels and films interrogated key metaphors, the perception of the Cold War in the US, but also in the USSR was structured around. Such metaphors were "dangerous predator," "paranoia," "infiltration," "arms race,"

---

113 Marvin Keith Booker, *The dystopian impulse in modern literature: fiction as social criticism*, 1. publ. ed., Contributions to the study of science fiction and fantasy (Westport, Conn. u. a.: Greenwood Press, 1994), 15.
114 Susan Sontag, "The imagination of disaster," *Commentary* 40, no. 4 (1965): 44.
115 Ibid., 48.

"iron curtain" and others. Bernard Wolfe's *Limbo* (1952) recoded "arms race" as a race between prosthetics or artificial limbs, undermining confidence in scientific progress, since those prosthetic limbs keep rebounding on their wearers.[116] Nick Boddie transforms the "Iron Curtain" metaphor into an "atomic curtain" in his 1956 novel which describes post-Holocaust America, not the Soviet Bloc.[117] In the same way the 1954 film *Them!* uses the metaphor of ants-as-monsters and ants-as-people to depict the Soviet society.[118]

American as well as Soviet literary dystopias went against the simple bipolar utopian sentiment. Their authors didn't support either side in its ideological struggle. They rather wanted to invalidate the conflicts overarching logical context. Gary Saul Morson distinguishes 'serial dystopias' from 'systemic dystopias'. "In the former a society is caught in the loop of equally undesirable revolutions and restorations; in the latter all parties in a given ideological struggle are presented as dystopian, thereby undermining any claim of moral superiority therein."[119] Both kinds of dystopias were applied to the Cold War.

Science fiction in the East increasingly diverged from official prescriptions and engaged in a critique of the regime and – as systemic dystopia – in questioning the Cold War itself and its assumption about a better future. The most important writers were the Strugatsky brothers in the Soviet Union and Stanislav Lem in Poland. Science-fiction found its "main readership in a key group of the communist society: young, urban male members of the technical intelligentsia and skilled workers, fostered by the system, but with a keen sense of belonging to a global scientific community."[120] Science fiction therefore was a social vision of the future with a potential to uproot its audience from the national and ideological settings they came from. For Soviet writers the dystopian character of the Soviet Union, as an inverted, not simply a failed utopia, had been made evident by nearly three decades of Stalinism. As a consequence, scientocracy – as narrated in science fiction novels – became a coded critique of contemporary party bureaucracy. Others like Stanislav Lem went even further. He used his science fiction novels to contribute to a general cognitive theory of knowledge beyond Cold War cognitive models (*Solaris*, 1961). Vladimir Voinovich introduced a critique of the linguistic control by the communist party

---

116 David Seed, "Deconstructing the Body Politic in Bernard Wolfe's 'Limbo'," *Science Fiction Studies* (1997).
117 *American science fiction and the Cold War: literature and film*, 2.
118 Ibid.
119 Maus, 73.
120 Patrick Major, "Future Perfect? Communist Science Fiction in the Cold War," *Cold War History* 4, no. 1 (2003): 73, 74.

into his novel *Moscow 2042* (1986). The toilet mutates to "natfunctbur," short for "Bureau of natural functions."[121]

On the US side the same held true for the science fiction critique of the "American dream." Particularly the 1960s and early 70s saw a massive disillusionment with an overly idealized national self-conception, that "form(ed) the core of international relations schemata such as the Cold War schema."[122] The linguistic expression of this self-image was the "nukespeak," mirroring Cold War language of the nuclear arms race,

> the language of the nuclear mindset – the world view, or system of beliefs – of nuclear developers. ... (This) mindset acts like a filter sorting information and perceptions, allowing it to be processed and some to be ignored, consciously or unconsciously. Nukespeak encodes the beliefs and assumptions of the nuclear mindset; the language and the mindsets continuously reinforce each other.[123]

Nukespeak was in the beginning a social vision of a better future with "euphoric visions of nuclear technologies" such as X-rays or radium. That changed when the war in Vietnam and the practices of the Nixon administration motivated young writers to use Science fiction for other purposes than to celebrate American progress.

Re-coding III: Postmodernism

Already Cold War dystopias like Joseph Heller's *Catch-22* (1961) deflated such idealistic self-images. The irrationality of 1960s America was mirrored in multiple unpredictable reactions to almost every action in *Catch-22* that render the cause-and-effect logic largely meaningless.[124] Displacing the Cold War of the early 1960s in a World war II setting, he reversed the values and assumptions of warfare: heroes desert, the rules of military conduct are corrupt, the purpose of war is irrational, the game is fixed. In 1961, Joseph Heller was one of the first writers to identify the irrationality of the Cold War based on the insane logic of militarism in the nuclear age.[125] In Heller's *Catch 22* "the enemy is anybody who's going to get you killed, no

121 Maus, 78.
122 Matthew S. Hirshberg, *Perpetuating patriotic perceptions. The cognitive function of the Cold War* (Westport, Conn. [u.a.]: Praeger, 1993), 17.
123 Stephen Hilgartner, Richard C. Bell, and Rory O'Connor, *Nukespeak. Nuclear language, visions, and mindset* (San Francisco: Sierra Club Books, 1982).
124 Maus, 81.
125 Peter J. Kuznick, *Rethinking cold war culture* (Washington, DC [u.a.]: Smithsonian Institution Press, 2001).

matter which side he is on. ... It doesn't make a damned bit of difference who wins the war to someone who's dead." Two years later Heller's example was followed by John Le Carrés *The Spy who Came in from the Cold.* 12 years later Thomas Pynchon's *Gravity's Rainbow* (1973) is also set shortly before and after the end of World War II, mirroring 1970s anxieties about war and total destruction. It takes Heller's point about the irrationality of war even further into philosophical nominalism and asks, "whether meaningful events are directed by a supremely competent mailman – a symbolic order or a 'Them' – or whether they are merely made meaningful by a discourse." The context of the Cold War was immediately at hand, when he "provides a cogent tableau of the myths of individual action and of collective action, both visibly dissolving in the face of public events." Taken together Pynchon recoded Cold War conspiracies as a discourse creating its own reality.[126] This resonated with the broader public since the Cold War was the high noon of conspiracies, real and imagined. The quest to "know your enemy" (David Engerman) knew hardly any limitation.[127] The enemy was to be found in places, where one would not expect him: he was the "enemy from within." The McCarthy era gave an example of how that worked politically. The Cold War figuration was displaced historically, spatially, socially and in other ways. Its aesthetic displacement allowed for new modes of imagination, conflating dominant political and subversive ideological positions. Popular culture imagining the Cold War relocated the political conflict into rituals of everyday life, most notably modern mass entertainment, serving ideological purposes.

Literature addressed Cold War anxieties collectively as well as individually, rendering accounts not only of the red menace but also of the "yellow peril," the US image of Communist East Asia. Richard Condon's novel *The Manchurian Candidate* of 1959 manifests the "Cold War orientalism" feeding into older stereotypes of Chinese immigration.[128] Fears of communist brainwashing fed suspicion, paranoia and anxiety typical of the Cold War era.[129] Cold War literature positioned itself against the backdrop of "containment culture" (Alan Nadel). The containment policies of the 1950s made the personal political.[130] It made the political

126 Timothy Melley, *Empire of conspiracy the culture of paranoia in postwar America* (Ithaca, NY [u.a.]: Cornell University Press, 2000).
127 Tiago Mata, "The enemy within. Academic freedom in 1960s and 1970s American social sciences," in *The unsocial social science?* (Durham, NC [u.a.]: Duke University Press, 2010).
128 Christina Klein, *Cold War orientalism. Asia in the middlebrow imagination, 1945–1961* (Berkeley, Calif. [u.a.]: University of California Press, 2003).
129 Hammond.
130 Robin; Alan Nadel, *Containment culture: American narrative, postmodernism, and the atomic age* (Durham, NC [u.a.]: Duke University Press, 1995).

Cold War narrative relevant in every aspect of life. Containment became domestic containment. "More than merely a metaphor for the Cold War on the home front, containment aptly describe[d] the way in which public policy, personal behavior, and even political values where focused on the home."[131] The historian Elaine Tyler May analyzed the *Kelly Longitudinal Study* with its interviews of 600 middle class men and women, forming their families in the 1950s, and pointed out, that "domestic containment" and Kennan-inspired political containment of communism were two sides of the same coin. The "homeward bound" Cold War culture saw women creating a secure "psychological fortress" in the apolitical, affluent, middle class suburban home containing all sorts of dangerous social forces like "women's sexuality, homosexuality, labor unions, and civil rights activism." They were all seen as disrupting American domestic security.[132]

Postmodernism tried to replace the binary language of "containment culture" (Alan Nadel) in its modernist disguise by "polysystemic mappings." Some critics interpreted the rise of American postmodernism as "a theoretical and artistic movement that called into question the containment paradigm itself." They claimed that by "challenging the dichotomous imagination of the Cold War, postmodernism proposed polysystemic cartographies that mediated among differentiated subjects and cultures according to the extravagant geography of 'zigging and zagging (sides), going ahead and doubling back, making loops inside loops.'"[133]

John Barth, Donald Barthelme, Richard Brautigan, Robert Coover, Ursula K. LeGuin, Thomas Pynchon, Ishmael Reed and Kurt Vonnegut used the satirical mode in their critique of the binary coding of Cold War culture.[134] Their "critifictional discourse" not only went against all ideological dichotomies, but also against the established form of the novel. It attacked outright "the vehicle that expressed and represented that reality: discursive language and the traditional

---

131 Elaine Tyler May, *Homeward bound. American families in the Cold War era*, Fully rev. and updated 20th anniversary ed ed. (New York, NY: Basic Books, 2008).

132 Barnhisel and Turner; May.

133 Marcel Cornis-Pope, "Postmodernism's Polytropic Imagination. Unwriting/rewriting the Cold War Narratives of Polarization," in *Narrative Innovation and cultural rewriting in the Cold War and after*, ed. Marcel Cornis-Pope (London: Palgrave, 2001), 3; Thomas Pynchon, *Mason & Dixon* (London: Jonathan Cape, 1997), 586.

134 After 1968 more writers emerged: Walter Abish, Raymond Federman, Kenneth Gangemi, Madeline Gins, Steve Katz, Clarence Major, Gilbert Sorrentino, and Ronald Sukeruck. They rejected all "mimetic realism and mimetic pretension" and went against the "silent agreement with the official discourse of the state" altogether. Raymond Federman, *Critifiction: postmodern essays*, SUNY series in postmodern culture (Albany: State University of New York Press, 1993).

form of the novel."[135] The critique of contents went hand in hand with a critique of form. The innovation of narrative strategies was not confined to the West or to the United States. Eastern writers also employed the postmodern narrative strategy to attack the foundations of the Communist hyperreality, while writing from the margins of society.[136] It is here that Hayden White's argument on the "content of form" applies most beyond historiography, since the formalism and transfiguration of the form of the novel went hand in hand with a critique of Cold War dichotomies in the West as well as of communism's ever more futile insistence on its hyperrealism. This formalism had content that undermined the credibility of the Cold War.[137]

"During the Cold War Utopia came to designate the program (...) which betrayed a will to uniformity and the ideal purity of a perfect system, that has to be imposed by force on its imperfect and reluctant subjects."[138] Instead irony was "the quintessential expression of late modernism and of the ideology of the modern as that was developed during the Cold War (whose traces and impasses it bears like a stigmata)."[139] Late Postmodernists like Frederic Jameson disrupted the bipolar thinking that had characterized Cold War culture. The impact of this development was obvious even within the narrative strategies. Postmodernism and de-storification took over from literary modernism.[140] Andrew Hammond points to four literary strategies in Cold War literature: narrative instability, ontological uncertainty, scathing self-reflexivity and suspicion of all forms of meta-narrative and historiography.[141]

There is another ring to the notion of uncertainty, that lay at the center of Cold War culture. Cold War actors were obsessed with uncertainty and chance from the early days of the nuclear age on. Uncertainty and chance could have disastrous consequences taking decision-making away from politics. This again collided with the scientific world view of communism, but also of Western modernization theory. "Stalinist objectivity" saw no room for chance in history. All

135 Ibid., 23, 32.
136 Cornis-Pope, 4.
137 Hayden White, *The content of the form narrative discourse and historical representation* (Baltimore, Md [u.a.]: Johns Hopkins University Press, 1987).
138 Fredric Jameson, *Archaeologies of the future. The desire called utopia and other science fictions* (London [u.a.]: Verso, 2005).
139 Ibid., 179.
140 Marcel Cornis-Pope, "National literatures and diasporas: towards a polycentric concept of culture," *World Literature Studies* 2, no. 1 (2010); M. Cornis-Pope, "Reading cultures: The construction of readers in the twentieth century," *College Literature* 26, no. 2 (1999).
141 Hammond.

political and economic changes occurred according to historical destiny. Jerzy Kosinski, a US writer of Polish descent and winner of the National Book Award, engaged with the motto "There is no chance, comrade!" in "The future is ours, comrade!" (1960). He associated 'chance' with American freedom and the denial of chance with Soviet totalitarianism, resonating the ideology of the Ford Foundation and the US establishment. The concept of chance circulated in Cold War literary culture, not only in the cultural Cold Wars of the 1950s.

Think tanks like the RAND Corporation tried to tame uncertainty by using game theory. Based on game theory and refined mathematical models Hermann Kahn came to the conclusion that 2 million dead in the US meant two years of economic recovery whereas 160 million dead resulted in a 10-year recovery period. The Cold War obsession with chance started on the front pages of the *New York Times*, game theory was first discussed in the comics section of *The New Republic*.[142] The shift from modernism to late modernism around 1960 goes along with a shift in looking at chance and uncertainty: where game theory could provide some certainty and validity in dealing with uncertainty, authors like Thomas Pynchon and Vladimir Nabokov use chance as tracers for the fault lines of Cold War culture. Thomas Pynchons *V.* (1963) and Vladimir Nabokov *Pale fire* (1962) gave it another twist, foregrounding the critique controlling cultural formations in the US. Pynchon and Nabokov dealt with chance and design, Pynchon in a critique of what he saw as the "tyranny of capitalist aesthetics," Nabokov exposing the homophobic narrative of postwar US culture.[143]

Both authors can be seen paradigmatically as examples for the rise of self-reflexivity in Cold War literature. Both turned on the literary conventions of the high modernism. Robert Genter has labeled this "late modernism." Marcel Cornis-Pope prefers to label it "early postmodernism."[144] These scholars observe a kind of cultural sea change in the early 1960s from high modernism to late modernism: in painting from Jackson Pollock to Andy Warhol, in literature from Jack Kerouac to Thomas Pynchon, and in literary criticism from Allen Tate to Paul de Man. The latter ones all shied away from what was evident to the former authors or painters. Robert Genter defines late modernism as follows:

---

142 Steven Belletto, *No accident, comrade chance and design in Cold War American narratives* (Oxford [u.a.]: Oxford University Press, 2012).

143 Joseph Kosinski and Irving R. Levine, *The future is ours comrade conversations with the russians* (London: The Bodley Head, 1960); Belletto; Thomas Pynchon, *V. a novel*, 4. impr ed. (Philadelphia u.a.: Lippincott, 1963); Vladimir Vladimirovich Nabokov, *Pale fire a novel*, 1. impr ed. (New York: Putnam, 1962).

144 Marcel Cornis-Pope, *Narrative innovation and cultural rewriting in the Cold War and after* (New York, NY [u.a]: Palgrave, 2001).

> Unwilling to abandon the literary and cultural revolution begun in the late nineteenth and early twentieth centuries by their modernist predecessors, whose original goal was to explore new forms of consciousness and unearth new forms of perception in the hopes of transforming the world at large, late modernists argued not only that the nature of the aesthetic form needed to be rethought in an age of mass media but that the general assumptions about the nature of subjectivity needed to be updated. They reformulated aesthetics as a mode of symbolic action – a deliberate attempt to use the aesthetic form to challenge the choice of lens through which individuals made sense of the world around them and to persuade them that the visions offered by the artist were not merely more poetic but possibly more liberating.[145]

At the center of this shift away from modernist to "late modernist" Cold War culture stood self-reflexivity, which was expressed through new literary techniques, the cracking open of traditional plot structures, exposing open ends and in general a higher awareness of the process of literary production and of the author. Thomas Pynchon stood for the "scathing self-reflexivity," that went along with the search for the nature of subjectivity. He, John Barth, John Hawkes and others wrote about the end of the subject with depthless and empty characters rejecting the heroism of high modernity. In cultural analysis authors like Jacques Derrida, Paul de Man and Roland Barthes went against the notions of the author and the text as the grounds for meaning. Its Cold War context was shining through in what they distanced themselves from: the high modernist belief in the autonomy of the arts as proof for a free society.[146]

Re-coding IV: Movies

Recoding the Cold War in popular movies was largely achieved through aesthetic displacements. While some movies directly reenacted the conflict between 'capitalists' and 'communists' on the screen, others displaced the conflict to other settings.[147] The cinematic displacement into a family setting was particularly thrilling. It evolved around the generational conflict of the "nuclear family" that emerged out of the civil rights movement.[148] As a result Cold War visual

---

145 Robert Genter, *Late modernism: Art, culture, and politics in Cold War America*, The arts and intellectual life in modern America (Philadelphia, Pa. [u.a.]: University of Pennsylvania Press, 2010), 4.

146 Ibid., 316.

147 Tony Shaw and Denise J. Youngblood, *Cinematic Cold War: the American and Soviet struggle for hearts and minds* (Lawrence: University Press of Kansas, 2010).

148 Frank Costigliola, "The Nuclear Family: Tropes of Gender and Pathology in the Western Alliance," *Diplomatic History* 21, no. 2 (1997).

culture transformed the conflict between "them versus us" into "we versus us," opening up internal differences regarding class, gender, and race. Movies could and did internalize the Cold War from a political conflict into a psychological drama.

Displacement of the Cold War in film often took on the form of Western and cowboy movies. The height of the early Cold War was the peak of Western movies. "The Western was *the* genre of the period after World War II." In the 1930s their strong moral message had reassured a depression ridden American audience. After 1945 Western movies portrayed US resistance against USSR aggression in historical disguise. John Ford's *Cavalry Trilogy* (*Fort Apache* 1948; *She Wore a Yellow Ribbon* 1949; *Rio Grande* 1950) was especially famous for visualizing the fear of external enemies, celebrating traditional American values and glorifying the military. Films like *The Searchers* (John Ford 1956), *Shane* (George Stevens, 1953), *The Alamo* (John Wayne, 1960 version), and particularly *The Man Who Shot Liberty Valance* (John Ford 1962) connected frontier morality with the Cold War.[149] The frontier Western heralded the individual citizen, that could stand above the law when defending his family, city or – by extension – his country. They emphatically dramatized freedom by showing "a hero who must disobey commands in order to save the command *structure*."[150] The moral impulse of John Ford's film was clear: the hero had to act alone to preserve the social order. The Hollywood Western provided a mythic landscape and a compelling narrative of American power during the Cold War. It reinscribed "the time-honored myth of heroic frontier individualism into the demands of uniting to defeat a common enemy, and thereby both proving and effectuating the nation's moral right to victory."[151]

The Western lost its prominent position in Cold War culture in the 1960s and was replaced by SciFi movies of the "Star Trek" and "Star Wars" type. The movie organizing metaphor of life on the frontier with all its enemies was kept and displaced into space. Producer Gene Roddenberry referred to Star Trek as a "wagon trek to the stars" and to its actors as "pioneers of the space age." The opening line of the first series ran "Space, the final frontier."[152] As Steven Belletto

149 Corkin; Richard Aquila, *The sagebrush trail: western movies and twentieth-century America*, The modern American West (Tucson: The University of Arizona Press, 2015).

150 Peter Baker, "Directions in left theory – cinema in the wake of the cold war," *Minnesota Review*, no. 41–42 (1994).

151 Arthur F. Redding, *Turncoats, traitors, and fellow travelers: culture and politics of the early Cold War*, 1. print. ed. (Jackson, Miss.: University Press of Mississippi, 2008), 134.

152 Susanne M. Maier, "Star Trek und das unentdeckte Land am Rande des Universums. Ein amerikanischer Mythos," in *Sinnwelt Film. Beiträge zur interdisziplinären Filmanalyse*, ed. Wilhelm Hofmann (Baden-Baden: 1996).

put it: "The Western goes galactic." The first *Star Wars (IV)* film came out in 1977. It transferred tropes and conventions of Western movies to another galaxy and tried to re-contextualize the US Cold War ethos. After Vietnam and – to a lesser degree – Watergate the object-specific meaning of "East versus West" had lost its meaning. The small planet earth was put in a multi-galactic perspective. Whereas the Western was a historical and legitimating myth, the *Star Wars* films presented the possibility of heroism, love, and success only, when all earthly social, historical and even natural realities are set aside.[153]

Another displacement in Cold War films were historical epics, most prominently in the 1950s, reenacting the Cold War antagonism of freedom versus dictatorship in biblical times and moralizing it at the same time. These moralizing historical displacements were a common feature of Cold War cinema. Historical epics as Cecil B. DeMille's *Ten Commandments* (1956), Stanley Kubrick's *Spartacus* (1960) or Anthony Mann's *The Fall of the Roman Empire* (1964) served as historical illustrations of a contemporary conflict. The Jewish emancipation from the tyrannical Pharaoh bore a direct resemblance to the US fight against Soviet atheism. The extremely conservative director Cecil B. DeMille, whose taste for biblical drama and proportions earned him the nickname "Apostle to Millionaires," articulated the film's message:

> The theme of this picture is whether men ought to be ruled by God's law or whether they are to be ruled by the whims of a dictator like Ramses. Are men the property of the state or are they free souls under God? This same battle continues throughout the world today. Our intention was not to create a story but to be worthy of the divinely inspired story created three thousand years ago: the five books of Moses.[154]

Re-coding V: Internalizing the Cold War

Another mode of displacement was the tendency to internalize the Cold War conflict into the society, the individual or gender roles. Political scientist Michael Rogin read its polarization as the third demonology of US society after slavery and socialism. These challenges were seen as subversions and answered by the

---

153 Steven Belletto and Daniel Grausam, *American literature and culture in an age of cold war. A critical reassessment*, New American Canon (Iowa City: University of Iowa Press, 2012), 191; Will Wright, "The Empire bites the dust," *Social Text* (1982).

154 Alan Nadel, "God's Law and the Wide Screen: The Ten Commandments as Cold War 'Epic'," *PMLA* 108, no. 3 (1993): 417.

US establishment with "counter subversions."[155] From the 1950s on invisible internal Soviet agents replaced the alien or African-American underclass as the target of Cold War counter subversion. It was the invisibility of its influence that distinguished the Communist Party from other legitimate opposition groups of the past. Rogin sees the most important impact of Cold War movies in the fact that it made visible three threatening changes:

> The first development was the rise of the national security state, which counteracted Soviet influence by imitating Soviet surveillance. The second ... arose from the simultaneous glorification and fear of maternal influence within the family. The third was the emergence of a mass society which seemed to homogenize all difference that makes subversives difficult to spot.[156]

Visual culture made two divisions visible that were constitutive for Cold War demonology: the distinctions between the free man and the state on the one hand and the free state and the slave state on the other. According to Rogin's interpretation of Cold War cinema, the first division was visually imagined by the second division: the division between the free man and the state was made visible through the division between the free and the slave state. Beyond both divisions lay the emotionally even stronger division between motherhood and communism, charging the domestic Cold War culture with gender roles.

The internalization of the Cold War threat was particularly evident when it came to the motives of the safety of the homeland and the security of the family. Most prominent are Alfred Hitchcock's comments on Cold War culture in *The Birds* (1963). Birds stood here for symbols of nuclear bombs and unprovoked attacks, mirroring a deep Cold War fear. Cinematic displacement showed communism as a threat to home and hearth, to the family as the psychological fortress, from which American citizens could defend their country. A particular threat to the family was also at stake in the newly established theme of the alien invasion that fed into paranoia. *Invasion of the Body Snatchers* by Siegel and Kaufman from 1956 is an example in place. John Frankenheimer's *Manchurian Candidate* (1962) addresses the motif of the ultimate "enemy from within," which is brainwashed and lives next door.[157] The "enemy from within" was represented in this genre

---

155 Michael Rogin, "Kiss Me Deadly: Communism, Motherhood, and Cold War Movies," *Representations*, no. 6 (1984).

156 Gilles Colpart, "America and the Soviet Union – The Cold war of cinema," *Revue du cinema*, no. 450 (1989): 3.

157 The "*Manchurian Candidate*" is particularly well researched. Cf. inter alia: S. L. Carruthers, "The 'Manchurian Candidate' (1962) and the Cold War brainwashing scare," *Historical Journal of Film Radio and Television* 18, no. 1 (1998); Gongzhao Li, "The Manchurian Candidate and brain-

as a force within the human psyche. The spreading fear of enemies from within catered to what Richard Hofstadter addressed as *The paranoid style in American politics* (1964).[158] This paranoia assumed that the enemy was already within the country, the family or even the individual psyche. It is this paranoia that led novelist and literary theorist Samuel Delany to suggest in his novel *Nevèrÿon* (1979) that the only hero left in Western civilization must always be a spy.[159] Accordingly the political witch-hunt of "containment culture" and the search for the enemies within aimed ultimately at the collapse of the public and private sphere.

Re-coding VI: Social sciences

From early on in the Cold War the social sciences engaged in the analysis of its actors and its very nature. That wasn't done for scholarly purposes, but rather to serve the political needs of the US administration. The social sciences provided important weapons in and paradigms for the understanding of the supposed enemy. Rather than being purely academic and scholarly objective, the social sciences of the early Cold War recoded the political antagonism in a scholarly fashion. Modernization theory provided a language to discern the Western societies as modern societies and distinguish them from all other societies as well as to win over the recently decolonized states in Africa and Asia. What modernism was for the arts modernization theory was for the social sciences. This aspect has been studied intensively.[160] The key point then was, that the social sciences and even modernization theory took on a new function, when the social sciences stepped out of the role they were supposed to play and recoded the Cold War from new perspectives.

washing: From Cold War paranoia to anti-terrorist paranoia," *Foreign Literature Studies* 29, no. 4 (2007); Jean Brugelle, "OSS 117," *Quinzaine Litteraire*, no. 974 (2008); Kirshner Jonathan, "Subverting the Cold War in the 1960s: Dr. Strangelove, The Manchurian Candidate, and The Planet of the Apes," *Film & History: An Interdisciplinary Journal of Film and Television Studies* 31, no. 2 (2001); Perucci Tony, "The Red Mask of Sanity: Paul Robeson, HUAC, and the Sound of Cold War Performance," *TDR: The Drama Review* 53, no. 4 (2009).

158 Richard Hofstadter, *The paranoid style in American politics and other essays*, [1st ed. (New York: Vintage Books, 1965).

159 John Nelson, *The American Political Science Review* 95, no. 1 (2001): 250; Melley.

160 Michael E. Latham, *Modernization as ideology. American social science and "nation building" in the Kennedy era*, New Cold War history (Chapel Hill, NC [u.a.]: University of North Carolina Press, 2000); Sebastian Conrad, "'The Colonial Ties are Liquidated': Modernization Theory, Post-War Japan and the Global Cold War," *Past & Present*, no. 216 (2012).

Cold War Sovietology had the function to help "know your enemy." Dressed up in academic language and university institutions it was serving both "Mars and Minerva." It became a national endeavor to analyze almost every aspect of Soviet life and present it in a Cold War manner to the American public. In the beginnings Soviet Studies were funded by government institutions and major private foundations so as to present scholarly evidence of a homogeneous Soviet threat to the US. One example was the "Harvard refugees interview project" referred to as "Russian interview project" (RIP) and paid for by the United States Air Force with one million dollars. At the initiative of Frederick Osborn this program was designed to figure out what made the new adversary tick. Members of the Truman administration felt that they did not understand their Russian counterparts. Behavioral sciences should solve the riddle.[161] The investigation team interviewed Russian displaced persons in Germany to find out whether the Soviet Union was stable or likely to break down. The US Air Force wanted a "working model of the Soviet social system" and proof of the aggressiveness of a fragile system without inner support.

The findings of the researchers Joseph Berliner and Clyde Kluckhohn refuted their funder's view of the Soviet Union. "In most respects Soviet society reflected the characteristics of a class society of the Western industrial kind."[162] The RIP did not prove that the Russian society was of socialist nature. Contrary to its loud ideological proclamations of a complete lack of historical precedents, the RIP saw Russian society as a stable industrial society, in many ways not so different from the US. Kluckhohn's team insisted that the USSR wasn't on the brink of collapse and had wide if not deep support from its citizens. US Forces wouldn't be greeted as liberators.[163] Merle Fainsod's analysis of the Smolensk archive delivered another blow to common convictions of the inner fragility of totalitarian party rule by a small elite of party rulers in the Kremlin. His findings contradicted the Soviet stereotypes in the US almost in every aspect.[164]

The rise of a generation of post-behaviorist social science scholars in the 1960s introduced new perspectives and made Cold War social sciences more reflective on the Cold War. The center of the research agenda shifted from explor-

---

161 An equivalent of 9 million $ in 2009.

162 *Tony Shaw, "Cinema, Television and the Cold War Introduction," Journal of British Cinema and Television 10, no. 1 (2013): 369; Joseph M. Bochenski, Soviet Russian dialectical materialism (Diamat) (Dordrecht, Holland,: D. Reidel Pub. Co., 1963), X.*

163 David C. Engerman, "Social Science in the Cold War," *Isis* 101, no. 2 (2010): 399.

164 James R. Arnold and Roberta Wiener, *Cold War. The essential reference guide* (Santa Barbara, Calif. [u.a.]: ABC-CLIO, 2012); A. L. Adamishin and Richard Schifter, *Human rights, perestroika, and the end of the cold war* (Washington, D.C.: United States Institute of Peace, 2009).

ing the stability, homogeneity and identity of a given society to analyzing social inequality, reproduction of social groups and access to political communication. Cold War social science transformed into social science of the Cold War, looking at the antagonism with its tools and concepts and not taking its methodology from a bipolar ideology.

Soviet studies benefited academic life as much if not more than national security. During the 1960s their belief in academic independence and neutrality while simultaneously being funded by the government was undermined. New cohorts of experts arrived and the division between the totalitarian and the revisionist approaches grew ever deeper. Soviet studies outgrew the know-your-enemy approach, gradually evolving into the study of Russia as an important world culture.[165] Instead of providing proof for a central control of the Soviet bloc, the new research made differences and distinctions visible within Russian society and politics. Since the 1960s it served less and less to buttress political claims against the enemy. Social scientists replaced anti-Communists in the Russian Centers. Sovietology's political lustre dimmed, when less partisan researchers began to make the heterogeneity of Soviet-style societies visible.[166]

Social science's role in the Cold War was ambivalent. First social scientists heralded modernization and economic development as key paradigms, but later they shied away from such grand narratives. They began to repudiate the teleologies underlying modernization and the dichotomy of "modern versus premodern/traditional." Instead plural, hybrid, and non-teleological approaches were favored. The competition of blueprints led to the emergence of a model of "multiple modernities." Social scientists did not simply defend Western democracy and market capitalism, they tried to transform it. Indeed, the Cold War gradually became an era of capitalist and communist self-reform.[167]

What was the impact of this recoding of the Cold War? Cold War culture became self-reflexive, it reflected on itself and provided models to put the Cold War into perspective. Once self-reflexivity – particularly in the social sciences – was a cognitive pattern, bipolar schemes of the Cold War could not be upheld. When in 1979/80 the political antagonism between East and West sharpened again, political actors could not count on the support of the arts and of culture in general.

---

165 Elena Osokina, "Know Your Enemy: The Rise and Fall of America's Soviet Experts," *Slavic Review* 70, no. 1 (2011): 207.

166 Shaw, "Cinema, Television and the Cold War Introduction."; Engerman.

167 Howard Brick, "Optimism of the Mind: Imagining Postindustrial Society in the 1960s and 1970s," *American Quarterly* 44, no. 3 (1992); *Transcending capitalism. Visions of a new society in modern American thought* (Ithaca [u.a.]: Cornell University Press, 2006).

4 Conclusion

Different concepts of culture reveal different Cold War cultures. The most common notion of culture refers to practices of representation. From this perspective Cold War culture was about various ways of representing the actors, the enemies and the conflict. These representations focused on competing forms of modernism in the East and the West. Representing Modernism in one way or the other was therefore a central feature of the cultural Cold War. A second concept of culture tries to make visible the production of meaning, the re-coding and re-imagining of the Cold War. In this view, Cold War culture wasn't a function of the conflict, but rather a field where its meaning was negotiated. These meanings changed over time. The most profound changes were the internalization of the Cold War and the reflexivity with which scientists came to look at the antagonism. These changes occurred mostly after the Cuban Missile Crisis offered a spectre of world-wide self-destruction. The Cold War turned into an object of cultural criticism. The Cold War cultures were never merely straightforward projections, simple or plain reproductions of Western or Eastern ideology. Over time, they entailed displacements, irony, hybridization and tragedy on both sides.[168] Due to such practices of hybridization, bipolar imaginaries such as "East" and "West" or "center and periphery" became blurred.[169] Sharpening them again ran against considerable resistance after 1979.

What did the Cold War produce culturally? What was its lasting impact? The Cold War's influence on Europe was more qualitative than quantitative. "It shaped existing disputes and older developments more than it inspired new trends."[170] The creative potential after 1945 came mostly from actors and movements that were only indirectly related to the Cold War, for instance the student rebellion in the 1960s or the new ideological debates after the end of the postwar boom in 1973. The end of the postwar growth produced more new ideas than the preceding Cold War confrontation. That becomes even clearer if one compares the cultural production of the interwar years with the Cold War, a period of relative peace and stability in Western Europe. Classical modernity reached its apogee in the 1920s and 30s, while postmodernism triumphed in the 1980s. The cultural Cold War

168 See Elisabeth Bronfen and Anne Emmert, *Hybride Kulturen. Beiträge zur anglo-amerikanischen Multikulturalismusdebatte*, Stauffenburg discussion (Tübingen: Stauffenburg-Verl., 1997).
169 Vittoria Borsò & Christiane Liermann & Patrick Merziger, "Transfigurationen des Politischen. Von Propaganda-Studien zu Interaktionsmodellen der Medienkommunikation – eine Einleitung," in *Die Macht des Populären. Politik und populäre Kultur im 20. Jahrhundert*, ed. Vittoria Borsò & Christiane Liermann & Patrick Merziger (Bielefeld: transcript Verlag, 2010), 20f.
170 Gienow-Hecht, 398f.

in many ways drew on older models and ideas. It hardly overcame them. It used them in new ways, assembled them in new assemblages or – to borrow a term from Claude Lévi-Strauss – Cold War bricolages.

George Orwell once remarked that the Cold War did generate a vocabulary of its own. The *lingua belli frigidi* knew mostly negative terms that stemmed from its bipolar logic. This vocabulary contained invectives like "'lackeys', 'pinkos', and 'running dogs', 'fellow-travellers', 'cliques' and 'deviationists', 'card-carrying', 'paper tigers', 'henchmen', 'stooges' and 'revanchists'". Other terms denoted states or cities: 'Formosa', 'Red China', 'Beijing', 'Pankow', 'Leningrad' or 'Karl-Marx-Stadt', now Chemnitz. The Cold War semantics comprised "central committees" and 'Five Year Plans' as well as 'Kremlinology'. Historical metaphors were held in especially high esteem. Brezhnev and other party leaders often used the phrase "History teaches us." Lenin knew history on his side, when he, "the thinking guillotine," quoted the Latin verse: *volentem ducunt, fata nolentem trahunt.* In October 1989 Mikhail Gorbachev made that the same point by warning that "latecomers will be punished by life."[171]

171 Fred Halliday, "'High and just proceedings': Notes towards an anthology of the Cold War," *Millennium-Journal of International Studies* 30, no. 3 (2001).

David Reynolds

Probing the Cold War Narrative since 1945: The Case of Western Europe

The master narrative of the Cold War emanated from the United States. It took several forms and emerged in a dialectical fashion – traditionalist approaches blaming Soviet expansion, revisionist critiques stressing American neo-imperialism, and post-revisionist attempts to reiterate Soviet responsibility while preserving the notion of American agency – but by the mid-1970s it had taken firm shape in America. Underlying all these various approaches was an essentially bipolar view of the Cold War. In 1945 Senator William Fulbright characterized the post-war world as "two big dogs chewing on a bone." In similar vein the political scientist Hans Morgenthau spoke of "two giants eyeing each other with watchful suspicion." This bipolar perspective extended to the writing of history as well: American historiography of the Cold War, at least until the 1980s, conveyed the impression that only the United States and the Soviet Union mattered. Projecting their struggle back from 1945 to 1917 – "Wilson versus Lenin" in Arno Mayer's phrase – served to inscribe the Cold War as the central story of whole twentieth century.[1]

In this essay I want to explore the response to that American bipolar narrative in three Western European countries – Great Britain, France and the Federal Republic of Germany. I shall look mainly at the Cold War era itself but will make reference, especially at the end, to the period since 1991. Two broad themes will be developed. First, how the historiography of the Cold War in each of these three countries challenged aspects of the overarching bipolar narrative generated in the United States. From the 1980s various scholars insisted that Britain, France and West Germany played an active role in shaping Europe's Cold War, rather than merely being passive recipients, even victims, of American policy. Secondly, I want to consider ways in which, in all three countries, the Cold War has been set within larger and longer patterns of international history, particularly themes of global decolonization and European identity. In other words, not merely probing the Cold War narrative but seeking to transcend it.

Let me start with Great Britain. "So far," wrote the historian Donald Cameron Watt in 1978, "there has been little or no serious writing on the Cold War in Britain." He urged British scholars to rectify the omission, stressing two exciting challenges.

1 Daniel Yergin, *Shattered Peace: The Origins of the Cold War and the National Security State* (London: André Deutsch, 1978), 223; Hans Morgenthau, *Politics among the Nations: The Struggle*

DOI 10.1515/9783110496178-003

First, the opening on a rolling annual timetable under the Thirty-Year Rule of the relevant British governmental archives – the papers of the Cabinet, Foreign Office and armed services – on which serious historical scholarship could be based. Watt drew particular attention to the cornucopia of newly-opened British documents for 1947 – perhaps the seminal year of the early Cold War, which saw the articulation of the Truman Doctrine and the inception of the Marshall Plan. A second stimulus to research, in Watt's view, was the passionate debate in America about Cold War history – sparked by the Vietnam War and the concomitant revisionist writings that questioned the fundamentals of US policy since 1945 and even 1917. The vast and well catalogued British archives offered rich new evidence, in Watt's opinion, on which to judge the revisionist case that the Cold War stemmed from American self-assertion as much as Soviet expansion.[2]

As Watt had hoped, the 1980s saw an outpouring of British scholarship, much of it seeking to position Britain at the center of the emerging Cold War by arguing that US policy in the 1940s was less clear-cut than American historians had suggested. On this interpretation America moved slowly and hesitantly into Cold War confrontation and European commitments, its progress depending crucially on Britain taking the lead. Fraser Harbutt, for instance, argued that Churchill's "Iron Curtain" speech in March 1946 played an "indispensable" part in Truman's shift from accommodation to confrontation, inspiring "the timing and much of the substance" of that re-orientation. Similarly, Anne Deighton argued that the British "led the way" in unifying the British and US zones in Germany and in forging a West German state, while Alan Bullock's magisterial study of Ernest Bevin, Britain's postwar Foreign Secretary, presented him as Washington's essential partner in turning the Marshall Plan and the Atlantic alliance from ideas into realities. According to Bullock, Bevin "secured the American support" necessary to underpin Western Europe's prosperity through the Marshall Plan and its independence by virtue of NATO and thereby "restore the balance of power in Europe."[3]

It should be noted that this 1980s conception among historians of Britain as the expediter of American Cold War commitments in Europe reflected the self-image of British policymakers in the 1940s. "It must be our purpose," asserted a Foreign

---

for Power and Peace (2nd edition, New York: Alfred A. Knopf, 1954), 339; Arno Mayer, *Wilson vs Lenin: Political Origins of the New Diplomacy, 1917–1918* (New York: Meridian Books, 1964).

2 D.C. Watt, 'Rethinking the Cold War: A Letter to a British Historian', *Political Quarterly*, 49 (1978), 446–56, quote 446.

3 Fraser J. Harbutt, *The Iron Curtain: Churchill, America, and the Origins of the Cold War* (New York: Oxford University Press, 1986), 284; Anne Deighton, *The Impossible Peace: Britain, the Division of Germany, and the Origins of the Cold War* (Oxford: Oxford University Press, 1990), 8; Alan Bullock, *Ernest Bevin: Foreign Secretary, 1945–1951* (London: Heinemann, 1983), 857.

Office memorandum in 1944, "to make use of American power for purposes which we regard as good," so that "we can help steer this great unwieldy barge, the United States of America, into the right harbour." This patronizing view is even more evident in a verse penned by an unknown British official during the 1945 negotiations for a post-war American loan:

> In Washington Lord Halifax
> Once whispered to Lord Keynes:
> It's true *they* have the money bags
> But *we* have all the brains.[4]

The parallels between 1940s policy and 1980s historiography highlight the seductive power of diplomatic archives, especially those as full and eloquent as the files of the British Foreign Office. It is tempting to take the aspirations of diplomats as statements of fact. Just as earlier American historiography had been overly preoccupied with the two big dogs, so some of the scholarship in Britain in the 1980s put too much beef on the British bone.

This conceit about utilizing America for Britain's own purposes also reminds us that the Cold War was not the sole or even the central preoccupation of British foreign policy in the half-century after 1945. London's real goal was to maintain Britain's position as a global force – until the end of the 1960s through the maintenance of imperial outposts and networks, thereafter by exploiting soft power to "punch above our weight" in the arena of world affairs. Integral to that strategy was the putative "special relationship" with the United States, especially for shoring up the European balance through America's economic support, military presence and nuclear alliance. A stable Europe, even one based on a balance of terror, would allow Britain to concentrate on its worldwide interests. For this reason, the forward policy of the 1940s, drawing the United States into European commitments, was followed for most of the Cold War by a more cautious attitude, seeking to restrain the United States from escalating European crises, especially over Berlin. Successive British governments were supportive of détente and ready from an early date to accept the division of Europe not merely as a *fait accompli* but as a welcome source of stability.

In short, the historiography about Britain and the world since 1945 has been less inclined than American scholarship to employ bipolarity as an over-arching

4 Terry H. Anderson, *The United States, Great Britain, and the Cold War, 1944–1947* (Columbia, MO: University of Missouri Press, 1981), 12–13; Richard N. Gardner, *Sterling-Dollar Diplomacy in Current Perspective* (3rd edition, New York: Columbia University Press, 1980), xiii.

theme. Instead the Cold War has been treated as one facet, albeit very important, of a narrative built around Britain's twentieth-century metamorphosis as a world power. As the documents were opened in the 1980s, scholars showed how Clement Attlee's postwar Labour government of 1945–51 worked assiduously to sustain Britain's position in an apparently bipolar world. In May 1947 Foreign Secretary Ernest Bevin dismissed claims that Britain had "ceased to be a great Power" and insisted that "we regard ourselves as one of the Powers most vital to the peace of the world." In an unprecedented move, Parliament maintained conscription in peacetime until the early 1960s, allowing Britain to keep nearly a million men in the armed forces. When the United States terminated wartime cooperation on nuclear weapons in 1945–6, Attlee committed Britain to building its own atomic bomb – becoming the third nuclear power in 1952. And although the British withdrew ignominiously from India and Palestine, the Labour Government and its Conservative successors in the 1950s built up Britain's position in the Middle East with bases and clients in a crucial arc from Egypt to Iraq and sought to maximize the dollar-earning capacity of the Sterling Area in countries such as Malaya and the Gold Coast. This was not mere hubris: at the beginning of the 1950s Britain was still the dominant economy in Europe, in both industrial production and total exports generating more than France and West Germany combined.[5] Bevin summed up the persistent globalism of British policymakers in 1950 when dismissing involvement in European integration. "Great Britain was not part of Europe," he declared; it was "not simply a Luxembourg."[6]

During the 1980s the opening of British archives therefore generated a series of works contesting a bipolar view of global affairs in the 1940s and 1950s. It also resulted in a more circuitous narrative than the familiar one about Britain's inexorable twentieth-century slide from imperial greatness. Instead, to quote Jack Gallagher, the story was one of "decline, revival and fall" of the British Empire, with the early Cold War energizing a new surge of globalism.[7] By the 1960s,

5 Alec Cairncross, *Years of Recovery: British Economic Policy, 1945–1951* (London: Methuen, 1985), p. 278.

6 David Reynolds, *Britannia Overruled: British Policy and World Power in the Twentieth Century* (2nd edition, London: Longman, 2000), 148, 186. Among major studies relating the Cold War to British globalism see Wm. Roger Louis, *The British Empire in the Middle East, 1945–1951: Arab Nationalism, The United States, and Postwar Imperialism* (Oxford: Oxford University Press, 1984) and John L. Kent, *British Imperial Strategy and the Origins of the Cold War, 1944–1949* (Leicester: Leicester University Press, 1993).

7 John Gallagher, *The Decline, Revival and Fall of the British Empire*, ed. Anil Seal (Cambridge: Cambridge University Press, 1982). For an example of this contextualization of Britain's Cold War within bigger narratives see John Darwin, *The Empire Project: The Rise and Fall of the*

however, the "revival" was over and the "fall" clearly apparent. Decolonization took hold in Africa and Asia, the Sterling Area gradually collapsed and the Cuban Missile Crisis dramatized the fact of bipolarity. When Dean Acheson, the former U.S. Secretary of State declared in 1962 that "Great Britain has lost an empire and has not yet found a role," the furious reaction in London showed he had touched a raw nerve. Following Britain's belated entry into the European Community in 1973, fifteen years after its essential structure had been forged by the Six, Cold War globalism, like the special relationship with America, was often presented as a distraction from Britain's essentially European destiny. Narrating how British leaders from Winston Churchill to Tony Blair viewed Europe, journalist Hugo Young called it a "story of fifty years in which Britain struggled to reconcile the past she could not forget with the future she could not avoid." In his view "no alternative" to Europe had existed in the previous half-century but Whitehall had refused to accept the reality. Brian Harrison's recent volumes about the years 1951 to 1990 in the "Oxford History of England," although acknowledging that the Cold War was "central" to the whole period, are structured around Acheson's comment, being entitled *Seeking a Role* and *Finding a Role?* Harrison explores various supposed alternatives to global *imperium*, including a Cold War "middle way" between capitalism and communism and the idea of Britain as cultural exemplar – a version of soft power – while noting that by 1970 none of these roles "carried conviction even within the UK." Harrison concludes his second volume by observing that "in 2007 Tony Blair left office with that holy grail, a world role for the UK, as elusive as ever," although he suggests that it did not matter to the British people because they "were fortunate enough within a political structure and culture that prescribed for them no collective role at all." Historian Sean Greenwood was less upbeat at the end of his overview *Britain and the Cold War*. Adapting the mordant words of W.B. Yeats on life itself, he argued that for Britain the Cold War was "a long preparation for nothing." Whatever the validity of this verdict, especially after the Brexit referendum of June 2016, it underlines my main point that the bipolar narrative has not been central to British accounts of the era since 1945.[8]

In France the Cold War had a more dominant place in post-war political and historical writing than was the case in Britain. One reason was the salience of the

---

British World-System, 1830–1970 (Cambridge: Cambridge University Press, 2009), chapters 12–14.

8 Hugo Young, *This Blessed Plot: Britain and Europe from Churchill to Blair* (London: Macmillan, 1998), 1, 171; Brian Harrison, *Seeking a Role: The United Kingdom, 1951–1970* (Oxford:

French communist party, the PCF, which regularly attracted a quarter of voters in the first post-war decade. This was in marked contrast to the United States where support for the communist party, and indeed for socialism, was miniscule. In other words, political forces that have been central to French post-war history, indeed to the history of much of continental Europe since 1945, were fundamentally alien to the experience of the United States. Hence the bipolar ideologization of the Cold War in America, where the political left per se was an essential element in defining the Soviet Other. In France, by contrast, the PCF was both an "incentive" to build and sustain an Atlantic alliance and also a "brake" that prevented France from waging the Cold War as wholeheartedly as the United States.[9]

It is also important to note that the dominant political discourse of post-war France was predicated on the bipolar narrative, especially the so-called Yalta Myths. Whereas the American version of this mythology, popularized by the Republican right, accused Roosevelt and the Democrats of "selling out" Eastern Europe to Stalin and communism, the French variant portrayed the Yalta conference of February 1945 as the division of Europe, even the world, by all of the Big Three – Churchill, Roosevelt and Stalin. This interpretation was pre-eminently an invention of Charles de Gaulle who bitterly resented his exclusion from the conference, even though at Yalta – thanks to the British – France was made an equal partner with the Big Three in the occupation regime for Germany. Volume three of de Gaulle's war memoirs, published in 1959, popularized his critique: at Yalta the Anglo-Saxons had abandoned Central Europe and the Balkans to "the discretion of the Soviets," bringing down the "iron curtain" over the whole of Eastern Europe. De Gaulle blamed this sell-out directly on France's exclusion from the conference because she was the real champion of European interests: there was, he insisted, a "correlation between France's absence and Europe's new laceration (*déchirement*)."[10]

Gaullist rhetoric entered the discourse of international history via Arthur Conte's book *Yalta, ou le partage du monde*, published in 1964. Conte concluded that Yalta "paved the way for the division of Europe" by sacrificing Poland; even worse it "sanctioned the great Asiatic tumult" because America sold out its Asian

---

Clarendon Press, 2009), 87, 544, and *Finding a Role?: The United Kingdom, 1950–1990* (Oxford: Clarendon Press, 2010), 549; Sean Greenwood, *Britain and the Cold War* (London: Macmillan, 2000), 196.

9 Georges-Henri Soutou, "France," in David Reynolds, ed., *The Origins of the Cold War in Europe: International Perspectives* (New Haven: Yale University Press, 1994), 120.

10 Charles de Gaulle, *Mémoires*, ed. Marius-François Guyard (Paris: Gallimard, 2000), 666–7, 788–9.

allies and encouraged the forces of revolution in China, Vietnam and elsewhere.[11] Few French scholars today accept such a crude characterization of Yalta. They acknowledge that the Soviet presence in Eastern Europe was already a fact because of the Red Army's advance and also admit that the conference yielded benefits for all three participants, not just Stalin. But such academic revisionism has done little to overturn conventional wisdom in France. The claim that Yalta marked the division of Europe and even the world became a cliché of French public discourse, informing many accounts of the Cold War. It has also been used as convenient shorthand by journalists in Germany and Britain.[12]

Not only did de Gaulle successfully promote his interpretation of Yalta, he used it as the intellectual basis of his diplomacy in the 1960s while President of the Fifth Republic. His was effectively an "anti-Yalta policy" intended to re-assert Europe's independence, under French tutelage, from the two superpowers. Thus his gradual disentanglement of France from NATO's integrated command because of its dominance by the United States, while his dramatic opening to Moscow in 1966 was followed by his denunciation of Moscow's suppression of the Prague Spring in 1968. Czechoslovakia, he declared, was evidence that "the government in Moscow has not dissociated itself from its bloc policy . . . imposed on Europe as a result of the Yalta accords, which are incompatible with the right of people to self-determination."[13] Thus in France as in Britain – albeit in different ways – historical interpretation was interwoven with contemporary diplomacy.

The polarization of French politics and the potency of the Yalta myth are two reasons why the Cold War was a central feature of French narratives of the era of 1945. Nevertheless, in France, as in Britain, the Cold War was located in larger and longer narratives. One was the question of France's imperial role. Anglo-French rivalry over India and North America had been the great global contest of the eighteenth century. The French empire, in its modern incarnation, dates back to 1830 and empire remained central to France after 1945: the wars in Indochina (1946–54) and then Algeria (1945–62) scarred French politics and society well into the 1960s, bringing down the Fourth Republic along the way. Both the Vietminh

---

11 Arthur Conte, *Yalta ou le Partage due Monde (11 février 1945)* (Paris: Robert Laffont, 1964), esp. 364–6.

12 Reiner Marcowitz, "Yalta, the Myth of the Division of the World," in Cyril Buffet and Beatrice Heuser, eds, *Haunted by History: Myths in International Relations* (Oxford: Berghahn, 1998), 80–91; André Fontaine, *History of the Cold War: From the October Revolution to the Korean War, 1917–1950*, transl. D.D. Paige (London: Secker and Warburg, 1965), chapter 10, p. 218. See also David Reynolds, *Summits: Six Meetings that Shaped the Twentieth Century* (London: Penguin, 2007), chapter 3.

13 Buffet and Heuser, eds, *Haunted by History*, 90.

in Indochina and the FLN in Algeria were supported by Moscow and its proxies, but these struggles were rooted in that larger imperial story.

But unlike Britain, France had a further major policy distraction – its relationship with Germany. Though entangled with the Cold War, this was rooted in a much longer trajectory of French history, including three catastrophic wars in 1870, 1914 and 1939. Two important books show how this issue has been addressed at different moments – one volume published in the era of detente, the other written after the Cold War.

Alfred Grosser published *Les Occidentaux*, his influential account of the Cold War Western alliance, in 1978, and the book was then translated into English. Grosser constructed the narrative around France and Germany – what he called the two *super-privilégiés* – and provocatively located both the Cold War and the Atlantic alliance within the question of Europe. The basic problem, Grosser argued – pace the Gaullists – was not US hegemony but what he called "the twofold nature of the Soviet Union" as "both a European country and a superpower, the only one on European soil." The minatory Soviet presence impeded creation of a European security system because that would be dominated by Moscow – hence the need to link Western Europe to the United States. For Grosser Europe's security deficit, so evident in the crucial years of 1945–9, had still not been resolved in the era of détente.[14]

By 2001, however, Georges–Henri Soutou could take a more positive view of the 1970s. His overview *La Guerre de Cinquante Ans*, on East-West relations 1943–90, interpreted the Cold War as a gradual and painful realization of two norm-defining moments. The first was the democratic order sketched out at Yalta in 1945, especially the Declaration on Liberated Europe, and then Potsdam, although this was not honored by Stalin and his successors. (Here, of course, was a very different take on Yalta from the Gaullist narrative.) Equally important was the structure of peaceful change and disarmament elaborated in the Helsinki accords and related détente agreements of the 1970s. The full realization of the Yalta and Helsinki visions in the Gorbachev era resulted in what Soutou termed "a new European order," although its character still had to be fleshed out in the twenty-first century.[15]

In the Federal Republic of Germany, historians were even slower to enter the Cold War debate. Access to documents was a bigger problem than in Britain and

---

14 Alfred Grosser, *Les Occidentaux: Les pays d'Europe et les États-Unis depuis la guerre* (Paris: Fayard, 1978), 3, 414.

15 Georges-Henri Soutou, *La Guerre de Cinquante Ans: Les Relations Est-Ouest, 1943–1990* (Paris: Fayard, 2001), 730.

France, not least because many of the archives of the National Socialist period had fallen into Allied hands under the occupation regime and were only slowly returned to Germany. 'Are we partners of the Allies or a colonial people?' fumed Georg Winter, director of the newly established *Bundesarchiv* in 1956. Before their return, the documents were microfilmed and used extensively by Western scholars to illuminate various aspects of the Nazi era: first fruits were works such as Alexander Dallin's *German Rule in Russia, 1941–1945* (1957), Raul Hilberg's pioneering account of *The Destruction of the European Jews* (1961) and Gerhard Weinberg's edition of Hitler's so-called Second Book (1961). German scholars, unable to travel abroad without governmental permission and funding, were at a disadvantage when, in the caustic words of Gerhard Ritter, the country's diplomatic files had been "given up without restriction to the whole world and every little college in America or Australia could photocopy them without further ado."[16]

In addition, the German historical profession in the 1960s was peculiarly affected by the turn to social history. Although this shift was evident in the United States and across all of Western Europe, it was more pronounced in West Germany than elsewhere – reflecting, perhaps, the post-Nazi era disenchantment with international power politics. Traditionalists such as Klaus Hildebrand who took a Rankean view of the centrality of political and diplomatic history were very much on the defensive. In the 1960s, with the social history of Nazism becoming a fertile field of research for contemporary historians, scholars writing about Germany and the Cold War, such as Ernst Deuerlein and Gerhard Wettig, were exceptions to the predominant trend of research.[17]

Nevertheless, in national life, the overwhelming importance of the Cold War was harder to deny than in Britain and France. The superpower contest was, after all, the main reason why there was by 1949 no longer one Germany but two – each aligned with and largely controlled by one of the rival blocs. The Cold War also helped each Germany to define a sense of identity – the GDR portraying itself as an "anti-fascist" state of workers and peasants, whereas the Federal Republic anchored itself in German ethnicity and culture and also in the wider community of "Western" values. In the 1950s the Cold War was central to party politics in Bonn, notably the clash between Christian Democrats and Social Democrats over

---

16 Astrid M. Eckert, *Kampf um die Akten: Die Westallierten und die Rückgabe von deutschem Archivgut nach dem Weltkrieg* (Stuttgart: Franz Steiner, 2004), 428, 464.

17 Wolfgang Krieger, "Germany," in David Reynolds, ed., *The Origins of the Cold War in Europe*, pp. 150–1; Klaus Hildebrand, "Geschichte oder 'Gesellschaftsgeschichte'? Die Notwendigkeit einer politischen Geschichtsschreibung von den internationalen Beziehungen," *Historische Zeitschrift*, 223 (1976), 328–57.

rearmament and Konrad Adenauer's policy of *Westbindung*, and also the more general controversy about whether West Germany was essentially a tool of the Allies.

Yet, although Germany was shaped far more profoundly than Britain or France by bipolarity, here too the Cold War was debated within larger narratives, especially about what it meant to be German. Always a pre-occupation of German intellectuals going back to the days of Goethe, Herder and Fichte, the controversy about German identity became a near "obsession" after 1945. It revolved above all around the fact of partition and the burden of guilt.[18]

First, partition: both the FRG and the GDR claimed to be the authentic Germany, faithful to the country's historic values. West Germany was always readier to locate its *Westbindung* in the longer patterns of German history – Adenauer invoked the Holy Roman Empire as a precursor of the European Union – but gradually the GDR also appropriated "difficult" Germans such as Luther and Bismarck into its political narrative. The fact of partition also placed a question mark over the goal of German unity, belatedly achieved under Bismarck but now destroyed in the Cold War. The détente agreements of the early 1970s, including the Bonn Republic's de facto recognition of the GDR, suggested to some that the unity issue had now been resolved.

One example comes from the philosopher-historian Ernst Nolte in *Deutschland und der Kalte Krieg* (1974) – a vast, rambling study described by the American scholar Felix Gilbert as "a Hegelian history in which events are determined by the logic of concepts." Nolte presented the Cold War as an "ideological and power-political struggle" waged by "militant universalisms" for "the future structure of a united world." He argued that this struggle, pre-figured in the American ideals of 1776, had been going on in earnest since 1917 and that its central arena since 1945 was the two Germanies, where the rival values of American liberalism and Soviet Marxism confronted each other in a divided country and a divided capital city. For Nolte the German treaties and Ostpolitik of the early 1970s suggested an end to the Cold War because partition was now accepted as a fact.[19]

A different perspective on the détente era was offered by the conservative military historian Andreas Hillgruber. In 1974 he published a slim overview of post-war German history which set the recent past into a traditional geopolitical framework of *Weltpolitik*. Hilgruber sketched out various scenarios for Germany

---

18 As discussed for instance by Mary Fulbrook, *German National Identity after the Holocaust* (Cambridge: Polity Press, 1999).

19 Ernst Nolte, *Deutschland und Kalte Krieg* (Munich: Piper, 1974), 39, 599–600; review by Felix Gilbert in *American Historical Review*, 81 (1976), 618–19.

in the 1970s, including continued partition, eventual reunification on terms benefiting either the FRG or the GDR, fuller absorption in one or other bloc, or even neutralization – akin to the Austrian solution of 1955.[20]

These books by Nolte and Hillgruber represented two different attempts, from the vantage point of the détente era, to locate divided Germany in a meta-narrative about the Cold War. Yet partition was not the only challenge to German national identity. On each side of the bipolar divide Germans had to address a peculiarly crushing burden of history and guilt – the Nazi past, the Second World War and above all the Holocaust. As the discipline of contemporary history took shape in West Germany – the *Institut für Zeitgeschichte* (*IfZ*) was founded in 1950 – it did so around the Hitler era. Although a reaction to the enormity of what had happened in those years, this process was facilitated by the unique availability of documentation thanks to the Allies' capture, opening and gradual repatriation of the archives. In 1956 the U.S. State Department files were accessible up to 1926 and the British Foreign Office files up to 1902, while documents from the Quai d'Orsay were closed after 1877. By contrast most of the records of the Nazi era between 1933 and 1945 were wide open for scholars. As William Langer of Harvard observed, "the historian could not ordinarily expect to have access to such records in less than fifty or a hundred years, and only the fortunes of war have brought this mine of information to our shores."[21]

Central to the British and American determination not to leave the Germans in unrestricted control of their archives was the desire to avoid a repeat of the "war guilt" arguments of the 1920s, when German historians mined their archives in support of Weimar's rebuttals of the Allied claim that the Kaiserreich had started the war in 1914. This remained the dominant view in West Germany even after 1945. Ritter and other national conservatives of the Front generation still asserted that the Great Powers had collectively "slithered" into war in August 1914. They went on to claim that Hitler's aggressive expansionism had been a tragic aberration from the course of German history – a glitch (*Betriebsunfall*) in the mocking words of Helmut Krausnick of the *IfZ*. American-based historians of modern Germany, often refugees from Nazism, were even blunter in their criticism of Ritter and his colleagues. What was needed, declared Hans Kohn, was not simply "new facts or documents" but "a new perspective" and "a different frame of values."[22]

---

20 Andreas Hillgruber, *Deutsche Geschichte, 1945–1975: Die "deutsche Frage" in der Weltpolitik* (2nd edition, Frankfurt/M: Ullstein, 1980), 173–4.

21 Eckert, *Kampf um die Akten*, 352–3, 435.

22 Astrid M. Eckert, "The Transnational Beginnings of West German *Zeitgeschichte* in the 1950s," *Central European History*, 40 (2007), 84–6.

It is in this context that the Fischer controversy should be understood. Fritz Fischer published *Griff nach der Weltmacht* in 1961, the year of the Berlin Wall, followed even more provocatively by *Krieg der Illusionen* (1967). His duel with Ritter, dean of the German historical establishment, became the professional *cause célèbre* of the 1960s, played up by major media outlets such as *Der Spiegel* and exploited as a left-right generational divide in German academic culture. Ritter was not an uncritical apologist of the Kaiserreich, having written extensively on German militarism, but he was essentially defending the Germany of his pre-war youth. Fischer, born in 1908, was twenty years younger: his distinctive perspective was shaped during the 1950s, on the one hand, by two semesters of study in the United States (which introduced him to the captured Nazi documents) and, on the other hand, by access through the GDR authorities to the Imperial German archives, which the Soviets had returned to Potsdam. Instead of presenting 1914 as a 'defensive war' by Germany, Fischer used his novel material and revisionist perspective to postulate an expansionist philosophy among German elites that stretched from the *Kaiserreich* back to Bismarck and on to Hitler. He also argued that their foreign policy had been consistently framed around domestic political imperatives. Elements of this argument were not new – they had been deployed by scholars such as Lewis Namier in Britain and Hans Gatzke in the United States. What was novel was the detailed archival base and the fact that *Griff nach der Weltmacht* was published in Germany by a German historian. The Fischer thesis – developed more dogmatically, though in different ways, by Immanuel Geiss and Hans-Ulrich Wehler – challenged the idea that Hitlerite expansionism was an aberration from the course of German history and asserted that it was the responsibility of the whole people rather than of a criminal few. Here was a direct assault on the fundamental fictions of Adenauer's Germany about the supposed oddity of the period 1933–45 – what Mary Fulbrook has called the official posture of "public penance" for Nazism but also "strictly limited liability."[23]

Such a posture became hard to sustain by the late 1960s, as student radicals openly denounced their elders from the so-called "silent generation" who had been complicit in Nazi crimes. But it was in the mid-1980s that the issue of guilt for Nazism became central to historical debate, shaping narratives of the Cold War. The so-called *Historikerstreit* was sparked by the social philosopher Jűrgen Habermas whose blistering article in *Die Zeit* in July 1986 attacked recent writings by Nolte, Hillgruber and others for "relativizing" Nazi crimes. Nolte had argued that Nazism was at root a "justified reaction" to Bolshevism and its "Asiatic deeds" – albeit a reaction that went too far. "Wasn't the Gulag Archipelago prior

23 Fulbrook, *German National Identity*, 59.

in history to Auschwitz?" he asked. "Wasn't 'class murder' by the Bolsheviks the logical and real precondition of 'race murder' by the Nazis?" Hillgruber's argument was couched more subtly and in a different form – evoking the Eastern Front in 1944–5 (where he had fought) as a *Götterdämmerung*-style struggle to protect Germany, Central Europe and European civilization from communist barbarity – but his underlying thrust was similar to that of Nolte. Both historians were using the Cold War (pre-dated to 1917) to exculpate, or at least explain, aspects of the Third Reich and to subsume the Nazi era in a larger and more positive version of German history.[24]

At a deeper level, as Hans Mommsen observed, the real "polarization" was not between two opposing sides in the Cold War but between two different methodologies for studying German history. Nolte, Hillgruber and their ilk were rooted in the *Primat der Außenpolitik* – a tradition going back to Ranke which assumed that geopolitics and external forces in general were the key determinants of historical change within nations. Their critics, often social historians, stressed the formative role of domestic pressures and societal tensions. These scholars presented German history as the exception to a supposedly European norm of modernization, whereas Nolte and Hillgruber sought to "normalize" Germany's past by comparing Nazi crimes with those of Soviet Russia and other countries.[25] Nolte asserted sensationally in *Deutschland und der Kalte Krieg* that most significant states apart from Britain and America have had their own Hitler era (*Hitlerzeit*), each with "its monstrosities and its victims."[26]

Even after 1989 attempts to understand Cold War Germany have drawn on these older debates and issues about unity and guilt. One example is Konrad Jarausch's *After Hitler: Recivilizing Germans, 1945–1955* (2006), which moves beyond the Cold War discourse of Americanization by developing the 1990s pre-occupation with "civil society." Writing from a transatlantic perspective, Jarausch offers a fresh narrative of Cold War West Germany, yet his ingredients remain those that pre-occupied scholars during the Cold War itself – Hitler, the Holocaust and the *Sonderweg* thesis. But, he asks presciently at the end, "does a continuing concentration on avoiding a repetition of the catastrophes of the

---

24 Richard J. Evans, *In Hitler's Shadow: West German Historians and the Attempt to Escape from the Nazi Past* (London: I.B. Tauris, 1989), 32, 60.

25 Hans Mommsen, "Stehen wir vor einer neuen Polarisierung des Geschichtsbildes in der Bundesrepublik?" in Susanna Miller, ed., *Geschichte in der demokratischen Gesellschaft: Eine Dokumentation* (Dűsseldorf: Schwann-Bagel, 1985), 71–82. See also the discussion in Charles S. Maier, *The Unmasterable Past: History, Holocaust, and German National Identity* (Cambridge, MA: Harvard University Press, 1988), 16–25

26 Nolte, *Deutschland und Kalte Krieg*, 601.

twentieth-century not somehow block the perception of the novel challenges of the twenty-first century?"[27]

I have suggested that, despite the importance of the Cold War for Western Europe in the second half of the twentieth century, once serious historiography got going in the 1980s many historians of Britain, France and Germany were disinclined to accept superpower bipolarity as *the* master narrative for understanding the years 1945 to 1989. In different ways they stressed the active role of Western European states in shaping the early Cold War (particularly Britain) and also in the later development of the conflict (Gaullist France). This approach was summed up in the phrase popularized by the Norwegian scholar Geir Lundestad who argued that if, as American revisionists claimed, NATO was a form of American imperialism, then it was "empire by invitation" – solicited and even shaped by the Europeans. In similar vein, the concept of "Westernization" – much used in recent years by German historians – is intended to suggest a narrative that, although configured by the ideological Cold War, embodies a two-way flow of values rather than one-way hegemonic "Americanization."[28]

I have also suggested that Western European scholars not merely probed the American Cold War narrative but tried to transcend it, by situating the Cold War within larger and longer frameworks. For historians in Britain and in France, once vast global empires enriched by trade and colonies, the complex process of decolonization has frequently provided the leitmotif. The consequence was a storyline starting well before 1945, into which specific Cold War struggles such as Malaya and Egypt, Algeria and Vietnam were then set. For France and Germany the era 1945–89 has often been located within the longer historical relationship between the two countries, stretching back through the wars of 1939, 1914 and 1870 to Napoleon and Louis XIV. Here the transcendent concepts are European integration and *Westbindung*, as the two countries finally buried the hatchet and learned to live together. In Germany Cold War polarization was peculiarly acute – embodied in two rival states – but even fervent anti-communists such as Ernst Nolte and Andreas Hillgruber rooted their interpretation of the Cold War in older

27 Konrad Jarausch, *After Hitler: Recivilizing Germans, 1945–1995*, translated by Brandon Hunziker (Oxford: Oxford University Press, 2006), 279.

28 Geir Lundestad, "Empire by Invitation? The United States and Western Europe, 1945–1952," *Journal of Peace Research*, 23 (1986), 263–77; Holger Nehring, "'Westernization': A New Paradigm for Interpreting West European History in a Cold War Context," *Journal of Contemporary History*, 4 (2004), 175–91. See also Anselm Doering-Manteuffel, *Wie westlich sind die Deutschen? Amerikanisierung und Westerisierung im 20. Jahrhundert* (Göttingen: Vandenhoeck and Ruprecht, 1999).

debates, notably the German question, and in older methodologies, such as the primacy of external forces in shaping German domestic history.

At several points we have seen how the détente agreements of the 1970s provided a platform from which to gain some perspective on the era since 1945 – this was true for Nolte, Hillgruber and Grosser. Yet we have also seen how Soutou, writing after the Cold War had ended, was able to frame both Yalta and détente within a different narrative about the evolution of democracy and disarmament. This underlines the point of Konrad Jarausch's question about how to construct twenty-first century narratives of the Cold War. Are frameworks derived from the last century still appropriate?

In considering this question, we should remember that in many European languages the term "history" is an extension of the word for "story." Telling a story successfully requires knowing how you will round it off: the endpoint defines the arc of narrative and also suggests the relevant details to be highlighted along the way. In writing contemporary history the endpoint is, however, an ever-moving target. Consider how perspectives on the wars of 1914–18 and 1939–45 shifted in the quarter-century after they ended. Twenty-five years on from the conclusion of the 'war to end war' took you through the Czech and Polish crises of 1938–9 and the fall of France to Stalingrad and Kursk. Inevitably the Second World War affected the narrative one then constructed about 1914–18 and its meaning. Similarly, moving twenty-five years on from the end of the Second World War gave Americans and Western Europeans very different perspectives on both Germany and Russia from those that prevailed in the twilight of the Third Reich, with West Germany now an ally and the Soviet Union a foe. In each of these cases the "post-war era" seemed clear: in the first case, 1918–39, it had become redefined as the inter-war era; in the second case, post-1945, as the Cold War.

Our problem today, a quarter-century from 1989–91, is that the character of the post-Cold War era is much harder to define. In 1995 the German President Roman Herzog declared that we were living in "a time which as yet has no name" [29] and his assertion remains essentially true, despite 9/11 and the "War on Terror." As we seek to define and to shape twenty-first century narratives about the Cold War era, the case studies I have mentioned may be prove suggestive.

In the first place, just as British and French writers related the Cold War to their retreat from empire, so imperialism and decolonization in turn are now being framed within larger and longer patterns of globalization, taking account of the shifting balance between Europe, the Americas and Asia over several cen-

---

29 Kristina Spohr-Readman, *Germany and the Baltic Problem after the Cold War: The Development of a New Ostpolitik, 1989–2000* (London: Routledge, 2004), 86, 113.

turies. The emergence of China in global politics – or rather its re-emergence when seen within the *longue durée* – has helped to push narrative construction in this direction. Likewise the recent implosion of North Africa and the Near East and the concomitant outflow of migrants across Europe highlight not just the legacies of the ill-judged American-British intervention in Iraq and the toxic fruits of the "Arab Spring" but also the longer-term historical failure of colonial and post-colonial state-building in these regions.[30]

Second, as we have also seen, French and German scholars regularly depicted the Cold War as the crucible for a Franco-German rapprochement located within a larger European identity. Since 1989 that integration project has spread eastward beyond the old "Iron Curtain" on a similar pacifying mission to embrace the former Soviet satellite states. As a result, the European Union now includes 500 million people from twenty-eight countries (twenty-seven after Brexit) and has extended right up to the edge of Russia. NATO has similarly pushed east, with the historic borderland of Ukraine as a particularly explosive flashpoint. This raises big historical questions. Are the EU and NATO, institutions forged as instruments of West European solidarity during the Cold War, appropriate to the whole continent in a post-Cold War era? And will Russia remain an alienated outsider or gradually be incorporated in a Europe-wide framework? Answers to these questions as the twenty-first century progresses will, in turn, suggest new narratives of the Cold War and its historical significance.

---

30 See Odd Arne Westad, "The Cold War and the International History of the Twentieth Century," in Melvyn P. Leffer and Odd Arne Westad, eds, *The Cambridge History of the Cold War* (3 vols, Cambridge: Cambridge University Press, 2010), 1: 7–8; also, on a more general plane, David Lowe and Tony Joel, *Remembering the Cold War: Global Contest and National Stories* (London: Routledge, 2013).

Vladimir O. Pechatnov

Changing Cold War Interpretations in Post-Soviet Russia

This paper is focused on changing narratives of the Cold War in the post-Soviet Russia as reflected both in scholarship and popular culture. These two realms are closely connected. So, what has changed and what has not in Russian perception of that epic conflict since its end? To simplify a bit, it is basically a story of three narratives (i.e. predominant mainstream trends in interpretations of the Cold War) replacing each other in the course of the last twenty years.

The first, primordial narrative was the standard Soviet version in its different variations – from the primitive to the more sophisticated ones. The Cold War was seen as having been imposed on the reluctant Soviet Union and its allies by the West headed by the United States. As Stalin commented to himself on the margins of one of his 1948 documents: “We are not waging the Cold War; it is being waged by the U.S. and its allies.”[1] This in a nutshell is a gist of the Soviet narrative. The basic American goal in this narrative was to deprive the Soviet Union of its well-deserved fruits of victory in World War II and, ultimately, to destroy the Soviet system by attrition and other means short of a big war. The basic motives behind that policy were perceived as a combination of ideology (class hatred towards Communism) and Realpolitik (to prevent Soviet domination of the Eurasian landmass). The tangible manifestations of American Cold War strategy were seen in the nuclear arms race, a ring of military bases around Soviet borders, NATO and other U.S. led military alliances aimed at the USSR.

The basic Soviet motive was described as a necessary defense against this global threat, as a continuation of the World War II struggle against fascism, this time represented by the U.S. “monopoly capital’s” drive for world domination. Just as in the United States the Cold War was described in terms of a continued struggle against totalitarianism, the Soviet version exploited the heroic narrative of the Great Patriotic War to legitimize its anti-American policy. Thus both sides rediscovered the new enemy as a different incarnation of the old one.

Moscow too had its own rough version of containment rooted in the general ideological vision of a hostile capitalist world, aggressive but inherently unstable, doomed to repeated circles of depression, war, and revolution. In this framework the basic Soviet strategy was to hold the line against the West and gather strength for a new showdown under a more favorable correlation of forces. But,

1 Russian State Archive of Social and Political History, f. 558, op.11, d.387, l.6.

DOI 10.1515/9783110496178-004

as Anders Stephanson pointed out, there was an important difference to this mirror imagery: the Soviet Union, as a weaker side in this conflict, held a more defensive posture – instead of trying to change the enemy's regime, it wanted primarily to force the U.S. into recognition of Soviet security interests including its new borders and sphere of influence.[2]

Naturally, this narrative went through some evolution as times changed. The crude original Stalin version was revised under Nikita Khrushchev. The new line was that given the changes in correlation of forces in the world there was no longer a fatal inevitability of major war; nor was there a situation of capitalist encirclement present any more. That's why a prolonged peaceful coexistence with capitalism was now declared both possible and desirable as a main guideline for Soviet foreign policy. Under Brezhnev the policy of détente came to be seen as a new stage in East-West relations transcending the Cold War itself. This change according to a modified narrative was caused mainly by the new strategic parity that led the West to finally recognize the post-WWII status quo in Europe and the USSR's legitimacy as a great power. The Soviet elite was now deeply pleased to run a superpower competing with the omnipotent United States in military might and global influence. The temporary recognition of this parity by Americans only reinforced this satisfaction. As President Richard Nixon said at the 1972 Moscow summit to his Soviet host, "You and I represent the two most powerful nations of the world... We are now at a stage where both our countries are equally strong and neither tries to dictate its terms to the other."[3] For the ordinary Soviet folks the U.S. was also a worthy rival enhancing their self-respect – after all, we were in the same super league with Americans and could therefore look down at the secondary players on the world scene. The national pride was flattered not so much by the waning confidence in the superiority of the Soviet model, as by the new superpower status and the feeling of competing with the all-powerful American giant. For a while it seemed that the Cold War ended with the honorable draw for the Soviet Union.

But if for the lagging behind USSR, this draw was close to victory, for the USA that had led the Cold War race for many years it looked like a defeat. So, when Washington under Ronald Reagan replaced détente with a new version of rolling

2 Anders Stephanson, "Cold War Origins," *Encyclopedia of American Foreign Policy.* Alexander De Conde, Richard Burns and Fredrick Logevall, Eds. 2nd Edition, New York: Gale Group, 2002, Vol.1, P.238.

3 *Soviet-American Relations. The Détente Years, 1969–1972.* David Geyer and Douglas Selvage, eds. Washington: GPO, 2007, P.836, 851.

back communism ("we shall bury you," American style) it resurrected the primordial Soviet narrative and gave it a new lease on life during early 1980s.

The second – let's call it a Revisionist Narrative emerged in the late 1980s to early 1990s with Michael Gorbachev's Glasnost and New Thinking. Began as a small and daring innovation, it soon became a new mainstream replacing the previous version. The mechanism of this replacement amounted to importing the orthodox Western Cold War narrative which in late Soviet times had penetrated a small circle of dissident intellectuals and liberal think tanks (Institute of USA and Canada, Institute of World Economy and International Relations). Then under conditions of glasnost it spilled over through mass media to a broad public hungry for alternative explanations.

Given its origins, it is not surprising that the revisionist narrative was almost diametrically opposite to the orthodox one. If back in the past the Soviets could do no wrong, now they could do nothing right. If then it was the West that started the Cold War, now all the war guilt laid on our side while the West wisely and moderately responded to the awesome Soviet threat. The United States with its vast preponderance of power, according to this view, "did not need a new global confrontation"[4] while the Stalinist system could not live without foreign enemies and expansion. The revisionist narrative emphasized Communist ideology and the nature of the Stalinist system as the main driving force behind the Soviet Cold War. With the first openings of Russian archives the biggest skeletons of Soviet foreign policy were soon out of the closet: Komintern secrets, Molotov-Ribbentrop pact, Sovietization of Baltics and Eastern Europe, Katyn, 1956 in Hungary and 1968 in Czechoslovakia, invasion of Afghanistan. Following the first – mostly journalistic phase of iconoclast accounts – there came an academic revisionism, when professional historians began to rethink the Soviet foreign policy experience, concentrating on blank spots and previously forbidden topics.[5]

The fitting ideological and political context for this new narrative was a massive rejection of the Soviet past and popular infatuation with all the things Western – way of life, ideas, institutions, etc. For many Russians, in particular its better educated intelligentsia their country was now a prodigal son on its way to finally rejoin Western civilization. The early 1990s marked the peak of Russian interest in and warm feelings towards the United States. America began to be

4 *Sovetskoye obshestvo: vozniknovenie, razvitie, istorichesky final.* Otv.red. Yuri Afanasyev, Vladimir Lel'chuk. Moscow, 1999, Tom 1, S.369.

5 Ilya Gaiduk, Maksim Korobochkin, Mikhail Narinsky (red.), *Kholodnaya Voina: Novye Podkhody, Novye Dokumenty*. Moscow, 1995; Leonid Nezhinsky (otv.red.). *Sovetskaya Vneshnaya Politika v Gody Kholodnoi Voiny (1945–1985). Novoye Prochtenie.* Moscow, 1995.

seen as a benign senior partner and a model for imitation. The American – a free individual endowed with civil rights and liberties – was now an antipode to the oppressed and servile Soviet "sovok" that had to be rooted out.[6] Romancing the West and repenting the Soviet sins was the motto of the day which deeply affected the Cold War image and legacy. But that context could not and did not last long.

The torturous way of Russian post-Communist development soon destroyed the two big illusions behind this euphoria – the first of a quick and easy transition to markets and democracy, and the second about a generous Western assistance in that process. Markets became synonymous with the downfall of production, skyrocketing prices and monopolization. Privatization meant the enrichment of the few and impoverishment of the many, democracy brought about corruption and manipulation, while freedom turned into lawlessness and chaos. Even though American values as such had little to do with this degradation, they were widely discredited. And the expected Western assistance boiled down to only loans, credits and a lot of bad advice on how to build democracy and a market economy. One of the first casualties of this frustrating transition became the Russian intelligentsia which had traditionally been a main base of liberal ideas and now felt abandoned and even betrayed by the West.

In foreign affairs, too, the early hopes for a quick integration into the Western community and for a warm embrace from the benevolent West (that should have been eternally grateful for the self-destruction of Communism and the end of the Cold War) failed to materialize. NATO expansion to the East and the advance of its infrastructure all the way to the Russian borders, a militarized regime change policy in the former Yugoslavia and then Iraq, active resistance to Russia-led integration of the post-Soviet space and cultivation of "colored revolutions" and anti-Russian forces there, – all these developments have caused a growing Russian concern. They have demonstrated that for the U.S. and its allies Russia's legitimate security interests were less important than expanding their own influence and locking in the Cold War geopolitical gains. For the Russians it has become clear that the end of the Cold War and of the great ideological divide hasn't done away with interstate rivalry and with old Western syndromes – an apprehension of a strong Russia and its image as a country alien and even hostile to Western culture and values. Growing vilification of Russia as a hopeless lost cause by Western mass media, experts and politicians disappointed with Russia's transition only reinforced this impression. For many in my country the Cold War is back, but this time it is being waged by the West against post-Soviet, post-Com-

6 Erik Chiraev, Vladislav Zubok. *Anti-Americanism in Russia: from Stalin to Putin.* N.Y., 2000, 42–43.

munist Russia.[7] This perception that first emerged in the late 1990s was reinforced by the crises over Georgia (2008) and Ukraine (2014–2015).

Another painful reality that affected Russian mentality is the unprecedented asymmetry of power between Russia and the West that has emerged since the end of the Cold War. The country that had been used to full sovereignty, self-sufficiency and great power status in a matter of several years turned into an ordinary, dependent and vulnerable state unable to seriously influence developments even in the neighboring countries. The amazing speed and unexpectedness of this downfall that had no visible causation (like a military defeat or a natural catastrophe) led certain people to look for some sinister "hidden hand" behind it and the former Cold War rival seemed the best candidate for that role. But even for those who did not subscribe to conspiracy theories this new combination of weakness, dependence and vulnerability created feelings of jealousy and offense toward the only remaining superpower – that is how the former long distance runner who had a fall and quitted the race is watching the leader that is still on the track.

As it often happens in such cases, the loosing side subconsciously strives for a psychological compensation and finds it in the old Russian complex of spiritual superiority over the West. Its main thesis is: "we may be not as rich and powerful as you, but we are surely pure and more spiritual." This contrast is being played upon by popular Russian comedians (Mikhail Zadornov in particular), Russian cinema ("Brother 2" and "Barber of Siberia") and current literary production.

Yet it would be unfair to reduce it to pure psychology. The failure of a Big Leap toward Russia's westernization revealed a huge inertia of Russian traditionalism in all of its aspects – political, economic and cultural. Despite vast changes of the recent years the main constants of Russian civilization in mass beliefs and patterns of behavior have remained intact and proved to be much more resistant to change than a political façade.[8] The growing realization of being different from others, of the fact that given Russia's unique geography, climate and history it can never become another America[9] created a wide audience for proponents of national exceptionalism. The resurgence of "the Russian Idea" becomes even more relevant given new challenges to Russian cultural heritage created by the expansion of mass American culture in the context of globalization.

7 Sergey Kortunov, "Kholodnaya Voina: Paradoksy Odnoi Stategii," *Mezhdunarodnaya Zhizn,* '1998, № 8; Yuri Golik, Vladimir Karasev, "Pochemy dazhe Democraticheskaya Rossia ne Ustraivaet "Svobodnyi Zapad?," *Polis,* 1999, N 3.

8 Eduard Batalov, *Russkaya Ideya I Amerikanskaya Mechta,* Moscow, 2009, S.319.

9 Andrey Parshev, *Pochemy Rossia ne Amerika,* Moscow, 1999, S.106.

These changes have deeply affected the whole political-psychological atmosphere in the country including analytical discourse. The search for a new Russian identity and national interests came into the forefront. Both were increasingly identified with the preservation of Russia as a great power possessing its own mode of development. It became fashionable to analyze international relations in terms of geopolitics and culture, but not ideology. The uncompromising rejection of ideology and practice of Soviet communism receded into the background.

Thus the ground was laid for a third Cold War narrative which may be called Post-Revisionism. It retained some features of its immediate predecessor – if only because certain facts are now impossible to deny (even though some weird characters still question the authenticity of Molotov-Ribbentrop pact or Soviet responsibility for the Katyn massacre). Yet this third narrative is different both in tone and substance from its predecessor. Gone is the former exposure and condemnation pathos. No less importantly, the post-revisionist narrative has a different focus. The sobering effect of the post-Cold War world played its role forcing people to rethink the origins and nature of Cold War itself. If the latter was solely about fighting Communism then, why are there still difficulties in the relations between Russia and the West now when there is not even a specter of communism left in Russia (when Russia indeed has become one of the most anti-Communist countries on Earth)? What are the long-term sources of Western (especially – American) conduct that make their relationship with Russia so difficult?[10] To what extent did Soviet foreign policy reflect legitimate national interests as opposed to those of the ruling nomenclature? What are changes and continuities between Tsarist, Soviet and post-Soviet Russia's foreign and defense policies? These questions have become central to the post-revisionist perspective.

In contrast to revisionists who emphasized ideological underpinnings of the Cold War from the Soviet side, post-revisionists downplay ideology and stress Realpolitik and socio-cultural factors for both sides of that great divide. One of the reasons for that shift is a new realization brought about by the post-Cold War Russian frustration with the West that was mentioned before. If the end of Communism has not led to harmony between Russia and the West then there must be other, enduring non-ideological reasons for this tension which had preceded and contributed to, but outlived the Cold War. Among those, Realpolitik and socio-cultural factors are being rediscovered as the most important ones.

According to the post-revisionist narrative, the central theme of Russia's foreign and defense policies over centuries has been the constant search for secu-

---

10 Alexey Bogaturov. "Istochniki Amerikanskogo Povedenya," *Rossia v Global'noi Politike*, 2004, № 6.

rity: defending its vast porous borders, securing a free access to blue seas, preventing an emergence of hostile coalitions with superior military capabilities. The main strategic goal was to provide a depth of defense along the whole perimeter of the Russian state. The Soviet period, in this view, was not radically different from the previous and successive ones, though it had some peculiarities. The Cold War then was basically a clash of the two security agendas – those of the Soviet Union and Anglo-Americans which competed for influence over strategically important areas of Central and Eastern Europe, the Far East, Northern Asia, and the Near and Middle East where WWII had created huge vacuums of power. That is how the whole trajectory of old Russian-Soviet-new Russian policy is described in recent authoritative accounts.[11] Reason d'etat has also been a favorite leitmotif of numerous memoirs of Soviet diplomats, intelligence officers and military commanders who profess to have been defending not the now discredited Communist ideology, but Russia's state interests.[12]

The social-cultural dimension is also very important in the post-revisionist narrative. In cultural-civilization terms Russia has always been a lonely country torn between East and West and never truly belonging to either. Ever since the 13th century its relationship with the West has been particularly difficult. For Russia a more prosperous, modern, and technologically advanced West was a cultural and security challenge, a source of many invasions through indefensible western frontiers. For the West the heart of "the Russian problem" – especially beginning in the 19th century – was a combination of huge natural and manpower resources with an alien authoritarian regime capable of using those resources freely against western interests.[13] Post-revisionists are now rediscovering this old divide regarding the Cold War as another chapter in a long struggle of civilizations between Orthodox authoritarian collectivist Russia and liberal individualistic Catholic/Protestant West. Nickolay Danilevsky's "Russia and Europe" which was the first elaborate exposition of this theme back in the 1870s is now again in fashion. The classical Russian debate of the 19th century between Slavophiles and Westerners has reemerged in a new incarnation which is often more extreme and intolerant

11 *Ocherki Istorii Ministerstva Inostrannykh Del Rossii.* Igor Ivanov (otv.red.). Tom 1–3. Moscow, 2002.

12 Anatoly Dobrynin. *Sugubo Doveritel'no: Posol v Vashingtone pri Shesti Prezidentakh SSHA*. Moscow, 1997; Georgy Kornienko. *Kholodnaya Voina: Svidetel'stvo Yeiyo Uchastnika*. Moscow, 1994; Sergey Akhromeyev, Georgy Kornienko. *Glazamy Marshalla i Diplomata: Kritichesky Vzglyad na Vneshnyu Politiky SSSR do i posle 1985 Goda*. Moscow, 1992; Nickolai Leonov. *Likholetye*. Moscow, 1995; Vadim Kirpichenko. *Razvedka: Litsa I Lichnosty*. Moscow, 1998.

13 This view was shared even by the founders of Marxism themselves (see Friedrich Engels's "Foreign Policy of Russian Tzars").

than its historic predecessor, especially on the new Slavophiles' side – people like Eduard Limonov or Alexander Prokhanov who regard the new Westerners as "enemies of the Russian people."

In a brilliant comparative analysis of "the American dream" and "the Russian idea" philosopher Eduard Batalov describes the huge value gap between these two credos emphasizing the enduring elements of the Russian idea – statism, collectivism, Eastern orthodoxy, messianism. "The Cold War," he concludes, "has also been a struggle of two national missions."[14] Veteran historian Viktor Mal'kov in his recent encyclopedic overview of Russian-American relations in the 20th century stresses continuity of geopolitical and cultural contradictions that bedeviled this relationship for decades.[15]

Post-revisionists also operate from a much broader documentary base than their predecessors. Over the last fifteen years numerous volumes of Soviet foreign policy documents have been published covering many aspects of Cold War history and many new documents have become available in our archives.[16] There has also been a virtual explosion of memoirs by former statesmen, high ranking diplomats, military and intelligence officials which has provided a human/eye-witness dimension to Cold War history.[17] One cumulative effect of this new evi-

---

14 Eduard Batalov. *Op.cit.*, S. 352.

15 Victor Mal'kov. *Rossia i SSHA v Dvadtsatom Veke: Ocherki Istorii Mezhgosudarstvennukh Otnoshenii i Diplomatii v Sotsiokul'turnom Kontexte.* Moscow, 2009.

16 *Sovetsko-Amerikanskie Otnoshenia. 1945–1948.* Otv.red. Grigory Sevost'yanov. Moscow, 2004; *Sovetsko-Amerikanskie Otnoshenia. Gody Razryadki. 1969–1976. Sbornik Documentov. Tom 1: May 1969–1972.* Moscow, 2007; *Vostochnaya Evropa v Documentakh Rossiskikh Arkhivov. 1944–1953. Tom 1–2.* Moscow-Novosibirsk, 1997–1998; *SSSR i Germansky Vopros. Dokumenty iz Arkhiva Vneshnei Politiki Rossiiskoi Federatsii.* Sostaviteli G.Kynin i I.Laufer. Tom 1–4. Moscow, 1996–2012; *Rusko-Kitaiskie Otnoshenia v XX veke. Dokumenty I Materialy. Tom IV. Sovetsko-Kitaiskie otnoshenia 1937–1945*, Kniga 2. 1945 (Otv.red. Sergey Tikhvinsky). Moscow, 2000; *Soveshania Kominforma. 1947, 1948, 1949. Documenty i Materialy.* Moscow, 1998; *Rossia i Afrika: Documenty I Materialy XVIII Century – 1960. Tom 2: 1918–1960.* Red. Appolon Davidson i Sergey Mazov. Moscow, 1999; *Blizhnevostochny Konflict, 1947–1956. Iz Dokumentov Arkhiva Vneshnei Politiki Rossiiskoi Federatsii. Tom 1–2.* Moscow, 2003; *Venskii Val's Kholodnoi voiny (Vstrecha N. Khrusheva i Dzh. Kennedi v Venne, 1961). Dokumenty.* Red. S. Karner, N. Tomilina, A. Chubaryan, B. Shteltsel-Marx, Moscow, 2011; *Rossia XX vek. "Prazhskaya Vesna" I Mezhdunarodnyi Krisis 1968 goda: Dokumenty.* Red. N. Tomilina, S. Karner, A. Chubaryan. Moscow, 2010.

17 Oleg Troyanovsky. *Cherez Gody I Rastoynia.* Moscow, 1997; A. Alexandrov-Agentov. *Ot Kollontai do Gorbacheva.* Moscow, 1994; Valentin Falin. *Bez Skidok na Obstoyatel'stva: Politicheskie Vospominania.* Moscow, 1999; Yuli Kvitsinsky. *Vremya i Sluchai: Zametki Professionala.* Moscow, 1999; Oleg Grinevsky. *Tysyacha odin Den' Nikity Sergeevicha.* Moscow, 1998; V.Musatov. *Predvestniki Buri: Politicheskie Krizisy v Vostochnoi Evrope (1956–1981).* Moscow, 1996(Научная книга); Viktor Israelyan. *Inside the Kremlin during the Yom Kippur War* (Penn State Press, 1996); Karen

dence has been to provide a much more complex and nuanced picture of the past in contrast to black and white images of revisionists. As is always the case with history, the closer you get to look at it, the more complicated it becomes; you begin to understand the ways of thinking and dilemmas of policy makers which in turn enhances your empathy (if not necessarily sympathy) toward them.

Another distinctive feature of the post-revisionist narrative is its reliance on comparative analysis of Soviet and American/Western policies in the Cold War.[18] Revisionists almost exclusively concentrated on the Soviet side using selected Soviet documents to make their case. As John Gaddis said, they were clapping with one hand. Now the trend is toward a broader view when Soviet policy is put into the framework of Cold War interaction. This naturally leads to a more comprehensive and balanced picture of the past. There is also a growing emphasis on studying U.S. and U.K. policy in Europe and the Middle East during the Cold War – a subject that had been neglected in contemporary Russian historiography.[19]

The post-revisionist narrative has not done away with other Cold War images and memories. It coexists with its predecessors and there are still lively debates going on between these different perspectives both among professional historians and the public at large.[20] Despite the current deterioration of Russia's relations

---

Brutents. *Tridtsat' Let na Staroi Ploshadi*. Moscow, 1998. Idem. *Nesbyvsheesya. Neravnodushnye Zametki o Perestroike*. Moscow, 2005; Vladimir Krychkov. *Lichnoe Delo*. Moscow, 1996; Pavel Sudoplatov. *Razvedka I Kreml': Zapiski Nezhelatel'nogo Svidetelya*. Moscow, 1996; Alexander G. Savel'yev and Nikolay N. Detinov. *The Big Five. Arms Control Decision-Making in the Soviet Union*, translated by Dmitriy Trenin and edited by Gregory Varhall (Westport, CT: Praeger, 1995); B. Chertok. *Rakety I Luidi: Goryachie Dni Kholodnoi Voiny*. Moscow, 1999; Vyacheslav Kevorkov. *Tainyi Kanal*. Moscow, 1997; Leonid Shebarshin. *Iz Zhizni Nachal'nika Razvedki*. Moscow, 1994; Idem. *Ruka Moskvy: Zapiski Nachal'nika Sovetskoi Razvedki*. Moscow, 1992; A.Feklisov. *Za Okeanom I na Ostrove: Zapiski Razvedchika*. Moscow, 1994.

18 One typical example is the author's «*Stalin, Ruzvel't, Truman: SSSR i SSHA v 1940-kh gg. Documental'nye Ocherki*. Moscow, 2006. Another comparative study of U.S. and Soviet policies in the early Cold War is "*Vstrechnymi Kursami: Politika SSSR i SShA na Balkanakh, Blizhnem i Srednem Vostoke, 1939–1947 gg*. Red. V.Yungbluid, A.Kostin. Kirov, 2014. See also Ilya Gaiduk's last book (*"V Labirintakh Kholodnoi Voiny: SSSR I SShA v OON. 1945–1965."* Moscow, 2012) – a pioneering study based on primary sources from both sides.

19 Lekarenko O., Volkov M., *Amerikanskaya Krepost' Evropa: Politika SShA po ukrepleneyu oboronnogo potentsiala stran Zapadnoi Evropy (1947–1955)*. Tomsk, 2009; Lekarenko O., *SShA i Protsess obyedinenia Stran Zapadnoi Evropy v 1955–1963 godakh*. Tomsk, 2012; Rumyantsev V., *Blizhnevostochnaya Politika SShA I Velikobritanii v 1956–1960 gg*. Tomsk, 2010.

20 A useful brief overview of academic debates is by Natalya Egorova in: Introduction *Kholodnaya Voina, 1945–1963: Istoricheskaya Perspektiva. Red. Natalya Egorova, Alexander Chubaryan*. Moscow, 2003, S. 9–10 (ОЛМА-ПРЕСС). For a more detailed review of these debates as they relate to different stages of the Cold War history see: Vladislav Zubok, Vladimir Pechatnov. "Otechest-

with the West, Russian historians continue to explore the Cold War in a scholarly way finding new avenues for research. Compared to the state of the field a dozen of years ago[21] there have been some positive developments in both research opportunities and new publications. The latter include new openings of archival material at the Russian State Archive of Social and Political History (RGASPI) where the Stalin papers, "Stalin's fund," has been digitized and made available to researchers, and at the Russian State Archive of Contemporary History (RGANI) which has recently opened many personal records of Soviet Party leaders from Nikita Khrushchev to Constantin Chernenko. Among the new research directions pursued by Russian historians are Soviet policy on European integration from the 1940s to the 1960s,[22] multilateral diplomacy during the Cold War,[23] the role of NGO's and public diplomacy,[24] Soviet policy in West Africa during the late 1950s and early 1960s,[25] and defense policies of Balkan members of the Warsaw pact.[26] There are also interesting new attempts to re-examine the entire Cold War period as a process of mutual learning, adjustment and cooperation between the United States and the Soviet Union.[27] The veteran authority on the Soviet Cold War policy in Germany, Alexei Filitov, produced an in-depth study of Germany in Soviet foreign policy planning from 1941 to 1990.[28] The leading Russian expert on Cold

---

vennaya Istoriographia Kholodnoi Voiny: Nekotorye Itogy Pervogo Desyatiletya," *Otechestvennaya Istoria*, 2003, N 4–5. The most recent round table discussion of the state of Cold War studies is in *Amerikanskii Ezhegodnik (The American Yearbook) 2014*. Moscow: Nauka Publishing House, 2014.

21 Vladislav Zubok, Vladimir Pechatnov, Op.cit.

22 Lipkin M., *Sovetskii Soyuz i Evropeiskaya Integratsia: seredina 1940-kh – seredina 1960-kh godov*. Moscow, 2011.

23 *Mnogostoronnaya Diplomatia v Bipolyarnoi Sisteme Mezhdunarodnykh Otnoshenii. Red. Natalya Egorova*. Moscow, 2012.

24 Natalya Egorova, Dvizhenie Storonnikov Mira s serediny 1950-kh do nachala 1960-kh gg: Ot Krizisa k Poisku Novykh Form in: *Mnogostoronnaya Diplomatia v Bipolyarnoi Sisteme Mezhdunarodnykh Otnoshenii; Idem. Vliyanie* Dvizhenia Storonnikov Mira na Politiku Yadernogo Razoruzhenia, 1950-e – 1960-e gody, *Novaia I Noveishaya Istoria*, 2015, N 6.

25 Sergey Mazov, *Sovetskaya Politika v Zapadnoi Afrike, 1956–1964. Neizvestnye Stranitsy Istorii Kholodnoi Voiny.* For the English version of this book see: *A Distant Front in the Cold War. The USSR in West Africa and Congo, 1956–1964*. Woodrow Wilson Center Press. Stanford University Press. 2010; Idem, *Kholodnaia Voina v Serdtse Afriki: SSSR I Kongolezskii Krisis, 1960–1964*. Moscow, 2015.

26 Artem Ulunyan, *Balkanskii Sheet Sotsializma. Oboronnaya Politika Albanii, Bolgarii, Rumynii i Yugoslavii (from mid-1950-s to 1980)*. Moscow, 2013.

27 Viktor Kremenyuk, *Uroki Kholodnoi Voiny*. Moscow, 2015.

28 Alexei Filitov, *Germania v Sovetskom Vneshnepoliticheskom Planirovanii, 1941–1990*. Moscow, 2009.

War historiography has recently published the first Russian textbook on Cold War history.[29] The writings of Russian historians are increasingly finding their way into authoritative Western journals and publications on the subject.

The search for truth about the Cold War goes on, but it will always be affected by the ever changing living experience of the Russian nation.

29 Natalya Egorova, *Istoria Kholodnoi Voiny, 1945–1991*. Vladimir, 2011.

Christopher R. Moran

Company Confessions: The CIA, Whistleblowers and Cold War Revisionism

In the 1970s, the Central Intelligence Agency (CIA) endured a "decade of horrors."[1] During this period, startling revelations emerged linking the Agency with a string of illegal activities, provoking public moral outrage and a level of scrutiny totally alien to an organization accustomed to limited accountability and operating in secrecy. In 1972, the CIA was required to fight off press allegations that it had been behind the Watergate break-in, as details surfaced showing that two of the so-called "plumbers," James McCord and E. Howard Hunt, had CIA connections.[2] On December 22, 1974, *The New York Times* carried a front-page story by Seymour Hersh revealing that the CIA had directly violated its charter as a centralized machine for the analysis of intelligence by engaging in domestic spying operations on American citizens. Several congressional investigations, the most famous of which was headed by Senator Frank Church of Idaho, confirmed the public's worst fears. Evidence showed that the CIA had, among other offences, sought to infiltrate and disrupt anti-Vietnam War groups, Black Panthers, and other domestic organizations while wreaking havoc with covert operations around the world.[3]

Intelligence scholars and Cold War historians have written at length about the trauma suffered by the CIA in the 1970s.[4] Considerable attention has been

---

1 David Canon, "Intelligence and Ethics: The CIA's Covert Operations," *The Journal of Libertarian Studies* 4, 2 (Spring 1980): 190.

2 Richard Helms to Dean A. Woodruff, August 16, 1972, Richard Helms Papers, 8/30/488, Lauinger Library, Georgetown University, Washington DC.

3 Richard Nixon to Richard Helms, October 24, 1983, Richard Helms Papers, 2/83/204, Lauinger Library, Georgetown University, Washington DC.

4 See Loch Johnson, *A Season of Inquiry: The Senate Intelligence Investigation* (Lexington, KY: University Press of Kentucky, 1985); John Ranelagh, *The Agency: The Rise and Decline of the CIA* (New York: Simon & Shuster, 1987); Gerald Haines, "The Pike Committee Investigations and the CIA," *Studies in Intelligence* Winter, (1988–89): 81–92; Loch Johnson, *America's Secret Power: The CIA in a Democratic Society* (New York: Oxford University Press, 1989); Rhodri Jeffreys-Jones, *The CIA and American Democracy* (New Haven, CT: Yale University Press, 1989); Katherine Olmstead, *Challenging the Secret Government: The Post-Watergate Investigations of the CIA and FBI* (Chapel Hill: University of North Carolina Press, 1996); John Prados, *The Lost Crusader: The Secret Wars of CIA Director William Colby* (New York: Oxford University Press, 2003); M.E. Bowman, "The Legacy of the Church Committee," *Intelligencer* 14,1 (2004): 27–34.

DOI 10.1515/9783110496178-005

given to the impact of reporters such as Hersh, and congressmen such as Church, on Agency efficiency and morale.[5] Memoirs by CIA veterans give a sense of the shock and pain inside Langley. Stansfield Turner, who had been appointed CIA Director in March 1977 to pick up the pieces, claimed in *Secrecy and Democracy* (1985) that the newly introduced congressional oversight had made staff "nervous."[6] In *The Night Watch*, David Atlee Phillips, a former Division Chief, claimed that he was a "happy man" before the sensational headlines broke.[7] The ensuing tumult, he confessed, "changed my life."[8] Indeed, Phillips took early retirement in 1975 so that he could respond in public to the charges being levelled against the Agency; he called this his "Last Assignment."[9]

While the CIA was undoubtedly wounded by revelations that surfaced in the press and in congressional hearings and reports, the most traumatic and confidence-shattering development was the emergence of whistleblowers and renegade writers. In the 1970s, the CIA was forced to deal with a largely new phenomenon: an increasing number of employees leaving the Agency and writing negative books. Earlier memoirs had been few in a number and were uncritical.[10] In 1963, fabled CIA Director Allen Dulles wrote *The Craft of Intelligence*, a part record, part instructional book on the value of intelligence for effective policy. Published within two years of the Bay of Pigs, the botched attempt by a CIA-trained force of exiles to invade Southern Cuba, the book had in fact been "ghost-written" by a team of CIA analysts for the purpose of restoring public faith in US intelligence.[11] Quite deliberately, it said nothing about the controversial subject of covert action; instead, it focused on the less sensitive issue of intelligence analysis, and elaborated on the difficulties of combating communist subversion. In the 1970s, everything changed. Suddenly, memoir production exploded. Devastatingly for the

---

5 See Cynthia M. Nolan, "Seymour Hersh's Impact on the CIA," *International Journal of Intelligence and Counterintelligence* 12,1 (1999): 18–34.

6 Stansfield Turner, *Secrecy and Democracy: The CIA in Transition* (New York: Harper & Row, 1985), 6.

7 David Atlee Phillips, *The Night Watch: 25 Years Inside the CIA* (London: Robert Hale, 1977), vii.

8 Ibid.

9 Christopher R. Moran, "The Last Assignment: David Atlee Phillips and the Birth of CIA Public Relations," *International History Review*, 35:2 (April 2013), 337–355.

10 A bibliography published by the Congressional Research Service in 1986 showed that, between 1949 and 1974, only 6 CIA memoirs were published. Wesley K. Wark, "Struggle in the Spy House: Memoirs of US Intelligence," in *Political Memoir: Essays on the Politics of Memory*, ed. George Egerton (London: Frank Cass, 1994), 312.

11 Christopher R. Moran, *Classified: Secrecy and the State in Modern Britain* (Cambridge: Cambridge University Press, 2012), 315.

CIA, many of these works were wholly given over to polemic, exposing blunders and abuses on an almost industrial scale.

These disclosures were particularly hurtful to the CIA because they came from "insiders," like Victor Marchetti, Phillip Agee and Frank Snepp, who had pledged themselves to a lifetime of reticence. CIA employees had signed a "Secrecy Agreement," a vow of perpetual silence, having been told countless times of the importance of keeping the secrets to which they had become privy. As a reporter for the *Washington Post* claimed in June 1972, by joining the CIA, a person "enters a Trappist monastery for the remainder of his natural life," speaking only when necessary.[12] The anguish caused by whistleblowers is well-captured in a speech by retired CIA Director John McCone, delivered to the annual convention of the Association of Former Intelligence Officers (AFIO) in San Diego in October 1978: "Probably the most serious [change] is the creation of a climate that has given licence to the Victor Marchetti's and the Phillip Agee's to set aside their vows to their country, and to preserve secrecy, to unveil – in books written for modest profit – information more damaging than that of most serious defectors."[13] In his peroration McCone declared: "No violation of trust, no defection to the other side, no damage from the acts of the [Kim] Philbys, the [Donald] Macleans or the Klaus Fuchses has been more damaging to our national interest and our security than the work of these men who prostitute their principles and make disclosures which places their close associates of many years in mortal danger."[14]

This chapter examines the story of three memoir writers, and considers the CIA's response in each case. The memoirists in question – Marchetti, Agee and Snepp – caused the CIA the most distress. Their publications disclosed the most sensitive material, generated the most public interest, and provoked the biggest reaction from the Agency. Two main arguments will be put forward. First, attempts by the CIA to control these apostate authors were too heavy-handed and backfired. Legal battles were fought, at high cost, and in full public view, bringing further opprobrium upon the Agency. Significantly, efforts by the CIA to enforce censorship opened up a serious constitutional question about freedom of speech. The First Amendment to the US Constitution protects the right of every American to speak his or her mind, irrespective of what that message might be. In trying to gag former agents who had quit and were now "telling it all," the CIA was seen by

12 Alan Barth, "Free Speech, Security and the CIA," *Washington Post*, June 16, 1972.
13 'John McCone: Speech to the Association of Former Intelligence Officers, San Diego, Hotel del Coronado, 2 October 1978,' The John McCone papers, BANC/MSS 95/20, Container 27:63, Bancroft Library, The University of California, Berkeley.
14 Ibid.

many to be pursuing a course of action totally foreign to the character of American law. In short, it was asking people to renounce a major part of their birthright.

Second, such critical memoirs added momentum to the burgeoning "revisionist" school of Cold War historiography. In the 1950s and much of the 1960s, the dominant view of the Cold War was that it had been caused by Soviet expansion in Eastern Europe and in other parts of the world. In his landmark 1959 work, *The Tragedy of American Diplomacy*, William Appleman Williams attributed the blame instead to US foreign policy which he characterized as being inherently imperialistic and a response to the unquenchable requirements of US capitalism.[15] Williams argued that the aim of the US was to secure an "open door" for American businesses abroad, an objective which led to empire-building and intervention in the domestic affairs of foreign states. In the context of US involvement in the ugly war in Vietnam, this thesis became quite popular; a host of works were published criticizing the expansionist tendencies of US power and capital.[16] Memoirs by disaffected CIA officers contributed to this new wave of historiography by describing a shocking range of unsavory clandestine political and paramilitary operations abroad. The rise and impact of historical revisionism was therefore substantially advanced by the "counter-tradition" of CIA memoir literature.

Marchetti

Victor Marchetti had enjoyed a successful 14-year career with the CIA. From a working-class ethnic background and starting at the bottom as a trainee, in 1966 he rose to be executive assistant to the deputy director, Admiral Rufus Taylor. In this capacity, he mingled with the CIA's senior bureaucrats, who resided on the seventh floor of its Langley headquarters. Indeed, he was one of the privileged few who had morning coffee with Director Richard Helms. For three years, he was privy to many of the CIA's most carefully guarded secrets, including information that was distributed to officials on a strictly need-to-know basis. However, the longer he served the CIA, the more disenchanted he became. He resigned in Sep-

---

15 William Appleman Williams, *The Tragedy of American Diplomacy* (1959; 50th anniversary edition, W.W. Norton, 2009).

16 Seminal 'revisionist' works include Walter LaFeber, *America, Russia and the Cold War* (New York: John Wiley & Sons, 1967); Gabriel Kolko and Joyce Kolko, *The Limits of Power: The World and United States Foreign Policy 1945–1954* (New York: Harper & Row, 1972); Thomas G. Paterson, *Soviet-American Confrontation: Postwar Reconstruction and the Origins of the Cold War* (Baltimore: The Johns Hopkins University Press, 1973).

tember 1969 disillusioned with the quagmire of Vietnam, the amorality of covert action in the Third World, and the bigoted "old boy network" that pervaded the CIA. "I was the lone ethnic," he later told news reporters, referred to by colleagues as the "Token Wop."[17]

Shortly after leaving the Agency, Marchetti wrote a spy novel, *The Rope Dancer*. Before its publication, a CIA officer vetted the text at Marchetti's home in Virginia, in keeping with the rules of the secrecy agreement. Since there was no objection on security grounds, publication went ahead in 1971.[18] Behind the scenes, however, CIA officials were vexed. Although the book had been marketed as pure fiction, the plot was unmistakably based on Marchetti's career, and the main protagonists were unflattering *roman à clefs* of real CIA officers, including Helms and James Jesus Angleton, the CIA's legendary chief of counterintelligence. Concerned that Marchetti was preparing to leak classified information, potentially to a foreign intelligence agency, Helms ordered that he be placed under surveillance. This operation, known as Project Butane, commenced on March 23, 1972 and lasted for about a month.[19] But Butane came up blank; no evidence was found linking Marchetti with enemy services, although secret photographs showed him meeting with Ben Welles from *The New York Times*.[20] With this, the CIA turned the surveillance operation over to the FBI. The Bureau agreed, but warned that, "Under such circumstances he could be the target of a recruitment attempt by the opposition, and it is not entirely inconceivable that he might choose to defect."[21]

Marchetti had no intention of defecting, but did plan to write a book and had circulated a proposal to various New York publishing houses, including Alfred A. Knopf. A copy was obtained by a CIA informant. For Helms and CIA's senior management, the proposal was "right out of a bad dream," since it planned to reveal how the Agency had violated its authority not only overseas, but domestically.[22] Previous experience with whistleblowers was limited, and had involved the CIA negotiating quietly with authors, with no thought being given to legal action. In

---

17 'The Whistle Blowers,' *Nation*, November 6, 1972.

18 Angus Mackenzie, *Secrets: The CIA's War at Home* (Berkeley: University of California Press, 1997), 43.

19 'CIA's "Family Jewels" Report,' May 16, 1973, 27. Declassified in June 2007 and available as a PDF file on the National Security Archive website: http://www.gwu.edu/~nsarchiv/NSAEBB/NSAEBB222/family_jewels_full_ocr.pdf

20 'CIA Spied on Spook Author,' April 9, 1979, http://jfk.hood.edu/Collection/Weisberg%20Subject%20Index%20Files/M%20Disk/Marchetti%20Victor%20CIA/Item%2027.pdf

21 Ibid.

22 Mackenzie, *Secrets*, 42.

July 1970, when confronted with *The Game of Nations* by former agent Miles Copeland Jr., Helms lamented that "in a democratic system one has a tough time with this kind of individual."[23] In the case of Marchetti, however, the CIA decided to test the legal waters. In late March 1972, it asked District Judge Albert V. Bryan for a court order requiring Marchetti to submit all his writings, even fiction, to the CIA for prepublication censorship, because prior restraint on publication was essential for the removal of "classified" material. The request hinged on the idea that Marchetti had signed a secrecy contract, which had the same legal weight as a commercial contract that prevented employees from disclosing trade secrets.[24] In a landmark move, Bryan sanctioned the request and issued a temporary injunction on April 18, 1972.

The significance of the order was not lost on the media and on civil liberties groups. This was the first time in US history that an injunction had been issued to enforce peacetime censorship before an author had written a single word. Marchetti was being punished for information that existed only in his mind. This action raised the question whether a US citizen should be required to surrender his or her freedom of conscience, of thought, in the manner prescribed by the CIA. In a leading article entitled "Free Speech, Security and the CIA," *Washington Post* reporter Alan Birth was indignant: "It is trying to impose a kind of preventive detention in the realm of ideas."[25] The weekly journal *The Nation* proposed that the case dramatized the "fact that the CIA is essentially an alien institution – alien to American custom, alien to the Constitution – and incompatible with both the form and the spirit of democracy."[26] The American Civil Liberties Union (ACLU) agreed to provide free counsel for Marchetti. The battle lines were drawn. The ACLU, led by Melvin L. Wulf, demanded that the injunction be lifted; the CIA, represented by attorneys from the Department of Justice, called for making the injunction permanent. The trial, which began on May 15, 1972, lasted less than eight hours. In a ruling of "immeasurable significance," Judge Bryan ruled in favor of the CIA, claiming that the secrecy contract signed by Marchetti constituted a relinquishment of his First Amendment rights.[27] Marchetti appealed to the Supreme Court, arguing that no contract should trump a constitutional right, but was defeated by a vote of 6 to 3.

---

23 Richard Helms to George Carroll, July 1970, Richard Helms Papers, 8/5/413, Lauinger Library, Georgetown University, Washington DC.

24 Mackenzie, *Secrets*, 44.

25 Alan Barth, "Free Speech, Security and the CIA," *Washington Post*, June 16, 1972.

26 "The Whistle Blowers," *Nation*, November 6, 1972.

27 Mackenzie, *Secrets*, 48.

This was not to be the last of the legal battle. Teaming up with John D. Marks, a former State Department employee, Marchetti produced a 400-page manuscript entitled *The CIA and the Cult of Intelligence.* As required, in August 1973, he submitted the text for censorship. After thirty days, the CIA, taking a very broad interpretation of what was meant by "classified," ordered Marchetti to remove 339 passages, roughly 20% of the book, ranging from single words to entire pages.[28] Marchetti and his publisher, Knopf, objected and immediately filed a suit. Once again, the parties found themselves in the courtroom of Judge Bryan. By March 1974, with public interest in the case at fever-pitch, CIA attorneys had agreed to reduce the number of deletions to 168. However, this concession only served to heighten the suspicion that the CIA's classification policy was *ad hoc* and capricious, with no consistently applied standards. Therefore Bryan announced that Marchetti's First Amendment rights had to be protected against the "whim of the reviewing official."[29] On March 20, Bryan decreed that of the 168 items, only 27 were valid. The CIA quickly filed an appeal. Determined not be dragged through the courts any longer, the authors boldly decided to publish the version with the 168 deletions. Embarrassingly for the CIA, Knopf published the book with 27 blank spaces, indicating the deletions. In the opinion of one reviewer, this "Swiss cheese quality curiously reinforced rather than diminished the book's credibility."[30] Knopf also set in bold typeface the reinstated 141 passages. Readers, therefore, knew exactly what information the CIA had regarded as "classified" and a threat to national security, if disclosed. Among the highlighted items was the detail that, between 1950 and 1955, the CIA had grown from 5,000 to 15,000 staff – hardly a "revelation that was likely to cost lives.[31]

Bryan's ruling was eventually thrown out by Chief Judge Clement. F. Harmsworth of the Fourth Judicial Circuit. In his estimation, the courts had no authority to determine what constituted a genuine secret, announcing that information was "secret" when "the legend was affixed to the document."[32] He also claimed that Marchetti had sacrificed his First Amendment rights when he signed his secrecy agreement. The CIA thus had reason to be pleased; the case had established a legal precedent that placed contract law above constitutional rights. Yet, this was a pyrrhic victory. The two year legal tussle had given unprec-

28 "$6 Billion a Year Spent on Spying, Authors Say," *Los Angeles Times*, June 19, 1974.
29 Mackenzie, *Secrets*, 51.
30 "Spy Story," *New Republic*, June 22, 1974, 8.
31 Victor Marchetti & John D. Marks, *The CIA and the Cult of Intelligence* (New York: Alfred A. Knopf, 1974), 46.
32 Mackenzie, *Secrets*, 52.

edented publicity to a book which, under ordinary circumstances, might have sunk without a trace. Marchetti was regularly invited to appear on national television and radio to air his grievances. According to the *New Republic*, the CIA merited a nod of gratitude for having unwittingly launched the book in the direction of the bestseller list.[33] It was marketed as the "First Book in American History to be Subject to Pre-Publication Censorship." Before it was even published, Knopf predicted that the "unusual legal complications around it will make for very large sales indeed."[34] Indeed, Marchetti received an advance of $45,000 – a huge sum for a public servant.[35]

The CIA and the Cult of Intelligence was a symptom of post-Vietnam disillusionment with America's ill-fated and morally-questionable attempts to remake the world in its own image. As it hit the press, there was already a growing body of revisionist scholarship on the Cold War, with authors challenging the traditionalist view that the US was morally superior and its foreign policy inherently benign. They typically presented the US as a cross between a "greedy colossus" and "school-bully," desperate to acquire raw materials and foreign markets under the auspices of a new international economic order. Written by former "insiders," Marchetti and Marks's account added a layer of authenticity and detail to this representation; it was revisionism straight from the horse's mouth. The basic thesis of the book was that an obsession with clandestine operations – illegal and immoral – had largely supplanted the CIA's authorized mission to coordinate and process intelligence. This obsession, the book contended, had led the CIA to fuel the Cold War. It prompted the CIA to conduct "back alley" struggles against communism in Iran and Indonesia in the 1950s. It encouraged the CIA to train Tibetan rebels to fight against the takeover of the country by Chinese communists. The book also contained strong hints that the CIA was, in effect, working for "corporate America." For example, it disclosed that the CIA owned and managed "proprietary organizations," including an airline that variously operated under the names of Air America and Rocky Mountain Air.

Marchetti's time in the spotlight brought him into contact with other renegades who were keen to spill the beans, some of whom had developed even stronger negative views about the CIA. Marchetti had hoped that his actions would win public support for a comprehensive review of the CIA in the congressional arena. More radical critics, however, wanted to see the Agency abolished. One of

---

33 "Spy Story," *New Republic*, June 22, 1974, 8.

34 Anthony M. Schulte to Victor Marchetti, February 12, 1974, Alfred Knopf Papers, KNOPF 796.1, Harry Ransom Center, Austin Tx.

35 Ibid.

these disgruntled former officers was domiciled in Great Britain. In September 1974, Marchetti travelled to meet this individual, who had his own memoir in the pipeline.[36] The person was Philip Agee, the most controversial whistleblower in CIA history.

Agee

Phillip Agee had been a CIA staff officer from July 1957 to November 1968. Eight of those years were spent undercover in Ecuador, Uruguay and Mexico. As a case officer on the streets in South America, he was more familiar with intelligence work overseas than the desk-bound Marchetti. CIA records, written after Agee's resignation, offer a negative assessment of the spy's employment and character. "During his career," considered one report, "Agee showed himself to be an egotistical, superficially intelligent, but essentially shallow young man."[37] Another report suggested that his "financial accountings were constantly in a poor state," and that he was "always borrowing money."[38]

The circumstances behind his resignation are disputed. According to the Agency, he was asked to resign by the US Ambassador in Mexico City because of family difficulties. CIA records suggest that the trouble originated when he separated from his wife after a string of "extra-marital affairs." In the tumult that followed this, Agee defied a court order and kidnapped his children from their mother, relocating them to Mexico where he lived with his mistress, "an American woman deeply involved in leftist activity."[39] The Ambassador's hand was apparently forced when Agee's wife threatened to reveal Agee's CIA connections if he did not return the boys.[40] CIA records emphasize that there was no evidence that Agee had become disenchanted. In a letter to the Director of Personnel on November 22, he attributed his resignation to a "personal crisis," before going on to say that "I will continue to hold in high regard the importance of the Agency's

---

36 Doug Porter and Margaret Van Houten, "CIA as White-Collar Mafia," *Village Voice*, June 16, 1975.

37 [Anon.], 'Phillip B.P. Agee,' Phillip Agee Papers, Box 5, Tamiment Library & Robert F. Wagner Labor Archives, New York University, New York.

38 [Anon.], 'Agee's Character,' Phillip Agee Papers, Box 5, Tamiment Library & Robert F. Wagner Labor Archives, New York University, New York.

39 [Anon.], 'Phillip B.P. Agee,' Phillip Agee Papers, Box 5, Tamiment Library & Robert F. Wagner Labor Archives, New York University, New York.

40 [Anon.], 'Personal Problems,' Phillip Agee Papers, Box 5, Tamiment Library & Robert F. Wagner Labor Archives, New York University, New York.

activities in the interests of the security of the United States."[41] Indeed, Agee was said to be excited by the prospect of assisting affluent Mexicans he had met through his work.[42]

Agee tells a different story. According to the renegade spy, his resignation was because of disillusionment with US foreign policy and the Agency's role in it. Specifically, he was distressed by the use of covert action in propping up anti-communist, military dictatorships. In his eyes, the CIA was the "secret policeman of capitalism," designed to facilitate the optimal conditions for multi-national corporate investment.[43]

CIA records suggest that Agee's disaffection only became known to them in November 1971, after he wrote a letter to a leftist Uruguayan newspaper accusing the CIA of meddling in Uruguayan elections.[44] Importantly, Agee's letter confirmed that he was writing a memoir. Upon hearing this, the CIA dispatched one of its top agents, Salvatore Ferrera, to befriend Agee, posing as a socialist journalist. By this time, Agee was living in Paris and progressing with his manuscript. In the summer of 1971 he had visited Havana to refresh his memory through Cuban sources where he received assistance from the Cuban Communist Party. Agee also conducted interviews with Cuban Embassy officials in London and Paris, some being Cuban intelligence officers.[45] In Paris, Ferrera introduced Agee to Leslie Donegan, a young American woman who claimed to be a graduate student. In reality, she too worked for the CIA. Donegan provided vital financial assistance to Agee, who was desperately poor, and in return was given a copy of the unfinished memoir to read. She also gave Agee a used typewriter, secretly bugged with microphones and transmitters. Regrettably for the CIA, Agee discovered the electronic apparatus and immediately left Paris for London.[46]

---

41 [Anon.] to Deputy Director for Plans, 'Mr. Phillip B.F. Agee and the CIA Expose in the Uruguayan Press,' Phillip Agee Papers, Box 5, Tamiment Library & Robert F. Wagner Labor Archives, New York University, New York.

42 CIA records propose that 'his grandiose scheme for making money in Mexico did not bear fruit'. Ibid.

43 P. Agee, *Inside the Company: CIA Diary* (London: Harmondsworth, 1975), entry for October 28, 1968.

44 [Anon.], 'Phillip B.P. Agee,' Phillip Agee Papers, Box 5, Tamiment Library & Robert F. Wagner Labor Archives, New York University, New York.

45 David Atlee Phillips, "The CIA Story – Irresponsible Critics and Suspect Sources," unpublished article, Scott D. Breckinridge papers, Box 1, University of Kentucky Archives, University of Kentucky (Lexington), Kentucky.

46 P. Agee, 'Affidavit,' Phillip Agee Papers, Box 7, Tamiment Library & Robert F. Wagner Labor Archives, New York University, New York.

Agee arrived in London in October 1972 and lived there until he finished his manuscript in May 1974. According to the *Mitrokhin Archive*, the book based on the secret notes taken by KGB defector Major Vasili Mitrokhin, Agee's text was prepared in conjunction with the KGB's "Service A, together with the Cubans."[47] Agee's KGB contact in London was said to be Edgar Anatolyevich Cheporov, London correspondent of the Novosti news agency. During this time, Agee claimed to have been subject to round-the-clock observation, presumably by British services acting at the CIA's request. "This surveillance," he recollected, "caused psychological pressures and fears of physical assault."[48] Unable to speak with Agee directly, Assistant CIA General Counsel John Greaney visited the spy's father in Tampa, Florida, and produced a copy of Agee's secrecy contract, as well as a document outlining the recent Marchetti court ruling.[49] Letters were also sent to potential publishers warning them that the Agency had a contractual right to review the manuscript before its publication and that the CIA was "gravely concerned as to its possible damage to the security of the United States."[50] But Agee refused to communicate.

To avoid the kind of censorship that had shredded parts of Marchetti and Mark's book, *Inside the Company: CIA Diary* was first published by Penguin in London, where it became a bestseller. The book jacket boasted that, unlike in Marchetti and Mark's redacted work, "There are no blanks in Philip Agee's." The CIA's bungled attempts to monitor Agee in Paris came back to haunt them as the front cover featured a picture of the impressively-wired bugged typewriter. Embarrassingly, the marketing campaign suggested that the book's completion was aided by Donegan. "It is no exaggeration to say," claimed Agee, "that the CIA itself financed me during the most critical period in writing the book."[51] Beginning with Agee's training at camp Perry, Virginia, *Inside the Company* presented an uncompromisingly negative picture of CIA activities and a revisionist interpretation of US foreign policy. As a case officer, Agee's duties were said to include bugging, blackmail, burglaries, hiring people to plant bombs, and bribing public officials, journalists, and union leaders. The core contention was that the US was

---

47 Christopher Andrew & Vasili Mitrokhin, *The Mitrokhin Archive: The KGB in Europe and the West* (London: Penguin, 1999), 300.

48 Ibid.

49 John Greaney to DCI, 'Meeting with Agee's Father, Burnet Franklin Agee,' Phillip Agee Papers Box 7, Tamiment Library & Robert F. Wagner Labor Archives, New York University, New York.

50 John Greaney to Anthony P. Brown, November 15, 1974, Phillip Agee Papers Box 2, Tamiment Library & Robert F. Wagner Labor Archives, New York University, New York.

51 P. Agee, 'Affidavit,' Phillip Agee Papers, Box 7, Tamiment Library & Robert F. Wagner Labor Archives, New York University, New York.

defending despots in Latin America, while ensuring that its states were kept in peonage to US investors under the ruse of "development." In an alphabetized Appendix, Agee identified some 250 CIA officers, as well as front companies and foreign agents.

The CIA deplored the book, calling it a "severe body blow" to the organization.[52] A review in the classified in-house journal, *Studies in Intelligence*, lamented that "a considerable number of CIA personnel must be diverted from their normal duties to undertake the meticulous and time-consuming task of repairing the damage done to its Latin American program, and to see what can be done to help those injured by the author's revelations."[53] The CIA was particularly appalled by the naming of names. Upon the publication of his book, Agee wrote that his intention was not to endanger the lives of CIA officers, but to "drive them out of the countries where they are operating."[54] He emphasized that publishing their names was not an act of espionage on behalf of the Soviet Union, but a political statement in the "long and honorable tradition of dissidence in the United States." This argument was rejected by former colleagues and officials. David Atlee Phillips, an erstwhile chief of Western hemisphere operations, predicted that Agee would be "responsible for the unnecessary death of an American intelligence officer abroad."[55] Agee's claim that CIA officers can "take care of themselves" ignored that their wives and children might also be targeted. Therefore he was "responsible for untold worry and even anxiety on the part of CIA families."[56] Writing for the *Spectator*, Miles Copeland, a former CIA station chief, called Agee's greatest sin the "betrayal of his former colleagues" and the rejection of the spy's code never to celebrate their successes, nor explain their failures.[57]

For six months, the CIA unsuccessfully tried to prevent the US publication of the book. It threatened legal action against Agee's US publisher, Stonehill, and the ACLU again became involved in defending the author's right to free speech. At one point, CIA Director William E. Colby told a house appropriations committee that government prosecutors were investigating the possibility of charging Agee

---

52 'Book Review of Inside the Company: CIA Diary by Phillip Agee,' *Studies in Intelligence*, https://www.cia.gov/library/center-for-the-study-of-intelligence/kent-csi/vol19no2

53 Ibid.

54 [Anon.], 'Inside the Company: CIA diary by Philip Agee,' Phillip Agee Papers, Box 5, Tamiment Library & Robert F. Wagner Labor Archives, New York University, New York.

55 David Atlee Phillips, 'The CIA Story – Irresponsible Critics and Suspect Sources,' Scott D. Breckinridge papers, Box 1, University of Kentucky Archives, University of Kentucky (Lexington), Kentucky.

56 Ibid.

57 "Book by Ex-CIA Man Links Latins to Spying," *New York Times*, January 14, 1975.

with treason.[58] The CIA eventually backed down, but by this time its actions had generated enormous public interest in the book and ensured that it became an another bestseller. “The CIA can blame only itself for this mishap,” considered noted espionage authority Ladislas Farago. “This is what they deserve for hiring an unstable young scout and making him perform some of the dirtiest tricks of the Cold War.... The wise men of Langley [should have] let his book die the natural death it so amply deserves.”[59]

There would be no improvement in the relationship between Agee and his former bosses. On December 23, 1975, Richard Welch, CIA Station Chief in Athens, was murdered by terrorists in front of his home as he returned from a Christmas Party. CIA Director George H.W. Bush accused Agee of identifying Welch and blamed him for the death. Stansfield Turner repeated the allegation in a letter to the editor of the *Washington Post* in December 1977, claiming that “shortly after the Agee book was published, one of the persons named in it was killed by terrorists.”[60] Agee disputed the charge for the rest of his life: “Welch was not in my book,” he stated in an interview, “I never knew Welch and I never published his name.”[61] Welch had in fact been named by several earlier publications, including *Counterspy*, a magazine popular among the East Coast radical chic.

Despite the refutation, Agee’s reputation never recovered. Later in the decade, he caused further consternation at Langley by founding the magazine *Covert Action Bulletin*, whose stated purpose was to “destabilize” the CIA by exposing its operations and personnel. General (Ret.) Richard G. Stilwell, representing the Association of Former Intelligence Officers (AFIO), called the magazine a “crime” and Agee a “traitor.”[62] Pressure from the CIA and AFIO eventually led the government to strip Agee of his passport and, in 1982, pass the Intelligence Identities Protection Act, popularly known as the “anti-Agee Bill,” which made it illegal to reveal the name of covert CIA officers even if the information came from open sources.

---

58 “Agee Book Draws Retaliation,” *National Guardian*, May 1, 1975.

59 Ladislas Farago to the Editors of Publishers Weekly, May 7, 1975, Ladislas Farago Papers, 807: Box 25, Howard Gotlieb Archival Research Center, Boston University, Massachusetts.

60 Stansfield Turner to the Editor (*Washington Post*), December 28, 1977, CIA Records Search Tool (hereafter CREST), National Archives II, College Park, Maryland

61 Jake Tapper, “White House Scandal ‘Ironic’ to Shamed Spy,” *ABC News*, October 1, 2003, http://abcnews.go.com/WNT/story?id=129392

62 Richard G. Stilwell to Griffen Bell (Attorney General), August 10, 1978, CREST.

Snepp

The CIA's struggle with whistleblowers climaxed with Frank Snepp. The Snepp case was the most significant of all the Agency's censorship battles, sparking a government lawsuit that culminated in a landmark Supreme Court decision on the reach and reality of the First Amendment with profound implications. Recruited out of Columbia University's School of International Affairs, Snepp had doubled as an analyst and counter-intelligence officer. From 1969 to 1975 he had been hand-picked for two tours of duty in Vietnam. In his final year he rose to be the CIA's chief analyst of North Vietnamese strategy. For his work, he was awarded the CIA's coveted Medal of Merit.

In his capacity as chief analyst, Snepp had been on hand for the fall of Saigon in April 1975; indeed, he escaped on one of the last American helicopters off the roof of the US Embassy. During his evacuation, he looked on in horror as many Vietnamese CIA agents were left behind, to their certain death. He could not shake the memory, and grew bitter at the tardy retreat by the CIA, which abandoned loyal Vietnamese nationals who had risked their lives by working for the Americans. Earlier, he had been shocked to discover that a North Vietnamese prisoner of war had been loaded onto an airplane and thrown out at high altitude over the South China Sea.[63] Back at Langley, he urged his superiors to produce an internal "after-action" report. His appeals fell on deaf ears. Snepp became more agitated when he learned that Ted Shackley, head of East Asia Division, was selectively leaking information to the press that gave, in his opinion, a spurious picture of the end of the war. Shackley was even said to be offering a friendly journalist the carrot of access to classified CIA files if he penned a "favorable" book about Saigon's fall – a "pack of lies in lieu of a true post-mortem."[64] Snepp's rage led him to write a short paper on the evacuation, which he shopped around headquarters, arguing that the CIA had left behind confidential documents that would help the communists identify the thousands of Vietnamese who had faithfully served the US cause. Those who read it treated it like a "skunk's carcass" and refused to act.[65]

Snepp's futile attempts to generate interest in an official investigation led him to write a book. He later explained to the press: "I thought it was a matter of

---

63 Frank Snepp, *Decent Interval: An Insider's Account of Saigon's Indecent End Told by the CIA's Chief of Strategy Analyst in Vietnam* (New York: Random House, 1977), 37–8.
64 Frank Snepp, *Irreparable Harm: A Firsthand Account of How One Agent Took on the CIA in an Epic Battle Over Free Speech* (Lawrence: University Press of Kansas, 1999), 21.
65 Ibid., 30.

honor. I tried to go through the system. I tried to prompt an internal report… and I had been turned away. The only thing that distinguishes the CIA from the Mafia or any criminal outlet is its commitment to getting the truth to Washington and to acknowledging the truth to itself. In the wake of Saigon's collapse, the CIA tried to cover reality with a lie."[66] Unlike Agee, he still believed in the CIA's mission, and considered the fingering of colleagues by name reckless and disgraceful. His primary objective was not to make money or expose agents, but to ensure that the US learned from its mistakes.

Snepp discusses the idea of a book with Bob Loomis, senior editor at the publishing giant Random House. Loomis had a reputation for successfully shepherding "hot" stories into print, having worked with Seymour Hersh on the journalist's historic report on the My Lai massacre, the mass murder of hundreds of Vietnamese civilians by US soldiers in March 1968. The two men met for the first time in a crowded and noisy New York restaurant, the "perpetual clatter of dishes providing a perfect mask for confidential tête-à-têtes."[67] Loomis agreed to support Snepp, but on two conditions. One, the book must not disclose sensitive secrets such as cryptographic data or agent identities; and two, the project must proceed with utmost secrecy. Experience had taught Loomis that any publisher who dared to print negative material about the Agency was playing a dangerous game. When in 1964, Random House had published Thomas Ross and David Wise's groundbreaking account of the CIA, *The Invisible Government*, the Agency had stolen galleys and threatened Loomis with espionage offences.[68] Accordingly, it was agreed that Snepp would never set foot inside Random House headquarters; throughout the book's editorial incubation, the men would meet in city parks, streets and restaurants.[69]

Though the CIA suspected that Snepp had authorial aspirations, it was oblivious to the Loomis connection. On January 26, 1976, Snepp was called to take a lie detector test, an indignity that led him to tender his immediate resignation. For the next 18 months, he worked tirelessly on his manuscript. The new CIA director Admiral Stansfield Turner tried in vain to get Snepp to give a written commitment not to publish anything without first submitting it to the Agency for review.[70] Snepp refused to do so because he believed that the book did not

---

66 "Q & A: Snepp tells of His War with the CIA," *The Washington Star*, unknown date.

67 Snepp, *Irreparable Harm*, 42.

68 Ibid., 43.

69 Carey Winfrey, "Random House Took Precautions to Keep its Publication of Book Secret," *New York Times*, November 19, 1977.

70 Snepp, *Irreparable Harm*, 106–7.

need to be vetted since it contained no secrets, and used unclassified materials. In November 1977, therefore, he published *Decent Interval* without prior review.

The book became a bestseller and generated a whirlwind of publicity, with front-page coverage in *The New York Times* and a "60 Minutes" exclusive. Still remaining the most detailed account of America's final days in Vietnam, the book was a classic piece of revisionism, questioning the wisdom and morality of US Cold War foreign policy. Snepp charged US officials like ambassador Graham Martin with constantly deceiving the public about the prospects for victory in Vietnam. He repeated what many of critics of Richard Nixon and Henry Kissinger had said of the Vietnam peace settlement in January 1973: Instead of amounting to "peace with honor," it merely constituted a "decent interval" before the inevitable Communist takeover. The book pilloried the CIA for heartlessly deserting its South Vietnamese allies to the mercy of any angry enemy, the implication being that the American Empire had no inclination to help local actors once the opportunity for overseas investment had dried up. *Decent Interval* is perhaps best seen as the culmination of the angry New Left historiography that had emerged in the 1960s and early 1970s. As John Lewis Gaddis and J. Samuel Walker have observed, by the late 1970s the glimmerings of a new school had appeared – "postrevisionism" – characterized by a "new consensus" that blamed neither the Soviet Union nor the United States for the Cold War, pointing instead to the inevitability of conflict owing to the power vacuum that had developed after World War Two.[71] Notable "postrevisionist" works by this point included: David McLellan's *Dean Acheson: The State Department Years* (1976); Michael Sherry's *Preparing for the Next War: Americans Plans for Post-War Defense* (1977); and Daniel Yergin's *Shattered Peace: The Origins of the Cold War and the National Security State* (1977).[72] Snepp's account, therefore, was tantamount to revisionism's last roar.

Turner felt personally betrayed by Snepp since he thought that he had secured an oral promise from the author to "surrender [the] manuscript."[73] In an interview with the *Washington Post*, Turner also disputed Snepp's claim that he

71 John Lewis Gaddis, "The Emerging Post-Revisionist Synthesis on the Origins of the Cold War," *Diplomatic History*, 7:3 (1983): 171–190; J. Samuel Walker, "Historians and Cold War Origins: The New Consensus," in Gerald K. Haines and J. Samuel Walker, eds, *American Foreign Relations: A Historiographical Review* (Westport, Connecticut, 1981): 207–36.

72 David S. McLellan, *Dean Acheson: The State Department Years* (New York, 1976); Michael S. Sherry, *Preparing for the Next War: Americans Plans for Postwar Defense* (New Haven, 1977); Daniel Yergin, *Shattered Peace: The Origins of the Cold War and the National Security State* (Boston, 1977).

73 Ibid., 137–8.

had loyally tried to encourage the CIA to examine its own failings.[74] At Turner's insistence, the Justice Department filed a lawsuit against Snepp in the same court in Virginia that had supported the Agency's suit against Marchetti. The government admitted that the book had not compromised any secrets, but built its case on different grounds. Snepp was sued for breaching his original secrecy contract, which the CIA argued contained a "fiduciary" obligation to obtain prepublication approval. Government lawyers also claimed that *Decent Interval* had "irreparably harmed" national security by creating the impression of a breakdown in CIA internal discipline that could jeopardize intelligence operations abroad. Speaking at the Naval Education and Training Center's change-of-command ceremony in June 1978, Turner defended his decision to prosecute, stating: "People who have been associated with us overseas have severed their associations" as a result of the book.[75]

The litigation attracted national and international interest. *Decent Interval* became a public issue of enormous symbolic importance, a test of First Amendment rights. But, from the trial's outset, Snepp was on the defensive. The septuagenarian presiding judge, Oren R. Lewis, was notorious for punishing anti-war activists and "made Genghis Khan look like a civil libertarian."[76] Snepp compared the experience to "being present at your own execution; you're watching the people put the bullets in the weapons and sight down the barrel."[77] Unsurprisingly, then, the CIA won the court verdict, with Lewis ruling against Snepp at every turn. The judge decreed that a retired CIA employee had no authority to decide unilaterally whether he or she had disclosed any classified information. The punishment was severe. Snepp was forced to surrender to the federal government all his profits from the book, described by Lewis as "ill-gotten gains." Stripped of every cent he had made in the nearly two years it took to write it, he was left on the brink of financial ruin. Lewis also imposed a lifetime gag order on Snepp, demanding that he submit all future writings to the CIA for censorship.

Snepp and his lawyers, which included ACLU attorney Mark Lynch, appealed to the Supreme Court to reverse the decision. The Court summarily refused to do so. In a milestone ruling it agreed with the District Court's decision that Snepp had violated his contract and, in doing so, had inflicted irreversible damage on present and future intelligence activities vital to national security. Accordingly,

---

74 Ibid.

75 Irene Wielawski, "Spy-and-tell authors damaging CI efforts, says Turner," *Providence Journal*, June 23, 1978.

76 Snepp, *Irreparable Harm*, 177.

77 'Radio TV Reports: Sunday Morning, March 28, 1982, to Public Affairs Staff,' CREST.

the gag order was allowed to stand, as was the garnishment of earnings. First Amendment purists were horrified, as were large portions of the media. Nat Hentoff of the *Los Angeles Times* exclaimed: "No court decision in history has so-imperiled whistle-blowers, and thereby, the ability of citizens to find out about rampant ineptitude and corruption in the agencies purportedly serving them."[78] *The Washington Post* criticized the Supreme Court for disposing of the case in a "casual, even cavalier manner," totally insensitive to the profound consequences it had for the ability of the government to stifle free speech.[79] The Snepp ruling provided the government with an authority it had never previously even claimed: the power to censor the publications of all employees, in any agency, who held or once held positions of trust. Moreover, it did not matter if the publication was harmless to national security; the ruling made it possible for the CIA or any other agency to silence its critics by simply convincing a court that the "appearance" of security had been imperiled. In one fell swoop, the Court had deprived government employees of the right to criticize the agencies for which they worked. In short, whistleblowers were required to follow their contract, not their conscience.

Whistleblowing Revisionism

The 1970s stand as the worst decade in CIA history. Set against the unpopular war in Southeast Asia and the Watergate scandal, the Agency was thrust into the limelight like never before, required to fend off attacks from a motley band of congressmen, civil liberties groups and investigative reporters, some of whom achieved national stardom on account of their public condemnations. Yet nothing stuck more in its craw than the emergence of whistleblowers. Interviewed in March 1982, Stansfield Turner referred to whistleblowers as the "Achilles' heel of intelligence in this country."[80] "If we can't keep secrets," he went on, "you can't have a good intelligence organization. People's lives are at stake. Your tax dollars are at stake."[81]

The problem of whistleblowers seemed to catch the Agency by surprise. Its clumsy efforts to purloin manuscripts, snoop on authors and install bugged typewriters were suggestive of a crisis with no easy solution. Ultimately, the CIA sought refuge in the panacea of the law, but this only served to attract criticism for

---

78 Cited in Snepp, *Irreparable Harm*, 344.
79 Ibid.
80 'Radio TV Reports: Sunday Morning, March 28, 1982, to Public Affairs Staff,' CREST.
81 Ibid.

trampling on First Amendment rights. In the late 1970s, with the Snepp case, the Agency generated fresh controversy by punishing a former agent who had written about ineptitude, but who had disclosed no classified information. Attempts to "police" whistleblowers ultimately fed into the larger discussion about whether the CIA, in a free society, had not become too powerful and a menace to democratic rights.

The memoirs that were published fundamentally challenged the celebratory story of US Cold War foreign policy, and reinforced the rise of academic revisionism. Holding up a mirror to the US, Marchetti, Agee and Snepp showed the primary objective of US foreign policy to be expansion, both territorial and economic, with the CIA as an obedient tool. US foreign policy was seen to be fueled not by any devotion to morality or democratic values, but rather by the desire to make the world hospitable for globalization, led by American-based multinational corporations. Whistleblowing memoirs also revealed the forgotten victims of US foreign policy, from the people who suffered under the authoritarian Shah of Iran, installed by the CIA in 1953, to the thousands of loyal collaborators who were betrayed and left behind in the killing fields of Vietnam. In short, "Company Confessions" were tragic monuments to Cold War revisionism.

Falk Pingel

The Cold War in History Textbooks: A German-German, French and British Comparison

Neither the cold nor hot war was on the pedagogical agenda of textbook authors and curriculum experts in the immediate postwar years. Instead both groups wanted to raise hopes in the young generation for a new peaceful international order. This was true in particular for Germany whose education systems were controlled by the Allied powers who wanted to convert German mind-sets which were supposedly influenced by a long militaristic tradition into peace-loving, or at least peace-respecting, co-operative attitudes. It did not fit into this aim if German education contributed to deepening the divide between the Allies or played them off against each other.

One of the first widely used German history textbooks, *Wege der Völker*,[1] followed this line of thought. The chapter dealing with the "World of Today" starts with a section, titled "The Will to Peace," and then leads with the following two sections cautiously to the problematic issue by using metaphoric language: "First Clouds on the Horizon" and "The World Divided anew." The first section deals with trials against war crimes and the foundation of the UN; the second one states, in contrast, that the UN cannot live up to its expectations because of the Soviet veto against atomic control. The third section gives a comprehensive view of the emerging postwar constellation: Europe is divided into two parts whose centers of gravitation lie in Washington and in Moscow with "its Asiatic hinterland." The 1951 edition chooses a soberer language for the headings with slightly revised content: "Years of Negotiation and Conferences," "Europe between East and West," "Changes in Asia." The chapter on "The World after the War – 1945 to 1954" in the 1955 edition still includes a section with the title "Preparing for Sustainable World Peace." Only thereafter can pupils read that tensions between the USA and USSR increased and a divided world was taking shape. Steps to peaceful international co-operation could not overcome but had to respect the dividing line that increasingly separated the East from the West of Europe.

1 Friedrich Schmidt, and Wally Schmelzer, *Das neue Gesicht der Welt: Vom Wiener Kongreß bis in die Gegenwart,* Wege der Völker: Geschichtsbuch für deutsche Schulen Vol. VII (Berlin: Pädagogischer Verlag Berthold Schulz, 1949), 431. The book series was developed in Berlin and originally used in both parts of the city; it was widely used in the forming years of the Federal Republic of Germany.

DOI 10.1515/9783110496178-006

Although the political and economic split became obvious in the late 1940s and threatened to turn into a military confrontation between the two superpowers with the Korean War, the educational agenda changed more slowly than the political one. Until well into the 1950s, unification remained a goal which seemed not to be out of reach according to the history textbooks of both German states. The division was not yet cemented, the Cold War had not yet become the leading paradigm for describing the postwar period. The first edition of the GDR history textbook concludes with a sub-chapter on "The fight for the unity of Germany." According to the text, the "policy of the imperialistic victorious powers" was still counter-balanced by the activities of the "world-peace camp."[2]

These introductory remarks suggest that history school books have some specific characteristics. They are considerably more influenced by political trends and educational philosophies than scholarly publications or university textbooks. Nevertheless, they have to acknowledge and reflect research findings. Furthermore, they have to represent the content in a way which can be understood and digested by youngsters of a certain age group in a limited time period defined by the lesson plan which allots to history teaching at lower secondary schools hardly more than two hours a week in Europe. A history schoolbook is, therefore, a highly selective medium that transmits, as a rule, a clear message to the pupils due to its underlying political assumptions and pedagogical objectives. These aims are mainly expressed in the curriculum and other related guidelines which teachers and textbook authors have to abide by. Normally, the ministry of education is the main agent of curriculum construction; however, parents' and teachers' associations, other interest groups, and public media may have a say as well.

The countries whose textbook representation of the Cold War will be examined here differ regarding the influence their ministries of education exert on the textbook market. The former German Democratic Republic had a centralized system where only one state-commissioned textbook was available per class and subject. The ministry was in full control of the curriculum and steered the whole process of writing and approval with the support of academic institutions. In the Federal Republic of Germany the curriculum offers methods and content guidelines, but teachers feel free to use the curriculum according to the needs of their specific classrooms. Each of the 16 federal states issues its own curriculum. The Standing Conference of Ministers of Education acts as a co-ordinating agency ensuring that a common structure is implemented country-wide. In principle, textbooks must be approved by the ministries of education, but an increasingly number of states

2 *Lehrbuch für den Geschichtsunterricht: 8. Schuljahr* (Berlin: Volk und Wissen Volkseigener Verlag, 1952), 321.

ask for expert reviews only in case that doubts have been expressed by teachers or the public. Although a small number of publishing houses has the biggest market share, the German textbook market is rather competitive and diverse.

In France and England, the state does not control the adoption of textbooks. However, France mandates a central curriculum for the whole country. Due to the strong state examination system, the methodological approaches and content areas do differ less than in Germany. The author's texts are shorter and often culminate in sentences than can easily be remembered. History and geography are covered in the same book. The textbooks are clearly structured, alternating between text, sources, illustrations, statistics, and "close-ups" which deal with specific topics in detail. In England, a "National Curriculum" covering England and Wales was only introduced in the 1990s against the background of Britain's accession to the EU. Only since then, a school book market comparable to other Western European countries has been established. Local "examination boards" set the criteria for passing school examinations and streamline the competency-based learning process as well as textbook representation in an otherwise free and competitive textbook market.

This analysis focuses on West and East German, French and English history textbooks, comparing the books of the defeated country with those of the two Western European Allies. As their curricula allows for a comparison only on the lower secondary level (comprising normally grades 5/6 to 10), the analysis is restricted to textbooks written for this age group. Concerning France only textbooks that appeared since the 1970s could be included because prior to this date the Cold War period was not part of the relevant curriculum. Since Britain developed a comparable textbook system only in the 1990s, the analysis of English books begins in that time period. To observe continuity as well as changes, relevant volumes from widely distributed German and French textbook series have been selected that were on the market for many years and re-edited several times. Only one of the series with a big market share could be taken into account per country for a certain time period with the exception of England because none of the series covered a longer time span there.

Although the postwar period is dealt with extensively in European textbooks since the 1970s, analytical studies have seldom focused on this topic. Since most of the textbook analyzes dealing with this period concentrate on the shaping of national and/or European identities, the Cold War plays only a minor role in this context.[3] This applies also to the extensive study of the portrayal of Germany

3 Hanna Schissler, and Yasemin Nuhoğlu Soysal eds., *The Nation, Europe and the World* (New York: Berghahn Books, 2005); Falk Pingel, *The European Home: representations of 20th century*

and the German question conducted by the Georg Eckert Institute for International Textbook Research in 1986 which is still the most detailed study of West and East German history, civics and geography textbooks.[4] The first critical analysis appeared in 1961, while a critical appraisal of U.S. history textbooks was published at the end of the Cold War.[5] The latest study was conducted by Brigitte Morand who analyzed the Cold War in French, German and U.S. (Upper) Secondary textbooks since the 1960s.[6] The results from the above literature will also be taken into account in order to provide a broader perspective.

The period of the Cold War forms part of contemporary history, making it particularly challenging to deal with in history textbooks. Traditionally, school books did not address the period of the contemporaries. The teaching of history was meant to lay the foundation for an understanding of the roots of present times looking back into a closed past on which clear and unambiguous interpretations could be based. In contrast, the interpretation of contemporary times was more ambiguous and politically controversial; it remained open to different future developments. Therefore, school history teaching has been more hesitant than scholarly research to accept contemporary history as an integral part of the discipline. Dealing with open, controversial issues became recognized as a teaching method only since the 1970s. In Germany the imperative of coping with the Nazi past and the division of the country made the teaching of contemporary history imperative. But in France, the contemporary times were not taught on the lower secondary level till the end of the 1960s. And in England the paradigm of Empire history hindered full recognition of the world's bipolar structure in the first postwar decades.

Europe in history textbooks (Strasbourg: Council of Europe, 2000); Falk Pingel ed., *Insegnare l'Europa. Concettti e rappresentazioni nei libri di testo europei* (Torino: Edizione Fondazione Agnelli, 2003); Falk Pingel, *UNESCO Guidebook on Textbook Research and Textbook Revision*, 2nd rev. and updated ed. (Paris; Braunschweig: UNESCO/Georg Eckert Institute, 2010).

4 Wolfgang Jacobmeyer ed., *Deutschlandbild und deutsche Frage in den historischen, geographischen und sozialwissenschaftlichen Unterrichtswerken der Bundesrepublik Deutschland und der Deutschen Demokratischen Republilk von 1949 bis in die 80er Jahre* (Braunschweig: Georg Eckert Institut für internationale Schulbuchforschung, 1986).

5 Mark M. Krug, "The Teaching of History at the Center of the Cold War: History Textbooks in East and West Germany," *The School Review*, Vol. 69, 4 (1961): 461–487; Dennis L. Carlson, "Legitimation and Delegitimation: American History textbooks and the cold war," in: *Language, Authortiy and Criticism. Readings on the School Textbook, eds.*, Suzanne de Castell, Allan Luke, and Carmen Luke (London: Falmer Press, 1989), 46–55.

6 Brigitte Morand, "Questions on the Comparative Method of European and U.S. Textbooks: The Example of the Cold War and the Berlin Blockade," in: *Yearbook: International Society for History Didactics, Vol. 32* (2011): 129–138.

The prelude

German history textbooks began to reflect the experience of the Cold War already in the 1950s. For authors on both sides of the divide, the "East-West conflict" threatened to cement the division of Germany which was still seen as a consequence of occupation and not yet regarded as an irreversible event. The main concern was that the political situation should be kept open for the re-unification of the divided nation. West and East German textbooks criticize Allied policy that led to the division of Germany and made the paradigm of "peaceful co-existence" illusionary. West German textbook authors therefore criticize Roosevelt's and Truman's "naive" trust in "peaceful co-existence with the Soviet Union." New West German textbooks that appeared since the mid 1950s openly deplore the results of the Allied peace conferences. "Thus, the German people has been torn into two parts by the disunited Allies of the war." The Oder-Neisse line is called "an illegal boundary."[7] In contrast, East German textbooks "approve of the Yalta and the Potsdam conferences," but criticize the Western Allies that they did not put Potsdam into practice. "The Potsdam agreement," says one textbook, "was in line with the best interests of the German people... It provided the groundwork for a democratic development."[8]

The clear anti-Soviet orientation of West German schoolbooks that appeared in the period of political and economic reconstruction after the Korean war is expressed in *Die Reise in die Vergangenheit* which became one of the most popular books for decades. The chapter on contemporary history is titled "Reconstruction and New Dangers"; one of the sections deals with "The New Global Divide – Germany as an Area of Conflict between the Superpowers." Only the Soviet Union is to blame for this development because of its systematic efforts to impose the Bolshevist system on the states occupied by it.[9] The underlying assumption of this formulation is that the real intentions of the Soviet Union were concealed by Stalin's peace rhetoric at the Allied conferences. Focal points of an early postwar

---

7 Mark M. Krug, "The Teaching of History at the "Center of the Cold War," 483 and Renate Riemeck: *Geschichtsbuch für die Jugend*, vol. IV (Mundus: Stuttgart, 1959), 86, quoted in Wolfgang Marienfeld and Manfred Overesch, *Deutschlandbild und Deutsche Frage in den Geschichtsbüchern der Bundesrepublik Deutschland und den Richtlinien der Länder,* in: *Deutschlandbild,* 1–118.

8 Krug, "The Teaching of History at the "Center of the Cold War," 484–85, quoting *Lehrbuch für Geschichte der 10. Klasse der Oberstufe* (Berlin: Volk und Wissen Volkseigener Verlag, 1960) 88–89.

9 Hans Ebeling, *Unser Zeitalter der Revolutionen und Weltkriege,* Die Reise in die Vergangenheit Vol. IV (Braunschweig: Westermann, 1961), 259.

narrative of tension and crisis are the arms race, the Korean War, the uprising of June 17, 1953, the anti-Soviet revolt in Hungary. Responsibility for the East-West conflict is assigned only to the Soviet Union.This line of thought remained unchanged in the following editions of the book till 1986!

Although the hope for peaceful coexistence had been replaced by the reality of conflict and tension, textbook authors did not yet label this development as "the period of the Cold War". The term Cold War is only used occasionally; textbook authors of the 1950s and 1960s preferred to speak of "tensions" or the "East-West-conflict". Until the mid-1960s no overall concept of the "Cold War" emerged. The world is represented through antagonistic relations that led to continuos "conflicts" between the superpowers such as the Berlin Blockade, Korean War, Cuban Missile Crisis and revolts within the Soviet empire such as 1953 protest in the GDR, 1956 in Hungary, 1968 in Czechoslovakia.

The edition of the GDR textbook which appeared in 1960 introduced a new chronological structure. The volume for grade 10 dealing with contemporary history now starts with the Second World War and the postwar era (and no longer with the First World War and the Russian Revolution). This change indicates that with the Soviet Union's victory over Nazism, the foundation of "people's democracies" in Eastern Europe and particularly in China, and the process of decolonization, a new epoch has begun: Imperialism is weakening and a "socialist world system" is emerging.[10] The Soviet Union fights for "peaceful coexistence and international détente." The crisis of imperialism and the rising sun of socialism represent the two leading antagonistic powers that govern the historic development in this new era. The peace-loving Soviet Union is the forerunner of a bright future whereas the spearhead of capitalism and imperialism, the USA, becomes more aggressive because it feels its leading position threatened. Accordingly, the book starts with the development of the USSR, and then goes with the other people's democracies including China and the GDR. Only the 1960 edition has sub-chapters on some Western European states such as Great Britain and France, whereas the following editions concentrate on the USA and West Germany.[11] The chapter on the "world peace movement" now concludes the book, referring to an overarching development that will unite the world in the end. This interpretation of the world remains almost unchanged till the last, 1988 edition of the book.

---

10 *Lehrbuch für Geschichte der 10. Klasse der Oberstufe* (Berlin: Volk und Wissen Volkseigener Verlag, 1960), 150–152.

11 The heading of this chapter in the 1960 edition is called "The fight of the German people against West German imperialism and militarism and for the national rebirth of Germany as a united, peace-loving democratic state."

In contrast to the Cold War model which balances two opposing powers, the socialist world interpretation shows a fundamental imbalance: the future is with socialism whereas imperialism represents a past that will be overcome. Therefore, socialist textbooks never speak of a "balance of terror." The term "Cold War" is only used sporadically and does not relate to the international constellation in general, but denotes the policy of imperialism which is destined to fail.[12]

The Bipolar Paradigm

A French book of 1972 delivers the motto for the new paradigmatic narrative: The chapter on "The US, the USSR and the Big European Powers" starts with two definitions meant for rote learning: "Since 1945 the life of the world is dominated by the two great powers, the USA and the USSR." And "the two Europes of the West and the East are separated by an iron curtain."[13] From now on, the term "Cold War" (*Kalter Krieg* in German or *Guerre Froide* in French) is often used for the time period ranging approximately from the late 1940s to the mid-1960s. In sharp contrast to West German textbooks, French authors empathize with the USSR whose achievements are underscored. The Soviet Union "liberated" the Eastern European countries, whereas the USA exercised her political dominance due to her economic strength. While the U.S. position seems to be based on mere power politics, the leading role of the Soviet Union is apparently built on positive values as well as the high esteem of her political leaders: "Due to their prestige, the communist parties gained all the key positions between 1946 and 1948."[14] The sympathy with the USSR fades away, however, in books that appeared after 1990.

The socialist countries are called "people's democracies" according to the official terminology, but their political systems are not explained in any detail, creating misunderstandings in pupils' minds. It is said that opposition movements emerged in Poland, Hungary and Czechoslovakia, yet their aims are not clarified. Only the position of Yugoslavia which developed an independent stand

---

12 See the chapter "Das Scheitern der imperialistischen 'Politik des kalten Krieges'" in: *Lehrbuch für Geschichte, 10. Klasse: Teil 1,* Oberschule und erweiterte Oberschule (Berlin: Volk und Wissen Volkseigener Verlag, 1966), 150.

13 Antoine Bonifacio, and Jean Michaud, *1789–1970: l'epoque contemporaine,* 3e (Paris: Classiques Hachette/Collection Isaacb, 1972); Antoine Bonifacio, and Jean Michaud, *1789–1970: L'époque contemporaine,* 3e (Paris: Classiques Hachette/Collection Isaac, 1976), 350.

14 Lucien Pernet et al. (ed.), *Histoire: Géographie,* 3e (Paris: Armand Colin/Classiques Hachette, 1980), 86.

vis-à-vis the Soviet Union and did not fit into the East-West divide is accentuated with a photograph of Tito and an interesting quotation, commenting on the Soviet intervention in Budapest in 1956. On the one hand, Tito speaks out against "counterrevolution" and "civil war," on the other hand, military intervention from outside is called a political "error."[15] The authors' sympathy seems to be with the "third way" of a "soft" socialism.

Once developed, the concept of the bipolar world order becomes so strong in French textbooks that it determines the structure of the whole chapter dealing with the time from 1945 to the present: "The capitalist countries since 1945" versus "the socialist countries since 1945." Both sides try to secure their own sphere of influence and develop parallel structures through economic and military alliances such as the EEC and NATO in the West and COMECON and the Warsaw Pact in the East. The problematic East-West relationship is described by referring to the most salient international crises such as the Berlin Blockade, the Korean War, the construction of the Berlin Wall and the Cuban Missile Crisis as "hot moments." The succession of crises gives the impression of being confronted with an almost permanent conflict situation.[16]

These topics constitute a set of content issues and interpretative models that can be found in French and German, and later on in English history textbooks as well. Yet, the bipolar configuration is particularly strong in French textbooks. The leading text provides a typical example by having the chapter "Two blocs face to face" accompanied by a double-paged map of "The Bipolar World." The entire globe is divided into blue and red areas referring to the "western camp" and the "Soviet camp," respectively. Only Finland, India, large parts of Africa and smaller parts of Southeast Asia are drawn in a neutral gray color. Political history is translated into a persuasive graphical representation of geopolitics.[17]

The chapters in French textbooks dealing with geography reflect the same structure as the history parts of the book. The cultural, economic and political geography of the contemporary world is broken down into three main chapters dealing with the EEC/EU, the USA and the USSR. Earlier than their German col-

15 Ibid.

16 Ibid. According to Carlson, *Legitimation and Delegitimation,* U.S. history textbooks displayed a quite similar structure of the postwar period.

17 Jean-Michel Lambin (ed.), *Histoire: Géographie,* 3e (Paris: Hachette Collèges, 1989), 162–163. The 2004 edition again uses the term but the map now shows the divided Europe only in blue and red with some green neutral spots like Finland and Spain [Vincent Adoumié (ed.), *Histoire: Géographie,* 3e (Paris: Hachette Éducation, 2004), 128.]; See further examples in Falk Pingel ed., *Macht Europa Schule? Die Darstellung Europas in Schulbüchern der Europäischen Gemeinschaft* (Frankfurt/M.: Diesterweg, 1995).

leagues, French textbook authors give particular weight to the West European dimension as a sub-set of the Western camp. The divided world is reflected in a highly selective curriculum that creates a relatively simple world view. In its center is still one's own nation but it forms part of a wider context that is shaped by the East-West conflict in a negative sense and the process of European integration in a positive, future-oriented way.

The interpretations of the reasons for the divided world differ slightly in West European books. Power politics and the preservation and expansion of the capitalist and the communist system respectively play a dominant role. A British book adds an interesting psychological explanation to these factors: A confrontational situation creates distrust on both sides which prolongs the conflict: "After 1945 the USSR and the USA were rivals locked in a struggle which became known as the Cold War. The basis of the Cold War was fear." Since the USSR had often been invaded from the West, the Soviet Union was "afraid of being threatened again" and the "western powers... were afraid that the USSR would try to spread the communist revolution throughout the world."[18]

Another book explains the ideological reasons of the conflict as "different beliefs. In the past, the USA and the USSR had always been very suspicious of each other. They had totally different beliefs about how a country should be run ... They were allies during the war only because they had the same enemy – Hitler's Germany."[19] Particularly English books underscore the long-term ideological sources of the antagonism. "The origins of the Cold War lay ... in the years between ... 1917 and 1941.... Once Germany had been defeated, the differences between capitalist USA and communist USSR became obvious once more." This explanation recalls Kennan's argument according to which the conflict would inevitably break out after the war and, therefore, the Western powers had to resume a preventive strategy (containment). However, it left the initiative to the Soviet Union which supported communist governments in Eastern Europe, since Truman and Churchill only responded to this challenge. [20] The Cold War unfolds according to

---

18 Nigel Kelly, and Rosemary Rees, *The Modern World: Heinemann Secondary History Project* (London: Heinemann, 2001), 182.

19 Ben Walsh, *Essential Modern World History,* History in Focus (London: John Murray, 2002); in a similar way argue John D. Clare et al. *GCSE History: AQA B Modern World History* (Harlow: Heinemann/Pearson Education, 2009), 60.: "The Allies were bound together only by the need to defeat their common enemies: the Nazis and the Japanese. They were divided by ideology. In fact, the two sides ...hated and feared each other." See also Colin Shepard, and Keith Shepard, *Re-Discovering Twentieth Century World: A World Study after 1900,* The School History Project (London: John Murray, 2004), 161.

20 Kelly, and Rees, *The Modern World,* 182.

an action-reaction scheme with the implicit message that coexistence between the capitalist and the socialist system is impossible.

French and German texts resort less to such schematic arguments that leave hardly any room for alternatives by focusing more on concrete analyses of crises situations. Underscoring that France did not participate in these decisions, French books date the reasons for the division back to the Yalta and Potsdam conferences that defined spheres of influence. Even though it is not explicitly stated, this starting point bears the implicit meaning that France is not responsible for the Cold War. In particular the German textbooks of the first postwar decades also emphasize that the USA offered material support for the reconstruction of the destroyed West European economies and the establishment of common Western organizations. Authors underscore that material help from the USA and the West European integration contributed to establishing positive feelings between former enemies. Thus, the psychological burden of the conflict with the East was counterbalanced by a rising Western European identity.

The Berlin crisis of 1948 is presented as the first instance of Soviet power politics and intransigence on the one hand and firm American support for the Western position on the other. Pictures of the airlift and, later on, of the Airlift Monument in Berlin become "ubiquitous" in French and West German (and also U.S.) textbooks.[21] By making them a graphic symbol of the East-West confrontation, textbooks contributed to forming this pattern of the collective memory.

The communist challenge and European cooperation represent focal points in the introductory remarks of a German history textbook. Its authors draw pupils' attention also to problems of the so-called underdeveloped countries – a feature which seldom appears so prominently in textbooks prior to the 1980s. Reflecting on the leading objectives of the book, the authors address pupils as follows: "It is decisive for your way of life to address the main issues of our time in a correct way; these are: the intellectual struggle with communism, European development, and support for underdeveloped countries."[22]

Parallel to the emerging image of a bipolar world in Western European books, the history texts of the GDR portray a decisive struggle between the "socialist world system" and an "increasingly aggressive imperialism." However, the books deal only in short sub-chapters with the Western world and international rela-

21 Brigitte Morand, "La Guerre Froide, une histoire partagée? Le blocus de Berlin dans les manuales allemands, américains et français depuis les années soixante," in: *La Fabrique de l'événement*, eds. F. Rouseau, and J.F. Thomas, (Paris: Michel Houdiard, 2009), 336–342.

22 Hans Heumann, "Unser Weg durch die Geschichte" Neubarbeitung, vol. 3: *Die Welt gestern und heute.* (Frankfurt: Hirschgraben, 1972). unchanged in the 1977 edition.

tions outside of the socialist system. With the editions of the 1960s the language becomes more derogatory and aggressive towards the imperialistic states than before. Culminating in the building of the Berlin Wall, the division is cemented in ideology as well as in reality. According to the new Teaching Program of 1959, the GDR is the "result of the lawlike development of society."[23] The building of the Wall is justified as a defensive measure against "the systematic preparation of a [West German] attack [on the GDR]" while the description of the FRG becomes overwhelmingly negative by accusing West Germany of being the "chief source of war in Europe." The FRG is depicted as an aggressive and militaristic state that threatens the very existence of the GDR. In contrast, the foundation of the GDR is characterized as "a turning point in the history of Germany and Europe."[24] The conflicting narratives of division in East and West German textbooks of the 1960s merely reflect the political reality in which each side claimed to represent the only legitimate German state.[25]

Rapprochement and Containment

The Cuban Missile Crisis is presented as the climax and turning point of the Cold War. Although the antagonistic relationship between the two blocs continued to exist, the concept of peaceful coexistence becomes, step by step, the leading paradigm as aptly expressed in the French textbook: "The Cuba crisis marks the end of the Cold War; the era of peaceful coexistence is approaching"[26] West German history books stress the process of European integration and deal with Franco-German and German-Polish reconciliation efforts. While tensions still arise, they are shifted to the periphery of the superpowers such as in Vietnam, Cambodia and Afghanistan. Though these proxy wars do not confront the superpowers directly, the risk of a "global war" is not yet banned.[27] It is an ambivalent and "difficult" peace, a "coexistence of the two systems under the shadow of the

---

23 Karl-Ernst Jeismann, and Erich Kosthorst, "Deutschlandbild und Deutsche Frage in den Geschichtlichen Unterrichtswerken der Deutschen Demokratischen Republik," in: *Deutschlandbild* (1986): 134, 146.

24 Lehrbuch für Geschichte, 10. Klasse, Teil 1 (Berlin: Volk und Wissen Volkseigener Verlag, 1966), 141, 149, 155.

25 Horst Siebert, *Der andere Teil Deutschlands in den Schulbüchern der DDR und der BRD: Ein Beitrag zur politischen Bildung in Deutschland* (Hamburg: Verlag für Buchmarkt-Forschung, 1970).

26 Jean-Michel Lambin (ed.), *Histoire: Géographie*, 3e (Paris: Classique Hachette, 1984), 140.

27 Ibid.

atomic bomb". Although the two superpowers still mistrust each other, the situation becomes less confrontational.[28]

In the context of summit meetings trying to reduce tensions, the role of individual politicians such as John F. Kennedy and Nikita Khrushchev is discussed who were involved in confrontations and had to take hard decisions: How do individuals act in a polarized political framework? What abilities do they have to create trust without running the risk of being naive and fostering illusions? How far did the leaders of the superpowers go in the Berlin or Cuba crises to preserve their "national interests"? Where they really about to bring the world at the brink of an atomic war? Was the awareness of this risk the strongest motivation for inspiring a policy of rapprochement after these crises had been managed?[29] In her analysis of French textbooks Brigitte Morand interprets a picture showing Leonid Brezhnev whispering something to Richard Nixon in such a manner: "The meeting of the Big Two is the culmination of détente and at the same time represents the joint domination of the United States and the Soviet Union over international affairs."[30] She contends: "This comment is representative of the narrative of the Cold War in French textbooks." Negotiations do not replace the antagonistic relationship but moderate it somewhat.

When the policy of détente gained ground during the 1970s, authors stress aspects anew that had already played a role in the immediate postwar years. Particularly in Germany, the new *Ostpolitik* of the Brandt government helped to revise the strong anti-Soviet attitude of West German history textbooks. The authors now show a more conciliatory attitude. *Reise in die Vergangenheit* includes a new chapter titled "The United Nations – Uniting the World?". A subsection of the chapter is devoted to new attempts at world peace.[31] In French textbooks of the 1980s similar chapters on a "new world order" can be found.

But authors writing after 1990 examine the renewed tensions more critically in a chapter titled "The Failure of Détente and the Collapse of Communism, 1970–

---

28 Jean-Michel Lambin (ed.), *Histoire: Géographie*, 3e (Paris: Hachette Collèges, 1989). and Klaus Bergmann et al., *Geschichte und Geschehen*, vol. A4 (Stuttgart: Ernst Klett Verlag, 1997), 134–135. The relations between East and West are labeled as "L'ère des méfiances" in Bonifacio and Michaud, *1789–1970: L'époque contemporaine*, 1972 and 1976, 371.

29 Hannes Adomeit, *Soviet Risk-Taling and Crisis Behavior: A theoretical and empirical analysis* (London: George Allen & Unwin, 1982); Stefan Karner et al. (ed.), Der Wiener Gipfel 1961: Kennedy – Chrutschow (Innsbruck: Studienverlag, 2011).

30 Morand, *Questions on the Comparative Method*, 2011, 133; André Gauthier et al., *Histoire, terminales* (Paris: Bréal, 1991), 88.

31 Hans Ebeling, *Die Reise in die Vergangenheit. Ein geschichtliches Arbeitsbuch* (1973) vol. IV: Geschichte und Politik unserer Zeit. ed. Wolgang Birkenfeld, (Braunschweig: Westermann, 1984).

1991." Both the invasion of Afghanistan by Soviet troops and Reagan's outspoken anti-communism plus the development of new weapons (cruise missiles) contributed to the "failure" of detente. The authors state that "Reagan actively began a new Cold War with the Soviets." Only Gorbachev's policy of perestroika led to "The end of the Cold War".[32] German books put less emphasis on the negative aspects of the 1980s and instead stress the democracy movements in the Eastern European states that helped to open the Iron Curtain. Looking back from the period of rapprochement, Western European textbook authors describe the 1950s and 1960s as the "Cold War" proper.[33] They use the term "Cold War" as a rule only from the 1970s/1980s on, when the "hot" phase of this war was already over and the period of "détente" was approaching.

With the 1970s, textbook authors began to regard the division of Germany as a matter of fact whose political recognition becomes the precondition for a peaceful rapprochement. Their colleagues in France or the Nordic countries juxtapose the political, economic and social systems of both states and discuss their pros and cons.[34] West German authors refrain from using the derogatory terms "Eastern zone" or "Soviet zone" when referring to the GDR. Nevertheless, re-unification remains a long-term political goal, a West German textbook of the 1980s expressed when citing a statement by Richard von Weizsäcker, then president of the Federal Republic: As long as the Brandenburg Gate is closed, the German question remains open.[35] The Berlin Wall has become a symbol not only for the division of Germany but also of the whole of Europe, and photographs of it are shown in many Western European textbooks.

Side boxes with sources from scholarly research sometimes present sophisticated arguments in order to allow students to compare claims and form their own opinion. *Geschichte und Geschehen* offers excerpts from speeches of leading politicians from East and West to familiarize pupils with conflicting statements

---

32 Clare et al., *GCSE History AQA B Modern World History,* 105–108.

33 "Die Reise in die Vergangenheit" uses the term "Cold War" in the 1986 edition for the first time! Cf. Derek Heater, *The Cold War* (London: Oxford University Press, 1965).

34 The German term is *Systemvergleich.* Wolfgang Jacobmeyer, ed. *Deutschlandbild und deutsche Frage in den historischen, geographischen und sozialwissenschaftlichen Unterrichtswerken der Bundesrepublik Deutschland und der Deutschen Demokratischen Republik von 1949 bis in die 80er Jahre* (Braunschweig: Georg-Eckert-Institut für Internationale Schulbuchforschung, 1986) See Brigitte Morand, "La problématique de la convergence entre les système de l'Est et de l'Ouest dans les manuels scolaires français des anées 1960 et 1970," in: *Revue d'Histoire Diplomatique,* No.1 (2008 B): 47–59.

35 Bernd Mütter et al. eds., *Die Menschen und ihre Geschichte in Darstellungen und Dokumenten,* Geschichtsbuch 4 (Berlin: Cornelsen, 1988), 237.

and develop their understanding of mutually exclusive positions.[36] In 1985 Ruth Sareik criticized this approach from a left-wing point of view: Despite a policy of détente and of de facto recognition by the "Treaty Concerning the Basis of Relations between the FRG and the GDR," textbook authors still kept the "German question" open and categorized the GDR as an undemocratic or totalitarian system. Such a description would not help to combat pupils' "extremely undifferentiated, aggressive and anti-Communist" images of the GDR.[37] Although some West German textbooks upheld the theory of totalitarianism, others dno longer referred to it. It was only revived in some books after the collapse of the Soviet Union and German re-unification.

According to the GDR history book, the 1970s showed the growing strength of the socialist world order: The imperialist policy of aggression had failed. The USA therefore had to accept a "policy of cooperation and restricted conflict" and adopt a "flexible" approach. Washington was forced "to avoid a direct military clash with the USSR" in order to secure its "survival."[38] Hence the Cuban Missile Crisis is not presented as a direct confrontation between the two superpowers, but as a one-sided "military attack" of the USA. The deployment of Soviet missiles is not even mentioned, indicating only the "unqualified" Soviet support for Cuba instead. The following period of détente is, therefore, interpreted as a defeat of imperialism and "a fiasco of the global counter-revolutionary counter-attack." Since the socialist system has developed into the global political power, the imperialist states are inclined to build international relations "on the basis of the principle of peaceful coexistence" – a policy that the Soviet Union has followed since 1945. The Helsinki Conference on Security and Co-operation in Europe (CSCE) has its roots in this approach.[39]

---

36 Peter Alter et al., *Geschichte und Geschehen,* vol IV (Stuttgart: Ernst Klett Verlag, 1987 and 1992), 138–139. Walsh uses a fictitious dialogue between Stalin and Truman over the German question. Ben Walsh, *Essential Modern World History*, History in Focus (London: John Murray, 2002), 164.

37 Ruth Sareik, "Anatomie eines Feindbildes: Für Schulbücher in der BRD war der kalte Krieg nie zu Ende," in: *Vergleichende Pädagogik*, Vol. 21, No. 3 (1985): 283–289. Citing Dieter Boßmann, *Schüler über die Einheit der Nation* (Frankfurt: Aubel, 1978); Siegfried et al., *DDR im Schulbuch*, (Köln: Pahl-Rugenstein and Radtke, 1983); Wolfang Rilling, and Rainer Rilling, "Hatte die Entspannungspolitik Auswirkungen auf die Schule? Schulbücher über die Beziehungen BRD – DDR – eine Inhaltsanalyse," in: *Demokratische Erziehung* (1981): 329–333.

38 *Geschichte. Lehrbuch für Klasse 10*, Teil 1 (Berlin: Volk und Wissen Volkseigener Verlag, 1971), 71.

39 *Geschichte. Lehrbuch für Klasse 10* (Berlin: Volk und Wissen Volkseigener Verlag, 1977), 193–207.

Consequently, the caesura indicating the epoch of the socialist world system is now clearly set with the year 1945. The 1971 edition of the "Lehrbuch" covering the period from 1945 on appears in two volumes, underscoring the importance of the entire postwar time period.[40] Only since the 1990s did curricula in Western European states adopt this chronological division of the curriculum which allots a whole school year to the time after 1945.

Textbook Consultations across the Iron Curtain

International textbook revision was one of the means to overcome enemy images and stereotyped presentations of different cultures, nations and other social and political groups in educational material.[41] However, delegates from Eastern European countries attended only some meetings organized by UNESCO in the immediate postwar years; later on they were only rarely involved in such consultations. The many projects of comparative textbook analysis and revision conducted on bi- and multilateral levels in Europe did not cross the iron curtain during the "hot" phase of the cold war.[42] Only the period of détente brought a notable change. The first successful example was set with the German-Polish textbook consultations that started in 1972 and published joint recommendations in 1975. The results were publicly and controversially discussed in Germany and Poland, and are being researched till today.[43] In the wake of this work the West German Georg Eckert Institute established further textbook commissions with socialist coun-

40 *Geschichte. Lehrbuch für Klasse 10*, Teil 1 and Teil 2 (Berlin: Volk und Wissen Volkseigener Verlag, 1971).

41 Falk Pingel, *UNESCO Guidebook on Textbook Research and Textbook Revision*, 2nd rev. and updated ed., (Paris; Braunschweig: UNESCO; Georg Eckert Institute, 2010).

42 Otto-Ernst Schüddekopf, in collaboration with Edouar Bruley et al., *History Education and History Textbook Revision* (Strasbourg: Council for Cultural Co-operation of the Council of Europe, 1967); Marina Cattaruzza, and Sacha Zala, "Negotiated History?: Bilateral historical commissions in twentieth-century Europe," in:, *Contemporary History on Trial: Europe since 1989 and the role of the expert historian* eds., Harriet Jones, Kjell Östberg, and Nico Randeraad (Manchester: Manchester University Press, 2007), 123–143.

43 *Die deutsch-polnischen Schulbuchempfehlungen in der öffentlichen Diskussion der Bundesrepublik Deutschland* Dokumentation, ed. Wolfgang Jacobmeyer (Braunschweig: Georg-Eckert-Institut für internationale Schulbuchforschung, 1979); "The Recommendations of the UNESCO Commission of the Polish People's Republic and the Federal Republic of Germany Concerning History and Geography Schoolbooks," with an "Introduction" by Władiyslaw Markiewicz, in: *Polish Western Affairs*, Vol. ~~14~~ XIX (1978): 78–103.

tries. Whatever the actual effects on textbooks themselves may have been, these consultations contributed to establishing mutual contacts and reducing mistrust.

However, the most ambitious attempt at textbook revision, the consultations between the two superpowers, failed in the end. The U.S.-USSR consultations show the limits of textbook revision due to the ambiguous relation between academia, pedagogy and politics in a period of still prevailing politico-ideological differences. After initial reservations the U.S. State Department accepted the idea of textbook consultations in September 1973 because they conformed with the wanted "renewal of the official cultural and educational exchange program between the two countries."[44] It took three years of preparatory talks with representatives of the USSR to sign a program of exchanging relevant history and geography textbooks for the years 1977–1979. After several meetings and analyses of textbooks a joint report was filed. However, it was not approved. The U.S. government withdrew financial and organizational support for further joint meetings in 1980 because of the Soviet invasion of Afghanistan. But the U.S. promoter of the idea, Howard Mehlinger, made strong efforts to renew the work when political prospects would be more propitious. In fact, in November 1985, the U.S. government renewed the Cultural Exchange Program and recommended the continuation of the joint textbook study. In spite of financial constraints during the Reagan administration, new textbooks could be exchanged and analyzed. Supported by an atmosphere of perestroika, a last meeting took place on November 1987 where Soviet scholars announced that their portrayal of the USA would change in future. U.S. participants also admitted that "American scholarship was greatly affected by the Cold War, resulting in an emphasis upon totalitarianism ...". Since they had almost no access to sources in the USSR, textbook images were "heavily influenced by émigré Soviet citizens and fundamentalist religious groups that are often very hostile to the Soviet Union."[45] Because of the political changes already under way, the participants decided that it did not make sense to publish the analyses of the old books. Rather, scholarly articles should be written to analyze the process of the consultations. In his unofficial

---

44 Howard D. Mehlinger, *School Textbooks: Weapons for the Cold War. A Report of the US/USSR Textbook Study Project (1977–1989)*, Vol. 2, copied typescript (1992) [Georg Eckert Institute, Library], 235–252.

45 Carlson, *Legitimation and Delegitimation*, 1989, 48. shares this critique stating that textbook authors justify official and wide spread anti-Communism in the general public and condemn the aggressive character of the USSR.

type-written report Mehlinger concluded: "The Project had very little direct influence on textbook content."[46]

These two examples of textbook consultations show that when the political situation was conducive, East-West textbooks talks were possible and could lead to joint results. In case of the Soviet-American negotiations, governmental approval was needed on both sides to start consultations. Furthermore, the work of the joint group was dependent on governmental financial support so that the political frame decided, in the end, on the success and failure of the whole project. Because of the political restrictions that had hindered their work, the participants concluded in their last meeting that, taking advantage of the new political freedom and open borders, further talks between scholars and textbook authors would no longer need governmental approval. They envisaged future textbook consultations as being organized by academic institutions or NGOs – a model which became widespread after 1990. But this approach has had, surprisingly, no effect on the U.S.-Russian textbook issue so far.

The End of the Cold War

The last edition of the East German history textbook which appeared in 1988 reflected the changes brought about with perestroika, if only to a limited extent. In no way did the authors foresee the total break down of Soviet rule and, as one of its consequences, the end of the East German state.[47] Surprisingly, this edition adopts "Western" terminology and uses the term "Cold War." However, the term does not denote a confrontation between two opposing powers but refers exclusively to the "imperialistic Cold War policy" of the USA. The concept is not explained further and does not indicate any change in interpretation.[48] Also the Berlin Blockade is mentioned in the 1988 edition of the GDR history book for the first time. Apparently, GDR authors did not dare deal with it in former editions, because the Blockade obviously increased tensions and led to a political defeat as

---

46 Ibid; Howard D. Mehlinger, "International Textbook Revision: examples from the United States," in: *Internationale Schulbuchforschung*, Vol. 7 (1985): 287–298; and Mehlinger, *Schoolbooks as Weapons*, 285.

47 Friedemann Neuhaus, *Geschichte im Umbruch: Geschichtspolitik, Geschichtsunterricht und Geschichtsbewußtsein in der DDR und den neuen Bundesländern 1983–1993* (Frankfurt: Peter Lang Verlag, 1998).

48 *Geschichte. Lehrbuch für Klasse 10* (1988) Berlin: Volk und Wissen Volkseigener Verlag, 129.

Stalin finally had to give in. Now this problem could no longer be concealed from East German pupils.[49]

The representation of the East-West relationship did not change much in the first half of the 1990s. The First World War and the Russian Revolution still constituted the decisive caesura between the past that has gone and contemporary history in most curricula. Only since the turn of the century, the curricula experts and textbook authors moved the caesura forward to 1945 or even 1990 when a new global age is said to have begun. The opening of the Berlin Wall now stands as a symbol for this new era and many textbooks of almost all European countries contain illustrations of this event.[50]

Nonetheless, in recent textbooks the old division continues to shape representations of the world in the long postwar period from 1945 to 1990. The binational German-French textbook titles its respective chapter "Europe in a Bipolar World (1949–1989)" and includes a conventional map with contrasting colors.[51] Also, descriptions of the Cold War crises, the superpowers' political and social systems as well as the division of Europe mirror the well-known structure of German and French books of the 1980s. The East-West conflict has become a leading term again, covering the whole postwar era which is divided into two or three phases, such as the "Cold War and Coexistence" or The Cold War proper (1945/48 – mid 1960s), détente (mid 1960s – mid 1980s), and reform and change (second half of the 1980s).[52] In addition arguments already developed in textbooks of previous periods are repeated and become almost ubiquitous: "Mutual mistrust" led to a protracted conflict between the two superpowers. The "Cold War ... informed world politics for about 40 years." However, the concept is still regarded as a "difficult" concept, needing further explanation. *Histoire/Géographie* poses the question: "What is the Cold War?" The answer refers to the action-reaction scheme

---

49 Morand, *Questions on the Comparative Method*, 2011, 134.

50 Daniela Bender et al., *Geschichte und Geschehen*, Sekundarstufe I, Vol. 4 (Leipzig: Ernst Klett Schulbuchverlag, 2005). and 2006 edition; Allan Tood, *Democracies and Dictatorships. Europe and the World 1919–1989* (Cambridge: Cambridge University Press, 2001).and Christian Bouvet, and Jean-Michel Lambin eds., *Histoire, Géographie-3e: Le monde d'aujourd'hui* (Paris: Hachette Education, 1999).

51 Guillaume Le Quintrec and Peter Geiss, *Histoire/Geschichte. Europa und die Welt seit 1945. Deutsch-französisches Geschichtsbuch Gymnasiale Oberstufe* , (Leipzig: Ernst Klett Schulbuchverlage, 2006) [*L'Europe et le monde depuis 1945*. Paris: Nathan], 64–65.

52 Bouvet and Lambin, *Histoire: Géographie*, 1999, 158, similarly Bergmann et al., *Geschichte und Geschehen*, 1997, 134.

and the calculation of limited risks. Each side multiplied provocations against the other side but tried to avoid open war.[53]

The action-reaction scheme has become the leading explanatory paradigm. No longer is one side right and the other wrong, but both argue legitimately from within their own system of values. This kind of argumentation is most clearly deployed in English history textbooks. Walsh confronts U.S. and Soviet arguments during the Cuban Missile Crisis under the heading "Why was Cuba so important?" – for both sides. Pupils are encouraged to give "one reason why the USA disliked Castro's government," "one reason why Khrushchev put nuclear missiles in Cuba," and "one reason why the USA objected." Interestingly, the positions of the Soviet Union and Cuba are personalized and represented by Khrushchev and Castro respectively whereas Kennedy's role is not mentioned as if U.S. public opinion were unanimous on the issue: "The USA was furious. It wanted to get rid of Castro quickly."[54] Clare et al. expressly ask "How close to war was the world in the 1960s?" and offer a surprising answer. Refering to latest research they state that it is some historians' "view of the Cold War, neither side had a single fixed agenda. Instead leaders stumbled through events. Often they did not fully understand what was going on: they were just trying to ‚come out on top'."[55]

Keeping equidistance from both systems is, however, not an unproblematic concept. After unification a debate arose in Germany whether presenting the GDR as a dictatorship which controlled every aspect of daily life would not violate the feelings of former GDR citizens. Textbook authors tried to take into account both aspects. On the one hand, they describe the totalitarian system and the role of the State Security Service (Stasi), on the other hand, they use interviews to show ways of adaptation to the system and the relative security most citizens enjoyed as long as they did not openly criticize it. [56]

French textbooks divide the world into three main areas: The West, the East and Europe. The East-West opposition has its roots in the Cold War era; due to the intensification of integration "Europe" now features as a separate politico-economic dimension which is treated in a chapter of its own which describes Europe as a supra-national entity. As the "West" is identified with the USA, the

53 *Geschichte und Geschehen* argues similarly in its 1997 and 2005 editions.
54 Walsh, *Essential Modern World History*, 2002, 182.
55 Clare et al., *GCSE History. AQA B Modern World History*, 2009, 89.
56 Ulrich Arnswald, Ulrich Bongertmann, and Ulrich Mählert ed., *DDR-Geschichte im Unterricht: Schulbuchanalyse, Schülerbefragung, Modellcurriculum* (Berlin: Metropol Verlag, 2006); Interview mit Hilke Günther-Arndt über den Wettbewerb "Vierzig Jahre deutsche Teilung – Zehn Jahre Mauerfall. Die Geschichte beider deutscher Staaten im Schulbuch" in: *Internationale Schulbuchforschung/International Textbook Research*, Vol. 22 (2000): 491–506.

"East" with Russia and "Europe" with the EU, the treatment of other Eastern European countries is reduced to only a few states that are located beyond the Eastern borders of the EU.[57] Moreover, decolonization and "third world countries" are taken into account in separate chapters. Already in the books of the 1970s, the chapter on the East-West confrontation is followed by a chapter dealing with "Asia and Africa since 1945."[58] Although the almost exclusive division of the world into these three or four entities seems to be a particular French feature, textbooks of other European countries often only deal with the USA and Russia in greater detail. Also, Europe is mostly understood as the European Union and identified with Western civilization. The expanded post-Maastricht EU-Europe is seen in contrast to a shrunken East, comprised of "Russian speaking Europe" such as Russia, Belorussia, Ukraine (and Moldova).[59]

The end of the East-West conflict has generated a subtler form of an East-West divide. No longer do the ideological differences divide the continent but a smaller East seems still to be different from an expanded West. It is represented as less democratic than the EU and more different in cultural traditions from the EU than the European states differ among themselves. Before the dissolution of the Soviet Union, Eastern Europe was equated with the members of the Warsaw Pact, and now it is defined as a negative entity: non-EU countries east of the EU. This reconfiguration has restored an older meaning to Eastern Europe as a geopolitical marker of difference.[60]

Empirical observations show that the division of the past still shapes the minds of pupils to a certain extent. Youngsters think that the East has always been somewhat detached from the West in terms of politics, economic development and cultural achievements. When a German secondary teacher asked pupils to draw a map of Europe, most depictions showed the contours of the continent vaguely but recognizably with most of the countries indicated. However, the Eastern European states were located far further East of Germany than one would have expected. One drawing placed even a large blank space between Poland and the Baltic States, Belorussia and Russia. The blank space certainly represents not a geographical, but a cultural lacuna and marks a geopolitical dis-

57 Morand, "Questions on the Comparative Method," 2011. See also *Histoire: Géographie*, 2004 and 2007 editions.

58 Bonifacio and Michaud, *1789–1970. L'époque contemporaine*, 1972 and 1976 editions, 358.

59 This finding is corroborated by Dmitrii Sidirov, "Visualizing the Former Cold War 'Other': Images of Eastern Europe in World Regional Geography Textbooks of the United States," in: *JEMMS*, Vol. 1 (Spring 2009): 44 f.

60 Larry Wolff, *Inventing Eastern Europe: The map of civilization in the mind of the enlightenment* (New York: Routledge, 1994).

tance of Western to Eastern Europe. To bridge this gap the teacher recommends in her summary: "The extension, completion and correction of the spatial image of Eastern Europe should be a first step towards creating a comprehensive representation of Europe in pupils' minds."[61]

61 Meike Schniotalle, *Räumliche Schülervorstellungen von Europa* (Berlin: TENEA Verlag für Medien, 2003), 255.

Paul Bleton

Machiavelli's Angels Hiding in Plain Sight: Media Culture and French Spy Fiction of the Cold War

Centripetal and globalizing forces shifted French pre-World War Two espionage fiction away from nationalism and towards the protection of the Western block. It developed within an ideological ground: a rightist core made of anti-Communism, racism, radical conservatism, and elitism. It expressed itself through heroes representing those values, elite fighters, alpha males, master spies, who seemed to inherit emblems of nobility, and were confident enough to assume that they lived in a natural order of society, which did not require explicit assessment; they showed complacence toward ex-colonial empire and smugness toward non-white people, and were less at war with communist theory than with the KGB's perverse agenda.

From a narrative point of view, paperback espionage fiction had inherited Manichaeism from popular literature, and two main types of plot from adjacent or previous genres: *adventure* (rush and pursuit), often in exotic places, and *investigation* (in the wake of a mystery). The former fitted perfectly the anti-communist program and the latter easily converted topical contemporary news as well as old ideological themes into fiction.[1]

Adventure: In *Agitation clandestine,*[2] a succession of unfortunate accidents alert a KGB spy ring in Cuba. Anton Blasick decides to eliminate whoever may put the ring in jeopardy. A killing game will ensue fought by him and his nemesis, the French agent Philippe Larsan, who naturally will win in the end.

Investigation: In *OSS 117 n'est pas aveugle,*[3] in order to understand the successive disappearances of three scientists working in a military facility, OSS (Office of Strategic Services) agent 117 assumes a false identity, works his way into the Russian-sponsored plot, thinks he has found a culprit only to discover that he has been out-maneuvered by the real traitor. Thanks to a doctored prestidigitation show, he succeeds in unmasking the real traitor.

---

1 For instance, notwithstanding his age, a reader of André Favières', *Menace asiatique,* La Loupe Espionage 64 (Lyon: Jacquier,1958); Gilles Morris-Dumoulin's, *Péril jaune sur la Place rouge*, Jean Bruce 63 (Paris: Presses de la Cité, 1960); or John Hery's, *La Guerre des jonques*, Espionnage 109 (Paris: Presses noires, 1967). would not have failed to recognize the ancient Yellow Peril ideologem, dating back to Kaiser Wilhelm II, which already had been extensively in use in French popular literature.

2 Michel Carnal, *Agitation clandestine,* Un Mystère. Jean Bruce 56 (Paris: Presses de la Cité, 1960).

3 Jean Bruce, *OSS 117 n'est pas aveugle*, Un Mystère, 320 (Paris: Presses de la Cité, 1957).

DOI 10.1515/9783110496178-007

In order to secure its readership's loyalty, the genre had to rely on diversity as well. It was to be found especially in the way each book boasted about being related to the true secret Cold War. For most, it was only an allusive background, others were technical footnote-ridden, or instilled with punctual verisimilitudes trying to establish links between fiction and actual episodes of the Cold War,

---

Opérations combinées[4] uses information on US Air Force spy-balloons. But the narrative is parsimonious on them, and gives them only a peripheral incidence. The plot, after American agents have swiftly realized that the intelligence they get from those balloons is actually controlled by the Soviets, concentrates on unmasking the Russian spy ring which had succeeded in countering their technology.

---

or conveyed to their readers the impression of having been sternly and extensively researched (e.g. Claude Rank) – in any case, lacking the necessary factual information, the reader would only be able to speculate on the appropriateness of the writer's knowledge and the reality of the secret war. In a totally different direction, some novels would play popular intertextual games.

Karacho Karachi[5] offers a dark and unusual variation on the old melodrama theme of the baby kidnapping. In Pakistan, which is courted by Americans and British to install a missile base in order to contain China's menace, information has leaked from secret meetings. Two hundred pages later, Rambert, a nato counter-spy, will unmask an improbable traitor: the trisomic son of Mouhrad Khan, the Pakistan officer representing his country in those negotiations. Actually, the beloved son was not Mouhrad Khan's but a Chinese midget agent surgically accommodated to delude the poor father – after the trisomic son had been discreetly disposed of.

On another level, some writers thought the dark universe of espionage should be taken with a grain of humorous salt (e.g. Charles Exbrayat).

Thus French spy fiction does not depart much from its British and American counterparts. Intimately linked to the Cold War, isn't it a case of media culture shaping national and social homogeneity, spy versus spy as riffs on the anti-communist program? Some of the studies dedicated to the genre seem to agree.[6] Nevertheless, instead of elaborating on such a disappointing similarity for

---

4 G. Livandert [Jean Libert and Gaston Van den Panhuyse], *Opérations combinées*. Espionnage, No. 260 (Paris: Fleuve noir, 1960).

5 Jean Crain, *Karacho, Karachi*, Espionnage, No. 20 (Paris: Presses noires, 1964).

6 Erik Neveu, *L'Idéologie dans le roman d'espionnage* (Paris: Presses de la Fondation nationale des sciences politiques, 1985); Paul Bleton, *Les Anges de Machiavel. Essai sur l'espionnage*, Etudes paralittéraires (Québec: Nuit blanche éditeur, 1994).

English-speaking readers, this essay will develop a two-pronged argument which will start from the assumption that Cold War anti-Communism was at the core of the French espionage fiction. First, instead of simply describing Cold War themes from the genre, it will focus on the obvious relationship between the Cold War and the genre from the composite point of view that can be culled from the bulk of espionage fiction – using an infra-thematic approach, so to speak. Building up a cultural history from a material ground and the history of cultural industries, it will attempt to reveal the underlying complexity of the situation.

Second, whatever the centrality of anti-Communist politics may have been, the success of spy fiction itself suggests a link to another type of consideration: the relevance of such stories for their public. How did fiction set in such an esoteric professional *milieu*, fighting secret battles involving enigmatic state apparatuses, about disquieting, apocalyptic, but fuzzy objectives come to catch the public fancy, especially within a very *exoteric* mass culture? This essay will contend that, as powerful as the centripetal and globalizing forces which built Western bilateral representations of the Cold War around a political, anti-Communist core may have been, they could not paper over new and inherited ideological differences, accentuated by their own centrifugal impetus, by their own heterogeneous vehicles (semiotic, generic, discursive...), and by their own cultural configurations, each of them not only complex, but also evolving.

The Cold War as Cultural Industry

The publishing industry of popular literature emerging from the Second World War was profoundly different from the one that existed before. Even though a few pre-war players survived, the spirit of the time had drastically changed, since French pop culture had elected America as a possible cultural model: this was the driving force behind the development of pop genres aimed at male readers (especially science fiction, crime thrillers, and espionage). In that general context, and since spy thrillers were seldom published *hors-collection*, a quick survey shows a massive production in the 20 first years of the period. Almost immediately, the paperback format asserted itself, and even though provincial publishers could try their luck for a time, the Parisian gravitational center rapidly took command of the industry. Here is a chronology of the larger *collections*, stating the quantity of respective titles.[7]

7 The word *collection* may be a *faux-ami*. In French, and in this paper, it will mean an ensemble of books that their publisher regroups around a common generic characteristic very obviously

Table 1: Important collections

chronological rank	collections	number of titles
1.	Fleuve noir, Espionnage 1951 to 1987	1904 titles
2.	L'Arabesque Espionnage 1954 to 1970	622 titles
3.	Librairie des Champs-Elysees, Le Masque, Dossiers secrets 1956 to 1957	19 titles
	Le Masque, Roman d'Espionnage 1957 to 1961	33 titles
	Le Masque, Espionnage 1961 to 1963	19 titles
	Le Masque, Espionnage 1962 to 1964	15 titles
	Le Masque, Service Secret 1964 to 1965	37 titles
4.	Atlantic (Grand Damier) Top Secret 1955 to 1962 198 titles	
5.	Les Elfes, Top Secret 1963	17 titles
6.	Galic, Carnets des services secrets 1961 to 1964 65 titles	
	Contre-espionage 1961 to 1962	21 titles
7.	Presses noires, espionnage 1964 to 1970	176 titles
8.	Euredif Espionnage 1969 to 1972	33 titles
9.	Presses Internationales, Jet Espionnage 1959 to 1965 73 titles	
	Choc Espionnage 1962 to 1963	23 titles
	Inter-Espionnage 1964 to 1971	210 titles
	Inter-Choc Espionnage 1964 to 1965	19 titles
10.	Fayard, L'aventure de notre temps 1956 to 1965	43 titles
11.	Flammarion, Agent secret 1964 to 1966	31 titles

L'Aventure de notre temps (Fayard) featured only one author, Pierre Nord, who was already a well-known espionage writer in the 1930's, and had himself been a practitioner of the *Spionspiel.* Le Masque (Librairie des Champs-Élysées), which published spy fiction before World War Two only haphazardly, decided to create specialized espionage *collection* lines in successive guises. It harbored mostly French writers, often featuring female heroes and humor. For their part, it is only progressively that les Presses de la Cité initiated a distinct espionage *collection*, responding to the huge success of Jean Bruce's series OSS 117 – which sold over 24 million copies for its combined 87 titles.[8] The most enduring of all these collections, *Espionnage* (Fleuve noir), published 1.904 titles. They featured recurring

stated for the reader's sake, with a straightforward name of the collection on the cover, homogeneity of the format, and of the art cover style.

8 After Bruce's death, OSS 117 was continued: 143 volumes (1966–1985) signed J. Bruce (J. for Josette, Bruce's wife), and 24 (1987–92) by their children François and Martine.

heroes who defended western values every week, frequently against malevolent Soviet spies, double agents, and naïve or ideological nationals.[9]

At the other end of the spectrum, here is a chronology of the small (and minuscule) *collections*:

Table 2: Small collections

chronological rank	collections	number of titles
1.	Etoile, série Choc 1949 to 1959	6 titles
2.	Champ de Mars, Moulin noir	18 titles
3.	C.P. E. Agent spécial 1952 to 1953	13 titles
	Guerre secrète 1955	4 titles
	Le roman d'espionnage 1955	8 titles
4.	Le trottoir, Espions et agents secrets 1952 to 1954	25 titles
5,	Flamme d'or, Missions secrètes 1952 to 1953	20 titles
6.	Roger Seban, Espionnage-Aventures Police 1953 to 1958	18 titles
7.	Nouvelles Presses Mondiales, Contre-espionnage 1954 to 1955	5 titles
8.	La Seine, Espions 1955 to 1956	8 titles
	Agents secret contre X 1956	8 titles
9.	Thill, Espionnage 1956	4 titles
	Stop Espionnage	4 titles
	Le Loup	4 titles
10.	Marcel Dauchy, Espionnage/Rouge et Noir 1957	4 titles
11.	Gerfaut, Chut espionage 1957 to 1959	8 titles
	Espionnage 1963 to 1964	8 titles
	Espionnate 1967 to 1969	30 titles
12.	Le Cobra 1959 to 1960	6 titles

In between them stood eclectic *collections* from a generic point of view which published spy thrillers but also crime thrillers, mysteries, or suspense novels.[10] Largely dedicated to American crime thrillers in translation, the Série noire nevertheless published a handful of French spy fiction. However, the impression made by Antoine L. Dominique, the first of these *Série noire* French authors of spy fiction, was quite deep, with his Gorille series going to 50 titles between 1954

9 Jean-Pierre Conty's *Mr. Suzuki*, Adam Saint-Moore's Face d'Ange, M.G. Braun's Alex Glenne, Alain Page's Calone, Richard Caron's TTX 75, Marc Revest's Bonder, Pierre Courcel's le Délégué, F. H. Ribes' Gérard Lecomte KB-09, Marc Arno's Kristian Fowey

10 La Chouette (Ditis), la Série noire (Gallimard), and Un Mystère (Presses de la Cité).

and 1961.[11] At les Presses de la Cité, even though its *collection Un Mystère* was mainly dedicated to American and British translations and mixed genres, this editor translated only a handful of foreign spy novels,[12] relying for this genre on French authors, sometimes under assumed Anglo-Saxon signatures.[13] The flag *espionnage* printed on the cover appeared only erratically at first, before getting used more consistently to reflect the actual content. In order to win its autonomy, a genre so closely related to the crime thriller had to build its own distinct identity, and thus rely on repetition (recurring heroes, cover art, thematic and stylistic choices, recognizable signatures, etc.).

Against *collections* as a commercial and cultural background which strongly and in a centripetal manner promoted generic conventions, individual books might get singled out by four modes of cultural distinction: prizes as recognition by the industry, translations as recognition by foreign cultures, best-seller status as recognition by the readership, and adaptations as recognition by other media. If espionage fiction did not rely much on prizes and was not often translated,[14] it is worth noticing that even in the Fleuve noir *collection*, four *séries* were distinctly out-selling the other ones: Gaunce, the Rank's polycephalic team, Coplan, and l'Agent spécial. But more importantly, when compared to the situation in the culture industries since the fall of the Berlin wall, in which espionage fiction seems to warrant only lackluster media integration, French cinema owed much to the adaptation of novels, as shown here against the total quantity of spy movies:

Table 3: Spy Films 1950–1962

1950–1962	1950	1951	1955	1956	1957	1958	1959	1960	1961	1962
Quantity	1	2	2	3	3	2	4	1	2	1
adaptations	1	2	2	2	3	2	4		1	1

11 This series was adapted to the silver screen three times, twice by Bernard Borderie and once by Maurice Labro. See, *Le Gorille vous salue bien*, directed by Bernard Borderie (1958; Les Films Raoul Ploquin); *La Valse du Gorille*, directed by Bernard Borderie (1959; Les Films Raoul Ploquin); *Le Gorille a mordu l'archevêque* , directed by Maurice Labro (1962 Gaumont). *Le Gorille* was also a TV 13-episode series in 1990.

12 Such as Peter Cheyney's.

13 Jean Bruce, Jean-Pierre Conty, G. Morris, Michel Lebrun, Alain Yaouanc, Michel Carnal.

14 Nevertheless Jean Bruce has been translated into 17 languages.

The percentage with an anti-Communist plot was surprisingly low, though, the actual competing camp(s) received often only a fuzzy definition, and the focus of the narrative was less Manichean anti-Soviet than anticipated.

While in *Action immédiate*[15] the final recipient of the stolen prototype of a new war plane and of the special alloy designed for it may be a Soviet country, this does not prevent Coplan from concentrating first on Lindbaum's gang and not on the KGB. In a more complicated fashion *La Valse du Gorille*[16] sets le Gorille in an awkward position, while he is trying to deliver le Vieux, his boss, from Lohn's hands (this head of the German secret service wanted to sell the pacifist professor Kelbel's invention on missiles to the highest bidder). He will have to alternatively fight and support Ted Parker, a discreet British agent, and Boris Armazian, his Soviet counterpart. And in Georges Lautner's comedy *L'Œil du Monocle,*[17] the British and Soviet spies after Hektor Schlumpf whose underwater expedition in Corsica seeks to recuperate German gold and documents dating back to 1944, ignore that he has an agreement with le Monocle who knows that the German would assuredly find documents embarrassing for the ex-Allies.

It actually took a Czech book in translation to inspire Henri-Georges Clouzot *Les Espions,*[18] a more classical Cold War story, and even then the Manichean West vs. Soviet battle was secondary to another confrontation of specialists vs. non-specialists.

Dr. Malic is paid to hide Alex, an agent, whose arrival in Malic's psychiatric clinic triggers lots of spying from two competing teams led by Kaminsky and Cooper. In a heavy and disquieting atmosphere, Malic mistakenly thinks he recognizes in Alex the inventor of a terrible atomic weapon, Vogel, and tries to divert the spies' attention in order to give the scientist a chance to escape. Such an unpredictable move by an amateur throws Colonel Howard's secret diversion plan: the real Vogel will be killed, and, disgusted, Malic will not even be able to denounce the evil spies' scheme to the police.

Finally, in the mediascape of the 1950s, radio, TV and comics were not real factors in the development of the genre. Original espionage comic strips[19] were rare, such as *L'Affaire Tournesol* (1956) by Hergé. Such a thinly veiled commentary on the Cold War seems not to have been fit for kids. But newspaper comics aimed at an adult readership featured spies only infrequently as well such as adaptation of

15 *Action immediate*, directed by Maurice Labro (1957; Gaumont).

16 *La Valse du Gorille*, directed by Bernard Borderie (1959; Les Films Raoul Ploquin).

17 *L'Œil du Monocle*, directed by Georges Lautner (1961; Les Films Borderie).

18 *Les Espions*, directed by Henri-Georges Clouzot (1957; Filmsonor).

19 BD (*bande dessinée*) will be used here instead of comics when applied to the Franco-Belgian format of the *album*.

three World War Two novels by Pierre Nord. More to the point, best-selling author Jean Bruce hosted a radio program on Europe 1 in 1962, in which he presented an OSS 117 *feuilleton* of the week with the actor playing the role of Hubert Bonnisseur de la Bath. But Bruce died in a car accident the following year. And on TV, the first recurring heroes appeared in small numbers and rather late in a 10-episode *Commandant X* (1962–1965) series by Jacques Antériou and Guillaume Hanoteau. Espionage was thus a matter for the novel and the cinema, the former topping the latter.

Crisis and Reconfiguration

With a box office grossing more than US $4,772,000 in France (almost five times its cost), *James Bond contre Dr. No* (1962) launched the hero's career on the silver screen. With its ups and downs, 007 not only reigned the spy cinema until the end of the Soviet block and beyond, but has been a factor in the evolution of the cultural industry as well. The James Bond series set off continental co-productions in which France participated, sometimes direct spoofs or imitations. From one to four a year, the number of espionage films jumped during the spy craze of 1963–67. It may come as a surprise that at the onset of *détente* the percentage of films dealing directly with a Cold War subject increased rapidly:

Table 4: Spy Films 1963–1967

	1963	1964	1965	1966	1967
Quantity	5	10	17	14	7
adaptation	5	2	5	9	3
novelization		2			
Cold War	5	3	3	7	4

But from a content point of view, the cinema of the spy craze seemed to be quite conservative, with all films falling either into the adventure or the comedy categories. Contrary to le Monocle, OSS 117 came back twice but with two separate directors, and two different actors. Neither Claude Rank nor Ernie Clerk, both serial writers, would be solicited by spy cinema more than once in that period, while Lino Ventura and Roger Hanin of le Gorille fame kept on spying on the silver screen, and Brigitte Bardot made her humorous début in the genre.[20]

20 In *Une Ravissante idiote*, directed by Edouard Molinaro (1963; Flora Film).

More importantly, the reduced readership of espionage novels led to a new spyscape. Readership in general was in decline, and part of the remaining readers left spy fiction behind, hooked by another type of war which was not secret. As if entering the post-colonial era, French pop culture went back to retrospective military fiction, when three major war *collections* cropped up in the middle of the spy craze. By the 1970s, small espionage *collections* had all disappeared, giving an opportunity to new or renewed players, but to no avail.[21] After the very slow emergence of its *collection* Espionnage, Presses de la Cité reacted to the changing context with a new *collection*, Espiorama, in which authors received tighter specifications, without much success.[22] Relying on more than one approach, Fleuve noir fared much better. To keep up with the spirit of the times, they asked their writers to address more leftist concerns. They also adopted an explicit identification on the covers of novels of their top series[23] and of new ones.[24] But with the exception of G.J. Arnaud, more critical of US international politics since the Chilean 1973 coup, these rightist writers failed to convince most readers, who did not follow them. The *collection* could not renew its inspiration, and finally the publisher had to throw in the towel in 1987.

Initially, Plon had built his *collection* Espionnage to harbor James Bond and six French series, but the success of Gérard de Villier's SAS led the publisher to reengineer that concept. 007 went his separate way, while Espionnage kept the French series and SAS gained its autonomy. The de Villiers' signature and his hero's very recognizable logo got through a few commercial reconfigurations, unchanged. SAS had not invented such a *série-collection*[25] but its success prompted other publishers to emulate the formula.[26] The series was translated into German, Russian, Turkish, and Japanese, and inspired a couple of films, as well as parodies, and a few comic books and strips. *Son Altesse Sérénissime* (His

---

21 Espionnage (Presses noires) tried a change in its appearance and became Espionnage (Eurédif), unsuccessfully. Série noire remained a multigeneric collection but at the end of the 1960s its espionage inspiration shifted from le Gorille to much more diverse authors: André Gex, Jean Delion, the sad and uninspired end of Jean Bommard's career, the unusual and skeptic pessimism of Francis Ryck's novels, etc.

22 It produced only 38 titles in 1971–1973.

23 Serge Laforest's "Gaunce et Tamara," Paul Kenny's "Francis Coplan" (and later "FX18," "k," "Paul Kenny"), Claude Rank's confusing mix "Combat de l'ombre," "Force M," "Série Force M," "Le monde en marche," "Priorité rouge," and others.

24 From unsuccessful ones (2 volumes Robert Travis' Lieutenant ZAC, 1996) to the relative success of the burlesque Espiomatic (102 volumes, by Vic Saint-Val alias Gilles Morris-Dumoulin, 1970–1979), through two James Bond series (13 volumes, 1979–82, then 12, 1996–1997).

25 A collection featuring only one reccurring hero.

26 It did not drive them very far, though.

Most Serene Highness), Malko Linge is an authentic Austrian prince, short on cash and working freelance for the CIA. SAS started defending the Western world in 1965 and was still at it just before his death in 2013. His creator, Gérard de Villiers, who lived until 83, was a prolific survivor of the genre: 200 paperback titles at the regular rate of 5 a year, each selling at an average of 200 000 copies. At least until the fall of the Berlin wall, French espionage fiction had restricted its new core to the single SAS *série-collection.*

While Non-serial literature may have taken possession of the genre slightly more often than before, the Cold War was only a very occasional theme, except for Vladimir Volkoff.[27] Beyond its impeccable style, *Le Retournement* (1979) struck a chord[28] thanks to its hero's status of cultural ambassador: his apparent advanced technical knowledge of secret warfare, his Russian-French biculturalism which conveyed credibility for the spy psyche of its heroes, and its strong mystical inspiration that gave an unusual and convincing religious twist to a standard *fabula*[29] – the title alluded to both espionage and religion. Comparable elements would be found in *Le Montage* (1982), which was very successful as well,[30] and which dealt with disinformation.[31]

If one considers the genre in a systemic perspective, it nonetheless becomes clear that espionage was abandoned to media culture, and, inside media culture, that paperback *collections* and cinema were clearly more responsive to espionage themes than comics or TV. Obviously, Artima's politics of adaptation had more to do with a business decision (extend the sales to non-book readers) than with

---

27 Under the pen-name Lieutenant X, Volkoff authored 40 juvenile novels from 1965 to 1986, in which Langelot [the Cherub], a young, facetious and yet staunchly patriotic second lieutenant working for the Service national d'information fonctionnelle (SNIF!), in competition with the (real) DST [Direction de la Surveillance du Territoire], is regularly pitted against current foes of the French secret services at the time. Thus part of the series dealt with Cold War themes.

28 The book sold more than 100,000 copies in France, and was translated into Spanish, Finnish, Portuguese, Italian, Swedish, German, Japanese, and English. Volkoff was awarded the Prix Chateaubriand, which is awarded to history books.

29 A *fabula* is a type of plots that readers recognize as typical, and that genres have elected to be a standard. One fiction may be exemplary for each *fabula.*

30 Translated into Italian, Dutch, Spanish, German, Swedish, English, Japanese, Polish, Russian, and Serbian. Volkoff was awarded the Grand Prix du roman de l'Académie française.

31 It was based on a suggestion by Alexandre de Marenches. Chosen by President Georges Pompidou, de Marenches had just tended his resignation at the head of the SDECE [Service de Documentation Extérieure et de Contre-Espionnage] to the new socialist president, François Mitterand.

an aesthetic choice. Cold War comics remained scarce, although at the end of the period *Soviet Zigzag*[32] gave an interesting new twist to the *Spionspiel* universe.

On TV not only the two simplistic models American espionage series (quasi-westerns[33] and super-heroes) but series such as the quasi-documentary and McCarthyite style of *I Led Three Lives* (1953–1956) as well were absent from French screens at the onset of TV's popularity,[34] and would have to share space with British ones when the spy craze reached the medium.[35] Starting its broadcast on the Deuxième chaîne de l'ORTF in 1967, the formula "humor plus soft hedonism plus gadgets" was typical of the 105-episode *Des agents très spéciaux*[36] and the 161-episode *Chapeau melon et botte de cuir.*[37] One cannot say that it was the formula "stern professionalism and gadgets" of the 171-episode *Mission Impossible* (Bruce Geller) that was emulated by a much shorter series in 1968,[38] nor that it was the formula "spoof of gadgets and professionalism" of the 138-episode *Max la Menace*[39] which inspired the humorous 13-episode *Espionne et tais-toi.*[40] And the six-episode *Coplan*[41] was a derivative of a successful paperback series by Paul Kenny. Espionage missed the opportunity to accompany the continuous surge of TV which was gradually taking the place of reading in the popular cultural practices.

Cinema took quite another road in keeping more regularly in touch with espionage. Adaptation remained important in the post-spy craze films and Cold War themes surfaced only occasionally:

32 Marc Barcelo (sc.) & Jean-Louis Tripp (ill.), *Soviet Zigzag*, "Une aventure de Jacques Gallard." (Toulouse: Milan, 1986).
33 007 may have been a huge success and become a model because he re-established a clear Manichaean narrative instead of the hues of grey world of double agents and indirect strategies.
34 The number of TV sets in France had dramatically risen from 10,000 in 1952 to 1,300,000 in 1960.
35 Actually, the American series followed, and accentuated, the spycraze curb: 9 in the 1950's, 7 in the 1960's, and only 3 in the 1970's.
36 *The Man from U.N.C.L.E.*, created by Norman Felton and Sam Rolfe (1965; Arena Productions).
37 *The Avengers*, created by Sydney Newman and Leonard White (1961; ABC Television).
38 *Les Atomistes*, created by Léonard Keigel (1968; Office de Radiodiffusion Télévision Française). Première chaîne, 26-episodes.
39 *Get Smart*, created by Peter Segal (1968; Talen Associates). Deuxième chaîne de l'ORTF.
40 *Espionne et tais-toi*, created by Claude Boissol (1986; Antenne-2).
41 *Coplan* (1989: Antenne-2).

Table 5: Spy Films 1968–1989

1968–1989	1968	1968	1970	1971	1972	1973	1978	1979	1980	1981	1984	1989
Qantity	3	1	1	1	3	1	2	1	1	2	3	1
Adaptat.s	1	1	1		3		1	1	1	1	1	1
Cold War	3		1		2					1	2	

Adventure might have remained a strong root for spy cinema, yet some directors departed from that law of the genre and dared develop other types of plots. For example *Le Serpent*[42] dealt with a labyrinthine disinformation scheme by which a false Russian defector, with the help of western traitors inside European intelligence agencies, aims at putting NATO's self-confidence in jeopardy. Here Verneuil adapted a Pierre Nord novel, itself commenting on a story of real espionage. The talented Gilles Perrault wrote the script, and Verneuil added international stars to his French cast. The sophisticated plot of seeing through an intentional fog in order to disassemble a disinformation scheme was a descendant of the investigation. Thanks to Sun-Tzu readers who published fiction, or non-fiction, or both,[43] disinformation has slowly grown to become a standard *fabula*, and opened new narrative horizons: reality might be manipulated as well as fiction.

To sum up, such a survey of the French spy fiction as cultural industry reveals centripetal forces that gave the genre its transnational unity such as the anti-Communist Cold War core and the ideological Manichaeism. But two additional centrifugal forces were also important: The media (popular literature, movies, TV, comics) were not equally concerned with espionage, and the history of the genre went through two distinct phases. The cultural industry is crucial, since from the perspective of the genre itself, 1962 is less the beginning of *détente* than the beginning of 007, and 1966, the date of France's withdrawal from NATO, is less remarkable than 1969, the date of the disappearance of most of the major paperback espionage series. Indeed, the important political and military ups and downs of the Cold War should be reconsidered in the light of these mutations in media culture.

42 *Le Serpent*, directed by Henri Verneuil (1972; Les Films de la Boétie).
43 E.g. Pierre Nord, Vladimir Volkoff.

The spy fiction as philosophical investigation

What could have been the meaning of the popular media spy genre for French readers and movie-goers? The often invoked concept that it was meant to help the general public to understand international politics is only convincing to a certain extent, but not entirely. While Nord's, Rank's, or de Villiers' *œuvres* may aptly claim to have a pedagogical intent, it is vastly less true in the case of the bulk of run-of-the-mill productions. The success of a whole pop genre dealing with secret agents and esoteric themes is utterly baffling. How was the genre perceived by its public from the onset of the Cold War to the fall of the Berlin Wall, making it so relevant?

The metaphysical dualism of Manichaeism offered a common ground to anti-Communism and pop fiction. As a vehicle for Cold War *Zeitgeist*, and as a rhetorical tool spy fiction was a way to adapt archaic oppositions rooted in western myths to the present as represented by the news media. The KGB's malevolent intention offered a global and single cause to the *cui prodest?* of Western inquisitive secret agents who, in the face of inexplicable events could possibly believe in sheer coincidence.

But even this core of the genre needs to be contextualized. While the basic anti-Communism endured for a long time,[44] French spy fiction had acquired its basic function long ago, as the expression of national military angst after the French defeat at the hands of Prussia in the war of 1870 that peaked during the colonial race of the 1880's, then just before WW1, and again in the 1930s.[45] Moreover, the ideological theme of anti-Communism had already been represented in 1930s spy fiction.[46] More importantly, from a political standpoint, the return of espionage in post-World War Two French popular culture had different roots from the development of British and American spy fiction. The international political configuration may have been the same for these three Western countries, but France was the only one that had to deal with the rise of a communist party to political prominence at the end of the 1940s. It would not be too far-fetched to

44 As distant as they may have been from a literary perspective, P.-S. Nouvel's *Le Guêpier de Formose* and Volkoff's novels shared a common political standpoint. P.-S. Nouvel, *Le Guêpier de Formose*, Espionnage, No. 514 (Paris: l'Arabesque, 1968).

45 On the history of the genre before 1945. See Paul Bleton, *La Cristallisation de l'ombre. Les origines oubliées du roman d'espionnage sous la IIIe République* (Limoges: PULIM (Médiatextes), 2011).

46 For instance in novels as diverse as Charles Robert-Dumas, *Ceux du S.R. L'Idole de plomb*, (Paris: Fayard, 1935); Jean Mauclère, *Grete Adamsohn: Espionne*, La Guerre secrète (Paris: Baudinière 1938); or Jean Bommart, *Le Train blindé N°4* (Paris: Éditions de Flore, 1948).

suggest that the genre's comeback was a reaction to this ascendancy of the *Parti communiste français*. While they accepted the disarmament of their patriotic militias in 1944, Communists won more than 26% of the vote, gained 159 *députés* in the 1945 elections, and were thus the dominant political force in the country, participating in government until 1947 and the outbreak of war in Indochina. Although they decided to return to playing the electoral game in 1948, the quasi-insurrectional strike of 1947 and the Czech coup in 1948 resulted in an ideological fear dividing the French public: the internal and external communist threat.

The resurgence of spy fiction had its roots in the French ideological landscape of the late 1940s and particularly in a popular nationalist anti-Communism. After the black years of occupation and collaboration, that ideology could only find a diffuse political expression because the Fourth Republic's institutional framework led to governments situated in the middle of the political spectrum, composed of social democrats.[47] It would take the advent of a new constitution drawn in 1958 by General Charles de Gaulle in the Fifth Republic to arrive at a clear bipolarization. And it would take even longer until the elections of 1987 to see the emergence of the ultra-rightist *Front National*, which captured the bulk of popular nationalist anti-Communism.

Such a powerful centripetal attraction by the anti-Soviet core did not prevent lots of other themes from emerging: There were internal political plots, mafia or crime stories (which sometimes worked with the good guys but were more often manipulated or used as a cover), terrorist groups, rightist and Fourth Reich plots, mad scientists, illegal traffickers in weapons, diamonds, counterfeit currencies or drugs, private dealers in secret intelligence, etc. Although seemingly unrelated themes were often understood as metaphors of the Soviet threat, such a thematic distance needs to be placed in its generic context, perhaps somewhat questioning the validity of the metaphor theory.

A quick glance at spy films – approximately 36% of the 96 espionage films of the period 1950–1990 dealt with the Cold War – reveals that Soviet competition was quite unevenly distributed: roughly 30% was situated in the periods before 1963 and after 1968 and more than 40% during the spy craze of 1963–1968, i.e. the first phase of *détente*! At the end of the 1960s, paperback novels and films went even further revealing a three-pronged disenchantment with American methods, government claims to protect their citizens, and with the *Spionspiel* itself.

---

47 SFIO (Section Française de l'Internationale Ouvrière) and MRP (Mouvement Républicain Populaire).

In *OSS 117 prend des vacances,*[48] the very American OSS 117 is first the target of forces he does not understand – he is kidnapped and replaced by a double, he flees to Rio, then escapes several attempts on his life. But everything gets clearer when he realizes he will have to shield Cuba against perfidious maneuvers, not of the United States apparatus but of rightist American billionaires helped by a shady French character, who have a plan to eradicate all life on Cuba by using acids and insects.

Behind the growing disenchantment[49] lay a deeper mutation. Departing from patriotic stoicism, its original dominant philosophical inspiration, espionage was disconnected from its transcendent value, the *Patrie*. During the Cold War spies kept on deceiving, killing, suffering at the hands of their foes, living outside the law, but within an assumed context of the values of *professionalism*. Specialists of the negative, Machiavelli's angels were required to obey government orders, and, more radically to follow the lethal rules of their trade. Fiction rewarded them in a more immanent fashion, allowing them well-earned sexual favors.

For the Benthamian version of hedonistic Utilitarianism the morality of the secret agent is actually irrelevant, since it is the action and its consequences that are weighed, and maximizing the welfare of a community is the only measure. The history of the genre tended to demonstrate that, in spite of the Cold War claim that the block would supersede the nation, such a community was actually much smaller than the patriotic solidarity of pre-World War Two fiction. In the reconfiguration of the genre, fictional professionalism constituted the intelligence community as a special group to which the reader could not compare himself. Rather, privy to their adventures, heroic deeds, and achievements, he is led to admire these specialists of the negative and their knowledge of the *arcanum imperii*, to delegate his authority to them, although (or because) the rules of democracy do not seem to apply to them – spy fiction as a twentieth century Cesarism.

Spy hedonism resided not only in their easy and repetitive promiscuity, but also in the notion that in international politics the well-being of the general

48 Pierre Kalfon, *OSS 117 prend des vacances* (Companhia Cinematográfica Vera Cruz, 1969). sc. Pierre Kalfon, and Pierre Philippe after Josette Bruce, featuring Luc Merenda, Edwige Feuillère. He made a bad but curious film out of Bruce's novel, with printed inserts, like in old silent movies or in Godard's films.

49 Second guessing the political intentions of allies' in spy fiction had its impact on another major worry for the French rightist psyche, the disappearing of the colonial empire which had already been infiltrated by Cold War themes. But it remained less disquieting than two other concerns regarding the power of the state: non-governmental players in a cryptic field, which was supposed to be a regal prerogative, and second-guessing the competence of the state apparatus itself.

public would be increased by actions maximizing the welfare of the intelligence community. Such freedom of action was awarded to that professional community, because it doubly represented the public – fighting for the good side and sharing the same values, despite the liberties spies were allowed to take. Spy fiction tried to reassure its public, and give it solace by expanding on common sense and drawing upon a doxa about human nature, natural hierarchies, conventional wisdom, and preprogrammed scholastics.[50] The adventure and the mystery, two of the main branches of popular fiction,[51] transited through the *Spionspiel* universe and reinvented ends and means of the Machiavellian maxim – a domination game in which spies, not anointed by the Prince anymore, but willing to comply professionally with the lethal rules of the game, were having to resort to violence, ruse, and deceit for the entertainment of their public.

That dominant trajectory, from stoicism to hedonistic Utilitarianism, has been the active force behind the spy craze. But its strength could not silence a much more pessimistic doubt. For a public which could either turn nostalgically to retrospective war fiction, or got worried to see that anti-Soviet Manichaeism did not have the complete answers to all the political challenges facing France anymore, the hedonistic and techno-optimistic axiology which had gradually come to prominence itself in contemporary society proved to be only a disguise for the cruel rules of *Spionspiel* and professionalism – and not a very credible solace.

Spy fiction as philosophical investigation then went a step further, and from the Machiavelli's angels hidden *praxis* considered the media culture itself not as a transparent ecosystem but as a problem to be approached either skeptically or cynically. The disinformation *fabula* epitomized a distrust towards the status of reality in the political world, the suspicion that it might have been fabricated, like a fiction. Actually, once doubt was aroused, it became multidirectional, and nothing seemed able to stop it, not even political affinities. Jean Mazarin's caustic irony threw suspicion at the seemingly ironclad French conservatism of Marcel Dassault. *Creuse, ma taupe...*,[52] revealed that the 88year-old Marcel L., leader of the French fighter-plane industry, had been coded Ton-ton by Guepeou 50 years ago, and may have been a forgotten Bolshevik mole!

---

50 See Erik Neveu, *L'Idéologie dans le roman d'espionnage* (Paris: Presses de la Fondation nationale des sciences politiques, 1985.

51 See John G. Cawelti, *Adventure, Mystery and Romance. Formula Stories as Art and Popular Culture* (Chicago, IL/London: University of Chicago Press, 1976).

52 Jean Mazarin, *Creuse, ma taupe...*, Engrenage, No. 106 (Paris: Fleuve noir, 1984).

Another skeptic *fabula* staged an opposition between specialists and amateurs. In *Peau de torpedo,*[53] amateurs caught in the sticky web of a *Spionspiel* might thrash all they want, they will not escape their fate.

Dominique, who in a jealous rage had killed her husband, unaware that he was an agent ordered to hide, has sought refuge in an old boat in Fécamp. She does not know that the police knew about the murder and the cryptic status of her late husband: they set a trap to catch the spy ring and she unknowingly acts as bait. And she is also unaware that Helen, head of her husband's spy ring, has sent two assassins in order to eliminate her.

An even more skeptic *fabula* showed specialists fighting among themselves. Being an agent did not shield them from anything.

In Robert Hossein's *Le Caviar rouge* (1984),[54] two ex-lovers are surprised to meet again for a tense night in a deserted but posh Genevan house. They were both agents, and it becomes apparent that Alex is on a mission to discover whether Nora, the only woman he ever loved, had recognized the man who accompanied another Soviet agent, le Caïman, supposed to be dead now. Le Caïman, who only faked his death, is actually sent to assassinate the man, a dissident physicist. If she had recognized him, she would have had to disappear. Youri, the head of the KGB mission had sent Alex, knowing that in the name of their old love, he could entice her to tell the truth, but Alex decides to lie to Youri and flee with Nora before their inescapable demise.

Spy fiction even became cynical when a *fabula* revealed the futility and toxicity of the *Spionspiel.* From the outside, in his Geromino series in the 1970's, Jean Amila pitted his non-conventional cop against secrecy and manipulations of the so-called *raison d'État.*[55] From inside, Philippe Lefebvre's *Le Transfuge*[56] illustrated the notion of a mortal game lacking significant stakes.

Corain, a businessman who frequently travels to the GDR is gradually reeled in by a French agent and convinced to help a Leipzig friend, Steger, to escape. A high-ranking civil servant critical of the régime, Steger is supposed to be a huge catch for the French DGSE (Direction Générale de la Sécurité Extérieure). Though Corain may become less ignorant, he will not reach the ultimate knowledge. At the end Steger will prove to be a hardline Communist mole cleverly implanted in their midst by the French agents themselves! Clément Tibère, character of Claude Pinoteau's *Le Silencieux* (1972), may be more familiar with the mores and tricks of spies, but he remains only a physicist, coerced into working for the Soviet Union, freed by MI5, pursued by KGB killers. He

---

53 *La Peau de torpedo,* directed by Jean Delannoy (1970; Comacico).

54 *Le Caviar rouge,* directed by Robert Hossein (1986; Philippe Dussart).

55 See. Paul Bleton, *"Geronimo as Translator," Belphégor. Littérature populaire et culture médiatique,* vol. II, n° 1 (2001), http://www.dal.ca/~etc/belphegor/vol2_no1/articles.

56 *Le Transfuge,* directed by Philippe Lefebvre (1985; Plaisance-Prestations).

may succeed in proving that maestro Korodine is a Soviet agent and hide microfilms in the music sheets of the symphony orchestra, but the KGB will kidnap him in order to get Korodine back in exchange.

What does present-day France inherit from the Cold War spy fiction? An ideological binarism, an Islamic foe simply replacing the Soviet one? While this is certainly so, with it come also all the centrifugal forces which gave the genre its complexity during the Cold War. On the one hand fictional spies were reassuring, because they could look behind the scenes, cater to public skepticism, reveal the hidden forces of international politics, and disclose the nature of information through exposing its double and entangled character of being at once a state secret and a salable commodity.

But, on the other hand, spy fiction of the Cold War also pointed to paradoxes in the media culture. Confronted by the genre's founding paradox of esoteric conflicts fought by secret agents, hushed up by governments, but publicized by very exoteric media, authors had to choose either entertainment or enlightenment on international problems. And due to the nature of media culture itself, they drove their public beyond a simple notion of government lies and propaganda. Through converting disinformation, a weapon of subversive war, into a popular narrative, they underlined how much readers were active in their own deception. Thus they taught a lesson of skepticism in the face of the all-conquering optimism of *communication* in the post-World War Two decades that witnessed the advent of technological sophistication and media culture ubiquity.

Christoph Classen

Enemies, Spies, and the Bomb

Cold War Cinema in Comparison: Germany and the US, 1948–1970

"Without the Cold War, what's the point of being an American?"[1] It is the American novelist John Updike who puts this poignant leading question concerning the relationship between national identity and the bipolar world order in the second half of the 20th century into his protagonist's mouth. The man who asks this question – Harry Angstrom, the protagonist of Updike's famous "Rabbit" novels – grew up during the Cold War, and when its end is on the horizon in 1989 he indulges in nostalgia. "I miss it," he says. "The Cold War. It gave you a reason to get up in the morning."[2] It is hardly a coincidence that the historian Stephen Whitfield quotes Updike (or rather Angstrom) in one of his essays.[3] Whitfield is the author of an influential book about US-American culture during the Cold War. First published in 1991, it puts a special emphasis on the Hollywood film industry and the movies produced there during this period.[4] In a slightly exaggerated way, it is possible to say that, unlike Updike's timid hero, the now firmly established concept of a "Cold War culture" does not mourn the end of this global conflict, but equally recognizes its importance. Without the Cold War, everything is nothing. In the meantime this concept has grown beyond the American context and has transferred to Europe, although significantly in Europe the term is used in the plural – "Cold War cultures."[5]

Indeed, there is a strong case for a Cold War culture approach. The Cold War was more than just a confrontation of two international blocs under the leadership of the US and the Soviet Union as hegemonic powers. The ideological fault lines also ran visibly through the blocs themselves – at least in the West. In many cases they created a vast and enduring gulf within the nationally constituted soci-

1 John Updike, *Rabbit at Rest* (New York: Fawcett Crest, 1990), 367.

2 Ibid., 293.

3 Stephen J. Whitfield, "The Culture of the Cold War," in *The Cambridge Companion to Modern American Culture*, ed. Christopher Bigsby (New York: Cambridge University Press, 2006), 256–274, here 272.

4 Stephen J. Whitfield, *The Culture of the Cold War* (Baltimore: John Hopkins University Press, 1991).

5 Annette Vowinckel, Markus M. Payk and Thomas Lindenberger, ed., *Cold War Cultures. Perspectives on Eastern and Western European Societies* (New York and Oxford: Berghahn, 2012).

DOI 10.1515/9783110496178-008

eties. A more or less obvious “Cold Civil War” took place within these countries, but the structure of the “fronts” was not always bipolar. Left-wingers of different hues fought each other as well as liberals and conservatives, and endeavored to mobilize the population for their respective political views in varying constellations and alliances.[6]

For a socio-historical perspective an analysis of the mass media and its contents is essential. They are a key source for these internal conflicts within societies, suitable for a reconstruction of contemporary mentalities and sensitivities. In the media everyday life and political norms merged, often implicitly. When the media expounded topics such as gender roles or religion, education or social norms, they would make an implicit (and often explicit) statement targeted at the model of society they perceived as antagonistic during the Cold War.[7] The media were always more than just a “mirror” of general political and social discourses or objects used to exert political influence. They were major players and protagonists in these internal conflicts of society and have to be viewed and interpreted as such. During the first two decades of the Cold War, which we will explore further in this article, cinema undoubtedly played a key role despite the impending rise of television as an all-pervasive mass medium.

As hinted above, the “Cold War culture(s)” approach also seems to harbor an inherent problem: it bears the temptation to interpret culture and cultural change primarily from the perspective of an ideologically rooted global conflict and to attach less importance to other factors. It must be borne in mind, however, that the structural conditions – for instance in the film industry – dated back into the period before 1945 and their impact persisted in the postwar period. The advanced postwar industrial and consumer societies also experienced a significant social transformation that encompassed all areas of life. While the bipolar conflict formed the backdrop for this transformation, it was hardly its sole reason. An example: if the film industry in the US and its products changed fundamentally since the 1960s (New Hollywood), this transformation occurred primarily because of internal change processes within society which had a very limited relation to the Cold War.[8] In addition, the term “Cold War” alone tends to homog-

6 See pars pro toto for the German case Patrick Major, *The Death of the KPD. Communism and Anti-Communism in West Germany 1945–1956* (Oxford: Oxford University Press, 1997).

7 Thomas Lindenberger, “Einleitung,” in *Massenmedien im Kalten Krieg. Akteure, Bilder, Resonanzen*, ed. Idem (Cologne et al.: Böhlau, 2006), 9–23.

8 See for example Stephen Powers, David J. Rothman and Stanley Rothman, *Hollywood’s America. Social and Political Themes in Motion Pictures* (Boulder and Oxford: Westview Press, 1996); Peter Krämer, *The New Hollywood. From Bonnie and Clyde to Star Wars* (London: Wallflower, 2005).

enize the topic. Without doubt it could have entirely different connotations in culture and film, depending on how, where and when it was used.

The following overview of the Cold War theme in the cinema will in no respect replace detailed empirical studies. Nevertheless, it should try to explore the problems of perspectivity and homogenization, and contribute to a differentiated view. To do this, I will use a comparative approach doing both: examine the impact of the Cold War on and representations of the conflict in US and European movies, focusing on West German productions in particular. Which shared patterns of perception can we reconstruct within the Western Bloc? How (and why) did they differ between individual countries? In addition to the movies themselves as cultural artefacts the comparison will also include an overview of the production structures in Hollywood and West Germany. While the aspect of political influence and censorship takes center stage, it may highlight the fact that, while film-making is always a political business, economic, technical, sector-specific and media-specific developments are also of great importance, whether they are global (for instance the challenge cinema faced during this period with the rise of television) or highly path dependent and national. How much was film production in the US and in West Germany really shaped by the Cold War?

Hollywood and German "Handwerk." Profit and Politics in the Film Industry after 1945

At a first glance, the positions of the film industry in the US and in West Germany at the end of the 1940s could not have been more different. In the US a well-established system of large studios existed that had controlled the market almost exclusively in the last three decades. In the late 1940s they attracted an audience of 90 million people per week on average to domestic cinemas. In postwar Germany the film industry had come to a standstill: many production facilities were destroyed, the staff was discredited or dispersed, and all production activities were subject to approval by the occupying powers. It was only in the early 1950s that small to mid-size companies, specialized in the production or distribution of films, began the cumbersome process of producing films for the domestic market in West Germany (FRG).

In 1945 the Allies had reserved the right to control both the reorganization and the conceptual orientation of German film production and distribution. Structurally, this represented a clear break with tradition. The Western Allies pursued a twofold aim in breaking up the Nazi film production structures consolidated in the Ufa-Film GmbH (UFI): they wanted to prevent a new government-controlled monopoly in the film industry like it existed in the Nazi era; alongside this political goal they also pursued economic interests in relation to their own film industries.[9] Only small production and distribution companies with limited capital were licensed in the British and American occupation zones. The fragmentation of the industry with medium-sized businesses contributed significantly to the enduring crisis of the West German film industry.[10]

The difficult financial situation, exacerbated by the breakthrough of television at the end of the 1950s, had direct consequences for film production. The undercapitalized production companies, distributors and cinema operators perforce targeted their activities at the domestic market and attempted to minimize entrepreneurial risks. As a consequence, they decided to stick with proven forms and formats. Rather than innovate, film-makers opted for a serial and rather unambitious production of genre movies. These productions were characterized by significant continuities to the escapist and ostensibly "unpolitical" movies of the Nazi era, not only with regard to actors, directors and cameramen.[11] As a result the production was hardly in line with the original aims of the re-education policy, but the difficult economic basis also made the industry – at least indirectly – vulnerable to political interventions.

The US film industry had suffered far less from the consequences of the war (and the depression). In the 1920s an oligopoly of eight studios had been established. By the end of the 1940s these eight studios obtained control over the entire exploitation chain from distribution to the cinemas. The crucial factor for the stability of this constellation was the financing the capital-intensive and high-risk film industry had received from Wall Street investors since the 1920s. These investors had no interest in independent productions that were exposed to incalculable risks.[12] This structure also resulted in risk prevention. As a matter of principle innovation, controversial topics and experiments were not in demand with investors and studio heads. These studio era films generally display conservative narratives and forms, confirm consensual norms and values, and show off

9 Under American pressure the government of the Federal Republic decided not to impose import restrictions on movies in the context of a GATT agreement in 1949/50; cf. Friedrich P. Kahlenberg, "Film," in *Die Geschichte der Bundesrepublik Deutschland. Kultur*, ed. Wolfgang Benz (Frankfurt am Main: Fischer Taschenbuch Verlag, 1989), 464.

10 Cf. Irmgard Wilharm, "Filmwirtschaft, Filmpolitik und "Publikumsgeschmack" im Westdeutschland der Nachkriegszeit," *Geschichte und Gesellschaft* 28 (2002): 267–290.

11 Knut Hickethier, "Das bundesdeutsche Kino der fünfziger Jahre. Zwischen Kulturindustrie und Handwerksbetrieb," in *Mediale Mobilmachung III. Das Kino der Bundesrepublik Deutschland als Kulturindustrie (1950–1962)*, ed. Harro Segeberg (Munich: Wilhelm Fink Verlag, 2009), 33–60.

12 Powers, Rothman and Rothman, *Hollywood's America*, 16.

their contractually bound star actors. Since the 1930s the underlying conservative trend of film production had been reinforced under the pressure of religious – particularly catholic – lobby groups. As a consequence the so-called *Production Code* (or *Hays Code*) was introduced in the 1930s. It proved an efficient basis for the suppression of scenes that involved violence or sexuality[13]

Against all appearances the US film industry was heading towards a crisis at the end of the 1940s. The oligopoly of studios came to an end, as the government threatened to break them up and trade unions exerted pressure on the companies. As a direct consequence the companies saw the need to raise their profile in competition and produced less, but more elaborate films.[14] They also placed great hopes in new sophisticated technologies. In the long-term the competition that arose with the emergence of television would prove even more decisive for the development of cinema. Not only was the number in cinema-goers in sharp decline from formerly 90 to 40 million per week by 1958,[15] but a shift in target audiences took place: television replaced cinema as mainstream family entertainment. The industry had to get used to an audience made up mostly of adolescents and young adults who had been socialized differently from the older generation and accordingly had different expectations with regard to movies and entertainment. While the large studios still maintained their influence particularly in the 1950s, the industry underwent a profound transformation. The usual business model established during Hollywood's infancy proved to be increasingly inefficient.

Overall the situation in Hollywood and West Germany were markedly different, but had more similarities than first it first seemed. The US had an established industry whose business model, although successful for many years, was in decline. The rise of television was the main cause for this decline and would create similar problems in Germany with a latency of about five years. In Germany the year 1945 marked a fundamental rupture. The new postwar cinema industry that was emerging under difficult circumstances struggled to consolidate. While this crisis was caused by entirely different circumstances – with the exception of the competition from television – on both sides of the Atlantic, industry reactions were curiously similar in many respects. Rather than striving for innovation and experiments, the major players turned to supposedly proven solutions and risk avoidance. Under these circumstances explicitly political themes were unpopular

---

13 Ibid., 18–19.

14 The number of movies produced declined from 383 in 1950 to 154 only ten years later; cf. Terry Christensen, *Reel Politics. American Political Movies from "Birth of a Nation" to "Platoon"* (New York: Basil Blackwell, 1987), 85–86.

15 By 1970 the number had halved to 20 million visitors per week; ibid., 112.

both in Europe and in the US. In the 1950s the number of political films was negligible, let alone films with a critical undertone.[16]

Political Interventions and Censorship

In political theory the relationship between politics and the media seems straightforward: in dictatorships the media are subject to the primacy of politics; in democracies they are able to work relatively independently. This applies in particular if they are privately organized and serve primarily their own economic interests. A closer look at Hollywood's history shows that reality is far more complex. In the early 1950s political interventions, anti-communist propaganda and prohibitions for supposed communists to exercise their profession reached a dimension in the US that is reminiscent of an authoritarian regime rather than a liberal democracy.

This includes above all the infamous activities of the "House Un-American Activities Committee" (HUAC) which amongst other groups also targeted Hollywood.[17] In 1947 HUAC opened an investigation due to suspected communist infiltration of the American film industry which continued until 1952. One of the reasons for their scrutiny was that Hollywood had produced several pro-Soviet films during the Second World War such as "Mission to Moscow"[18] at the express request of the Roosevelt administration. These films were intended to raise public support for the military alliance with the Soviet Union. The questioning of film industry employees by HUAC resulted in the denunciation of numerous supposed communists on the studios' pay roll. In the increasingly hysterical climate of fear and denunciation people totally lost sight of the distinction between liberals – and there would have been many in Hollywood –, former communist sympathizers and actual active members of the Communist Party (CPUSA). Hence it was possible to turn an initial suspicion that lacked substance into a successful case.

---

16 Ibid., 71–72; the socially critical "Rubble films" created under Allied supervision did not go down particularly well in the Federal Republic. Compared to the so-called "Überläufer" films (literally: defector), superficially unpolitical movies dating from the Nazi era that were only shown in cinemas after the Second World War, the contemporary "Rubble films" that were in line with the re-education policy were unsuccessful at the box offices. The autonomous production in West Germany (FRG) followed the latter line of tradition; cf. Kahlenberg, 472.

17 For a general review on the activities of HUAC see Walter Goodman, *The Committee: The Extraordinary Career of the House Committee on Un-American Activities* (New York: Farrar, Straus & Giroux, 1968).

18 USA 1943, director: Michael Curtiz.

This was significant in view of the considerable public attention the scrutiny of prominent show business personalities such as Harry Belafonte, Charlie Chaplin and Orson Welles received. After the investigation they found their names together with several hundred other actors, screenwriters, directors and musicians on a blacklist prepared by producers under the enormous pressure exerted until the mid-1950s. Once blacklisted, people were often banned from working in the entertainment industry for years.[19] The first people summoned before HUAC, the famous "Hollywood Ten," who had refused to give evidence citing the 5th Amendment, were sentenced to imprisonment. Others left the country. Charlie Chaplin was refused re-entry in the US at the instigation of Edgar J. Hoover. This communist witch hunt was orchestrated by a flurry of brash anti-communist movies.[20]

A closer look illustrates that the postwar anti-communist paranoia was not spawned by the beginning of the Cold War. The fear of an impending communist revolution that had gripped the US dated back to the Russian October uprising in 1917. The first temporary investigating committees were established during this period of the "Red Scare." Founded during the Second World War under the presidency of the Democrat Franklin D. Roosevelt, the House Committee on Un-American Activities had targeted Hollywood for the first time in 1938, years before the Cold War began.[21] For obvious reasons at that time particularly fascist groups have been under observation. The term "un-American" – which has never been defined – indicates that the open confrontation of the superpowers from 1947 on fueled the fear of an existing threat to the American identity. Ultimately, however, it stems from a deeply ingrained insecurity in relation to the cohesion and foundations of America as an immigration society when put under pressure by social change processes.[22]

These fears were deeply rooted in society which indicates that the issue cannot be reduced to a simple antagonism between politics and Hollywood during this period. In many cases the studio managements showed themselves cooperative because they sympathized with the right-wing camp and not only because they feared political consequences or damage to their image which would have

---

19 For a comprehensive portrayal of HUAC's activities in Hollywood see Larry Ceplair and Steven Englund, *The Inquisition in Hollywood: Politics in the Film Community, 1930–1960* (Urbana and Chicago, IL: University of Illinois Press, 2003).

20 Cf. below in this article.

21 Cf. Murray B. Levin, *Political Hysteria in America: The Democratic Capacity for Repression* (New York: Basic Books, 1971).

22 Cf. Thomas Mergel, "'The Enemy in Our Midst'. Antikommunismus und Amerikanismus in der Ära McCarthy," *Zeitschrift für Geschichtswissenschaft (ZfG)* 51 (2003): 237–258.

negatively impacted their businesses. The generation of studio moguls active in the 1950s generally came from an immigration background. The experience of their own rise to power often resulted in an excessive patriotism.[23] Even among the creatives a fundamental agreement with anti-communist and anti-liberal attitudes was widespread. Under the impression of the war and Roosevelt's interventionist politics the "Motion Picture Alliance for the Preservation of American Ideals" (MPAPAI) was formed in 1944, a conservative and influential Hollywood lobby group. Initially anti-totalitarian, the group committed itself increasingly to the fight against communism after the end of the Second World War. Among its members were numerous prominent actors, directors, managers and publicists including Walt Disney, John Wayne, Ronald Reagan and Ayn Rand. They managed to promote their stance prominently in the public sphere and to gain the necessary support for HUAC's investigations. A large number of films were found to contain allegedly implicit communist messages, and the group publicized a kind of "political supplement" to the Production Code written by Ayn Rand. The supplement suggested film-makers use a blatant glorification of right-wing political views such as "Don't smear wealth" or "Don't glorify failure."[24] The management of the studios that largely controlled film production at the time had no communist leanings whatsoever. Moreover, fear led many liberals or CPUSA sympathizers or supporters to cooperate with excessive zeal. Consequently, the anti-communist witch hunt encountered little resistance for a long time and the allegations seemed increasingly plausible.

While HUAC hearings and the ensuing blacklisting took anti-communist fervor to a new level, Hollywood traditionally had strong political ties, and censorship under the *Production Code* was part of the daily routine, albeit rarely for political reasons.[25] During the war much of Hollywood had been a willing contributor in the production of patriotic propaganda which – unlike in Germany – did not have a bad public image in the US after 1945.[26] In the postwar years multiple

---

23 Powers, Rothman and Rothman, *Hollywood's America*, 18.

24 The Motion Picture Alliance for the Preservation of American Ideals, ed., *Screen Guide for Americans* (Beverly Hills, CA, 1947).

25 US legislation played a vital role in the enforcement of the Code and the industry's general vulnerability to political intervention. Initially the law did not recognize film as an artistic medium, refusing to afford it the protection provided by the constitutionally guaranteed right of freedom of speech under the First Amendment. This was only corrected by a 1952 landmark decision of the United States Supreme Court – the so-called "Miracle Decision."

26 Cf. Clayton R. Koppes and Gregory D. Black, *Hollywood Goes to War. How Politics, Profits and Propaganda Shaped World War II Movies* (Berkeley and Los Angeles, CA: University of California Press, 1990).

more or less informal “state-private networks” continued to shape the relationship between film producers and official organizations such as the State Department, the Pentagon, the CIA, the FBI and the USIA.[27] Building upon wartime predecessor organizations, a civil propaganda infrastructure began to emerge in 1947 whose responsibilities included the distribution of Hollywood productions abroad.[28] These organizations supported the production of a fair number of films and sometimes initiated film projects or intervened in shaping content. A prime example is the significant initiative and influence of the CIA and USIA on the British screen adaptations of George Orwell’s novels “Animal Farm” (1954) and “1984” (1956) to achieve an expressly anti-communist interpretation.[29]

Postwar West Germany undoubtedly had a history of state-controlled film production, but it did not see any anti-communist campaigns comparable to HUAC’s activities in Hollywood. Allegations of communist leanings could nevertheless be detrimental to film-makers. These negative consequences seem to have been limited to a few individual cases such as the director Wolfgang Staudte and the film producer Walter Koppel. Based in Hamburg, Koppel was the owner of the production company *Real-Film*. In the immediate postwar period he was indeed briefly an active supporter of the German Communist Party (KPD) and the Association of Persecutees of the Nazi Regime (VVN), reputed as close to the KPD.[30] In Staudte’s case his work for the East German state-owned film production company DEFA and his refusal, as a matter of principle, to publicly distance himself from communism was sufficient to cause professional difficulties.[31] An instrument used as leverage against “fellow travelers” were German federal guarantees (Bundesbürgschaften), granted in two waves to boost the ailing film industry between 1950 and 1955. The federal government underwrote deficit guarantees that enabled the notoriously cash-strapped film producers to take out bank loans to fund their projects. The project was then assessed by a guarantee committee (Bürgschaftsausschuss). In theory, the grants should have been made solely based on economic criteria, but the reality looked different: pressure from

27 Tony Shaw, *Hollywood’s Cold War* (Edinburgh: Edinburgh University Press, 2007), 4.
28 Ibid, 24–26.
29 Whitfield, “Culture,” 261; Laurence Zuckerman, “How the Central Intelligence Agency Played Dirty Tricks With Our Culture,” *New York Times*, March 18, 2000.
30 Cf. “Gesinnungs-Prüfung – Ein süßer Stoff,” *Der Spiegel* 33 (1951): 7–10.
31 For Staudte cf. Ulrike Weckel, “Begrenzte Spielräume: Wolfgang Staudtes Filme und deren Rezeption im Kalten Krieg,” in *Massenmedien im Kalten Krieg*, ed. Thomas Lindenberger (cf. footnote 3), 25–47.

the ministry of the interior resulted in an amalgamation of political and economic criteria.[32]

The guarantee for a – totally unpolitical – natural history film was only granted once Staudte had withdrawn as a director.[33] In addition to the political past of the management team under Koppel, *Real-Film* – at the time one of the largest German production companies – was also reproached for its cooperation with DEFA. While the company was able to refute these allegations, it was excluded from receiving government subsidies for years.[34] A project featuring UFA actress Marika Rökk raised objections from the ministry of the interior because she had starred in a dance film shot in the Soviet-occupied zone of Austria. Before the film could go ahead, Rökk had to declare that she would not work for the communist East in the future.[35] The German film industry had neither a blacklist nor forced denunciations. Nevertheless, a rumor of communist sympathies could limit work opportunities significantly in 1950s Germany.

Beside individual "politically suspect" people, projects struggled to take off if the government considered them as harmful to the Federal Republic's image.[36] East-West German cooperation was also rejected. One production company requested support for a pan-German screen adaptation of Thomas Mann's novel *Buddenbrooks* because Mann had made the film rights conditional on an East-West cooperation. However, the relevant ministry advised that the East German DEFA was "a state-controlled film company" tasked with "propagating historical materialism as shaped by Marx, Lenin and Stalin, destroying civil order and preparing the dictatorship of the proletariat." A joint production was therefore out of the question.[37] In consequence of these constraints, production companies simply abstained from proposing politically controversial topics. The principle of the guarantees, states media researcher Stephan Buchloh, acted "like a prompt for self-censorship."[38] The same can be said for the *Wiesbadener Filmbewer-*

---

32 Stephan Buchloh, *"Pervers, jugendgefährdend, staatsfeindlich". Zensur in der Ära Adenauer als Spiegel des gesellschaftlichen Klimas* (Frankfurt am Main and New York: Campus Verlag, 2002), 249–251.

33 Ibid., 27–28.

34 Ibid., 253–254.

35 Ibid., 255–256.

36 These cases mostly referred to critical appraisals of the Nazi past; cf. Knut Hickethier, "Kino," 38.

37 Quoted from Walter Euchner, "Unterdrückte Vergangenheitsbewältigung: Motive der Filmpolitik in der Ära Adenauer," in *Gegen Barbarei. Essays – Robert M. W. Kempner zu Ehren*, ed. Rainer Eisfeld and Ingo Müller (Frankfurt am Main: Athenäum, 1989), 346–359, here 352.

38 Buchloh, *Zensur*, 261.

tungsstelle, the German board that evaluated and rated films. The quality ratings had a significant impact on marketing opportunities, entitling the production company to tax privileges until 1971.

The inherited state-authoritarian outlook of the German administration is also evident in censorship. Working more or less covertly and without a clear legal basis, an interdepartmental committee for East-West film matters (Interministerieller Ausschuß für Ost/West-Filmfragen)[39] controlled the import of any films from the East.[40] Until the cessation of its activities in 1966, the committee refused import licenses to 130 films, while others could only be shown if certain conditions were met.[41] The refused films included various prestigious East German propaganda projects but also Eastern European documentaries, children's and cultural films. The most prominent case is undoubtedly the screen adaptation of Heinrich Mann's novel *Der Untertan* (in English *The Kaiser's Lackey*, *Man of Straw* or *The Subject*) shot in 1951 by Wolfgang Staudte for DEFA. The film was shown in West German cinemas not before 1957 – and then only in a shortened version.[42] A large number of films were not admitted for public showings in the Federal Republic because the committee believed they "glorified communism" or styled their historical protagonists as spearheads of the proletariat.[43] It was not the topic of the films alone that determined whether an import license was granted or not; a refusal would for instance also be justified if an Eastern bank was involved in the funding.[44]

A comparison of political influences illustrates the strong impact of historically developed political cultures and practices. Both America and West Germany perceived communism as a significant danger, but governments and societies of

39 This was the official name since 1956. Prior to this date correspondence refers to the interministerial committee for the appraisal of films produced in the Soviet Union or countries under Soviet influence, including the Eastern zone (Interministerieller Ausschuß für die Begutachtung von Filmen sowjetischer Produktion bzw. sowjetisch beeinflußter Staaten, einschl. der Ostzone).

40 In 1955 the committee included representatives of the following federal institutions: the ministry of foreign affairs (Auswärtiges Amt), the ministry of the interior, the pan-German ministry and the ministry of economics as well as the press and information office and the Federal Office for the Protection of the Constitution.

41 Buchloh, *Zensur*, 225.

42 Cf. Weckel, "Begrenzte Spielräume," 31–33; for the committee's motivations cf. also "Plädoyer für den Untertan," *Der Spiegel* 47 (1956): 59–61.

43 This was the internal justification in the case of the DEFA film *Genesung* (in English "Recovery"), directed by Konrad Wolf, in 1954, and for refusing the commercial exploitation of the DEFA-produced film "Ludwig van Beethoven," directed by Max Jaap cf. Buchloh, *Zensur*, 226.

44 Ibid.

both countries responded differently. After the historical rupture of 1945 political influence on the film industry in West Germany were perforce limited to indirect interventions. One of the most powerful instruments to exert influence was the granting or withdrawal of subsidies. Censorship in particular is also marked by an enduring state-authoritarian outlook: the government focused predominantly on the control of actual or alleged propaganda from the Eastern Bloc. The state cast itself in the role of a concerned patriarch, tasked with protecting its citizens from communist influences. The production of critical films was perceived as a danger for Germany's battered reputation abroad and had to be prevented whenever possible.

Hollywood had cultivated good relationships with political entities and government institutions even before the war in order to safeguard its business models. Political alignment stood therefore not necessarily in contrast to economic success, but was considered a prerequisite. The fear of a communist infiltration of film studios was widespread both in political circles and society as a whole. Under these circumstances there was no systematic resistance against the wide-ranging political impositions – quite the contrary: the US civil society approved of them, whether by conviction or opportunism. Unlike in Germany this approval was not based on a patriarchal authoritarian tradition, but rather on populist tendencies linking older scandalizations of the media-driven shift in values with uncertainties about the foundations of American identity. This resulted in an aggressive discourse that represented "communism" in stark opposition to "Americanism," creating a much stronger momentum than in Germany. The consequences for individual creatives suspected of communist leanings could nevertheless be similar in both countries: they would struggle to find work in the film industry, whether in Hollywood or in West Germany.

Representations of the Cold War in Feature Films: Three Paradigms

Any attempt to obtain an overview over Cold War films in the US and West Germany reveals a major imbalance. In the Federal Republic hardly any cinema feature broaches the subject of the Cold War. In the US film industry the situation was different, but this cannot solely be attributed to the larger number of movies produced in Hollywood during the first two decades of the conflict. A more likely cause is that the resentments against political entertainment were (and still are) traditionally less pronounced in the US than in Germany. Until the mid-1960s the number of films that explicitly deal with Cold War themes remained in the low double-digit range in Germany. Most of these films have been forgotten today. By contrast, the much vaster US film production during the same period included many films considered as classics today such as Stanley Kubrick's satire *Dr. Strangelove*, John Frankenheimer's *The Manchurian Candidate* or Billy Wilder's *One, Two, Three*.[45]

The following section will reconstruct some characteristic patterns in the way films dealt with the Cold War until the mid-1960s. The choice of films is neither representative nor complete, but is based on a pragmatic approach and includes some either very famous or successful productions. The patterns applied follow an ideal type and cannot always be considered exclusive: some films may equally well be classified differently.

Red or Dead: Anti-Communism & Identity

The first ever Hollywood movie that focused on the Cold War was released in May 1948, only a few months after the conflict between the two victorious Allied powers of the Second World War had evolved into an open conflict: *The Iron Curtain*.[46] The spy thriller produced by Twentieth Century Fox is based on a true story. It adapted the memoir of a Soviet defector who had fled to Canada in 1945, providing the authorities with comprehensive espionage and infiltration plans for the country. The film seemed a perfect fit at a time when the entire American public was gripped by anti-communist hysteria and HUAC wanted to uncover a similar strategy for the US. The form and contents of the film were modelled on previous comparatively successful anti-Nazi films produced by the studio during the war which had also used the themes of espionage and counter-intelligence.[47] The film delivered its anti-communist message in the guise of a spy thriller, but achieved a mixed response from both critics and audience. Contrary to the producer's high expectations, box office receipts only just covered production costs.[48]

---

45 Tony Shaw's book *Hollywood's Cold War* lists roughly 340 productions until 1990. Although his list includes various productions without any direct link to the Cold War, we can still assume a low three-digit number of relevant films. Unlike *Dr. Strangelove* neither Frankenheimer's nor Wilder's films were popular with the audience when they premiered in the 1960s. Their significance is based on retrospective evaluations.

46 U.S. 1948, director: William A. Wellman.

47 Examples are *The House on 92nd Street* (1945) and *Confessions of a Nazi Spy* (1939); cf. Daniel J. Leab, "The Iron Curtain (1948). Hollywood's First Cold War Movie," *Historical Journal of Film, Radio and Television* 8, no.2 (1989): 162–176.

48 Ibid.

With its lack of commercial success, the movie shared the fate of numerous other anti-communist films produced in Hollywood until the mid-1950s to impress on the audience the dangers of communism in their own country.[49] Many similar films such as Warner's low-budget production *I was a Communist for the FBI*[50] – also based on an autobiographical publication of a former communist – suffered from the extremely black and white depictions taken from the weaker gangster dramas of the *film noir* era: communists and trade unionists were widely portrayed as criminal and ruthless, as "gangsters whose sole purpose in life is to spend their days drinking champagne and eating caviar at the expense of trusting workers" commented a German newspaper in a scathing review.[51] Melodramatic elements used in films such as Howard Hughes' production *I Married a Communist*[52] – the said husband is blackmailed by his former comrades because of his communist past and finally murdered – had no effect on the whiff of blatant anti-communist propaganda around these films. Audiences were well aware of this despite attempts to market the movie as "action-sex melodrama."[53]

Later representatives of this genre did not fare any better in this respect, for instance the long forgotten movie *My Son John* produced in 1952 by the catholic director Leo McCarey. However, the depictions of communists gained an interesting new facet. The film portrays an average American family, the Jeffersons, with profoundly patriotic and religious parents and two brothers serving their country in Korea. The black sheep of the family is the eldest son John, an arrogant intellectual working for the government in Washington. He is also a mama's boy, and there are hints that he is homosexual. When the FBI exposes John as a communist spy, his mother suffers a health breakdown, leading him to renounce communism. Before he is able to openly announce his conversion, he is murdered by his former comrades. A statement recorded before his death survives as a stark warning against communism to the next generation.

---

49 Depending on the sources, bibliographical references cite around 50 to 60 films which fit into this category.

50 USA 1951, director: Gordon Douglas.

51 Rudolf Thome, *Süddeutsche Zeitung*, April 26, 1965; reprinted in Stiftung Deutsche Kinemathek, ed., *Kalter Krieg: 60 Filme aus Ost und West* (Berlin: Stiftung Deutsche Kinemathek, 1991), 261.

52 USA 1949/50, director: Robert Stevenson.

53 Hughes withdrew the movie after a negative response to the premiere in the fall 1949 and relaunched it the following year with the new title *The Women on Pier 13*, emphasizing the melodramatic rather than the political aspect. The movie was still no great success; cf. Daniel J. Leab, "Hollywood im Kalten Krieg," in *Kalter Krieg: 60 Filme aus Ost und West*, ed. Stiftung Deutsche Kinemathek (Berlin: Stiftung Deutsche Kinemathek, 1991), 204–226, here 212–214.

The most interesting aspect in this film is the construction of "being un-American" as an illegitimate part of the "good," patriotic, godly and upright-conservative America. Being un-American means a mixture of presumptuous intellectualism, atheism and infringement of the reputedly natural gender hierarchy opposing the traditional family values. Anti-modern, conservative and anti-liberal discourses that opposed social change culminated in a concept of the communist as the enemy. All of this had existed before the outbreak of the Cold War. Only a few years before, Hollywood had allocated the role of the latent homosexual intent on destroying the traditional American family to another enemy: the Nazi spy.[54]

In any case *My Son John* reveals that the "Red Scare" of the early 1950s in the US was simultaneously an anti-modern crisis discourse on the very heart of American identity. This indirectly also answers the controversial question whether these movies, none of which was a box office success, were only launched to prove the producers' politically unobjectionable convictions to HUAC's anti-communist inquisitors.[55] The examples mentioned here show little evidence of this. If anything, these films epitomize a broad social discourse, with the producers positioning themselves according to their own convictions and by all appearances hoping to make profits along the way.

It is difficult to find similar films in the West German context. The film that best fits the bill of communism as a threat to society from within is *Menschen im Netz* (in English *People in a Net* or *Unwilling Agent*).[56] It is a story about a husband released after years of imprisonment in communist East Germany who realizes that his wife has secured his freedom by giving in to blackmail and working as a communist agent. The film ends no less tragic than its American counterparts: the wife pays with her life for her communist entanglement. *Menschen im Netz* is very similar to many American films shot in the first half of the decade in insinuating the threat of clandestine communist diversion, in portraying communist agents as criminals and in highlighting the success of counter-espionage. Unlike in *My Son John*, however, the threat does not stem from the very heart of society, but from the machinations of a hostile intelligence service using criminal

54 Cf. Ronny Loewy, "Der Lächerlichkeit preisgegeben. Nazis in den Anti-Nazi-Filmen Hollywoods," in *Lachen über Hitler – Auschwitz-Gelächter? Filmkomödie, Satire und Holocaust*, ed. Margit Fröhlich et al. (Munich: Edition Text + Kritik, 2003), 125–132.

55 This view is supported by older research, cf. Nora Sayre, *Running Time: Films of the Cold War* (New York: Dial Press, 1980), and was firmly rejected recently, among others by Tony Shaw.

56 FRG 1957, director: Franz Peter Wirth. In the 1960s the film's theme was also used as a basis for a series of television dramas entitled *Die fünfte Kolonne* (FRG 1963–1968, in English *The Fifth Column*) created by the same authors and producers.

methods to abuse people's weaknesses. It was a reflection of the actual situation in divided Germany where Eastern and Western intelligence services antagonized each other, and a call for vigilance in the face of communism. However, the criminal and cynical machinations of Eastern intelligence services could hardly be considered as a serious ideological challenge for the social order of the West.

Blatantly anti-communist films were rarely successful with the audience in West Germany. It is therefore not surprising that producers were reluctant to make films focused on these themes. The few exceptions were realized by independent producers such as the openly anti-communist Gerhard T. Buchholz who, by his own admission, made his films to promote a free and democratic reunification of Germany.[57] In the early 1950s he produced two films focusing on the "conversion" of convinced communists and their subsequent flight to the West: *Postlagernd Turteltaube*[58] and *Weg ohne Umkehr*[59].

In the satire *Postlagernd Turteltaube* (literally "Poste restante: Turtle Dove") a convinced communist bets his sister, who is living across the border in the West, that the citizens of the young GDR have a rock-solid confidence in their state. He loses his bet when all the residents of his apartment building flee to the West for trivial reasons. Their flight causes him to lose confidence in the system. Completed in 1953, *Weg ohne Umkehr* (in English *No Way Back*) has a similar construction, but with a tragic plot. Here it is the continual harassment and the cynical activities of the Soviet intelligence services that persuade a Russian engineer and his German girlfriend to flee to West Berlin. Their successful flight has no happy ending: no one is safe from the persecution of the communist intelligence services, not even in the West, is the gloomy message at the end of the film. Any interpretation of Buchholz' films needs to take into account the historic backdrop of two German states vying for the "better" system. The outcome of this struggle only became more obvious a few years later. In addition to Buchholz' strong support for the West and against the conditions under communist regimes, his films openly argue against the pacifist attitudes and ideas about neutrality popular in West Germany at the time and expressed strongly in the nascent debates around rearmament. While some critics commented Buchholz' films favorably, the audience's response was lukewarm.

---

57 Cf. "Komödie gegen die Angst," *Der Spiegel* 24 (1952): 30–31; Buchholz (1898–1970) who was working as a screenwriter from 1937 and contributed to the screenplay of *Die Rothschilds* (D 1940, director: Erich Waschneck) was rumored to have a close relationship to the Pan-German Ministry (Gesamtdeutsches Ministerium (BMG)); cf. ibid. and: "Gesinnungs-Prüfung – Ein süßer Stoff," 7–10.

58 FRG 1952, Director: Gerhard T. Buchholz.

59 FRG 1953, Director: Victor Vicas.

The screen adaptation of Heinz G. Konsalik's melodramatic bestselling novel *Der Arzt von Stalingrad* (in English *The Doctor of Stalingrad*) was an altogether different case. The film was an immediate box office hit in Germany.[60] The film's topic – German prisoners of war in Soviet captivity – proved very popular at the time. Just a few years earlier, in 1955, the last German soldiers returned from the Soviet Union after the German Chancellor Adenauer had successfully negotiated their release during a state visit to Moscow. The film consistently portrayed German prisoners of war as victims of communist cruelty and despotism, accompanied by a multitude of entrenched racist and anti-Slavic stereotypes.[61] The steadfast humanism of the German soldiers and, consequently, their intellectual and moral superiority over the totalitarian tyranny of their communist guards was presumed as a fact. The film alludes to the widespread need in the German population to retrospectively give a meaning to the war and to overcome the defeat. The differentiation from communism was also accompanied by an old concept of German identity based on a reputedly superior race.

Beyond Anti-Communism: Overcoming the Conflict or Nuclear Armageddon?

By the 1960s the different and often unsubtle varieties of anti-communism were spiraling out of control in films produced in both countries. The reasons for this were different and can be attributed both to the political level and to the two countries' societies and film industries. Politically, the policy of detente initiated in the wake of the Cuban Missile Crisis undoubtedly had a considerable impact, because it encouraged understanding rather than confrontation. In Hollywood, the explicitly anti-communist phase had ended in the mid-1950s, both because the "Red Scare" had largely fizzled out by this time and because these films were just not popular. The decline of the studio system also increased opportunities for independent productions. In Germany blatantly anti-communist films had been the exception rather than the rule and the film industry showed other clear signs of change. The wave of extremely popular and unpolitical "Heimatfilme" –

60 FRG 1958, director: Géza von Radvanyi.
61 Cf. also Georg Wurzer, "Antikommunismus und Russlandfeindschaft vor und nach 1945. Die Romane der Bestsellerautoren Erich Dwinger und Heinz G. Konsalik," *Jahrbuch für historische Kommunismusforschung* 24 (2011), 49–60.

a genre of feel-good films that feature rural settings, unspoiled nature, and firm values – came to an end.[62]

The theory of archetypal forms of narration makes a basic distinction between comedy and tragedy.[63] Both are visible in films shot in the 1960s that focus on the nuclear threat. The first form is characterized by an optimistic telos: in the end the protagonists will overcome all obstacles and head towards a promising future. Other films have a tragic narrative: the protagonists are doomed to fail because of the political circumstances in the nuclear era and their consequences.

A prominent example of optimistic comedy is the satire *The Russians are Coming, the Russians are Coming* produced in 1966.[64] The movie tells the story of a Soviet submarine that stranded off the coast of Massachusetts as a result of an accident. The situation escalates due to misunderstandings and stupidity on both sides, and the Soviet captain threatens to destroy the nearby coastal town. In this tense situation a child from the town runs into trouble and is saved by the joint effort of Americans and Russians. The conflict is overcome, and both parties depart on friendly terms. The film was a great success both with critics and at the box office. With box office takings of $ 7.75 million the film was the second most successful Cold War film after *Green Berets*, John Wayne's notorious justification of the Vietnam War.[65] Today the film is still considered as proof that Hollywood had a political change of heart in the 1960s about confronting communism.[66] In *The Russians are Coming, the Russians are Coming* de-escalation occurred because the film did not address communism, but de-politicized the conflict: the situation is resolved on a purely human level.[67]

The trend to de-politicize is also visible in many other comedies produced during this period, some even before the Cuban Missile Crisis. Top of the list is Billy Wilder's screwball comedy *One, Two, Three*[68] in which communists and capitalists, Americans, Soviets and Germans are indiscriminately made the butt of derision. People nevertheless found it hard to laugh about this fast-paced story

---

62 Cf. Johannes von Moltke, *No Place Like Home. Locations of Heimat in German Cinema* (= Weimar and Now: German Cultural Criticism, 36) (Berkeley, CA: University of California Press, 2005).

63 Northrop Frye, "The Archetypes of Literature," in *Criticism: The Major Statements*, ed. Charles Kaplan and William Anderson (New York: St. Martin's Press, 1991), 500–514.

64 USA 1966, director: Norman Jewison.

65 USA 1968, directors: John Wayne and Ray Kellogg.

66 Cf. review by Tony Shaw, "The Russians Are Coming The Russians Are Coming (1966): Considering Hollywood's Cold War "Turn" of the 1960s," *Film History* 22 (2010): 235–250.

67 Ibid, 244–245.

68 USA 1961.

that jumps between East and West in the period just after the wall was built in Berlin. The success of the six-part French-Italian coproduction *Don Camillo und Peppone*[69] across Western Europe can also basically be attributed to a trend to de-politicize. The shift of the global conflict to an Italian provincial town and to a slapstick confrontation between a catholic priest and a communist mayor makes the conflict palatable for the cinema audience. To achieve this, the conflict had to be harmonized and banalized as a purely human conflict of two both clever and headstrong (and therefore very similar) protagonists.

The implicit idea to use "humanity" to make the challenges of the Cold War surmountable or at least bearable is opposed by a number of dystopian films which focus on the failure of the atomic balance. The first of these films was *On the Beach*, produced by independent director and producer Stanley Kramer before the Cuban Missile Crisis.[70] It tells the story of the fruitless attempts of a submarine crew to find a permanently inhabitable living space on earth after a nuclear war. The initial scenario of a recent nuclear catastrophe is reminiscent of the later and even more successful production *Planet of the Apes*. This film was deliberately marketed as a science fiction adventure as Twentieth Century Fox feared the movie would flop with the audience if it was interpreted as a political statement.[71]

Two other equally dystopian US productions focused on the potential risk of a nuclear war triggered "by accident." Sidney Lumet's classic movie *Fail Safe* (1964) and Stanley Kubrick's black satire *Dr Strangelove or: How I Learned to Stop Worrying and Love the Bomb* (also 1964) were released almost simultaneously and featured variations on the same theme: a technical or human failure triggers a US bombing raid which cannot be stopped even by desperate measures. The combination of technological "safeguards" meant to prevent the outbreak of a war and human narrow-mindedness leads irreversibly into a catastrophe. Both movies were obviously inspired by the dynamics of the Cuban Missile Crisis. They were much applauded by critics, but only Kubrick's parody (which was released first) was also a box office success.

Future scenarios of a nuclear catastrophe were not evoked in West German movies of the 1950s and 1960s. One possible reason is that, unlike the US, Germany had no nuclear arms. There are, however, other dystopian visions of humankind without a human future. The most impressive representative of this genre is probably Helmut Käutner's 1955 border drama *Himmel ohne Sterne* (in

69 F/I 1952–1971.

70 USA 1959.

71 USA 1968, director: Franklin J. Schaffner.

English *Sky without Stars*).[72] The plot focuses on the fate of a young mother torn between her responsibility for her frail parents in East Germany and for her young son living with the parents of her lover who died in the war. A new love for a border guard from West Germany complicates the plot. All attempts of the protagonists to escape this situation between the fronts of the Cold War lead to further entanglement. In the end only no man's land, an area which has not yet been blocked off and is only controlled sporadically, is the lovers' sole refuge. When the border between the two German countries is sealed off for good, even this refuge is lost. During an attempt to cross the border into the West the lovers are shot and the son is orphaned.

The film's protagonists are victims of the political situation which leaves them with no way out. Like a noose the small border area tightens around them and leaves no room for a shared future. It is conspicuous that the discourse creates an antagonism between "politics" and "human beings." The border becomes a *factum brutum*, an inhuman principle for which apparently no one is responsible. By contrast, the protagonists epitomize love, humanity and solidarity. Their failure symbolizes the lack of hope for both these principles and the young generation of Germans. The film concludes with the resigned prediction that in the end all will be victims.

Käutner's film is therefore far more than just a maudlin lament for the lost national unity. Consistent with the national sensitivities after the lost war, it portrayed all Germans as victims of policies outside of their control. History seems to repeat itself here. "Good" people are again the victims of "evil" politics just like in the Nazi era. The theme of rejecting responsibility for the past leaves a visible imprint on the present.

Himmel ohne Sterne was not the only film that portrayed the man on the street as a victim of politics. The ostensibly contrasting comedy *Genosse Münchhausen* (literally "Comrade Münchhausen") produced by the comedian Wolfgang Neuss[73] conveys a very similar message: Farmer Puste is literally catapulted between East and West, a pawn of the competing superpowers. The essence of the story is that the man on the street is not only reduced to an object of an absurd and totally exaggerated competition between two systems by "higher powers," but he is also paying the bill.

---

72 FRG 1955; cf. on this film Michael Schaudig, "Vom Pathos im Niemandsland. *Himmel ohne Sterne* (BRD 1955): Helmut Käutners 'filmsemiotische Diskussion' des geteilten Deutschland," in *Mediale Mobilmachung III. Das Kino der Bundesrepublik Deutschland als Kulturindustrie (1950–1962)*, ed. Harro Segeberg, (Munich: Wilhelm Fink Verlag, 2009), 305–336.

73 FRG 1962, director: Wolfgang Neuss.

The Cold War as a Thrill: Spies and Escapes

One last and important category of films needs to be included here: the spy and escape thrillers which came to the cinemas in the 1960s. Many of them – the Bond movies in particular – were elaborately staged action films. They used the technical capabilities of cinema to distinguish themselves from television which was not able to visually match them at the time. Unlike the previous category, most of these films had no ambition to take a critical view on society. They exploited the fact that the audience was obviously fascinated by the aura of the clandestine, of secret meetings and deceptive appearances which characterized the intelligence services during the Cold War. It was a perfect choice for the commercial media which targeted the widest possible audience.[74]

Ironically one of the most famous spy thrillers, the British classic *The Spy Who Came in from the Cold*[75] only fits this bill to a limited extent. While the screen adaptation of John le Carré's novel uses classic suspense elements, it could equally be defined as a tragic dystopia. The hero – British agent Alec Leamas played by Richard Burton – is exposed to a cynical play around a double agent that defies all notions of moral superiority the West claimed during the Cold War. The film conveys the message that the end does not justify the means, and the intelligence services' activities show that both East and West operated on the same low level with regard to the moral values they put into practice.

This primarily self-critical message is the exception rather than the rule in this subgenre. More typical movies are Hitchcock's classics *North by Northwest* (1959) and *Torn Curtain* (1966). Hitchcock was primarily interested in creating a sophisticated suspense, while the political level was significantly less important. The audience would have been aware that the Soviet intelligence services were behind the spy ring at the heart of *North by Northwest*, but this fact is never explicitly mentioned. Unlike *The Spy Who Came in from the Cold*, both films leave no doubt that those who support the West are on the good side, but that is the extent of Hitchcock's political message. The Cold War mutated essentially into a backdrop whose main purpose was to create suspense as well as a clandestine and realistic aura.

The same can be said for the James Bond series. It is remarkable how much the films tone down Cold War references in comparison to Ian Fleming's original

74 Cf. Eva Horn, *The Secret War. Treason, Espionage, and Modern Fiction* (Evanston, IL: Northwestern University Press, 2013).
75 UK 1965, director: Martin Ritt.

novels. Of the Bond movies produced in the 1960s, *From Russia with Love*[76] is the one that focuses most on the conflict between East and West. Even in this case Bond's opponent is a *former* KGB agent. She works for the terrorist organization S.P.E.C.T.R.E., which often challenges both East and West in the films, while Bond collaborates with a young KGB agent. The plots of the 1960s Bond films are never based directly on the conflict between the two political camps. It is likely that the film-makers de-politicized the movies to avoid controversy and related economic risks. Their objective was to earn money with good entertainment, and political issues were obviously still considered as an obstacle to profit. The Bond films nevertheless propagated subliminal messages relating to the superiority of the West and the blessings of capitalist consumer markets in particular.[77]

In Germany individual producers endeavored to jump the bandwagon to benefit from the enthusiasm for the successful spy films. More common, however, was another type of action film relating directly to the situation in the divided Germany: escape films. One of the first films about an escape attempt from the GDR was the low-budget production *Flucht nach Berlin* (literally "Flight to Berlin") in 1960.[78] After the Wall had been built a further three action films came into the cinemas simultaneously, all of them based on true stories: the German-American co-production *Tunnel 28*[79] was a film about the escape of 28 GDR citizens to West Berlin through a tunnel they had dug themselves.[80] The film also included a love story, adding drama by keeping the audience in suspense on whether the meticulously prepared escape is going to fail through treachery at the last minute. Produced in 1963, *Durchbruch Lok 234* (in English *The Breakthrough*) recounts the spectacular escape of an engine driver on his train shortly after the wall was built.[81] Lastly, *Verspätung in Marienborn* (in English *Stop Train 349*) also focused

---

76 UK 1963, director: Terence Young.

77 Cf. Bodo Mrozek, "Im Geheimdienst Seiner Majestät, des Kapitalismus. Helden der Popkultur: Spione und Agenten im Kalten Krieg," in *Heldengedenken. Über das heroische Phantasma (Merkur Special Volume 724/725)*, ed. Karl-Heinz Bohrer and Kurt Scheel (Stuttgart: Klett-Cotta, 2009), 982–988.

78 FRG 1960, director: Will Tremper. This was based on the serialized novel *Komm mit nach Berlin – Geschichte einer Flucht*, published in the German magazine *Stern* between May and October 1959; cf. Tremper's autobiography Will Tremper, *Meine wilden Jahre* (Frankfurt am Main: Ullstein, 1993), 522–524.

79 FRG/USA 1962, director: Robert Siodmak.

80 The story was based on the escape of 28 people from Glienicke/Nordbahn to Berlin-Frohnau on January 24, 1962; cf. Marion Detjen, *Ein Loch in der Mauer. Die Geschichte der Fluchthilfe im geteilten Deutschland 1961–1989* (München: Siedler Verlag, 2005), 442–443.

81 FRG 1963, director: Frank Wisbar.

on an escape attempt: a US military duty train is held by Soviet soldiers until the Americans hand over an East German refugee who had slipped aboard the train.[82]

Most of these films follow the same pattern as prison films. The Eastern Bloc is portrayed like a prison, and the plot focuses largely on the tension-filled preparation and execution of the escape.[83] There is little room for the exploration of different motives or the "cost" of the decision. All stories are consistently told from a Western perspective. Any reasonable and courageous individual would naturally want to escape from a communist regime. Against this backdrop an in-depth appreciation of the social reality in "real socialism" seemed obviously obsolete.

Cold War Cinema in Comparison: A Conclusion

Overall this brief overview of film production in the US and West Germany or Europe respectively confirms our initial hypothesis that Cold War culture was subject to considerable change and differed significantly between the two countries.

While the structural prerequisites in the film industry were very different in both countries after 1945, the fundamental issue encountered by producers – the high level of investment required and the incalculable risks – seems to have promoted similar risk prevention strategies: avoiding controversial topics and sticking to proven solutions. Nevertheless, the number of movies dedicated to aspects of the Cold War theme differs considerably. Very few West German films addressed the topic explicitly. Those who did were in most cases initiated and funded by independent film-makers. In Hollywood, Cold War films also formed a minor part of the overall production, but the number of films produced was much higher, both generally and proportionally in terms of the annual output. The fact that the relationship between politics and entertainment was traditionally established before the Cold War would have been of some importance. By contrast, Germany had – even in the Nazi era – mostly produced "unpolitical" entertainment films. For a long time politics was a "no go" in German postwar films; in the

82 *Verspätung in Marienborn*, FRG/F/I 1963, director: Rolf Hädrich; cf. on the background Will Tremper, *Große Klappe. Meine Filmjahre* (Berlin: Rütten & Loening, 1998), 93–102.

83 Cf. Rainer Rother, "Feindliche Brüder: Der Kalte Krieg und der deutsche Film," in *Deutschland im Kalten Krieg 1945–1963*, ed. Dieter Vorsteher et al. (Berlin: Argon Verlag GmbH, 1992), 101–112.

US political themes were possible, at least if the presentation was in alignment with the consensual mainstream.

Political influence and censorship motivated by an anti-communist stance affected film-making in both countries. Assuming a straightforward antagonism between politics and the film industry would be naive; Hollywood in particular maintained a close relationship to the political arena. The scope and type of interventions differed significantly. In the US society and the media contributed to, evoked and supported a paranoid atmosphere which created considerable pressure to act and to make a mark, causing significant repressions. In Germany interventions were limited to individual measures which occurred more or less clandestinely. They clearly reflected an inherited state-authoritarian outlook.

Anti-communist policies in the US and in West Germany were only similar at a first glance. The fear of a communist infiltration and of a serious challenge to national identity reflected in the anti-communist movies of the early 1950s only surfaces rarely in German films. West German cinema production tended to focus on the challenge posed by the country's division or to process the Second World War defeat against the Soviet Union. Entrenched racist and anti-Slavic prejudices amalgamated with the anti-communist concept of the enemy.

In the 1960s different perceptions of the Cold War began to emerge. Especially in the US film-makers questioned the simple geographical or ideological attributions of "good" and "evil." US and British movies critically addressed the policy of nuclear deterrence and the Western self-image. The blatant anti-communism of movies such as John Wayne's "Green Berets" was the exception rather than the rule. This was contrasted by a marked trend to de-politicize films. The spy thriller genre in particular reduced the Cold War to a captivating backdrop. The shift to commercially motivated action movies can also be observed in 1960s West Germany, but the escape theme linked to the division of Germany was much more prominent than espionage stories. Specific experiences also structured plots in other respects. Marked by the war and the Nazi era, the German past shaped a pessimist view on the Cold War, for instance in Helmut Käutner's films.

While detente clearly influenced many movies such as *The Russians are Coming, the Russians are Coming*, attributing this change solely or primarily to the changed political circumstances would be too simplistic. The competition emerging with the rise of television was a decisive factor which resulted in a liberalization and reorientation of cinema production. It also contributed to the evolution of the spy thriller to action films laden with special effects such as the Bond movies. The different Cold War cultures were closely linked with other social developments such as mediatization and seem to reveal as much about the historical experiences and sensitivities of the respective societies as about their perception of the political situation during the Cold War. Not only did the climate of the Cold

War influence film and culture but also different national political-cultural traditions and social experiences were significant when it comes to the perception of and even understanding what Cold War actually meant.

Jennifer Dickey

Remembering the American War in Vietnam

In the fall of 2003 the United States Congress authorized the Vietnam Veterans Memorial Fund (VVMF) to construct "an education center 'at or near the Vietnam Veterans Memorial Site'" on the National Mall in Washington, D.C.[1] This new Education Center was conceived by VVMF founder Jan Scruggs as an interpretive center for the adjacent Vietnam Veterans Memorial. At the Education Center, visitors could "put a face to the more than 58,000 names" that appear on The Wall, as the Vietnam Veterans Memorial is known, learn about the history of The Wall and the Vietnam War, and see some of the 400,000 objects that have been left at The Wall since its opening in 1982.[2]

Writing about the Education Center in 2012, historian Meredith Lair posited that the proposed interpretive center offered "an emerging narrative of the Vietnam War that combines the familiar tropes of the 'Lost Cause' and the 'Good War.'" The proposed interpretive plan included "a linear, military history of conflict that is defined by universal, voluntary sacrifice and a benevolent partnership between citizens and state," hence comparisons to World War II. Yet it also "cast the Vietnam War as a futile yet noble struggle," just as the American Civil War had been reframed in the late nineteenth century, thereby purging from the master narrative all of the "unsavory aspects" of the war. Lair, who served as a consultant for the New Jersey Vietnam Veterans Memorial Foundation and as a "special guest" for several planning meetings for the Education Center at The Wall, noted that curators and fundraisers for the project "must balance public expectation of an affirming, patriotic narrative with professional obligation to share inconvenient and unpleasant truths."[3] Such is the case for curators everywhere who struggle to meet public expectations while oftentimes presenting "inconvenient and unpleasant truths." It is a struggle of paramount importance, at least in the United States, where studies show that for information about the past, the public

1 Michael Neibauer, "Decade-long saga over $115M underground National Mall construction project nears resolution," *Washington Business Journal*, June 24, 2015, accessed March 2, 2016, at http://www.bizjournals.com/washington/breaking_ground/2015/06/decade-long-saga-over-115m-underground-national.html.

2 Campaign for the Education Center at The Wall, accessed March 2, 2016, at http://www.vvmf.org/education-center. The Wall lists the names of the men and women who died while serving with the U.S. armed forces during the Vietnam War or who remain missing.

3 Meredith Lair, "The Education Center at The Wall and the Rewriting of History," *Public Historian*, Vol. 34, No. 1 (2012), 35–36.

DOI 10.1515/9783110496178-009

trusts museums and historic sites above all other sources.[4] Whatever the outcome of the debate about interpretation of the Vietnam War at the Education Center at The Wall, there is no doubt that the war will be framed in terms of individual sacrifice and the Cold War. It is a master narrative that sanitizes the war, gives agency to the American soldiers who died fighting the war, and generally simplifies the war into a valiant struggle by those soldiers against communism, an ideology that threatened the very existence of the United States of America and its version of freedom for four decades following World War II.

Such interpretations of the Vietnam War have become commonplace in the United States. At the National Museum of American History in Washington, D.C., the Vietnam War is interpreted as "a protracted and divisive war against Communist expansion in Southeast Asia."[5] The proposed National Vietnam War Museum in Mineral Wells, Texas, has as its mission statement, "to promote an understanding of the Vietnam Era, while honoring those who served." According to the museum's website, "The war in Vietnam was one of many flags," although only the flags of the United States and its allies (Australia, New Zealand, Philippines, Republic of Korea, Thailand, and the Republic of Vietnam) are presented on the website.[6] And although the museum promises to include a section on the history and culture of Vietnam, the war itself will be framed in the context of the Cold War.[7]

A master narrative of the war has also emerged in museums and historic sites in Vietnam. Much like in the United States, the story of the war is told in a remarkably consistent way. Unlike in the United States, there is no framing of the war as part of a larger, global conflict known as the Cold War, and there is almost no recognition of the more than 3 million Vietnamese soldiers and civilians who were killed during the conflict beyond the broad notion of the collective, heroic sacrifice. While communist ideology is ever present through language and symbols, there is no broader interpretation offered that situates the conflict as a "hot war" in the context of the "Cold War." The war, known in Vietnam as the War of National Salvation Against the Americans, or the American War, is instead

4 Roy Rosenzweig and David Thelen, *The Presence of the Past: Popular Uses of History in American Life* (New York: Columbia University Press, 1998), 20.

5 "The Price of Freedom: Americans at War," National Museum of American History brochure, 2010.

6 "About the National Vietnam War Museum," accessed March 1, 2016, http://www.nationalvnwarmuseum.org/the-museum-today.html.

7 "Museum Themes," accessed March 1, 2016, http://www.nationalvnwarmuseum.org/development-plan/museum-themes.html.

framed as the story of a glorious victory by a united Vietnamese people against an imperialist oppressor.

This chapter focuses on sites in and around Ho Chi Minh City, formerly Saigon, that offer interpretations of the American War. Included in this study are the three most visited tourist sites in Vietnam – Reunification Palace, the War Remnants Museum, and the Cu Chi Tunnels – as well as the less-visited Ap Bac Relic Reserve. Each of these sites presents a celebratory master narrative that adheres to what historian Hue-Tam Ho Tai has described as "the single most important theme in Vietnamese historiography," that of "national unity achieved through heroic sacrifice."[8] This is a narrative that is aimed principally at foreign tourists and one with which the local population generally does not engage. These museums and historic sites in Vietnam make up what anthropologist Christina Schwenkel has described as "transnational sites of memory" that are shaped by globalization as much as by historical events or ideology.[9]

In this now-thriving nation that corporate investors refer to as "the emerging star of Asia," the American War is commemorated in museums, at battlefields, and in cemeteries. The North Vietnamese victory of 1975 is re-enacted each year on April 30 and interpreted year-round at numerous sites in and around Ho Chi Minh City. Almost an entire floor of the Ho Chi Minh City Museum is devoted to an exhibition on the "revolutionary struggle for independence." The Ho Chi Minh Campaign Museum celebrates "the determination of the Party, and the people as a whole, to liberate the South and reunify the country." The two most popular museums for western tourists in Ho Chi Minh City, however, are Reunification Palace, and the War Remnants Museum. Although both sites cast the war as a struggle for national unity against the United States and its "puppet regime" in South Vietnam, the tone of each museum is quite different. Reunification Palace celebrates the "Vietnamese victory," while the War Remnants Museum offers a more somber look at the causes and effects of the decades of war that ravaged Vietnam in the twentieth century.

Reunification Palace, formerly known as Independence Palace, served as the office and residence for the president of the Republic of Vietnam (South Vietnam) from 1966 to 1975.[10] It was here that a North Vietnamese Army tank crashed through the gates on April 30, 1975, signifying the end of the Republic of Vietnam and the

---

8 Scott Laderman, *Tours of Vietnam: War, Travel Guides, and Memory* (Durham: Duke University Press, 2009), 162.

9 Christina Schwenkel, *The American War in Contemporary Vietnam: Transnational Remembrance and Representation* (Bloomington: Indiana University Press, 2009), 146.

10 *Vietnam Heritage Magazine*, No. 2, Vol. 1, March 2011.

beginning of the "reunification" of North and South Vietnam into a single nation. Two tanks from the same battalion as the tank that crashed through the gate are displayed on the side lawn of the palace. The building, designed by award-winning Vietnamese architect Ngo Viet Thu, was completed in 1966 on the site of a previous French colonial palace that was badly damaged by bombs in a 1962 coup attempt. Today the former presidential palace is managed by the central government as a monument to the "reunited nation" of Vietnam.

The *Lonely Planet* guidebook to Vietnam reports that "[t]ime has stood still here since April 30, 1975," and at first glance, this might appear to be the case.[11] The main floors of the palace have been preserved as they were during the occupancy of Nguyen Van Thieu, who served as the president of the Republic of Vietnam from 1967 until 1975. The mid-1960s furnishings that presumably belonged to President Thieu are all there. Signage in Vietnamese, English, French, and Chinese above the entry doors to the various spaces identifies each room by function – Cabinet Meeting Room, Gambling Room, Movie Theatre, Library, Office of the President. In the spring of 2014, additional interpretive signage was added to facilitate self-guided tours through the building. The new reader rails, presented in Vietnamese, French, and English, were created by a team of French designers and curators and funded by the French government as part of a collaboration in honor of the fortieth anniversary of the two countries' diplomatic relationship.[12] The thirty-five reader rails positioned throughout the building present visitors with background information on such innocuous subjects as the architecture of the building as well as heroic stories of the "liberation of Saigon" in April of 1975.[13]

While these new reader rails help guide visitors through the palace, the main interpretive exhibit is a single room in the basement that provides the present-day context for the palace as "a historical and cultural relic" that "contributes to a modern and evolving Ho Chi Minh City and is part of the foundation of and continuance of the Socialist Republic of Vietnam."[14] Using laminated, framed photographs and text panels in Vietnamese and English, the exhibition tells the story of the struggle of Vietnam to push out the "French colonialists" followed by the "American imperialists." The caption for a photograph of President Diem with U.S. Ambassador Frederick Nolting is presented as a meeting to "discuss the

---

11 Nick Ray, *Vietnam* (Footscray, Victoria, Australia: Lonely Planet Publications, 2014), 304.

12 N. Nga, "Self guided tour opens at Vietnam's Reunification Palace," *Thanh Nien News*, 27 April 2014, accessed March 7, 2016, http://www.thanhniennews.com/travel/selfguided-tour-opens-at-vietnams-reunification-palace-25665.html

13 "New Face of the Independence Palace Cultural – Historic Site," accessed March 7, 2016, http://ditich.dinhdoclap.gov.vn/en-us/gioi-thieu/oi-moi-lo-trinh-tham-quan.aspx

14 Text panel, main exhibition, Reunification Palace.

plan to increase the American military interference in Vietnam, Sep. 1962." The caption beneath a photograph of the tank crashing through the gate of the palace reads, "At 10:45 AM, Apr. 30, 1975, the first tanks [sic] of the Liberation army enters Independence Palace." A text panel, quoting from a political report of the Central party Executive Committee at the IVth Communist Party Congress, perhaps best frames the "official" version of the events of April 1975 with the following statement:

> Time will fly but our people's victory in the cause of anti-American Resistance to save our country shall make one of the brightest pages in our national history, a radiant symbol of the complete victory of the revolutionary heroism and human mind, which shall be entered in the world history as a brilliant feat of arms in the XXth century, an event of great international important [sic] & profoundly contemporary in nature.

Through this panel, the reason for the preservation of this cultural relic becomes clear. Showing visitors the relative opulence and excesses of the South Vietnamese regime enhances the significance and meaning of the military victory by the North. In 2010 the official website for Reunification Palace described the building as "the headquarter [sic] of Saigon Government, a place witnessing the merciless war by foreign military interference in Vietnam, a place producing the Republic of Vietnam President Nguyen Van Thieu's many policies which betrayed the people." Recounting the events of April 30, 1975, the website concluded that "Under the leadership by Vietnamese Communist Party our army and people have realized President Ho Chi Minh's aspirations: The people of 2 South-North parts have been reunited in one home. Vietnamese people's spirit and will of national independence and unification have successfully won."[15] While many Americans recoil at this interpretation of the U.S. intervention in Southeast Asia, no one can deny the enormity of the accomplishment by the Vietnamese Communist Party in achieving an objective that the United States spent over 120 billion dollars to prevent. Politics aside, the perseverance of the party is remarkable.

Most visitors to Reunification Palace forego the docent-led tour and wander on their own through the spacious palace. Guidebooks in a variety of languages are available at the entrance, and although the English translations found in the basement exhibition hall are generally grammatically incorrect, the message is clear. In May 2011, I opted for a docent-led tour and was led to the large conference room on the main floor where the docent introduced the site as "the headquar-

---

15 "Cultural Historical Relic of the Palace of Independence," accessed December 28, 2010, http://www.dinhdoclap.gov.vn/index.htm. This particular text, which was on the official website of the site in 2010, is no longer accessible online.

ters for the anti-communist cabinet set up by the U.S. government." The docent explained that "since 1954, Vietnam was divided into two governments, North Vietnam and South Vietnam. North Vietnam was independent. South Vietnam was under the French government, and then the U.S. Army came." The first president of South Vietnam was "controlled by the U.S. Army until 1963, when the U.S. Army staged a coup to remove Diem and put in a new president" who, according to the docent "made the war become fiercer." The U.S. Army was "defeated in Vietnam and forced to sign the Paris Agreement." President Thieu resigned and was followed in quick succession by two other presidents, the last of whom stepped down on April 30, 1975, when the "tank of the Vietnam Army attacked the building." In the immediate aftermath of the "liberation of Saigon," continued the docent, "all of the people who worked for the South Vietnam government fled to the USA with the U.S. Army. All of these people live in California today. Vietnam got independence. The South Vietnam army was destroyed completely." Following this introduction, my group of twenty-three visitors, most of whom were from Thailand, was led through the building with little additional narration beyond a recitation of the name of the various spaces that we were seeing. One exception was the map room adjacent to the president's office, where, according to the docent, President Thieu "met with military advisers to make plans against the Vietnamese people."[16]

The majority of the visitors to Reunification Palace are foreign tourists, clearly the museum's target audience. The story they find there is of the struggle of the Vietnamese for self-determination and unification. Although the Communist Party, which still controls the government of Vietnam, is lauded for its achievement of Ho Chi Minh's dream for a united Vietnam, and the United States is criticized for its "imperial aggression," no broader Cold War context is presented. This is not surprising, given, as Christina Schwenkel has noted, that "There is a marked absence of Cold War discourse [in Vietnam] since the 'American War' in official Vietnamese history was not fought for communism, but against imperialism."[17] The message that comes across most clearly in the designed exhibitions (as opposed to the preserved historic spaces and furnishings) at Reunification Palace is the importance of national unity rather than communist ideology.

A short walk from Reunification Palace is another of Ho Chi Minh City's most visited sites – the War Remnants Museum. The museum, first established in 1975 as the Exhibition House for U.S. and Puppet Crimes, served as a place to display documentation of the atrocities committed by the American and South Vietnam-

16 Docent, Reunification Palace, Ho Chi Minh City, Vietnam, May 13, 2011.

17 Schwenkel, 7.

ese governments. The name was changed in 1990 to the Exhibition House for Crimes of War and Aggression. Shortly before Vietnam resumed diplomatic relations with the United States in 1995, the Exhibition House became the War Remnants Museum in an effort to appeal to the anticipated masses of western tourists expected to flock to Vietnam.[18] Historian Scott Laderman describes the War Remnants Museum as "ground zero for the touristic contest over postwar memory."[19]

Located in a building once occupied by the U.S. Information Service, the War Remnants Museum focuses "on war crimes and aftermaths foreign aggressive forces caused for the Vietnamese people."[20] The museum features an array of military armaments and equipment in the courtyard, including a UH1 helicopter, the workhorse of the American military during the war in Vietnam. A reconstructed "tiger cage" modeled after those in which the South Vietnamese government held and tortured NLF prisoners during the war is offered as evidence of the atrocities perpetrated by the South Vietnamese regime. The main building houses several permanent and temporary exhibits, one of which, "Requiem–The Vietnam Collection," originated in the United States. The Requiem exhibit features a collection of photographs shot by photojournalists in Vietnam who were killed during the conflict. Photographers Horst Faas and Tim Page, both of whom covered the war, compiled the photographs for a book published in 1997.[21] A traveling exhibition based on the book, organized by the Kentucky Requiem Project Steering Committee, soon followed.[22] In March of 2000 Faas and Page traveled to Hanoi, where the exhibition began a two-week run.[23] In April 2000 the Requiem exhibition opened at the War Remnants Museum in Ho Chi Minh City as part of the 25th anniversary celebration "of the liberation of the south and the reunification of the country."[24]

The exhibition is divided into five sections – A Distant War, Escalation, The Quagmire, Last Flight, and Final Days. Each section features indelible images of Vietnam, mostly of the war and violence that wracked the country from the 1950s until 1975. The framed images are accompanied by text in Vietnamese

---

18 Schwenkel, 164.

19 Scott Laderman, *Tours of Vietnam: War, Travel Guides, and Memory* (Durham: Duke University Press, 2009), 161.

20 War Remnants Museum brochure, 2009.

21 Horst Faas and Tim Page, eds., *Requiem by the Photographers Who Died in Vietnam and Indochina*, (New York: Random House, 1997).

22 Schwenkel, 53. "Requiem: Photographers Who Died in Vietnam and Indochina," November 23, 1997, accessed March 7, 2016, http://www.cnn.com/US/9711/23/vietnam.exhibit/.

23 Horst Faas, "'Requiem' Exhibit Travels to Vietnam," The Digital Journalist, accessed March 7, 2016, http://digitaljournalist.org/issue0004/faas1.htm.

24 Schwenkel, 50.

and English – short captions for the photographs, and brief biographies for each photographer who was memorialized. Images from over 130 photographers from eleven countries are displayed. First envisioned as a temporary exhibition, Requiem has become a permanent display at the War Remnants Museum. The exhibit concludes with a wall of portraits of the photographers whose work is featured in the exhibit and thus puts a human face on the death toll of the war.

In the adjacent gallery an exhibition entitled "Historical Truths" offers visitors insight into the "causes, origins and processes of aggressive wars." The exhibition chronicles the history of the French and American Wars in Southeast Asia beginning with Ho Chi Minh's Declaration of Independence from September 2, 1945. The featured artifact is a copy of Ho Chi Minh's address to the Vietnamese people in which he asserted that "the entire Vietnamese people are determined to mobilize all their physical and mental strength, to sacrifice their lives and property in order to safeguard their liberty and independence." The exhibition uses photographs, graphics, maps, and text panels to make the case that the U.S. intervention in Vietnam, which included financial and materiel support of the French between 1950 and 1954, was imperialistic and illegal. Excerpts from the 1954 Geneva Conference spell out the temporary nature of the demarcation line between the north and south and reinforce the principles of "independence, unity, and territorial integrity" promised to Vietnam. In an effort to make the case that the U.S. knowingly violated the terms of the Geneva Agreement, American voices are invoked, such as that of Oregon Senator Wayne Morse, who declared in September 1965:

> In Vietnam, we have totally flouted the rule of law, and we have flouted the United Nations Charter. Ever since our first violations on the Geneva Accords, starting with the imposition of our first puppet regime in South Vietnam, the Diem regime, we have violated one tenet after another of international law and one treaty obligation after another, and the world knows it.

Harsh criticism is levied against the Johnson administration for its "fabrication" of the Gulf of Tonkin incident and the ensuing escalation of the war.

On the ground floor of the museum, the Vestiges of War Crimes and Aftermaths exhibition recounts such horrors as the Son My (My Lai) massacre, the devastating effects of relentless American bombing, and the use of toxic chemicals. Visitors are informed that more than three million Vietnamese were killed during the war, including two million civilians, and that generations of Vietnamese have suffered the after-effects of such toxic chemicals as Agent Orange. The message is conveyed primarily through photographs and text panels. A concrete sewer pipe is the central artifact for the story of the 1969 massacre at Thanh Phong Village allegedly carried out by American troops including U.S. Senator Bob Kerrey. The pipe served as the hiding place for three young children during the massacre. The focal point of the Agent Orange exhibit is a glass tank containing two deformed fetuses.

The War Remnants Museum is run by the department of Culture, Sports, and Tourism of Ho Chi Minh City and received more than 700,000 visitors a year in 2013 and 2014.[25] As is the case throughout Vietnam, all city departments fall under the auspices of the People's Committee of Ho Chi Minh City and its chairman, who also sits on the Communist Party Committee of the city. Despite the Party's loosening of some aspects of control in the last two decades, it remains the overseer of the government at both the local and national levels. The Party controls the message in the museums throughout Vietnam, whether they are operated by the local government, as is the case with the War Remnants Museum, or the national government, as with Reunification Palace. Predictably, the museums glorify the victors and condemn the Americans. Such an approach should come as no surprise. While the War Remnants Museum and Reunification Palace might benefit from a more nuanced presentation, they certainly offer insight into the victor's perspective on one of the defining conflicts of the second half of the twentieth century.

Approximately forty-five miles north of Ho Chi Minh City lies the Cu Chi Tunnel Historic Site, an underground city constructed by Vietnamese liberation forces during the campaign against the French that began in the 1940s. During the American War, the tunnel network was expanded to cover more than 100 miles. Located in a free-fire zone, the area around Cu Chi was the site of some of the most vicious fighting during the war. Today it is one of the most visited historic sites in Vietnam. Christina Schwenkel describes the site as a "commercialized transnational public space for the consumption of a multisensory 'Viet Cong' experience," at which "wartime secrets are divulged and the invisible enemy revealed as young men dressed as guerrillas escort visitors through a day in the life of a typical fighter living underground."[26]

Each day busloads of tourists arrive at Cu Chi, where they are led into the jungle to see the remnants of this underground city that was an important base of operation for the National Liberation Front during the war. The site, which was abandoned for several years after the war, was developed as a tourist destination by the Vietnamese government in the 1990s. Portions of the narrow, claustropho-

---

25 Thuy Vi, "Inside Vietnam's war museum, some truths are still hard to face," *Thanh Nien News*, March 25, 2015, accessed on March 7, 2016, at http://www.thanhniennews.com/travel/inside-vietnams-war-museum-some-truths-are-still-hard-to-face-40296.html.
26 Schwenkel, 88.

bic tunnels that were once navigated by the Vietnamese guerillas were widened to accommodate foreign visitors, and concession stands and gift shops were added. Pavilions where an introductory video could be shown were built, and models of the various weapons used by the guerillas, such as the fabled "tiger trap," were constructed.

Upon arrival, visitors are led to one of the film pavilions where they are shown a model of the tunnel network and a film that explains that the Cu Chi area was once known as a "peaceful place with shady trees, fruit trees, and hundreds of rubber trees," on the outskirts of Saigon, which was "the central city of the Americans." The "ruthless Americans decided to kill these peaceful people thousands of miles from the USA," and "like a crazy batch of devils, they fired into women and children. The bullets of Washington, DC, fired into peaceful people." In Cu Chi, the "simple peasant people" became "heroes for killing Americans" and "stopped all attempts of American soldiers" using such traditional weapons as bamboo sticks.[27] Using reenactment footage shot by Soviet filmmakers in the 1960s, the film relates how these "simple peasants" with a "rifle in one hand and a plow in the other" fought the enemy and made "Cu Chi a treacherous target for Americans." The film proclaims that "No architect could design such a system," and "anyone who went into the system had to admire the communists."[28]

Visitors are then taken to one of the "hidden" entrances to the tunnels, where a guide dressed in the familiar "black pajamas" of the guerillas demonstrates how residents of the tunnels were able to "disappear" into the underground network. Visitors are afforded an opportunity to squeeze into the tiny opening, which is quickly revealed to be a bit small for most westerners. Peals of laughter ensue as group after group of overweight foreigners arrive at the opening and attempt to fit through the hole with little success. Visitors are then paraded past a tiger trap, a trap door over a pit filled with bamboo spikes, followed by a mock-up of an above-ground guerilla campsite and a disabled, abandoned American tank. The "Self-Made Weapons Gallery" features more than half a dozen "traps" rigged with metal and wood spikes in front of a crude mural that shows American soldiers caught in the contraptions. Additional displays include a "military workshop" where mannequins are engaged in scraping gunpowder from unexploded American bombs to make land mines. Perhaps the most popular and talked-about part of the tour is the National Defence [sic] Shooting Range, where for a dollar per bullet visitors can fire an AK-47 or an M16. Adjacent to the shooting range is a gift

---

27 Introductory Film at the Cu Chi National Tunnel Historic Site, Cu Chi District, Ho Chi Minh City, Vietnam, 2011.

28 Introductory film at the Cu Chi Tunnel Historic Site, Ben Dinh, Vietnam, May 15, 2011.

shop that sells a variety of beverages, including rice alcohol, snacks, and souvenirs such as Zippo lighters and miniature helicopters and tanks made from beer and soft-drink cans. The tour continues through a workshop where a young man in guerilla attire is making rubber-soled sandals from old tires, which visitors can purchase for about two dollars. An opportunity to crawl through a section of the tunnels, which has been enlarged to accommodate the larger physique of the foreign visitors, is followed by more gift shops, the last of which has posted on its wall a certificate recognizing the Cu Chi Tunnels as one of the ten most unforgettable sites in Ho Chi Minh City.

Fifty miles southwest of Ho Chi Minh City lies another historic site, the Ap Bac Relic Reserve. Described by historian Neil Sheehan as "the first great battle of the American war in Vietnam," Ap Bac was the site of a ferocious day of fighting between the Army of the Republic of Vietnam (ARVN) and guerillas from the National Liberation Front on January 2, 1963.[29] It was at Ap Bac where Lieutenant Colonel John Paul Vann, a top American advisor to the ARVN, would "learn the mettle of the Vietnamese he had been sent to defeat" when, according to Sheehan, "350 guerillas stood their ground and humbled a modern army four times their number equipped with armor and artillery and supported by helicopters and fighter-bombers."[30] Several UH-1 and CH-21 American helicopters were shot down by the guerillas, and three armored personnel carriers were disabled by the guerillas.

Although historians differ on the significance of the Battle of Ap Bac in the history of the war, following the unification of Vietnam in 1975, the central government recognized the site as historic and created the Ap Bac Relic Reserve. Located near the tiny Mekong Delta hamlet of Ap Bac, the Reserve includes the vast expanse of rice paddies where the American helicopters unloaded ARVN soldiers during the battle. Concrete markers in the shape of helicopters and armed personnel carriers mark the spots where the American weapons of war under the control of ARVN troops were disabled or destroyed by guerilla fighters. Nearby is the memorial-site pavilion containing the graves of three guerillas killed in the battle along with several implements of war, including what became perhaps the single most ubiquitous symbol of U.S. military involvement in Vietnam, a UH-1 helicopter. A large, Socialist-realist statue featuring three guerillas atop a disabled personnel carrier is located in the center of the pavilion, and a nearby "Ap Bac Victory" marker informs visitors that "The victory has stated the indom-

29 Neil Sheehan, *A Bright Shining Lie: John Paul Vann and America in Vietnam* (New York: Vintage Books, 1989), 199.
30 Sheehan, 262.

itable will of Vietnam People. The unconquerable force of the people's war was an alarm for the collapse of Ngo Dinh Diem Regime with the strategy of 'Special war' of American Emperor."[31] Although the English translation on the monument is less than perfect, the meaning is clear. The interpretation, presented in Vietnamese and English, reinforces the message conveyed at other war-related sites throughout Vietnam. The three graves are symbols not of individual sacrifice but rather represent the collective members of the National Liberation Front who died at Ap Bac.

Few visitors make it to the Ap Bac Relic Reserve. Poor road conditions and the site's location in a remote area make such an excursion difficult. The online travel guide, Rusty Compass, highlights Ap Bac as one of two "bookends" to the American War in Vietnam, the other bookend being the rooftop of the apartment building in downtown Ho Chi Minh City from which American helicopters evacuated personnel in April 1975. Rusty Compass founder and travel writer Mark Bowyer describes Ap Bac as a "picture of timeless rural Vietnamese life" where "farmers work in lush rice paddies while children cycle along narrow paths to school" with the "only indicators of its rise to global attention five decades ago" being the "markers that resemble militaristic playground decorations." Rice farmers continue to labor in the fields of Ap Bac in the shadow of these markers, seemingly oblivious to the occasional visitor to the site of the battle that, in the words of Bowyer, would serve as "a terrible omen for the deadly 13-year journey the United States was about to embark on in Vietnam."[32] For the current regime in Vietnam, however, the Ap Bac Relic Reserve is a site of victory, as proclaimed on the historic marker and the entrance gate to the site.

The subject of war and remembrance in Vietnam has been the focus of study for numerous scholars in the past decade. A collection of essays edited by Harvard professor Hue-Tam Ho Tai entitled *The Country of Memory: Remaking the Past in Late Socialist Vietnam*, published in 2001, was one of the first efforts that dealt with remembrance of the war in Vietnam. Reflecting on how the "officially sanctioned" sites of memory have failed to meet the needs of the local population, historian John Bodnar reminds us that "Traditions of public debate over commemoration or monuments did not exist in totalitarian regimes."[33] This is certainly evident in the state-controlled museums and memorial sites in and around

---

31 Inscription on the Ap Bac Victory monument, Ap Bac Relic Reserve, Tien Giang Province, Vietnam, 2010.

32 "Bookends to a war: Ap Bac and that Saigon rooftop," Rusty Compass, accessed February 8, 2012, http://www.rustycompass.com/insights/152-bookends-to-a-war-ap-bac-and-that-saigon-rooftop.

33 Hue-Tam Ho Tai, *The Country of Memory: Remaking the Past in Late Socialist Vietnam* (Berkeley: University of California Press, 2001), x.

Ho Chi Minh City where the interpretive message is the state-sanctioned master narrative of the American War. During my visit to Ho Chi Minh City in May 2011, a university professor expressed to me her dissatisfaction with museums as sites of learning or memory. "I don't go to museums," she said. "They are nothing but propaganda, and I am sickened when I see school children forced to go there. What is shown there is not my experience. I lived through the war, and what is shown in the museums was not how I remember it."[34]

An American acquaintance living in Ho Chi Minh City with family ties to Vietnam echoed those sentiments, stating, "The master narrative is that of the party, not what the Vietnamese people know or believe. That's why the people don't go to museums. School children are marched through there, but no one else goes. That's part of the reason no one in this country wants to study history. What they are taught in school and at museums does not coincide with their life experience. There are no private museums here. All the museums are controlled by the local or national government, so there is no independent voice, no engagement with scholarship. South Vietnam is given no agency in the master narrative. It's always cast as 'the puppet regime.' There is no place in public life for discussion of history beyond the master narrative, and that narrative stops in 1975."[35]

A serendipitous conversation with a group of university students at the post office building in Ho Chi Minh City seemed to confirm the idea that museums and history are of little interest to the younger generations in Vietnam. "I don't like history; it's boring," explained a young woman who was studying accounting at a local university. She and two of her friends were lurking around the old French colonial post office, which is today a magnet for tourists, on a weekday afternoon in order to encounter Americans with whom they could practice their English. "We don't go to museums," the three women said, although one of them admitted she had visited the War Remnants Museum with a group from her school. "I didn't like it," she said. "It had nothing to do with me."[36]

In his 2009 book, *Tours of Vietnam: War, Travel Guides, and Memory*, historian Scott Laderman recounts how comment books at the War Remnants Museum provided an outlet through which visitors could express their opinions about the museum, and perhaps more importantly, about the war that remains

34 University Professor (name withheld to protect the identity of the individual), conversation with the author, May 11, 2011.

35 University employee (name withheld to protect the identity of the individual), conversation with the author, May 12, 2011.

36 Students at the Ho Chi Minh Post Office, conversation with the author, May 18, 2011.

controversial in the public memory.[37] The museum offered exposure "for the first time to a narrative of the war with which they were previously unfamiliar," notes Laderman. This narrative, which "placed Vietnamese rather than American experiences at its center," proved destabilizing to some visitors and infuriating to others.[38] Laderman recounts how the comment books served as a forum in which "an international dialogue on peace and justice" unfolded among "ordinary people," making the museum "a space more akin to the World Social Forum."[39] The comment books have also emerged "as a site of witness," according to Laderman, in which visitors could record "their revulsion at the suffering caused by the war." Perhaps the most interesting aspect of the comment-book forum, however, was the intranational debate among American visitors who began responding to other visitors' comments.[40]

The prospect of a wholesale revision of the interpretive message at the museums and historic sites discussed in this chapter seems unrealistic under the current regime in Vietnam. In 2009, I was asked to co-curate a traveling exhibition on the history of U.S. diplomatic relations with Vietnam – a history that dates back to the 18th century – for the United States Consulate General in Ho Chi Minh City. While the story of American/Vietnamese relations was compelling, equally as compelling was the process of putting together an exhibit in a country that has a different view of that history. Although the Vietnamese government has no control over what the U.S. government says and does within the confines of the U.S. Consulate, the exhibit would be displayed to the public at a reception held off site in celebration of American Independence Day. Officials at the Consulate were advised by their counterparts in the Vietnamese government that our exhibit should not venture beyond 1954, the year that the Viet Minh defeated the French at Dien Bein Phu and the First Indochina War ended with an agreement at the Geneva Accords to divide Vietnam provisionally into two sections, North and South. The state department staff and I were uncomfortable with this limitation, but not wanting to create an international incident, we decided to present the history only up to 1941. Everything that followed was considered too controversial to present from an American point of view in a public setting in Ho Chi Minh City.

The site of the U. S. Consulate in Ho Chi Minh City is itself a place steeped in history. It is the same piece of land where the United States opened its new

37 The comment books referenced by Laderman were from 2002. In recent years during renovations to the building and exhibits, comment books were not available.

38 Laderman, 152.

39 Laderman, 176–177.

40 Laderman, 167.

Embassy in September 1967 – the very Embassy that was attacked in January 1968 during the Tet Offensive. The property, which was abandoned by the United States in April 1975 when the South Vietnamese government collapsed, was reclaimed by the United States following the resumption of diplomatic relations with Vietnam in 1995. The old Embassy building, which had fallen into a state of disrepair, was razed and new buildings constructed on the site to serve as the Consulate General. However, several historic landscape features were preserved, including the round flower beds that once graced the front lawn of the Embassy. In 2002, Ambassador Ray Burghardt had installed in one of the flower beds a replica of the bronze memorial marker that recognized "the brave men who died January 31, 1968, defending this Embassy against the Viet Cong." The individuals are listed by name, rank, and branch of service.[41] Just outside the perimeter wall of the Consulate General compound, no more than thirty feet from the bronze marker that recognizes the Americans who died during the attack on the Embassy, is a memorial marker commemorating the event from the Vietnamese perspective. The Vietnamese text on the red granite marker reads, "The Motherland remembers and the People are forever grateful to the Saigon-Gia Dinh Sector special forces fighters who heroically fought and died for national liberation in the assault on the U.S. Embassy on January 31, 1968 – Lunar New Year of the Monkey." No individual names are listed.

The sites discussed in this chapter, three of which are among the most frequently visited tourist sites in the country by foreigners, will remain of little interest to the Vietnamese people. By presenting a past that seems irrelevant to much of the local community, the directors and curators of these sites have missed an opportunity to engage with that population. Rather than instilling a sense of pride and patriotism in the people, these sites are mostly perceived by locals as mere magnets for tourists who need to have their perspectives broadened through exposure to a version of history that places Vietnamese nationalism at its center. Such a broadening of the mind, especially for American tourists, is admirable, but whether that is indeed the goal of these sites remains the subject of debate. Most American tourists, however moved they may be by the plight of the Vietnamese people during decades of warfare, dismiss much of what they encounter in the museums and historic sites as party doctrine through the use of propaganda. Observant tourists will see few locals at these sites, but they will not likely question why the Vietnamese are not there. These sites from which the party's master narrative is being disseminated ultimately fail to reach the very people whom

---

41 The names listed on the marker are Charles L. Daniel, James C. Marshall, Owen E. Mebust, William M. Sebast, and Jonnie B. Thomas.

they were designed to serve – the Vietnamese. The history presented at these sites, rather than serving as an inspiration or source of contemplation, becomes nothing more than a part of the tourist economy that has become increasingly important in Vietnam.

Globalization and the reintegration by Vietnam into the world economy have transformed the country.[42] However, the museums and historic sites continue to frame Vietnamese history in the narrowest of terms. Western tourists flock to Vietnam in search of "authentic" experiences, and they inevitably encounter the narrative of the American War as presented at Reunification Palace, the War Remnants Museum, and the Cu Chi Tunnels. A few intrepid travelers even make it to the Ap Bac Battlefield. What they encounter at these sites often leaves visitors feeling that they have just been subjected to an interpretation of history that is divorced from the world at large. Yet in some ways, the interpretation of the American War at these sites in Vietnam is no more stilted and biased than is the interpretation of the Vietnam War at museums and memorials in the United States. The biggest difference, perhaps, is in the audience. In Vietnam, two-thirds of the population was born after the reunification of Vietnam in 1975. According to Thomas Fuller of the *New York Times*, "among the young there is gratefulness that they are coming of age now, when the country is at peace after so many centuries of wars, occupation and entanglements with foreign armies."[43] This younger generation has little interest in their nation's struggle against foreign powers that dominated its history in the nineteenth and twentieth centuries. A Pew Research Center poll published in 2015 reported that seventy-eight percent of Vietnamese "had a favorable opinion of the United States," while among those under the age of thirty, a favorable opinion was held by eighty-eight percent.[44]

American veterans who have returned to Vietnam often find the experience to be cathartic. Some of them have even retired to Vietnam. Such is the case with Larry Vetter who counts among his friends Vietnamese war veterans, some of whom fought against the Americans during the war. For Vetter, "It's mind-boggling how much they accept Americans." Nguyen Tien, a former Vietcong fighter

---

42 Vietnam became a member of the World Trade Organization in January 2007.

43 Thomas Fuller, "Capitalist Soul Rises as Ho Chi Minh City Sheds Its Past," New York Times, July 20, 2015, accessed March 2, 2016 at http://www.nytimes.com/2015/07/21/world/asia/ho-chi-minh-city-finds-its-soul-in-a-voracious-capitalism.html?_r=0.

44 Thomas Fuller, "War Veterans Lead the Way in Reconciling Former Enemies," *New York Times*, July 5, 2015, accessed March 2, 2016 at http://www.nytimes.com/2015/07/06/world/asia/war-veterans-lead-the-way-in-reconciling-former-enemies.html.

who was imprisoned and tortured by America's allies in South Vietnam and is now friends with Vetter, explains, "We have closed the door on the past."[45]

In the United States, the Vietnam War continues to cast a long shadow. Americans still struggle to make sense of this Cold War conflict that cost the nation so much blood and treasure. The memory of the Vietnam War in America has been shaped by numerous forces, including film and literature, but among the most important is the Vietnam Veterans Memorial in Washington, D.C. The Memorial and its forthcoming Education Center will continue to impart a great sense of sorrow and sacrifice to those who visit the site, framing the war, as Meredith Lair described, as a "futile yet noble struggle."[46]

U.S. Colonel Harry Summers, in his book *On Strategy: A Critical Analysis of the Vietnam War*, recalled a conversation with his North Vietnamese counterpart in April 1975 in which Summers stated, "You know you never defeated us on the battlefield." Colonel Tu replied, "That may be so but it is also irrelevant."[47] Regardless of the outcome on the battlefield, the United States lost its war in Vietnam when the nation-state that it had worked so hard to create collapsed on April 30, 1975. More than four decades later, the burden of history weighs heavily on Americans who still struggle to understand how, as Howard Zinn once wrote, "the wealthiest and most powerful nation in the history of the world made a maximum military effort, with everything short of atomic bombs, to defeat a nationalist revolutionary movement in a tiny, peasant country – and failed."[48]

45 Ibid.
46 Lair, 35.
47 Harry G. Summers, *On Strategy: A Critical Analysis of the Vietnam War* (New York: Ballantine Books, 1995), 1.
48 Howard Zinn, *A People's History of the United States*, accessed March 2, 2016 at http://www.historyisaweapon.com/defcon1/zinnimvivi18.html.

Muriel Blaive

"The Cold War? I Have it at Home with my Family"

Memories of the 1948–1989 Period Beyond the Iron Curtain

> If I had to sum up in a single sentence what I have learned over the years about how historical work on international politics should be done, it would be this: The key to doing meaningful work in this area is to find some way to get conceptual and empirical issues to link up with each other.[1]

Ever since its inception, Cold War history has been characterized by a top-down approach. It has centered on political history, while for decades only Western archives were accessible and only the Western public sphere benefited from a genuine degree of freedom. This specific constellation has informed and determined the Cold War history paradigms: It has resulted in a geographical asymmetry, with a predominance of studies relating to the West in general and to the U.S. in particular; it has also resulted in a methodological asymmetry, with political and diplomatic history leaving less space to social, everyday life, or oral history. Studies dealing with the social and cultural reception of political events concerned almost exclusively the Western European/American side,[2] while the "cultural turn" was extended to the former East only recently. Overall, Cold War history has been either "conceptual" (theoretical, speculative) or "empirical" (documenting), but the inscription of the vast corpus of theoretical Cold War literature into social history, especially concerning East Central Europe, is still to be fully achieved.

---

1 Marc Trachtenberg, *The Cold War and After: History, Theory, and the Logic of International Politics* (Princeton, NJ: Princeton University Press, 2012), vii.

2 See Annette Vowinckel, Marcus M. Payk, Thomas Lindenberger, "European Cold War Culture(s)? An Introduction," in *Cold War Cultures. Perspectives on Eastern and Western European Societies*, ed. Annette Vowinckel, Marcus M. Payk, Thomas Lindenberger (New York: Berghahn, 2012), 2. See also Marsha Siefert, "East European Cold War Culture(s). Alterities, Commonalities, and Film Industries," Ibid., 25.

Many thanks to Martin Brown and Thomas Lindenberger for their critical remarks on this text, as well as to the latter for allowing me to reproduce passages from two of our common articles. This article is published in the frame of the research project "Rulers and Ruled...," supported by the Grant Academy of the Czech Republic (GACR) number 16-26104S.

DOI 10.1515/9783110496178-010

This article intends to raise awareness of these asymmetries by looking at the Cold War from the bottom up, from an oral and social history, and from a formerly "Eastern" perspective. It proceeds from an oral history study undertaken at the Czech border to Austria in the town of České Velenice in 2006–2008.[3]

České Velenice is a small town (3.500 inhabitants) but was lying directly atop the Iron Curtain, like East Berlin, with a Forbidden Border Zone no wider than a few meters. Before 1918, České Velenice was only a suburb of the Austrian town of Gmünd, as the ethnic and historical border to Bohemia was running ten kilometers further north. But when the Austro-Hungarian Empire was dismantled in 1918–1920 and Czechoslovakia created with the support of the Western powers, the borders of the new state were conceived in order to promote its economic development. They stretched all the way to České Velenice because it housed an important factory for locomotive repairs and because its predominantly Czech workers constituted a Czech-language island in an otherwise Austrian environment. Due to these workers' struggle for their national and language rights since the late 19th century, the factory's passage of ownership into Czech hands emphasized and symbolized the Czechoslovak national victory over the Austrian centuries-long domination.[4]

The Austrian population of Gmünd was resentful, angry and frustrated, and in many instances never really accepted the loss of this territory.[5] As a result of the redrawing of the borders, a sizable German-speaking minority was left behind in České Velenice. After 1945, these historical Austrians were tagged as "Sudeten Germans" and expelled towards Austria. Many of them resettled in Gmünd, just a few hundred meters from their former homes.

The "Cold War" as Western Concept

The České Velenice/Gmünd project[6] was based on the assumption that border towns were a place of increased politicization and our research would document

3 I led 40 semi-directive interviews with town people on their everyday life at the border before and 1989, as well as on their perception and image of Austrians and of themselves. The quotes presented here are issued from these materials and M.B. stands for Muriel Blaive. My colleague Berthold Molden led a similar study on the other side in Gmünd.

4 Muriel Blaive, "České Velenice, eine Stadt an der Grenze zu Österreich," in Muriel Blaive, Berthold Molden, *Grenzfälle. Österreichische und tschechische Erfahrungen am Eisernen Vorhang* (Weitra: Bibliothek der Provinz, 2009), 140–142.

5 Berthold Molden, "Aussenposten des Westens. Das 20. Jahrhundert im Gedächtnis der Grenzstadt Gmünd," in Muriel Blaive, Berthold Molden, *Grenzfälle*, 30–32.

6 Originally designed by Berthold Molden, it was taken over by Libora Oates-Indruchová in

the perception, and presumably the importance, of the Cold War in the eyes of the border population on both sides. In fact, this starting point reflected the Western intellectual paradigm of the Cold War. For decades, academic expertise on the Cold War was centered on the United States and on its international relations with the Soviet bloc – and was almost exclusively of Western provenience. John Gaddis' supposedly "new" Cold War history only endeavored to reestablish the Soviet bloc as a superpower worthy of an equal scrutiny. Its scope was only marginally enlarged to social and cultural history rather than international and diplomatic history: "The 'new' Cold War will be multi-archival, in that it will at least attempt to draw upon the records of all major participants in that conflict. ... It will thus be a truly international history ..."[7] The novelty was meant to be the opening of the ex-Soviet archives; intellectually, the working concept remains essentially unchanged.[8]

Although mainstream scholarship on the Cold War has significantly evolved in recent years,[9] Western academic elites and the wider public have continued to think of the Cold War mainly as an aggressive power contest between the US and the USSR, in which two (implicitly equal) superpowers sought to demonstrate a superior vision of modernity or humanity. But as seen in the highly successful exhibit *Cold War Modern* at the Victoria & Albert Museum in London in 2008,[10] this "egalitarian" vision also tends to convey the impression that everyday life in all its aspects, including consumption and design, fulfilled a similar role on both sides.

It did not. Consumerism was a highly political issue in the East,[11] whereas it represented the antidote to politics in the West. Even when promoted, commis-

2010 – see the description of this project under http://ehp.lbg.ac.at/node/375 (last accessed May 28, 2016.)

7 John Lewis Gaddis, *We Now Know. Rethinking Cold War History* (Oxford: Clarendon Press, 1997), p. 282.

8 For other examples of hugely popular works, but which lack in methodological innovation, see Anne Applebaum, *Iron Curtain: The Crushing of Eastern Europe, 1944–1956* (New York: Doubleday, 2012); (although not relating strictly to the Cold War) Antony Beevor, *Stalingrad* (New York: Viking, 1998); Antony Beevor, *The Fall of Berlin*, 1945 (New York: Viking, 2002).

9 See for instance the major work Melvyn P. Leffler, and Odd Arne Westad, ed., *The Cambridge History of the Cold War* (Cambridge: Cambridge University Press, 2010).

10 *Cold War Modern, Design 1945–1970,* Exhibit at the Victoria & Albert Museum, London (UK), September 2008–January 2009, curated by David Crowley and Jane Pavitt. For a more detailed critique of this exhibit, see Muriel Blaive, "Utopian visions. The 'Cold War' and its political aesthetics," *ZeithistorischeForschungen/Studies in Contemporary History,* vol. 5, n°2 (2009), 313–322, last accessed May 27, 2016, http://www.zeithistorische-forschungen.de/site/40208849/default.aspx.

11 The Khrushchev doctrine, laid out in the famous 1959 "Kitchen Debate," promised that the USSR would "catch up with the West." See Ruth Oldenziel, Karen Zachman, *Cold War Kitchen.*

sioned or instrumentalized in the context of the superpower competition, Western design also meant a benefit for citizens in their everyday lives. The Vespa scooter, for instance, was not only good-looking and symbolic of Western prosperity but defined a genuine way of life for generations of Westerners. In contrast, the 1954 East German P70 coupé made a good impression in international design contests but was mass produced only as the ubiquitous Trabant, whose practicality for its users was in no way comparable to that of a standard Western car.

The often simplistic Western vision of the Cold War was retrospectively validated by the collapse of Communism. Three elements are particularly emblematic of this vision of "winners'" history. The first example is the periodization of the Cold War and the frequent assumption that it stopped with the negotiations for limiting nuclear weapons (the SALT treaties signed between the USA and the USSR in 1972 and 1973). Despite détente, the communist regimes did not come to an end at this time and this artificial "end of the Cold War" meant nothing to the people in the Eastern bloc as far as their everyday lives were concerned.

Another implicit or explicit Western assumption is that the consumerist enthusiasm of the 1950s, the nuclear fear at the beginning of the 1960s, the protests at the end of the 1960s, or the Flower Power movement in the 1970s are integral part of the Cold War atmosphere. Political activism in the West in the 1960s has been erroneously paralleled with the democratization movements in the East, a misunderstanding climaxing with the Prague Spring in Czechoslovakia.[12] Even though the 1968 movements did manifest on both sides of the Iron Curtain a collective rejection of what was perceived as oppressive and all-pervading ideologies, the bourgeois democracy so despised by Rudi Dutschke, Daniel Cohn-Bendit and their peers represented nothing less than a dream come true for the people in Czechoslovakia and, presumably, other Eastern bloc countries.[13] The Western leaders of the 1968 movement were young and looking towards the future; the Eastern leaders were middle-aged and primarily intent on repairing the mistakes of the past.

Finally, in the West the Cold War retroactively became a source of amusement. President Reagan, for instance, cracked one of his most famous jokes in 1984 during a sound check for his weekly radio address, amidst audible laughter:

Americanization, Technology, and European Users (Cambridge: MIT Press, 2009), in particular "Part 1: Staging the Kitchen Debate: Nixon and Khrushchev, 1949 to 1959."

12 See for instance Jeremi Suri, *Power and Protest: Global Revolution and the Rise of Detente.* (Cambridge, MA.: Harvard University Press, 2003).

13 See Jürgen Danyel's article "Rudi Dutschke in Prag oder die Schwierigkeiten der westdeutschen Linken mit dem tschechoslowakischen Experiment," Conference *Der Prager Frühling 1968. Zivilgesellschaft – Medien – Politische und kulturelle Transferprozesse*, Prague, June 15–17, 2008.

"My fellow Americans, I'm pleased to tell you today that I've signed legislation that will outlaw Russia forever. We begin bombing in five minutes."[14] Central and Eastern European humor was of a more bittersweet nature. Though some claimed it "laughed communism out of existence,"[15] emblematic Eastern films of New Wave directors such as Jiří Menzel and Miloš Forman did not describe the Cold War but rather depict life under communism. In the former East, "Cold War" is no more synonymous with the period from 1945 to 1989 than "Real Existing Socialism" would be in the former West. Moreover, "The superpower, bilateral rhetorical images still potent in characterizing American-Russian relations are often tautological, and limit an appreciation of the active role of Europeans from both sides of the 'Curtain.'"[16]

As Patrick Major and Rana Mitter have noted, it is time for a "conscious change in our boundaries of what Cold War history means"; it is time to research its social and cultural aspects not just as an "afterthought to the analysis of high politics."[17] Cold War history paradigms demand to be renewed by balancing what has been so far an almost exclusive interest in international and diplomatic history with questions addressing the social and cultural experience of the people,[18] especially on the Eastern side of the Iron Curtain. This article contends that a study of everyday life challenges these paradigms.

Everyday life history must be approached as an introduction to social history of communism, not as an illustration of the "old" or "new" Cold War history. John Gaddis' recent discovery of the massive extent to which East German women were subjected to rape by Red Army soldiers is a case in point. "The rapes," he writes, "dramatized differences between Soviet authoritarianism and American democracy in ways that could hardly have been more direct. Social history, even gender history, intersected with humanity to make diplomatic history."[19] But the mass rapes had been discussed in German-speaking academic literature at least

---

14 August 11, 1984, audio track freely available on YouTube under the title "Reagan Bombing Joke," last accessed May 27, 2016, http://www.youtube.com/watch?v=Zv13ZnkpWos.

15 Ben Lewis, *Hammer & Tickle: A History of Communism Told through Communist Jokes* (London: Weidenfeld & Nicolson, 2008), cover jacket.

16 Marsha Siefert, art.cit., 44.

17 Patrick Major, Rana Mitter, "East is East and West is West? Towards a Comparative Socio-Cultural History of the Cold War," in *Across the Blocs. Cold War Cultural and Social History*, ed. Patrick Major, Rana Mitter, (London: Frank Cass, 2004), 1. See also the very interesting work produced by the Aleksanteri Institute in Helsinki, for instance Autio-Sarasmo, Sari, and Brendan Humphreys. *Winter Kept Us Warm: Cold War Interactions Reconsidered*. Helsinki: Aleksanteri Institute, 2010.

18 As argued also here Patrick Major, Rana Mitter, Ibid., 2.

19 Gaddis, *We Now Know*, 287.

since 1965[20] and were even known in English-speaking journalistic literature.[21] Moreover, in everyday life of Central European populations normative assumptions and choices were not always as clearly laid out as when a brutal rape was committed by an enemy soldier. Everyday reality placed people amidst a complex set of values, choices, and obligations which did not always prompt easy moral choices.

If the home front is as integrated as "social history in its broad sense of the 'ordinary' and 'everyday'" in the "extraordinary circumstances" of the Cold War,[22] the issues at stake are complex: Can one speak of a public opinion, or at least of a "popular opinion" (Paul Corner[23]) in the case of Communist societies? Can one assume that a "domestic consensus for Cold War," putting a "premium on conformity of ideas," reigned in Eastern European societies the same way it did in the U.S.?[24] Can one find a comparable "nexus between high politics and everyday society" which would help us understand the "social disciplinary aspects of America's Cold War"?[25]

Local studies and oral history are a priceless tool for discussing these questions. In fact, it took no more than a few hours to discover a striking discrepancy in perception between the Western conception of the Cold War and the one prevailing in the former Eastern Europe. When posing the standardized question in České Velenice: "How have you experienced the Cold War?" the answers instantly illustrated the fact that this academic term is not part of Czech daily vocabulary. Interviewees as a rule watched with awe and were at a loss for an answer. Olga Rájová (age 59), one of the first to be asked, made this point with a touch of humor:

> M.B. Did you ever speak at home of the Cold War?
> O.R. No, no [laughter.]
> M.B. What word would you use to describe the Cold War, then?
> O.R. The cold war? I have it at home with my family.[26]

20 Erich Kuby, *Die Russen in Berlin* (Munich: Scherz, 1965).

21 See Cornelius Ryan, *The Last Battle* (New York: Simon & Schuster, 1966).

22 Major, Mitter, *Across the Blocs*, 3.

23 Corner, Paul, ed., *Popular Opinion in Totalitarian Regimes: Fascism, Nazism, Communism.* (Oxford: Oxford University Press, 2009).

24 Major, Mitter, *Across the Blocs*, 4.

25 Ibid., 4.

26 Muriel Blaive, "České Velenice, eine Stadt an der Grenze zu Österreich," in Muriel Blaive, Berthold Molden, *Grenzfälle*, 156.

Most interviewees were smiling at the incongruity of the question. As an abstract notion, the Cold War was not completely unknown since it is now taught in school and occasionally referred to in the media. But it is in no way the concept spontaneously used to refer to the 1948–1989 period. The standard category of reference is instead "life under communism."

The Human Dimension of Policing the Border

While the interaction between the population and the communist authorities was complex, two of its most striking forms were denouncing and informing. Informing generally implied a regular, often paid or materially compensated, relationship to the secret police and was, as such, a social practice typical of communism. Although also practiced everywhere, denunciation was considered by the authorities as the cornerstone of an efficient surveillance of the border. Sheila Fitzpatrick and Robert Gellately defined it as a form of

> spontaneous communication from individual citizens to the state (or to another authority such as the church) containing accusations of wrongdoing by other citizens or officials and implicitly or explicitly calling for punishment. Typically, denunciations are written and delivered privately to an addressee rather than published. They are likely to invoke state (or church) values and to disclaim any personal interest on the part of the writer, citing duty to the state (or the public good) as the reason for offering information to the authorities.[27]

The normative ambivalence implicit in the activity of denouncing was crucial for the local popular opinion's apparent support to regime policies concerning the guarding of the border: Just as the French language opposes *dénonciation* to *délation*, denunciation can have a positive connotation (good, public-spirited) and a negative one (treacherous, self-interested.) It makes all the difference between a disinterested accusation guided by patriotic motivations and an interested one guided by the search for a personal reward.[28] Most importantly, the mere existence of the first type of motivation sufficed to morally justify the massive practice of the second.

The communist regime's policy concerning the border population focused on one model type of citizen: the civilian helper of the border guards, i.e. the

27 Sheila Fitzpatrick, Robert Gellately, "Introduction to the Practices of Denunciation in Modern European History," *Journal of Modern History,* Vol. 68, No. 4 (December 1996): 747.

28 Sheila Fitzpatrick, "Signals from Below: Soviet Letters of Denunciation of the 1930s," *Journal of Modern History*, Ibid., 832.

Auxiliary Border Guard. The Iron Curtain, the emblem of the Cold War, was not a "technological monolith" but the "accumulated actions of residents who lived along it," it was a "living system" reminding us of the "human dimension" of the border.[29] Auxiliary Border Guards epitomize this human dimension with all its qualities and flaws.[30]

Czechoslovak Minister of the Interior Rudolf Barák began the 1956 bill concerning the Auxiliary Border Guards (Pomocní pohraniční stráž or PPS) with a poetic sentence: "The protection of the state borders from the infiltration of spies, saboteurs, terrorists and other enemies of our state and of the whole camp of progress is the duty of each and every citizen."[31] His high hopes for the civilians of the border regions, the special target of this "duty call," rapidly became clear: "With the civilian population inhabiting the border territory, the ... Border Guard Units (PS) ... have substantial resources at their disposal to help them secure the state border."[32] The "Statute of Auxiliary Border Guards" therefore meant to "judiciously and fully use the borderland population" to achieve this aim. The propagandist claim that the border was preventing capitalist spies from flooding into the country rather than honest citizens from getting out was particularly dear to that minister.[33]

The text of a speech to be read in front of Auxiliary Border Guards and Border Guard Units across the whole nation in the mid-1950s also points out a special bond:[34] "Without the purposeful help of the borderland population, the border

---

29 Edith Sheffer, *Burned Bridge. How East and West Germans Made the Iron Curtain* (Oxford: Oxford University Press, 2011), 167.

30 This passage, part of my research project on České Velenice, is largely reproduced from the article: Muriel Blaive, Thomas Lindenberger, "A Dictatorship of Limits: Border Control as a Paradigmatic Practice of Communist Governance," in Jana Osterkamp, Joachim von Puttkamer, eds., *Sozialistische Staatlichkeit*, (Oldenburg: Oldenburg Verlag, (Bad Wiessee Tagung des Collegium Carolinum 2009), 2011), 185–188.

31 "Návrh tajného rozkazu ministra vnitra," 1956, no shelf mark, archives of the Czechoslovak Ministry of the Interior in Brno-Kanice.

32 Ibid.

33 At the Central Committee meeting of March 29–30, 1956, he claimed that hidden and vicious enemies kept trying to invade the Czechoslovak territory by all possible means. They were passing the Iron Curtain "underwater in diving gear" or "above our heads in hot air balloons." See Fond 01, sv.44, aj.49, 29–30 March 1956, 4. Diskuse, l.511, s. Barák, 241–244, Archives of the Central Committee of the Czechoslovak Communist Party (ÚV KSČ.)

34 The places where the described incidents took place are not named; however, it is evident from the topographic description that at least a few of them occurred in České Velenice, and most were typical situations partly or largely reproduced in Secret Police (StB) material concerning this town. Hence all of the following situations could have played out in České Velenice and can be read as such.

guards' work is much more difficult. The cooperation of the population is a considerable help ...; fully instructed inhabitants are their best allies."[35] Without their help "it would have taken a lot more time, effort and means to accomplish the same operation." Locals had a "sixth sense" for spotting the difference between "incomers and autochthones" and for "unmasking the enemy who is trying to pass the state border, especially towards abroad" [sic].[36]

A number of edifying examples illustrated this special bond. Gamekeeper L. was lying in wait in August 1954 when he noticed, in the late afternoon, an "unknown man" hiding in the woods. He ordered his wife to cover him with a small rifle and he stepped forward to check the man's ID. Upon seeing that this person did not have a permission slip allowing him to enter the Border Zone, he called the border guards. The interrogation revealed that the man had intended to pass the border illegally: "Gamekeeper L. gave proof of his attention, vigilance and watchfulness towards an unknown person walking around in a markedly guarded way" and acted in an "exemplary way," with a real "border guarding spirit," worthy of an Auxiliary Border Guard.[37]

H., also an Auxiliary Border Guard, was having a postprandial walk one evening in April 1955 when he noticed two young men sitting at the border of the woods in the vicinity of the train station. Conspicuously enough in his eyes, they were carrying backpacks. He went to ask them what they were doing in the Border Zone. "Because he ascertained inconsistencies in their story," he "energetically bid them to follow him" to his home, where he called the border guards. The two boys were arrested and as it turned out, they were students with bad results in school who wanted to escape abroad for fear of their parents' reaction. Again, the report was full of praise: Citizen H. showed "determination and courage" when he stood up to "two trespassers of whom he couldn't have known whether they were armed or not" and "energetically delivered them to the border guards."[38]

Auxiliary Border Guards were also useful during their working hours. F. was at his work post in his factory, watching the border guard patrol passing by, when he saw an unknown person approaching the fence in hiding. He ran out of the factory to share his discovery and the man was caught. The speaker again underlined the usefulness of such watchful citizens: had F. not actually seen the man, the patrol would probably never have found him as he was well hidden in

---

35 Přednáška Výsledky činnosti PPS při ochraně státních hranic v r.1955 – příklady správné i nesprávné činnosti," no date (1956?), no shelf mark, archives in Brno-Kanice, p. 1.

36 Ibid., 1.

37 Ibid., 2.

38 Ibid., 2.

a bush.[39] Other examples of watchful locals were given. These model citizens, however, needed to be properly instructed and to learn tricks such as to never step over a trespasser's fresh trace so as not to complicate the dogs' work.

Another case symbolizes the crossing of the line from armed surveillance to civilian denunciation: In May 1955 a man was sitting in a pub and he tried to chat the waitress into telling him details about the exact location and disposition of the fence. Finding these questions "suspicious," the woman phoned her husband, an Auxiliary Border Guard. He in turn jumped on his motorcycle and went to alert the border guards. Although the professional units missed the man, who had already left the pub, the husband saw him on his way back and arrested him without fight. As the paper commented, the "involvement of family members testifies to the fact that the protection of the state border is becoming an almost natural thing for all the border population."[40]

The role of women was held in high esteem: "As a matter of fact, our women are a lot more vigilant and they have a finer aptitude at recognizing outsiders and their behavior, allowing them to size up trespassers of the state borders or men with something suspicious on their minds."[41] In July 1955, forest employee K. noticed a man at the edge of the woods behind the school. She did not hesitate and went to the border police to warn them. While they were looking for him, the said "trespasser" came across another women, B., who was in turn the mother of an Auxiliary Border Guard. She promised to give him bread and led him in the direction of the border guards until they were spotted and he was arrested. Again, the "courage" and the "intelligence," if not the "outright genius" of "our women," who outmaneuvered "much stronger men" into being caught, was enthusiastically hailed.[42]

Sometimes, the well-oiled denunciation mechanism jammed – not that it helped the "trespassers," who were all caught in the end anyway, at least in the cases described here. "Good" denunciation work spared time and energy; "bad" work demanded more effort, albeit for the same result. For instance, when an unknown man came knocking at Auxiliary Border Guard J.'s door and asked him the way to the border, he refused to show it to him and threatened to denounce him to the police. "Obviously, the trespasser didn't wait" until the police was brought in by J.'s brother-in-law and it took twelve hours to catch him "whereas

39 Ibid., 5.
40 Ibid., 3.
41 Ibid., 4.
42 Ibid., 4.

it would have taken only a few minutes to do so if J. had acted sensibly and with initiative."[43]

And finally, the Minister praised children and especially the Pioneers for their dedication and usefulness in catching "trespassers." The border police held seminars on the "importance of surveying the state border" for the children's benefit and got a "very positive feedback":

> Schoolchildren thus all became small Auxiliary Border Guards and brought the border police on the trace of many trespassers. A young Pioneer naturally tends to escape the attention even of a vigilant trespasser, who then doesn't hide from him, and children are obviously spending a lot more time outdoors, where they have better chances to run into a trespasser and to notify the border police of his presence.[44]

The Cooperation Between the Local Population and the Authorities

In a town where everyday life was so closely connected to the guarding of the border, locals did collectively entertain a privileged relationship with the Secret and Army Police and practiced denunciation on a regular basis. Why? Without attempting in any way to excuse inexcusable behavior, one should realize that their motivations were complex and not always, or not only, morally reprehensible.

Part of them lay in patriotic feelings. The surveillance of the Iron Curtain was predicated on inventing and perpetuating an enemy, a common foe uniting the regime and its population. In the Czech case, in view of recent and older history the "natural" enemy was Austria/Germany, i.e. it was situated just across the border. The barbed wire fence of the Iron Curtain was highly reminiscent of a similar barrier hastily put together in 1938 by the last democratic regime in Czechoslovakia as a defense against Hitler's Greater Germany before the cataclysm of the Second World War.[45] Most people also gave credit to the Communist regime and to its Soviet ally for liberating them from German occupation and for protecting them from such an invasion ever occurring again – a "credit" artfully

43 Ibid., 6.

44 Ibid., 7.

45 See the pictures in Alena Jílková and Tomáš Jílek, eds., *Železná opona. Československá státní hranice od Jáchymova po Bratislavu 1948–1989* (Prague: Baset, 2006).

entertained by an unrelenting Communist propaganda depicting revanchism as the core value of (West) German and Austrian society.[46]

The regular, and highly publicized, arrest of alleged "Western spies" trying to penetrate Czechoslovak territory might appear today as testament to a ridiculous Communist folklore, but this propaganda delineated a useful potential for moral ambivalence. Its impact on people's perceptions is still visible today. The 37-year-old director of the local train repair shop Jakub Obědval was 18 years old in 1989 and his father was the (Communist) director of the said factory. When asked if local citizens guarded the border against the people trying to escape or against the outside enemy trying to leak in the country, he eagerly answered:

> Both. *Both.* That's just what I wanted to say. The fact is, if you want, that agents were leaking on both sides of the border, and agents came in. And ... they would be tough and they would shoot at the border.

I have as yet not come across any documented case of such agents penetrating Czechoslovak territory by force but such an argument testifies to the fact that even the most unlikely propaganda could serve as justification or self-justification if it fulfilled a social need.

Another motivation mentioned by the interviewees was the fear of what the escapees were willing to do to anyone trying to stop them. The Czech audience under Communism was periodically reminded of a highly publicized case in 1953 which became even more controversial after 1989: that of the sons of Josef Mašín, a Czech national hero for his partisan activities during the Second World War, who was eventually executed by the Nazis. While fleeing West in 1953, the Mašín brothers and their friend Milan Paumer killed six people: one Czech militiaman, two Czech policemen, and three East German border guards. Their case has raised passionate debates in the Czech Republic since the Velvet Revolution. Some see them as anti-Communist hero fighters worthy of the state decorations they were handed, others consider them petty criminals who deserve to be arrested.[47]

As the daughter of one of these brothers points out in her exculpatory account, armed struggle against Nazi oppression has been canonized by the Czech nation as "moral and necessary," but the public is much more ambivalent about armed

46 For a more detailed analysis of pan-Slavism and anti-Germanism as a core value of the Czechoslovak communist regime, see Muriel Blaive, *Une déstalinisation manquée. Tchécoslovaquie 1956* (Brussels: Complexe, 2005).

47 For a description of their flight, see Barbara Masin, *Gauntlet. Five Friends, 20,000 Enemy Troops, and the Secret that Could Have Changed the Course of the Cold War* (London: Green Hill, 2006).

resistance to the Communist regime. The Mašíns resorted to the same fighting methods as their father, but they have been subjected to a heated "political debate on morality."[48] The existence of this discussion points to a genuine level of legitimacy for the Communist regime because people would rather defend the regime against criminals than suspected criminals against the regime. As Pavel Rychetský, then Minister of Justice, put it in 1995: "A fight against totalitarianism is okay, but nobody may die as a result."[49]

Although they did not explicitly refer to it, the widely publicized Mašíns' case certainly contributed to many of the interviewees' contemptuous perception that these criminals, real or imagined, who wanted to escape to the West after having committed different misdeeds would then be treated there as political refugees. The United States government did grant political asylum to the Mašín brothers. Jakub Obědval explained:

> We are all against shooting. But like I said, it was a question of life and death. ... There were cases when the people didn't escape because of political reasons but because they were swindlers or because they killed somebody and they could be armed. There were such cases and not just a few, people who had done something and had to escape to the West and there they were greeted like political escapees. Isn't that so?

Olga Rájová (59-year old) used to work outdoors, right at the gate marking the border on the railroad tracks to Austria. She got quite scared once when she bumped into a dozing soldier at four in the morning, who suddenly woke up and pointed his gun at her:

> Well, I almost made a mess in my pants, because in the night, like this, well, I was scared. But I wasn't afraid of [the soldiers], rather, I was afraid of those who would want to use this road to escape, I was afraid of our own people. Because you never know who you meet, who you run into.

Escapees were not only running away from dictatorship but also from petty events in their daily lives.[50] Vojtěch Ripka and his team have led the only comprehensive study to date of escapees killed at the border.[51] Their work shows that in

48 Ibid., 337.

49 Ibid., 337.

50 Duane Huguenin, "Mutations des pratiques répressives de la police secrète tchécoslovaque (1956–1968.) Du recours à la force au contrôle social," *Vingtième siècle*, Vol. 96, No. 4 (2007): 163–177.

51 Vojtěch Ripka, Tereza Mašková, *Železná opona v Československu. Usmrcení na československých státních hranicích v letech 1948–1989* (Iron Curtain in Czechoslovakia. People Killed at the State Border in the Years 1948–1989), (Prague: Ústav pro studium totalitních režimů, 2015).

numerous cases, people escaped for personal rather than political reasons; quite a few escapees were petty or serious criminals. Furthermore, as in many other instances, the better documented East German case is enlightening. It appears that the fear of "trespassers" was shared by border guards. GDR border police supposedly considered Czech escapees in particular as good marksmen who did not hesitate to shoot. Their "fearsome reputation grew to the point that troops would not move forward without armed personnel carriers supporting them."[52]

In her study of the small East German community of Sonnenberg, Edith Sheffer cites a local report from 1959–1960 according to which 12% of defectors to the West were thought to have left either because, or in anticipation, of a police investigation. More often than not, the trigger was a minor infraction such as a brawl in a pub or an assault.[53] Undercutting many Cold War historians who never even considered everyday negotiation between the people and the communist authorities, she claims that town people would even bluff about intending to leave in order to gain better apartments or working conditions.[54]

Whether the proportion of people escaping for petty and/or criminal reasons really was 12% is not of real substance here. What matters is that the existence of such cases, of which interviewees were aware, provided moral ground for the local people who engaged in denunciation or in informing. Even if only one escapee in eight had immoral and illegitimate motivations to get out, the mere fact that not all escapees were freedom-craving, decent people but could also be small-time crooks, swindlers, or assassins who passed themselves off as political refugees in the West, was enough to justify this social practice of denunciation. This context relativized the political dimension of the practice. As Jakub Obědval expressed it:

> J.O. Some people [denounced escapees] to help protect public and their own property.
>
> M.B. Which is not necessarily political...?
>
> J.O. Exactly, which may not necessarily be understood as something political, something linked to political beliefs.

Other motivations for obeying the "denunciation duty" predicated by the guarding of the border include of course, and perhaps primarily, fear of what the authorities might do to the concerned citizens if they were caught failing at their

52 Barbara Masin, *Gauntlet*, 324.

53 Edith Sheffer, *Burned Bridge. How East and West Germans Made the Iron Curtain*, 145.

54 For these "flight negotiations," see Ibid., 147.

surveillance task and abstained from denouncing a potential escapee. Important was also anticipation of support from the regime for securing a decent life for their families (children studying, good living conditions, etc.), as well as genuine support for socialism in Czechoslovakia – a motivation easy to discard today as misplaced idealism but which must not be underestimated.

These and many other motivations combining the carrot and the stick, voluntary, semi-voluntary, repressive, and potentially or concretely threatening dimensions constituted a gray zone of everyday life under a dictatorship. They interacted within one and the same person so that a unique and distinct motivation would rarely prove relevant to a black and white retrospective judgment. Jakub Obědval expressed this ambivalence in a meaningful way:

> M.B. So the border between good and bad is not always clear?
>
> J.O. It isn't. Why should it be? Nothing is like this in life. Where is the border between good and bad? Can we draw a thick line? It's not possible.

From (Self)-Protection to (Self-)Policing

This impossibility to draw a thick line between "good" and "bad" makes all the difference between Cold War history in the former West and the history of Central and Eastern European countries and societies under communism. East of the Iron Curtain it is a history "without heroes,"[55] which did not neatly oppose two camps presumably representing the "good" and the "bad" side, but which divided each society and in time, each individual, as they were caught in the vagaries of everyday survival under a dictatorship.

The surveillance system established to fight against the candidates to emigration rapidly led to the establishment of a self-surveillance system, geared at the local population to monitor itself and to "voluntarily" entertain a climate of terror turned against its own body. It was a simple, efficient, and mainly unavoidable logic: Any local who would fail to denounce a potential escapee and who would thus endanger the efficiency of guarding the border would have to be denounced by another local. A (self-)protecting gesture thus led to a (self-)policing practice.

The interviewees collectively estimated that perhaps up to half of the town population was spying on behalf of the secret or border police, a high percentage

55 Wendy Z. Goldman, *Inventing the Enemy: Denunciation and Terror in Stalin's Russia* (Cambridge: Cambridge University Press, 2011), 298.

which is rather impossible to measure and confirm, but which is not unrealistic in view of German findings currently being worked out at the research department of the Federal Commissioner for Stasi Files (BStU) in Germany and elsewhere.[56]

The climate of mutual denunciations intensified by the border proximity is aptly described by Josefa Kramárová, a 38-year-old railway station employee:

> M.B. Why was the regime so tough here and not elsewhere?
>
> J.K. Because people created this among themselves. They made it worse.
>
> M.B. Because they collaborated with the border guards, the Militia, the Secret Police?
>
> J.K. Yeah, they simply went too far. The people themselves denounced each other. They simply made it worse. Not the regime but the people made it tougher for themselves in this regime. People created this themselves!

Olga Rájová (59-year-old industrial photographer) holds a similar view:

> O.R. Here every other person was an "Auxiliary," either with the border guards or with the police. They denounced each other, they hid things from one another, they envied each other.
>
> M.B. What would they denounce, for instance?
>
> O.R. Small crap things, I would say. Nobody had any relationships, there was nothing here, actually everything was monitored.

In effect, this study of everyday life under Communism in České Velenice reveals the elements of a tacit social contract: the town was allowed to continue to exist after the war despite its proximity to the border because it was highly industrial, a workers' stronghold, and because it symbolized the Czech national project. People also benefited from improved material conditions compared to the rest of the country. In exchange, the border population was strongly expected, and outright compelled, to take part in the border guarding.

This shows that the Communist regime carved sources of legitimacy for itself that leave no space to the champions of a dogmatic totalitarian approach. České

---

56 See for instance Gerhard Sälter, *Grenzpolizisten, Konformität, Verweigerung und Repression in der Grenzpolizei und der Grenztruppen der DDR 1952–1965* (Berlin: Ch. Links, 2009). We might add that according to Edith Sheffer, in East German Sonnenberg one in ten male borderland residents already served as (visible) Voluntary Border Helpers or Police Helper. See Edith Sheffer, *Burned Bridge*, 186.

Velenice's situation was not the result of an abstract "totalitarian" system, but of a real, concrete, compromise on a daily basis. State repression played a crucial role in initiating this particular atmosphere, and without it this state of affairs would not have endured, but actual violence was not resorted to on a massive scale. The regime lasted in time and was rooted in society only because the people themselves participated in the repression policy – this was true for the entire communist bloc. These instituted practices of self-control and denunciation at the border epitomized the application of Communist governance.[57] The claims exerted by the state on the local population because of the Iron Curtain proximity helps to reveal the social mechanisms of compliance and servility, as well as the population's *Eigen-Sinn* or "sense of oneself."[58] But this case also documents that people would indulge in, or resign themselves to, or surrender to, collaborating with the communist regime if and when they could find a form of moral (self)-justification for it. Purposely creating problems for a fellow human being, including putting him/her at risk to end up in the hands of the police, in jail, or even shot dead if he/she was intending to pass the border, rarely was, as far as I could infer from the interviews, a purely "evil" act; people tended to justify their behavior in their own eyes with at least some form of self-rationalization. This is where a well-targeted regime propaganda played a crucial role. Even the least credible arguments became useful if they fulfilled a social need.

Can this exacerbated political climate really be considered as the Eastern avatar of the Cold War? This study suggests the following answer: Only insofar as

---

57 For a more detailed analysis of border guarding as a case study of communist governance see Muriel Blaive, Thomas Lindenberger, "Border Guarding as a Social Practice; A Case Study of Czech Communist Surveillance and Hidden Transcripts," in Marc Silberman, Karen E. Till, Janet Ward, *Walls, Borders, Boundaries. Spatial and Cultural Practices in Europe* (New York: Berghahn, 2012), 97–112.

58 "Eigen-sinn – Key term in Lüdtke's analysis of workers' everyday life, denoting wilfulness, spontaneous self-will, a kind of self-affirmation, an act of (re)appropriating alienated social relations on and off the shop floor by self-assertive prankishness, demarcating a space of one's own. There is a disjunction between formalized politics and the prankish, stylized, misanthropic distancing from all constraints or incentives present in the everyday politics of Eigen-Sinn. In standard parlance, the word has pejorative overtones, referring to 'obstreperous, obstinate' behavior, usually of children. The 'discompounding' of writing it as Eigen-Sinn stresses its root signification of 'one's own sense, own meaning.' It is semantically linked to aneignen (appropriate, reappropriate, reclaim)." See Alf Lüdtke, ed, *The History of Everyday Life: Reconstructing Historical Experiences and Ways of Life* (Princeton, NJ: Princeton University Press, 1995), 313–314. In layman's terms, the regime could not control everything in everybody's life, which implies that individuals could carve spaces of micro-resistance, but also that some collaboration or support of the regime was voluntary and genuine.

it is considered in its specific social and socio-political context, that of everyday life under communism – a context in which the notion of cold war can be devoid of its political significance and reappropriated as an everyday conflict between husband and wife ("The cold war? I have it at home with my family.") The border guarding situation was more about the social practice of domination under Communism than about world overreach. It illustrates Communist rule and the managing of Communist state legitimacy more than superpower competition. It reveals more of the Communist Party's prerogatives in defining the limits of societal activity and of society's everyday negotiation of this rule than of equality in the space and arms race.

The notion of Cold War applied to the Communist experience is misleading because of its predominantly top-down perspective. Seen from this political angle, the Communist state would be regarded primarily as an institution of repression. What the study of České Velenice shows, however, is that repression was inextricably accompanied by self-repression, i.e. by the constant "integration of the controlled into the activity of controlling."[59] A large part of the adult population was not only policed but policing to some degree. The České Velenice population was also actively co-defining the terms of the Communist rule, as testified by the number of picturesque popular demands which were negotiated with the Communist authorities in defiance of the usual understanding of dictatorship: For instance traditional Saturday afternoon dancing teas were organized in the midst of the Forbidden Border Zone under Stalinism; local families had continued access to the said Forbidden Zone to gather blueberries and mushrooms amidst border guards patrols; or the No Man's Land between the two rows of barbed wire marking the Iron Curtain was turned into a zone of public amusement, since it is where the local swimming pool was oddly situated.[60]

This is why it is inappropriate to see the Cold War seen as "a contest of good versus evil."[61] As John Gaddis points out, when examining "the gap between popular and academic perceptions of the past today ... historians seem to want to tell the public what its memories ought to be. A little self-scrutiny might be in order here, to see whether we are treating the distant past and the recent past in exactly the same way."[62] The inequality in treatment between East and West needs

59 See Thomas Lindenberger, "Creating state socialist governance: The case of the Deutsche Volkspolizei," in Konrad Jarausch, ed., *Dictatorship As Experience. Towards a Socio-Cultural History of the GDR* (New-York: Berghahn, 1999), 130.

60 Muriel Blaive, "České Velenice, eine Stadt an der Grenze zu Österreich," in Muriel Blaive, Berthold Molden, *Grenzfälle*, 137–203.

61 John Gaddis, *We Now Know*, 287.

62 Ibid., 287.

to be urgently remedied but the point hardly is to bring the archival study of the Communist political elites to the Western level; it rather resides in the questioning and examination of the normal people's involvement in the establishment, maintenance and perpetuation of the Communist regime over several decades.

As both the Austrian and the Czech interviews show, the source of hostility which still exists today between České Velenice and Gmünd originated already in 1918, and not in the Cold War. The Austrian/Czech border has stood as a symbol of the Communist-capitalist, East-West divide, while Gmünd was even known as the "Berlin of the Waldviertel." Yet when studied in greater detail, this border has primarily marked the collapse of the Habsburg Empire and it is still remembered as such. This border tells the story of 1918, not of the Cold War.

The Displacement of Memory

As the interviews abundantly demonstrate, the "Eastern Cold War" is a history without heroes. But a discrepancy seems to be growing between the living memory of the communist times, which leaves little or no place to the "Cold War" as a concept, and the media, historical, and political approach to this recent history. Ever since 1989, Central European post-Communist elites have tended to dismiss the Communist past as a unilateral dictatorship of one camp (Communist party members; Secret Police informers) over the other (the rest of society), in order to maximize the political and electoral benefit of a starch anti-Communist ideology. They have generally refrained from launching an investigation into the actual practices of domination.[63]

These countries, many of which have since become members of the European Union, now show a tendency to dismiss their Communist past and to adopt instead the Western Cold War memory. The reactions which the exhibit *Cold War Modern* sparked in the Polish and Czech media are an interesting case in point. Far from objecting to the discrepancy between "Eastern" exclusive design (as represented in international trade-fairs) and the "Eastern" way of life (where these beautiful objects never materialized), the Czech reviewers were flattered to see some of their countrymen, though they were regime artists, remembered in the West. Even a Czech Communist propaganda poster from the 1950s entitled "Build

63 See for instance the general philosophy informing the activities of the Polish Institute of National Memory (IPN), of the Czech Institute for the Study of Totalitarian Regimes (ÚSTR) until 2013, of the Slovak Institute for National Memory (ÚPN), etc.

the Nation – You Shall Strengthen Peace" was now fondly acclaimed in Prague as a piece of art worthy of representing the country.

Co-curator David Crowley gave the Czech press agency ČTK an interview in which he spoke of his will to "show that there were many talented people" in the East. He testified to his intention to "overthrow the usual image of greyness and shortages" under Communism.[64] This discourse was well received in the Czech media. It shows that a form of pride was waiting to be restored in this former Eastern bloc country for having "been part of history," even if the battle was fought on the wrong side and by partly or largely illegitimate leaders. It demonstrates also that a new historical narrative is gaining momentum on the losers' side of the former Iron Curtain. Just like the "new Cold War history," it perpetuates a retroactive success of the West at the risk of anachronism: that of conquering the minds via a progressing and uncritical "self-Westernization" of historical perception. In Hungary for instance, a statue of Ronald Reagan was erected in 2011 on Budapest's Freedom Square – the same square where another monument pays tribute to the Red Army. Reagan was being honored by his "role in bringing the Cold War to a conclusion, and for the fact that Hungary regained its sovereignty in the process."[65]

One can of course speculate as to how representative these reviewing journalists and memory reinventions are for the proverbial public opinion. But judging by historians' interests and scientific paradigms both in the former East and in the West, such reactions could well signal the upcoming victory of the concept of "Cold War" in communicative memory on a trans-European scale. Rather than opposing a specific post-Communist narrative of the Cold War, it could be that the American/Western narrative is simply expanding in an Eastern direction.[66] Marsha Siefert cites for instance the West German film *The Lives of Others* (2006), which depicts a "typical" East German story of interaction with the Secret Police.[67] This movie became a benchmark for both "East" and "West" Germans, marking the beginning of a reconciliation of memories that establishes the Cold War period as a common past of both Germanies. This Western interpretation of Eastern events might be historically objectionable, but it proved appealing to the

64 The ČTK (Czech press agency) article "A London exhibit examines the role of design under the Cold War," published on September 28, 2008, was reproduced or quoted in numerous Czech magazines and newspapers.

65 See Marsha Siefert, art.cit., 43.

66 Ibid., 43.

67 Ibid., 43.

wider public both in the former East and in the former West since it provided a "redemption for Eastern Europe."[68]

The path to redeeming former Eastern Europe via the appropriation of the Western memory of the Cold War could not be better symbolized than by the enthusiastic praise that appeared in the Polish press for another exhibit at the Imperial War Museum: It was entitled *For Your Eyes Only – Ian Fleming and James Bond*. One could indeed make the claim that a "James-Bondization" of history is at work in former Eastern Europe. It is no coincidence that the Coke Zero commercial produced to capitalize on the James Bond film *Skyfall* in 2012, aptly entitled "Unlock the 007 in You," is taking place nowhere else but in Prague.

This advertising spot stars a youthful anti-hero, who seduces a young woman by quietly humming the James Bond theme while standing at a bar. When she is hastily taken away by her presumed "villain" boyfriend, the bogus hero resolves to snatch her back with quaint and limited means – in order to share a Coke Zero with her.[69] The James Bond reference is reduced to comical everyday life level. Not only does Coke Zero stand for the Martini cocktail, but a washed-out, banal Golf convertible suffices as get-away for the villain, while a smoking old moped replaces the gadget-loaded Aston Martin for the pursuit of the would-be hero. The chasing scene and purposely clumsy stunts depart from Café Slavia, the landmark meeting-point for Czechoslovak dissidents under Communism.

In sixty-three seconds, this advertisement offers a reinterpretation of Cold War history, rich with symbolism. It shakes and stirs a mixture of metaphors from the former West and from the former East, invoking at once the famous dissidents, the no less famous "power of the powerless" dear to Václav Havel, and the mythical James Bond figure. By parodying courage for one's ideas or values, it reintroduces the missing "Eastern" sense of humor into European collective memory, gently mocking dissidents and James Bond against one another. By so doing, it creates a proxy Cold War memory out of thin air and unlocks the 007 in each and every Czech. The hybrid, ex-post facto humanized type of hero modeled on the improbable James Bond is now suitable for consumption – on both sides of the former Iron Curtain. How long will it be before the middle-aged woman, whose answer provided the title to this essay, unlocks the 007 in her family and actively incorporates the concept of Cold War in her experience of Communism?

---

68 Ibid., 43.

69 "Unlock The 007 In You – New Coke Zero Commercial," YouTube video, last accessed May 27, 2016, https://www.youtube.com/watch?v=hwpRFh0Jkhk.

Wayne D. Cocroft

Protect and Survive

Preserving and Presenting the Built Cold War Heritage

This essay considers the efforts to protect and present the built legacy of the Cold War represented by its military installations and also discusses examples of museum-based interpretations of the Cold War. The militarism engendered by the Cold War quickly spread to the civilian world, notably in "post-war" state funded science and technology programs, and the utopian visions played out in large public housing schemes. For the purposes of this paper Cold War monuments are narrowly defined as those sites and places that reflect the most obvious expression of the Cold War military standoff.

Protection in the United Kingdom

In the United Kingdom, heritage legislation is administered by each of the four home countries, England, Wales, Scotland and Northern Ireland. In all four there is a long tradition of protecting historic monuments; and sites associated with warfare ranging from prehistoric hillforts to 19th century coastal fortifications are prominent on the lists of protected places. In England official recognition of the historical value of Cold War monuments began in the early 1990s, at first through a program of site recording to enhance the National Monuments Record.[1] This coincided with other projects to identify and protect key sites from the two world wars; in many cases sites played a role in all three conflicts or represented the evolution of a theme across the "short" twentieth century, such as, air defense. In the choice of places that might be put forward for protection decisions were guided by established selection criteria, which are particularly rigorous in regards to recent sites.[2] Internationally, when comparing efforts to protect Cold War sites

1 Wayne D. Cocroft, "Defining the National Character of Cold War Remains," in *A Fearsome Heritage Diverse legacies of the Cold War* ed. John A. Schofield and Wayne D. Cocroft (California: Left Coast Press, 2007), 107–128; Wayne D. Cocroft, *Cold War* (London: English Heritage, 2001).

2 "Designation Listing Selection Guide: Military Structures," https://content.historicengland.org.uk/images-books/publications/dlsg-military/military_final.pdf/; "Designation Scheduling Selection Guide: Military Sites Post-1500," https://content.historicengland.org.uk/images-books/publications/dssg-military-post1500/130423_Modern_Military_Post_1500_SSG_final.pdf/

DOI 10.1515/9783110496178-011

it is critical to understand the legislative background that guides the protection of sites. In most cases it will be concerned with protecting the tangible, physical, traces of the past. A distinction also needs to be drawn between sites that meet the criteria for legal protection and others that may offer opportunities for academic study, but which ultimately may be lost. The materiality of the sources studied by architectural historians and archaeologists, either for academic or heritage management purposes, introduces a bias in favor of military and technological themes. Some topics, such as spying, that in the popular imagination defined one of the key characteristics of the Cold War, has by its nature left few, if any, physical traces. Similarly, the legacy of the western peace movements is essentially an intangible heritage.

Geographically, the United Kingdom's Cold War infrastructure was concentrated in England and especially in its eastern counties. To date about 60 Cold War sites have been protected in England, including late 1950s Thor missile sites (Figure 1), emergency government bunkers, radar stations, research and development establishments, 1980s cruise missile shelters, and small monitoring posts.

Fig. 1: Harrington Northamptonshire, between 1959 and 1963 this site was occupied by three Thor intermediate range ballistic missiles, these were raised to alert during the October 1962 Cuban missile crisis. The site is listed. © Historic England 1741/23

In Scotland and Wales similar infrastructure was found, but in far lower numbers and fewer structures have been protected in these countries.[3]

Management and Conservation

As increasing numbers of 20th century sites are protected they are raising many issues about the philosophy and practicalities regarding their conservation. Bunkers are complex machines, supported by generators and air conditioning plants, and their adaptation for public access may conflict with preservation goals, present day health and safety concerns, disabled access, and fire regulations. Recent conservation work at the scheduled 1950s atomic bomb stores, at Barnham, Suffolk, has raised questions about the ethics of using endangered hardwoods in like-for-like reconstruction work, and consideration of the point at which any attempt to repair damaged concrete panels and posts should be abandoned and new items cast (Figure 2).

Fig. 2: Barnham, Suffolk, early 1950s atomic bomb store, conservation on this scheduled monument has included the conservation of its watchtowers and the replacement of sections of its outer fences. © W D Cocroft

3 In Scotland, a 1950s central government War Room and two local authority emergency bunkers, personal communication Elizabeth McCrone, Historic Scotland, Missile testing facilities at Aberporth and Caerwent personal communication Jonathan Berry, *Caring for Military Sites of the Twentieth Century* (Cardiff: CADW, 2009).

Many Cold War installations were sited in places now valued for their natural beauty. At the Needles, Isle of Wight, the independent conservation body the National Trust acquired the important coastal chalk landscape in the mid 1970s. Initially, the significance of the late 1950s rocket test facility went unrecognized and most of it was cleared. More recently, work by volunteers, supported by engineers who worked on the rocket program, has led to a renewed interest in the abandoned research site and displays have been installed.[4] Likewise, at Orford Ness, Suffolk, the National Trust acquired the former atomic weapon research site primarily for its importance as the largest vegetated spit in Europe. At the time of acquisition the significance of the research facility was poorly understood, and initial discussions considered if it might be removed. These enigmatic modern ruins set against the natural beauty of the spit are now equally appreciated for their aesthetic qualities as for their technological significance (Figure 3).[5] A conservation regime of benign neglect is being pursued, which extends to minimal

Fig. 3: Orford Ness, Suffolk, the former Atomic Weapons Research Establishment site was originally acquired by the National Trust primarily for its significance as the largest vegetated coastal spit in Europe. © Historic England DP070004

4 Wayne D. Cocroft, *The High Down Test Site Rocket Test Site* (Swindon: English Heritage Research Report 90, 2007).

5 Louise K. Wilson, *A Record of Fear*. (Cambridge: National Trust/Commissions East, 2005).

on-site interpretation. For those who wish to know more there is a small exhibition, guided tours and an online report.[6] Similarly, in Lithuania, the United States, and Russia abandoned Cold War installations within existing National Parks are being incorporated into tourist trails.[7]

For heritage managers one of the practical challenges in conserving Cold War sites is the scale of some places, which conveys to current and future generations the enormity of the perceived threat. At Corsham, Wiltshire, the former Central Government War Head Quarters was established in the late 1950s in a former Bath stone quarry with accommodation for the Prime Minister and up to 4000 civil servants. When it was declassified in 2004, it still contained most of its original fittings and stores necessary to sustain it for many weeks (Figure 4).

Fig. 4: Corsham, Wiltshire, Central Government Head Quarters, the war cabinet's operations room, in the event of the war in the early 1960s this would have been the heart of the United Kingdom's emergency government. © Historic England DP147820

Today, the various wooden fittings and furniture, and paper stores represent a fire hazard, and in the very aggressive underground environment organic matter also

6 Wayne D. Cocroft and Magnus Alexander, *Atomic Weapons Research Establishment, Orford Ness, Suffolk Cold War Research & Development Site* (Swindon: English Heritage Research Report-10, 2009).
7 Zemaitija, Lithuania, Valdai National Park, between Moscow and St Petersburg, Russia.

provides sustenance for potentially harmful spores and moulds. To safeguard a future for the areas of key historic interest new uses need to be found for the mine to justify the high cost of forced ventilation needed to maintain a stable environment.[8] Although areas of the complex might be designated, its long-term survival is dependent on establishing a common understanding of its historic value with the owners, in this case the Ministry of Defence, which needs to reconcile continuing defense uses with a requirement to derive income from commercial partners.

In England, local authorities are responsible for most of the day-to-day management of the historic environment, they also have powers to create conservation areas and identify features of historic significance for inclusion on local lists. At former RAF Upper Heyford, Oxfordshire, during the latter stages of the Cold War, United States' nuclear-armed F111s stationed there were a key NATO asset tasked with hunting down Soviet SS20 missiles and other high value targets in Eastern Europe; its landscape is a physical expression of the doctrine of Flexible Response (Figure 5). Here the airfield has been designated as a conservation

Fig. 5: Upper Heyford, Oxfordshire, the 'hardened' landscape of a former United States Air Force base. It is protected as a Conservation Area, with key features protected as listed buildings and scheduled monuments. © Historic England 18517/25

8 "Corsham – A Cold War Secret," last accessed May 30, 2011, http://corsham.thehumanjourney.net/.

area, and within it the most significant features have been scheduled and listed. Conservation area status defined through the local planning process is able to ensure that the historic interest of an area is maintained, while allowing change to take place, which may in part include demolition and the construction of new buildings.

In the United Kingdom, listing is primarily designed to protect the special interest of a structure or site, and does not necessarily imply that there will be public access, funds for repair work; nor is it intended to prevent structures from being adapted for new uses. Only a small percentage of Cold War sites will be formally designated as historic structures. Many will be demolished, but some will find new uses. Some bunkers are meeting new threats as secure accommodation for computer server farms. Hardened aircraft shelters are being put to more prosaic uses with internal racking for paper records, or converted to house agricultural processing machinery. Abandoned military bases are also valued as modern ruins by urban explorers who seek places that aren't necessarily too safe, or mediated by expert groups with signs and guidebooks. Their ruination is also an inspiration for many artistic interventions.[9]

Presentation and Access

The lists in the appendices reveal that many of the principal publicly accessible monuments overwhelmingly represent the Cold War through former military facilities. In presenting Cold War sites to the public in most cases sufficient information needs to be imparted to place the location in its political and military context. To explore other themes different institutions and media are more appropriate. In Germany, the DDR Museum, Berlin, Zeitreise DDR-Museum, Dresden, and the museums of the Haus der Geschichte der Bundesrepublik Deutschland are rare examples of the documentation of everyday life during the Cold War. While, the allure of the closed world of the spy is sufficient to support a number of commercial spy museums.[10]

---

9 Klaus Honnef, Manfred Sieloff, and Jurgen Strauss, *Geisterstadt Konversionkunst in Wünsdorf-Waldstadt* (Potsdam: Strauss, 1998); Jane Wilson and Louise Wilson, *Stasi City, GAMMA, Parliament, Las Vegas Graveyard Time* (London: Serpentine Gallery, 1999); John Kippin, *Cold War Pastoral: Greenham Common* (Newcastle-upon-Tyne: Blackdog Publishing Limited, 2001); Louise K Wilson, *A Record of Fear* (Cambridge: National Trust/Commissions East, 2005).

10 Dedicated spy museums are found in Washington DC, USA, Tampere, Finland, and Potsdamer Platz, Berlin; the Imperial War Museum London has a gallery devoted to spying and the Allied

Only a small number of Cold War sites will be developed into museums or tourist attractions. In the United Kingdom, there are currently eight large Cold War bunkers open to the public, and they fall into three broad categories, ones receiving some public subsidy, purely commercial ventures, and ones owned by private individuals or trusts. On closure most were stripped of their equipment, and one of the first questions that needed to be addressed was if a structure was to be restored to its operational form, or its spaces filled to create a general Cold War museum. The latter may in part be a commercial decision to attract visitors, but also provides a valuable educational role in setting the structure in its wider historical context. In the early 1990s, the new museums had easy access to vast quantities of discarded military equipment and civil defense stores, and have been instrumental in saving many artefacts that lie outside of the national collections.

At the former Royal Observer Corps (ROC) Headquarters at York, English Heritage took the decision that the aim should be to conserve the structure to reflect its appearance when it was stood down in the early 1990s (Figure 6).[11] Fortunately,

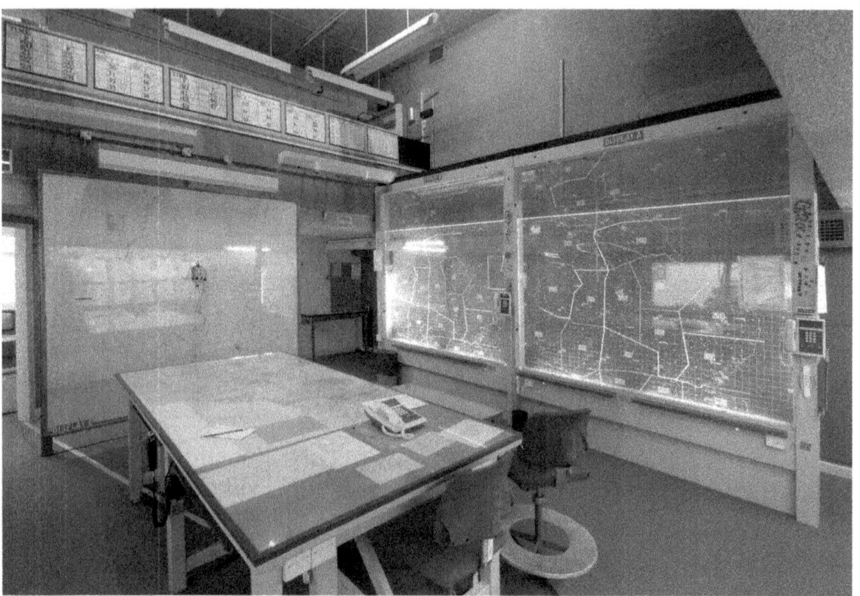

Fig. 6: York, Royal Observer Corps Headquarters, this is owned by English Heritage and is open to the public as a Guardianship monument. © Historic England N070184

Museum, Berlin, has a section of a late 1950s western espionage tunnel.

11 Roger J C Thomas, *York Cold War Bunker* (London: English Heritage, 2010).

most of its specialized equipment had been left in place and smaller items were easily replaced. On arrival in the former canteen visitors are shown an orientation film on the Cold War, with a parental guidance rating, but otherwise the bunker is presented and preserved as was in its last years of operation.[12] Information was originally fed to headquarters buildings such as this by a network of 1500, three or four person underground monitoring posts, and they represent by far the most numerous type of bunker in the United Kingdom. Their function was to confirm that the country had been attacked with nuclear weapons, and then to monitor the spread of the resulting fallout. Their small size and relative cheapness also makes them affordable for small groups, such as ex-ROC members, and to private individuals, who may wish to preserve them.[13] For many types of high tech military equipment, such as radars and missiles, the built infrastructure and equipment was an integral system, but in very few instances have fully equipped sites passed directly from service use into active preservation. This may be due to secrecy at the time of closure, the lack of appreciation of historical significance, environmental legislation, or disarmament treaties that required evidence of destruction.[14] In a few instances, sites have been kept intact at Gubel near Zug, Switzerland. A Bloodhound air defense site is preserved complete with its missiles and radars, and close to the Golden Gate Bridge, San Francisco, the National Parks Service has preserved a complete Nike air defense site.[15] A more spectacular presentation close to Tucson, Arizona, is a Titan II inter-continental missile, which sits complete in its silo, except for a hole cut in its nose cone to confirm to spy satellites its decommissioned status.[16] An insight into the equivalent former Soviet missile forces silo is provided by the, Strategic Missile Forces Museum, Pervomaysk, Ukraine.[17]

At RAF Neatishead, Norfolk, in the early 1990s when the control room was decommissioned through the initiative of the local RAF personnel, the original 1970s

---

12 Keith Emerick, "The ROC HQ at Acomb Presenting the Recent Past," *Conservation Bulletin* 44 (2003): 45–6.
13 Mark Dalton, *The Royal Observer Corps Underground Monitoring Posts* (Monkton Farleigh: Folly Books, 2011), 170–211.
14 Joseph P. Harahan, and John C. Kuhn, *On-site Inspections Under the CFE Treaty* (Washington DC: On-Site Inspection Agency, 1996), 316.
15 Marcus Cassutt, "Military Deterrence Versus Museum Attraction – The 'Bloodhound' Guided Missile Installations in Switzerland," in *On Both Sides of the Wall Preserving Monuments of the Cold War* ed. Leo Schmidt, L and Henrietta von Preussen (Berlin: Westkreuz-Verlag, 2005), 99–102; Paul Ozarak, *Underground Structures of the Cold War* (Barnsley: Pen & Sword, 2012), 170–173; "News – Militärhistorische Stiftung des Kantons Zug," last accessed July 7, 2010, http://mhsz.ch/.
16 "Titan Missile Museum," last accessed June 1, 2011, http://www.titanmissilemuseum.org/.
17 "Museum SRF – Branch of the National Military History Museum Ukraine," last accessed June 22, 2012, http://www.rvsn.com.ua/en/

Fig. 7: Neatishead, Norfolk, preserved 1970s air defense control room, which is open to the public. © Historic England BB98/10082

equipment was left in place (Figure 7). It presents the visitor with an authentic Cold War front line, from where Soviet incursions were monitored and interceptor aircraft scrambled over the North Sea. On the same site, the last Cold War era high power surveillance radar remains protected as a scheduled monument – the last of its type in Europe. Large preserved bunkers, such as Neatishead, can present a bewildering experience to the non-expert visitor. It's a place from where war would be waged remotely and plotted on a Second World War style tote board. In many cases the military role of bunker interiors may not be obvious from the rooms formerly filled with complex data handling equipment, and now often stripped bare. Here, they are able to draw on a group of knowledgeable volunteers to explain the complex systems. But, as with earlier preserved industrial sites, the long term sustainability of these sites is dependent on attracting new generations of volunteers.[18] For many of the current volunteers, and a wider group of sup-

---

18 Neil Cossons, "Industrial Archaeology: The Challenge of the Evidence," *The Antiquaries Journal* 87 (2007): 1–52.

porters, these museums also provide an important social function. For some they allow them to recapture something of the cameraderie of the services, to practice perhaps obsolete skills, and to explain the increasingly distant Cold War.

Preserved sites and derelict Cold War installations are all places of memory, for the people who were stationed there or lived nearby, and for veterans who served elsewhere. Conversely, for many visitors, who may have lived through Cold War, they offer an insight into a closed, secret, and bewildering lost world.

All lie within living memory, but realising their stories often requires the collaboration between many specialists, and is highly dependent on the willingness of national heritage cultures to engage with the recent past. Despite their relatively modern age many sites are virtually historically invisible, and in many cases the details of their operations may be unknown. Where former personnel can be found their knowledge is often restricted to a particular task over a short period of time, and offical secrecy often contrains what they can say. If a base was occupied by foreign troops finding people to describe life within them may be even more difficult. Established methods of historic building investigation and archaeological analysis may add another dimension to the understanding of these places, and is particularly insightful where it can be combined with other methods of analysis, such as oral testimony.

Museum Presentations of Cold War Military Materiél

With the end of the Cold War an enormous quantity of war materiél and military infrastructure suddenly became surplus to defense requirements. Even before the events of 1989, treaties designed to ease tensions in Europe, had rendered many fighting vehicles, warheads, missile systems, and supporting installations, subject to scrapping, demolition, or more rarely static display.[19] The withering of the Iron Curtain quickly allowed hitherto unobtainable Warsaw Pact equipment to move to the West either by gift, or by simple purchase.[20]

During the 1990s, large amounts of Cold War military equipment entered into museums, and most types of characteristic items from West and East are found

---

19 Harahan and. Kuhn *On-site Inspections*, 316.

20 Otfried Nassauer, "An army surplus – The NVA's heritage," in *Coping with Surplus Weapons: A Priority for Conversion Research and Policy* eds. E J. Laurance and H and Wulf (Bonn: Bonn International Center for Conversion, 1995), 42–45.

as multiple examples in public and private collections. Many military museums are closely associated with a particular branch of the armed services and may have narrow collecting interests, perhaps restricted to aircraft or armored fighting vehicles. In so doing they limit their ability to exhibit the integration of technological systems that is a feature of modern warfare. There is also a long tradition of government research establishments maintaining collections, or museums, to celebrate past achievements and foster esprit de corps, as well as providing a practical training resource. Some remain closed to the public, while others in the United States, have formed the basis of the National Atomic Museum in Albuquerque and Atomic Test Site Museum in Las Vegas. In a number of cases, some of the largest preserved Cold War artefacts, submarines, have formed the centerpieces of attractions (Figure 8) (*see* appendix 5).

Fig. 8: Peenemünde, Germany, U461 a 1960s Soviet Juliett class submarine that was equipped with cruise missiles is preserved and open to the public. © W D Cocroft

To date, few museums have presented a narrative of the Cold War combining military artefacts with a wider social and political discourse. An early example of this approach was the 1990s post-war gallery at the Imperial War Museum, London. Far more ambitious is the National Cold War Exhibition, Cosford, Shropshire, which was opened in February 2007, growing out of the need for the Royal

Air Force Museum to find accommodation for many of its post-war aircraft.[21] The exhibition is housed in a huge purpose-built structure, designed by Fielden Clegg Bradley; the two juxtaposed triangular constructions symbolic of the fractured Cold War world (Figure 9). The stated aim of the exhibition is to inform and

Fig. 9: Cosford, Shropshire, the National Cold War Exhibition. © W D Cocroft

educate, although the economic benefits of such a large attraction were one of the motivations behind its construction.[22] In its exhibition halls set among the aircraft are displays, themed kiosks, and audio-visual presentations that reflect the wider political, cultural, and social history of the Cold War. The Smithsonian Institution's National Museum of American History in Washington DC, took a similar approach in its exhibition *Fast Attacks and Boomers: Submarines in the Cold War*, which opened in 2000. Alongside displays on the technology and Cold War foreign and military policy, the exhibition explored life on-board, and the lives of those left behind on shore.[23]

---

21 Opened February 7, 2007.

22 Royal Air Force Museum, *Forty-Year Winter: National Cold War Exhibition* (London: Newsdesk Communications, 2007), 6–7; "Home – National Cold War Exhibition," www.nationalcoldwar exhibition.org.uk Funding for the venture was through the Heritage Lottery Fund and Ministry of Defence, but considerable contributions were also made through economic development bodies, including European sources.

23 Barton C. Hacker, "Objects at an exhibition: reflections on 'Fast attack and Boomers'," in Barton C. Hacker, and Bernard Finn *Materializing the Military* (Science Museum: London, 2005), 141–148.

Germany

During the Cold War, Germany was one of the most militarized landscapes in the world. It is also in Germany where there is the greatest concentration of preserved and accessible Cold War sites, especially in former East Germany, where many are being actively promoted as part of tourist trails (*see* appendix 2).[24] They may be split into two broad categories, firstly are those places associated with remembering the repression of the East German regime and their Soviet allies. Secondly, are the more obvious military facilities, where there is a preponderance of former command bunkers. The memorial sites tend to be publicly funded and are preserved as monuments to those who suffered and died within them, and their principal purpose is to educate current and future generations. In the former administrative districts of East Germany, a federal commission maintains the surviving Stasi records, usually in former Stasi buildings with some public access. These sites present extraordinarily difficult presentation challenges, places where history is still very raw, the ownership of the heritage disputed, and where presentation is hotly contested. In 2006, at the Hohenschönhausen prison memorial, Berlin, 200 former Stasi employees protested, denouncing former prisoners as common criminals and objecting to the description of East Germany by the memorial as a communist dictatorship.[25] In Potsdam, Amnesty International maintains the former Soviet KGB prison and a local initiative has preserved the Stasi prison at the Lindenstrasse.[26]

In the former East Germany there are at least eight preserved bunkers that are open to the public. The motivations of the new owners and operators are very different. In Leipzig, the Citizen Committee that originated in the late 1980s protest movement manages the former Stasi headquarters and its associated emergency bunker at Machern to impart political education. Elsewhere, an identical bunker is run as part of a commercial venture. Other bunkers are preserved for their military technical interest, some are formally recognized as cultural monuments, and are supported by active volunteer associations.

From its construction in 1961, the Berlin Wall that split the western and eastern sectors of the city became the most potent symbol of the Cold War divide.[27] In

---

24 German National Tourist Board 2009, *Welcome to the Country without Borders*, last accessed September date 2009, www.germany-tourism.de.

25 Anna Funder, "Tyranny of terror," *The Guardian Review*, May 5, 2007, 14.

26 "Gedenk- und Begegnungsstätte – Herzlich Willkommen" http://www.kgb-gefaengnis.de/.

27 Gordon L. Rottman, *The Berlin Wall and the Intra-German Border 1961–89* (Oxford: Osprey, 2008), 34–35., see also the essays by Hope Harrison and Sybille Frank in this volume.

1989, after the opening of the Wall there was an understandable desire to sweep it away and re-unify the city. A few sections were protected by the ailing East German regime, but most of the fortification was cleared away, although more sections have subsequently been protected.[28]

During in its 28 year history, the Wall was substantially rebuilt on at least three occassions. In the 26 years since its fall a similar dynamism has been evident in the various incarnations of memorials and interpretation schemes. The former crossing point at Checkpoint Charlie is now no more than a location with few authentic traces of the border fortifications (Figure 10). To its north, at

Fig. 10: Checkpoint Charlie, Berlin, July 2011, visitors are presented with a confusing impression of one of the Cold War's most iconic locations. © W D Cocroft

Bernauer Strasse, is the only surviving section of the Wall complete with its rear wall and patrol path, here a 46 million Euro project opened in August 2011 to commemorate the division of the city and its people.[29] Elsewhere, in the city and

28 Axel Klausmeier, "Interpretation as a Means of Preservation Policy or: Whose Heritage is the Berlin Wall?," in *Europe's Deadly Century,* eds., Neil Forbes, Robin Page, and G Perez, G (Swindon: English Heritage, 2009), 97 –105.
29 Ibid., 97; the first part of the monument was designed by Stuttgart architects Kohlhoff & Kohlhoff.

its hinterland, despite continuing losses, sections of the border fortifications may still be traced and tourist trails are being promoted.

Along the former inner German border, there are at least 24 border museums, and some sections such as the main border crossing point at Marienborn and a section of the border defences at Mödlareuth are officially recognised as monuments.[30] In former West Germany, there are far fewer dedicated Cold War museums. At Ahrweiler, near Bonn, after initial plans to seal the former West German government bunker a museum has been created and parts of it are accessible to visitors. Further south, in Bavaria in 2003, a catalogue was created of its prepared and static military barriers, and five are protected.[31]

Baltic initiatives

During the Cold War the Baltic represented a microcosm of the East-West standoff. Today, with an increasingly assertive Russia and rising political tensions the memorialization of the Cold War is inextricably linked with current security concerns and the desire by recently independent nations to affirm their national identities through stories of oppression and liberation (Figure 11).

In the event of war Denmark, as the key to the Baltic, would soon become a battlefield with critical military centers assaulted with tactical nuclear weapons. To resist such an attack from the early 1950s, with assistance from her NATO allies, the country invested heavily in her defenses and shelters to protect her civil population. The Danish Agency for Culture recognized that the story of the Cold War is integral to the understanding of the development of post-war Danish society. To decide which places should be identified for designation leading experts were commissioned to identify 25 sites through which the story of Denmark's Cold War could be told.[32] These include coastal fortifications, Stevns Fort and Langelands Fort that guarded the Baltic; both have pursued a careful collecting policy of only acquiring objects that illustrate the nature of the Cold War in the Baltic region.[33]

---

30 Deutsch-Deutsches Museum Mödlareuth http://moedlareuth.de/

31 "Dr Gerhard Ongyerth Bayerisches Landesamt für Denkmakflege 15-3-04," last accessed June 22, 2012 www.blfd.bayern.de.

32 Morten Stenak, Thomas Tram Pedersen, Peer Henrik Hansen, and Martin Jespersen, *Kold Krig* (Denmark: Copenhagen: 2013).

33 Langelands Museum and the Initiative Group, *Historically Valuable Installations from the Cold War Period* Typescript report (Denmark: Langelands Museum, 2006); another Danish fort is preserved at Stevnsfort complete with Nike surface to air missiles.

Fig. 11: Gdansk shipyard, Poland, the monument to striking workers killed by the security forces in 1970s and the dockyard gates are important symbols of the country's road to freedom. © W D Cocroft

Other designated places include civil defense centers and a government bunker at Regan Vest. To the north during the Cold War Sweden pursued a policy of armed neutrality supported by a strong, independent, state led arms industry. Along the Baltic coast her sovereignty was guarded by rock-hewn shelters worthy of any James Bond film, including underground aircraft hangars and a naval base. In the 1990s, during the decommissioning of her coastal defences the National Property Board had the foresight to identify three coastal sites sites as historic monuments, two have been preserved by private groups.[34] Postwar allegiances and alliances are also represented though military architecture. In Sweden, British

---

34 The National Property Board sites are at Victoria, Fortress Hemso and the Red Mountain Fort, a fourth at Femöre is run by a volunteer group. "Femorefortet – The Femore Fortress, "http://www.femorefortet.se/Femorefortet-eng.htm. A private museum is based at the battery at Helsenborg, "Beredskapsmusett – Kanonerna på Djuramossa," accessed June 22, 2012, www.beredskapsmuseet.com.

supplied Bloodhound missile bases were installed, and in Denmark the Ejbybunkeren copied contemporary 1950s British designs; later Nike and Hawk missile batteries supplied by the United States mirrored similar sites elsewhere.[35]

In recent years, the Baltic Initiative Group has sought to bring together former protagonists to promote a wider awareness of the significance of "sites from the period of the Cold War."[36] Its main aim is to promote cultural understanding through the preservation of authentic sites, while recognizing cultural tourism will be crucial for their survival.[37] To tell this story the group has identified two broad themes, firstly, an understanding of the balance of power in the region, which will be explored through military installations. Secondly, the nature of the communist regimes of Eastern Europe and the road to independence, whose story is represented not only by the secret police installations, but also civic buildings, sculptural monuments, and former closed towns.[38]

In Europe, it is striking that the preservation and presentation of Cold War sites has a distinct north European bias. This may in part be attributed to the past proximity of the former Iron Curtain and the familiarity of a constant military presence. Over the last decade, it is also in northern Europe where we have witnessed a greater willingness to apply traditional archaeological techniques to the study of the recent past. In a number of countries state and local heritage agencies have compiled inventories of places created or associated with the Cold War, which have been used to select sites for protection. In England, the initial selections were made based on identifying representative examples of site types using criteria common to monuments and buildings of all periods. In Denmark, a different approach was taken by establishing an agreed history of the country's Cold War experience and protecting monuments to reflect this narrative. Elsewhere –as the appendices listing principal preserved and publicly accessible sites indicate – the memorialization of the Cold War through its physical infrastructure has to date largely been a matter of chance, rather than national or local policies to select a sample of representative sites.

Alongside official initiatives to protect Cold War sites for their military and technological significance, or commemorative value, many individuals and groups have acquired abandoned Cold War facilities. The motivations of these

35 Ibid. 32, 136–39.

36 Johannes B. Rasmussen, *Travel Guide Traces of the Cold War Period: The Countries around the Baltic Sea* (Denmark: Norden, 2010).

37 Langelands Museum and the Initiative Group, *Historically Valuable Installations from the Cold War Period* Typescript report (Denmark: Langelands Museum, 2006), 4.

38 Ibid., 6.

enthusiasts and collectors who have a passion for obsolete Cold War technology are many and varied. For some it is a private or group pursuit, although many wish to share their interest of a secret world that was outside of most people's experience and is increasingly chronologically distant with a wider public. Many of these people had a personal connection through their professional lives and often form the backbone of volunteer organizations that support the operation of preserved sites. As time passes this direct connection with the Cold War will diminish and with greater historical understanding new values will emerge around surviving sites. By analogy with the remains of earlier conflicts the passing of generations with direct associations creates a greater interest in the surviving physical remains and an increase in their archaeological significance as a source of evidence.

In many of the newly independent states that lay within the Eastern Bloc the memory of this period is dominated by communist inspired social engineering. In these, as in many other countries, the military bases were invisible and inaccessible to the civil population, and are reminders of an "all too-recent and unloved past."[39] State and local authorities have chosen to preserve sites associated with political repression, often presented as memorials to their victims and places of political education and discourse. In these countries the histories of their armed forces as displayed in official museum often emphasizes their origins to the period of inter-war (1919–1939) independence, often to the exclusion of their post-war history. Although, this often abundantly event in extensive, but sparsely interpreted, collections of Warsaw Pact armaments. Other organizations and individuals have seen the commercial potential of acquiring decommissioned Cold War sites and equipment; and tourism to its "battleless" battlefields is ensuring the survival of many installations.[40] Sites in this category have often been chosen for pragmatic reasons of accessibility, or their locations within existing national parks, rather than the best examples of particular site types.

The archaeological record of the Cold War is far greater than preserved and publicly accessible sites. The memory of the role many places played during the Cold War has yet to be documented by many national and local heritage agencies and its value recognized through research. Military infrastructure has been adapted and modernized for new roles in the post-Cold War world. Elsewhere, former military airfields have aided the growth of cheap air travel and provided large brownfield sites for university campuses, industry and housing. Bunkers

---

39 Bryan Ayers and Ilir Paragoni. "Industrial heritage in Albania," *Industrial Archaeology Review* 37 (2015), 111–122.

40 Bruce Prideaux, "Echoes of War," in Ryan, C eds. *Battlefield Tourism History, Place and Interpretation* (Amsterdam: Elesiver: 2007), 20.

have been reused as secure computer server farms, converted into houses and veterinary surgeries. Other once high tech sites now provide accommodation for agricultural activities, or due to their remoteness lie abandoned subject to metal stripping, vandalism and natural decay. As archaeological monuments they all possess the potential to reveal more about their individual stories and offer in the future opportunities for public access. Superficially, the Cold War bunkers, missile sites, and airbases of West and East may appear similar, but the value placed on these structures is a reflection of each nation's experience of the Cold War and the willingness of heritage cultures within them to recognise the historical value of structures of the recent past.

Principal Cold War museums and publicly accessible places

Appendix 1: Cold War museums in the United Kingdom

Bentwaters, Suffolk, 1980s USAF hardened command bunker and airfield –http://www.bcwm.org.uk/

Cosford, Shropshire, The National Cold War Exhibition (part of the Royal Air Force Museum) http://www.rafmuseum.org.uk/

Gravesend, Kent – 1950s Civil defence bunker –http://www.gravesham.gov.uk/index.jsp?Articleid=2807

Hack Green, Cheshire – 1950s radar bunker, and later Regional Seat of Government (private) – http://www.hackgreen.co.uk/

Holpmton, Yorkshire – 1950s radar bunker and later RAF occupation (private) –http://www.rafholmpton.com/

Kelvedon Hatch, Essex – 1950s air defense control bunker, and later Regional Seat of Government (private) http://www.secretnuclearbunker.com/

Mistley, Essex – 1950s Anti Aircraft Operations Room (private) – closed

Neatishead, Norfolk – RAF Air Defence Museum and 1970s control room –http://www.radarmuseum.co.uk/

Orford Ness, Suffolk – 1950s and 1960s nuclear weapons test site atomic (National Trust) – http://www.nationaltrust.org.uk/orford-ness/

RAF Upper Heyford, Oxfordshire – 1950s to 1990s USAF air base, including command bunkers http://heymuseums.co.uk/036495/RAF_Upper_Heyford_Heritage_Centre

The Needles, Isle of Wight – 1950s rocket test site (National Trust) –http://www.theneedlesbattery.org.uk/

York, 1960s Royal Observer Corps Group Headquarters (English Heritage) – http://www.english-heritage.org.uk/daysout/properties/york-cold-war-bunker/

Anstruther, Scotland – 1950s radar bunker, and later Regional Seat of Government (private) – http://www.secretbunker.co.uk/

Appendix 2: Cold War Museums in Germany

Border museums

Deutsch-Deutsches Museum, Mödlareuth www.moedlareuth.de
Checkpoint Bravo http://www.checkpoint-bravo.de/
Checkpoint Charlie Mauermuseum Museum Haus am Checkpoint Charlie http://museum-haus-am.checkpoint.org
Point Alpha – www.pointalpha.com
Dokumentationszentrum Berliner Mauer www.berliner-mauer-dokumentationszentrum.de
Grenzlandmuseum, Eichsfeld www.grenzlandmuseum.de
Grenzland-Museum, Bad Sachsa www.gm-badsachsa.de www.sehenswert.de/grenzland-museum www.bad-sachsa.de/grenzland-museum
Kühlungsborn, Mecklenburg-Vorpommern www.ostsee-grenzturm.com

Military museums

Militärhistorisches Museum der Bundeswehr, Dresden www.mhm.bundeswehr.de
Luftwaffenmuseum der Bundeswehr Berlin-Gatow www.luftwaffenmuseum.com
Cottbus www.flugplatzmuseumcottbus.de
Finowfurt http://www.luftfahrt-museum-finowfurt.de/

Bunkers

Ahrweiler, Ahr Valley – West German government bunker museum www.regbu.de
Berlin, Gesundbrunnen, Berlin Unterwelten, West Berlin Atomschutzbunker http://berliner-unterwelten.de/tour-3.15.1.html
Eichenthaler, Bunker 302 Troposphärenfunk bunker www.bunker-302.de
Dienstelle 391 Der Bunker http://www.dienststellemarienthal.de/z_frames.html
Harnekop, Baudenkmal Bunker-Harnecop www.atombunker-16-102.de
Kossa, Denkmal Militär-Museum www.bunker-kossa.de
Zossen-Wunsdorf www.garnisonsmuseum.de
Wollenberg 301, Troposphärenfunk bunker http://www.bunker-wollenberg.eu/
Machern www.runde-ecke-leipzig.de

Post-war Germany

Berlin, Tränenpalast, Border Experiences Everyday life in divided Germany www.hdg.de
Berlin, Alltag in der DDR www.hdg.de
Berlin, Blackbox Kalter Krieg www.zentrum-kalter-krieg.de
Berlin, DDR Museum www.ddr-museum.de

Berlin, The Spy Museum, Potsdamer Platz www.spymuseumberlin.com
Dresden, Zeitreise DDR-Museum www.ddr-museum-dresden.de
Leipzig, Stiftung Haus der Geschichte der Bundesrepublik Deutschland Zeitgeschichtliches Forum www.hdg.de

Ministerium für Staatsicherheit – Stasi

Federal Commissioner for the records of the State Security Service of the former German Democratic Republic www.bstu.bund.de
Information on Stasi regional office archives and museums may be found at http://www.bstu.bund.de/DE/InDerRegion/_node.html;jsessionid=DBF675A8837CDF310DB4112F5899F6D6.2_cid134
Bautzen, Stasi prison www.gendenkstaette-bautzen.de
Berlin, Forschungs und Gedenkstätte Normannenstrasse www.stasimuseum.de
Berlin, Hohenschönhausen, Stasi prison www.stiftung-hsh.de
Berlin, Informations- und Dokumentationszentrum der Bundesbeauftragten, Wilhelmstrasse www.btsu.de
Dresden, Gedenkstätte Bautzner Strasse www.bautzner-strasse-dresden.de www.stsg.de
Machern, Museum im Stasi-Bunker www.runde-ecke-leipzig.de
Leipzig, Musuem in der Runden Ecke, Bürgerkomitee www.runde-ecke-leipzig.de
Potsdam, Ausstellung in ehemaligen KGB-Gefängnis Potsdam, Leistikowstrasse 1 www.kgb-gefaengnis.de
Rennsteighöhe, Bunkermuseum Waldhotel www.waldhotel-rennsteighoehe.de
Torgau, Closed Juvenile Detention Centre, www.jugendwerkhof-torgau.de

Appendix 3: Other European Cold War Museums

Austria, Wurzenpass, Carinthia – Border fortifications www.bunker.at
Belgium, Command Bunker Kemmelberg The Royal Museum of the Armed Forces and of Military History in Brussels is http://www.klm-mra.be/klm-new/engels/main01.php?id=outside/cdob/kemmelberg
Czech Republic Olomouc – 1950s Municipal Civil Defence bunker http://www.outsideprague.com/olomouc/nuclear_bomb_fallout_shelter.html
Czech Republic, Prague – Civil Defence bunker www.rt.com/news/prague-bunker-party-venue/
Czech Republic, Misov, SS-20 missile shelters
Denmark, Langelands Fort – http://www.langelandsfortet.dk/
Denmark, Stevnsfort – http://www.aabne-samlinger.dk/oestsjaellands/koldkrigsmuseum/
Estonia, Tallin, The museum of occupation and the Fight for Freedom http://www.okupatsioon.ee/
Finland, Tampere – The Spy Museum www.vakoilumuseo.fi
Hungary, Budapest, nuclear bunker http://www.sziklakorhaz.eu/en
Hungary, Budapest, The House of Terror http://www.terrorhaza.hu/en/index_2.html

Latvia, The museum of occupation of Latvia, Riga www.occupationmuseum.lv
Lithuania, Gruta Parkas, leisure park with Soviet era statues http://www.grutoparkas.lt/
Lithuania, 1980s Soviet TV bunker, KGB themed experience www.sovietbunker.com
Norway, Bodo, – National aircraft museum http://luftfart.museum.no/Engelsk/
Russia, Bunker 42 Taganka, Moscow http://www.bunker42.com/index.php?lang=en
Sweden, The Red Mountain Fort http://www.sfhm.se/smha/ListPage____2244.aspx?epslanguage=EN&ObjectID=2276
Sweden, Victoria Fortet http://www.sfhm.se/smha/ListPage____2244.aspx?epslanguage=EN&ObjectID=2278
Sweden, Hemsö Fortress http://www.sfhm.se/smha/ListPage____2244.aspx?epslanguage=EN&ObjectID=2271
Sweden, Femöre Fortet http://www.femorefortet.se/Femorefortet-eng.htm
Sweden, Fort Helsenborg www.beredskapsmuseet.com
Sweden, Aeroseum http://www.aeroseum.se/english/index.html
Ukraine, Pervomaysk, Strategic Missile Forces Museum http://www.rvsn.com.ua/en/

Appendix 4: North America

Cooperstown, North Dakota, Ronald Reagan Minuteman https://oscarzero.wordpress.com/thehistoricsite
Launch Control Facility Delta-01 http://www.nps.gov/mimi/index.htm
Golden Gate Bridge San Francisco, Nike missile site, http://www.nps.gov/goga/nike-missile-site.htm
Tucson, Arizona, Titan II missile silo http://www.titanmissilemuseum.org/
Diefenbunker, Canada http://www.diefenbunker.ca/

Appendix 5: Submarine museums in Europe

Belgium, Zeebrugge, U480, Soviet Foxtrot class http://www.info-toerisme.be/Toerisme/Belgie/Fotosite/Zeebrugge%20U-480(1).html
Denmark, Langelandsfort, *Springeren,* Danish Tumleren class, http://www.langelandsfortet.dk/
Denmark, Tøjhusmuseet, *Saelen,* Royal Danish War Museum, Danish Tumleren class http://www.orlogsmuseet.dk/info/eng.htm
France, Cherbourg, French, *Le Redoubtable* SSBN http://www.citedelamer.com/en/exhibition-of-la-cite-de-la-mer/le-redoutable-the-largest-submarine-open-to-the-public-in-the-world/
Germany, Hamburg, U434, Soviet Tango class, www.u-434.de
Germany, Peenemünde, U461, Soviet Juliett class, www.U-461.de
Germany, Sassnitz, Mecklenburg, HMS *Otus,* British Oberon class, http://www.hms-otus.com/
Russia, Kaliningrad, B413, Soviet Foxtrot class http://www.konigsberg.ru/eng/kaliningrad/cultures/museum-of-world-ocean.htm
United Kingdom, Chatham, Kent, HMS *Ocelot,* British Oberon class, http://www.thedockyard.co.uk/Home

United Kingdom, Gosport, Hampshire, HMS *Alliance*, British A class http://www.historicdockyard.co.uk/site-attractions/off-site-attractions/hms-alliance?gclid=CIGMj7T-lMoCFQqdGwodDnUCvw

United Kingdom, Rochester, Kent, U475, Soviet Foxtrot class http://www.sovietsub.co.uk/ (closed)

United Kingdom, Plymouth, HMS *Courageous*, British nuclear powered Valiant class https://devonportnhc.wordpress.com/warshiptours/

Hope M. Harrison

Berlin's *Gesamtkonzept* for Remembering the Wall

Memory of the Cold War and particularly the years of the country's division have been contested in Germany. This chapter will examine united Germany's approach to remembering, depicting, and commemorating the structure that stood at the frontline of the Cold War: the Berlin Wall. Just as the Berlin Wall represented a key dividing line while it stood, in post-Wall united Germany there are a broad range of often emotionally charged views about how to see the rise and fall of the Berlin Wall in retrospect and how the Wall should be depicted and commemorated now. A certain consensus was reached in 2006 when the Berlin Senate backed a "Master Plan [Gesamtkonzept] for Remembering the Berlin Wall." While officials agreed on the importance of highlighting the history of the Wall in the capital city, exactly how to do that and which parts of the history should be privileged were matters of ongoing debate. This chapter will explore the origins, composition, and implementation of the *Gesamtkonzept* as well as the debates surrounding it.

With both Germany and Berlin divided between the democratic, capitalist West and the communist East during the Cold War, the Berlin Wall built by the communist regime in 1961 came to serve as a world-wide symbol of the depth of the Cold War struggle.[1] From the West, it was seen as an evil representation of the oppressive nature of the East German communist regime itself and was compared to Nazi concentration camps in its brutal, sometimes lethal method of imprisoning people. Its forward and rear walls and "death strip" in between encircled the 146-kilometer border around West Berlin so as to prevent East Germans from escaping into the "show window of the West." From the East, it was called "an anti-fascist protective barrier" built to defend the East Berliners and East Germans from a West German attack and thus to "keep the peace" at the frontline between East and West Germany and between the Warsaw Pact and NATO.[2]

With such contrasting views of the Berlin Wall for the 28 years it stood, it is not surprising that there remain differing views, although they are not so simply

1 For an elucidation of the decision to build the Berlin Wall, see Hope M. Harrison, *Driving the Soviets up the Wall: Soviet-East German Relations, 1953–1961* (Princeton, NJ: Princeton University Press, 2003).

2 On differing East and West German descriptions of the Berlin Wall, see Pertti Ahonen, *Death at the Berlin Wall* (NY: Oxford University Press, 2011).

DOI 10.1515/9783110496178-012

divided into eastern and western approaches. Not least, there are of course contrasting perspectives among people who lived in the German Democratic Republic (GDR, East Germany) ranging, for example, from people who served the regime by helping to maintain the Berlin Wall to others who were imprisoned for trying to escape. Germans also have varying outlooks on the fall of the Wall in November 1989 and how it should be portrayed, with some seeing it as the painful collapse of a system they had worked to uphold and others in both east and west seeing it as the joyous, long awaited demonstration of the triumph of freedom over tyranny. For those of the latter outlook, there is debate about the relative weights of the protesting East Germans (whether by taking to the streets or leaving the country) versus the strength and attractiveness of the Western democratic, capitalist system in bringing about the collapse of the Berlin Wall and the communist regime behind it followed by the unification of Germany on Western terms.

The German historical memory of the Berlin Wall is further influenced by broader international, European, and national contexts. Internationally, the US and its Western Allies, including many people who lived in West Germany, believe that the collapse of the Berlin Wall, the East German communist regime, the Soviet regime, and the Cold War generally represented a triumph of the Western democratic, capitalist way of life and a defeat for communism. The Western notion of freedom won; Soviet tyranny lost. From this perspective, the Wall and communism were evil and ultimately and righteously were overthrown by good. This view has predominated in public, political discourse in Germany since 1990, causing resentment among some from the former GDR.

Communism, however, is not the only part of the recent past that Germans and Europeans have been grappling with. The Nazi past in Germany and Europe has also been a focal point in public memory, with multiple effects on the German process of dealing with the historical memory of the Berlin Wall. For Western Germany and other countries in the West who were not occupied or attacked by communists after World War II, the Nazi past is the more salient one and thus demands and commands more public attention. This gives rise to the conviction that any focus on communism and its crimes and victims is somehow an effort to downplay the importance and unique nature of the crimes and victims of the Holocaust. This is obviously a particular flashpoint in Germany, the home of Hitler's Nazi regime, and memory of the Berlin Wall has at times been caught in the crossfire of this debate. On the other hand, for many people who suffered in Eastern Germany and countries of the former Soviet bloc, it is the more recent communist past that must be faced and accounted for. This spotlight on the communist past includes a debate over agency and the relative responsibility of local, in this case East German, communists versus the Soviet leadership in carrying out atrocities – such as shooting people who tried to escape across the Berlin Wall.

All of these issues are visible when studying the evolution of German approaches to the historical memory of the Berlin Wall. The *Gesamtkonzept* of 2006 represented a turning point in the historical memory of the Berlin Wall, because initially, for years after the fall of the Wall, there was no great public interest in remembering or commemorating the Berlin Wall. After all, one of the rallying cries of Germans on the streets in late 1989–90 was, "*die Mauer muss weg!*" – "the Wall must go!" Most Berliners and Germans wanted to get rid of the Wall as soon and as completely as possible. They were glad to leave this brutal, deadly part of their history in the past and move on. And they certainly did not want to see the Wall standing in its old spot or fight to preserve some of it now that they had a choice. In the wake of German unification on October 3, 1990, there were streets, train lines and neighborhoods to rebuild and reconnect that had been separated by the Wall for 28 years. The few people who called to preserve parts of the Wall so that future generations would have some sense of what they lived through were drowned out by the overwhelming majority's desire to get rid of the Wall.[3]

In the first fifteen years after the fall of the Wall, some lonely voices succeeding in getting parts of the remaining Wall placed under historic landmark protection and in creating a Berlin Wall Memorial, but these moves did not garner much attention or support. In addition, a double row of cobblestones was installed in the pavement in some areas to mark where the Wall had been in the center of the city, and a Wall trail (Mauerweg) for walking and biking around the outskirts of Berlin was established on the former path of the Wall. Official support, however, for a serious and thorough grappling with the history of the Berlin Wall and a related commemoration of the Wall was lacking. In Germany, as in many countries, only high-level official support ensures widespread attention to and funding for commemorative initiatives.

The German reluctance to confront the Berlin Wall as part of the East German communist past stemmed from a fear that doing so would indicate a diminishing commitment by newly united Germany to the historical commemoration of the Nazi regime and its victims. In part fueled by awareness that Germany's neighbors were watching closely to see that this united Germany was different from the last one, German officials went out of their way to demonstrate their under-

3 Willy Brandt was one of the few who called to preserve some parts of the Wall for future generations to know what it had been like. "Rede von Willy Brandt am 10. November 1989 vor dem Rathaus Schöneberg," Bundeszentrale für politische Bildung, March 23, 2009.

standing of the serious and unique nature of the crimes committed by the Nazis and their sense of responsibility for dealing with this past and making sure the past was not repeated. A fundamental indication of German recognition and contrition came with the 2005 dedication of the massive Monument to the Murdered Jews of Europe (widely referred to as the Holocaust Memorial) in the center of Berlin near the Brandenburg Gate.

The Nazi past is related to another explanation for delayed official attention to the commemoration of the Berlin Wall. As Germans were still grappling with themselves as perpetrators of Nazi crimes, confronting another set of crimes and victims related to the Berlin Wall took a kind of energy most Germans did not have, especially since the process of integrating the former GDR into the united Federal Republic of Germany (FRG) occupied more resources than expected. The one exception to this was trials of former East German border guards and their military and political superiors for the "shoot to kill order" at the Berlin Wall and the broader East-West German border.[4] The trials, however, were largely an effort to wrap up unfinished business with the Berlin Wall, not part of a desire to keep the past alive in some way so as to commemorate it and continue to grapple with that part of German history.

A further connection between the Nazi and communists pasts with relevance for the historical memory of the Berlin Wall is the happenstance double importance of the date November 9: the date of both the Nazi attack on Jewish synagogues, homes, and businesses in 1938 (*Kristallnacht* or the "Night of Broken Glass"), and the date of the opening of the Wall in 1989. If the Wall had fallen on November 8 or 10 or nearly any other date, it is very likely that date would have been chosen as the day for German unification a year later. Yet, due to November 9, 1938, there was no way the Germans could or would do this. The double importance of the date is part of the reason it took Germans so long to embrace a large-scale celebratory commemoration of the fall of the Wall.

Finally, official reticence in delving into the history of the Berlin Wall also was due to the fact that since 2001, the Berlin city-state government (as distinguished from the federal government and its parliament, the Bundestag) had been ruled by a "Red-Red" coalition between the Social Democrats (SPD) and the Party of Democratic Socialism (PDS). Since the PDS was the successor party to the old East German communist ruling party (the Socialist Unity Party, SED) which backed the Berlin Wall, this governing coalition preferred to keep discussions of

4 On the Wall trials, see A. James McAdams, *Judging the Past in Unified Germany* (NY: Cambridge University Press, 2001), and Roman Grafe, *Deutsche Gerechtigkeit: Prozesse gegen DDR-Grenzschützen und ihre Befehlsgeber* (Munich: Siedler, 2004).

the history of the Wall out of the public eye as much as possible. They knew that at a minimum the opposition (particularly the conservative Christian Democratic Union, CDU) would seize upon any mention of the Wall to criticize the PDS and the ruling coalition – even though the CDU had also done very little to commemorate the Wall in the 1990s when it held power.

The tenure of discussions about the Berlin Wall, or, more aptly, the lack of much public discussion about this history would change abruptly on the fifteenth anniversary of the fall of the Wall. In the autumn of 2004, the controversial initiative of a private citizen to commemorate the victims of the Wall prompted a broad public debate that served as the impetus for a major official commitment to the historical commemoration of the Berlin Wall. Two years later, the Berlin Senate, in close coordination with the Bundestag, adopted the "*Gesamtkonzept* for Remembering the Berlin Wall."[5]

The Origins of the Gesamtkonzept

On October 31, 2004, the director of the private Checkpoint Charlie Museum, Alexandra Hildebrandt, unveiled 1,065 wooden crosses in memory of people killed at the Berlin Wall and along the entire former East German border. In addition to the crosses, which soon increased in number to 1,075, Hildebrandt had 200 meters of the Berlin Wall re-installed at Checkpoint Charlie (described in more detail in the chapters by S. Frank and H. Hochmuth in this volume). Hildebrandt herself is from Ukraine but became a German citizen when she married the human rights activist and former member of the Nazi resistance, Rainer Hildebrandt. He had founded the Checkpoint Charlie Museum and passed away in January 2004, leaving his wife in charge.

Alexandra Hildebrandt used her new memorial in this central location to chide the Berlin government for not having done enough to commemorate victims of the Wall.[6] Many of the "Wall Crosses" had a picture of a person killed trying to escape, their name, dates of birth and death, and the reason for their death,

5 Dr. Thomas Flierl, Endredaktion, "Gesamtkonzept zur Erinnerung an die Berliner Mauer: Dokumentation, Information und Gedenken," June 12, 2006. Hereafter referred to as *Gesamtkonzept*, last accessed on August 15, 2016, http://www.stiftung-berliner-mauer.de/en/uploads/test/gesamtkonzept.pdf.

6 Alexandra Hildebrandt's booklet for the press, "Freedom Memorial at Checkpoint Charlie Square: 'All they wanted was freedom'," distributed at the 143rd press conference of the Working Group of the "Registered Association August 13" on Tuesday, June 28, 2005.

such as "shot while trying to escape" or "drowned after being shot." Members of victims associations from the former GDR were very grateful to Hildebrandt, and tourists and members of the media from Germany and all over the world flocked to see the "Freedom Monument," as Hildebrandt called it.[7] Many found it a very powerful and moving site and long overdue.

Yet controversy also accompanied the "Freedom Monument" and Hildebrandt's statements about it. In response to a reporter's observations that her rows of crosses were somewhat reminiscent of the rows of large blocks that would form the future Holocaust Memorial, Hildebrandt declared, "That is a monument for the victims of the first and ours is for the victims of the second German dictatorship."[8] "With this, we bring a counterpart to the Holocaust monument."[9] This claim elicited much criticism from politicians, journalists, members of the Jewish community, and others. Although she later backpedalled,[10] many never forgave her for what they felt (even if she did not mean) as a slight to the victims of the Holocaust.

Hildebrandt refused to answer questions about how she had arrived at her number of victims of the Wall, leading many observers to urge that professional research be devoted to ascertaining the correct number of people killed at the Wall, their personal backgrounds and how best to commemorate them as well as a broader plan for dealing with the memory of the Berlin Wall. All parties, including much of the public, the media, experts, and Hildebrandt herself, felt that the government should play a central role in commemorating the Berlin Wall and its victims and needed to formulate a plan to do so.

At the same time, four Bundestag members proposed that a "Central Site of Memory for the Berlin Wall" be created at the Brandenburg Gate.[11] Representing

---

7 Thomas Loy, "Botschaft mit Kreuzen. Wie gedenkt man der Mauer – lieber authentisch oder mit Gemüt?" *Der Tagesspiegel*, November 2, 2004; Guntram Doelfs, "Checkpoint: Besucher wollen dauerhafte Kunstaktion," *Berliner Morgenpost*, November 8, 2004.

8 Stefan Schulz, "1065 Holzkreuze für die Opfer der Teilung und des Mauerbaus," *Berliner Morgenpost*, October 26, 2004. See also Sven Felix Kellerhoff, "1065 Holzkreuze, 2700 Betonstelen. Gerade ein Kilometer liegt dazwischen: Was hat der Checkpoint Charlie mit dem Holocaust-Mahnmal zu tun?" *Die Welt*, November 2, 2004.

9 Jana Sittnick, "Die Frau meint es ernst," *taz*, October 30, 2004.

10 For Hildebrandt's backtracking a few days later, see Joachim Stoltenberg's interview with her, "Ein Leben wider das Vergessen," *Berliner Morgenpost*, November 7, 2004.

11 Draft proposal, "Ort des Erinnerns," Deutscher Bundestag, 15. Wahlperiode, "Antrag der Abgeordneten Carl-Ludwig Thiele (FDP), Stephan Hilsberg (SPD), Franziska Eichstädt-Bohlig (Bündnis 90/Die Grünen), Werner Kuhn (CDU), et al., Gelände um das Brandenburger Tor als zentraler Ort des Erinnerns an die Berliner Mauer, des Gedenkens an ihre Opfer und der Freude über die Überwindung der deutschen Teilung," November 4, 2004.

the former East and West and four political parties – the Free Democratic Party (FDP), the SPD, Alliance 90/the Greens, and the CDU – they argued that the joyful pictures of November 9, 1989 broadcast around the world made the Brandenburg Gate the site most associated with the Berlin Wall. They wanted more information to be available at the Gate about the Wall, including both the 28 years during which the Gate was closed and surrounded by the Wall and also the peaceful, celebratory opening of the Wall at the Gate.[12]

With public discussion now everywhere about the Berlin Wall, the members of the Berlin Parliament became active as well. On November 11, 2004, the parliamentary groups of the CDU and Alliance 90/the Greens pushed the Berlin Senate to come up with a plan to do more to remember the Berlin Wall. The CDU's proposal was the more ambitious of the two, calling on the Senate to formulate a plan for the public reckoning with both the Nazi and communist-East German dictatorships in order to respond to the "desire of Berliners and national and international visitors for more information on the dimensions and course of the Berlin Wall in the heart of Berlin."[13] The Greens' proposal was centered on the Wall and the need for a plan which would "keep the division of Berlin and the remembrance of its victims alive in the cityscape." It called on the Senate to work with the federal government and the relevant districts of Berlin to come up with a "*Gesamtkonzept*" for "documenting the Berlin Wall as evidence of the division of Berlin, including preserving the remaining pieces and making them more visible and understandable."[14]

The Berlin Parliament met on November 11 to commemorate the fifteenth anniversary of the fall of the Berlin Wall. Party politics and the legacy of the division made for a raucous, emotional, often hostile discussion of how to deal with the history of the Wall. Berliners in the parliament had lived through the division, had experienced the Wall when it stood as a deadly border. These were not theoretical discussions about how to handle a distant past but emotional outpourings mixed with politics, a potent combination.[15]

---

12 Author's interviews with Carl-Ludwig Thiele and Werner Kuhn on November 11, 2004, Franziska Eichstädt-Bohling on November 19, 2004, and Stephan Hilsberg on November 22, 2004.

13 Dringlicher Antrag der Fraktion der CDU, "Gesamtkonzept zur öffentlichen Darstellung und Aufarbeitung der jüngsten Deutschen Zeitgeschichte in der Hauptstadt Berlin," Abgeordnetenhaus Berlin, 15. Wahlperiode, Drucksache 15/3378, November 11, 2004.

14 Dringlicher Antrag der Fraktion Bündnis 90/Die Grünen, "Die Teilung Berlins und die Erinnerung an ihre Opfer im Stadtbild wach halten," Abgeordnetenhaus Berlin, 15. Wahlperiode, Drucksache 15/3377, November 11, 2004.

15 Aktuelle Stunde, "Bilanz 15 Jahre nach dem Mauerfall – die Einheit gestalten und der Opfer gedenken," Abgeordnetenhaus Berlin, 15. Wahlperiode, Plenarprotokoll 15/59, 59. Sitzung vom

Members of the opposition parties, particularly the CDU and FDP, were sharply critical of the PDS having a role in the Red-Red coalition government in deciding how to treat the Berlin Wall now. One of the positions held by the PDS was that of the cultural senator, Thomas Flierl, who would oversee the plan for commemorating the Wall. Opposition to his role was heightened by the revelation that one of the candidates he was considering for an important position had worked for the East German secret police, the Stasi. PDS parliamentarians were repeatedly shouted down and interrupted when speaking. Some representatives called loudly for Flierl's resignation or for the mayor to fire him.[16]

This uproar put Governing Mayor Klaus Wowereit (SPD) on the defensive. Since coming into office in 2001 his strategy had been to do the minimum necessary in public with regard to the Wall, because his coalition with the PDS made him vulnerable to criticism on matters concerning the GDR. When he laid wreaths in honor of victims at the Berlin Wall Memorial on Bernauer Strasse on the annual anniversaries of the rise and fall of the Wall, he was heckled for being in coalition with the PDS and thus suspected of not wanting to truly come to terms with the GDR past, including the Wall. Yet in private, he met regularly with members of victims groups.

In the parliamentary session on November 11, 2004, Wowereit adopted a position somewhere in the center of the debate about policy on Wall memory. On the one hand, he argued that the already existing Berlin Wall Memorial site at Bernauer Strasse was sufficient, since it attracted more than 1,000 visitors every day and that therefore nothing new needed to be created. He also argued that "Berlin really has no lack of memorials and sites of memory." On the other hand, he agreed that, "we must connect [the sites] better and integrate them into a common plan so they attract more attention." Accordingly, he announced that the Senate would work on a city-wide plan for remembering the Berlin Wall. The fact that 40% of Berliners under the age of 30 did not know what happened on November 9, 1989 demonstrated that something more needed to be done.[17]

11. November 2004, 4922–4941.

16 Martin Lindner (FDP) called for the mayor to remove Flierl from his post, ibid., 4930.

17 Ibid., 4933–34.

Motives for the Gesamtkonzept

The motives for paying more attention to the Berlin Wall ranged from personal, family connections to the border to "democratic education," lessons of history, tourism, and moral and historical responsibility. For many Germans, remembering the Berlin Wall was a personal, emotional issue, a part of their own lives. Since they had lived through the years of division, many felt this history was receding with fewer and fewer reminders of it. In their proposal the Bundestag members lamented that "the memory of the division of Berlin, Germany and the world threatens to disappear." Noting that "an entire generation was influenced by the division of Germany and the world," they argued, "there is a great need to remember."[18] It felt strange and somehow wrong to them that it was nearly impossible for their children or grandchildren to understand or feel what it had been like.[19] Bundestag member Carl-Ludwig Thiele spoke of how hard it was to explain to his seventeen year old son what the death strip at the Wall had been like: "Young people who see remains of the Wall in Berlin today often wonder: People couldn't get over *that*? The world was divided by *this* wall?"[20] More explanation was necessary.

Another reason for wanting more attention to the history of the Berlin Wall was the desire to extract from it certain lessons of history. Policymakers and others emphasized the need to preserve pieces of the Wall as part of the "civic education" of young people who did not experience it. The predominant argument was that pieces of the Wall are "elements for living memory of a dictatorship which part of Germany had to put up with for 40 years."[21] "In the interest of democracy," politicians argued that young people should know about the kind of communist system in the GDR that created the deadly Berlin Wall.[22] The freedoms they took for granted, including travel all over the country and beyond, had not always existed and were in fact severely limited while Germany was divided. With the legacy of "two German dictatorships in the 20th century," policymakers and others often speak of the importance of fostering a post-unification "democratic

18 "Ort des Erinnerns" draft proposal, November 4, 2004. See note 11.

19 See in particular the comments of Carl-Ludwig Thiele, Bundestag, Plenarprotokoll 15/163, March 10, 2005, 15,309; Bundestag Ausschuss für Kultur und Medien, Protokoll 15/60, Wortprotokoll 60. Sitzung, June 15, 2005, 14; and Bundestag Plenarprotokoll 15/184, June 30, 2005, 17,447–48.

20 Carl-Ludwig Thiele, Bundestag Plenarprotokoll 15/184, June 30, 2005, 17,447.

21 Uwe Lehmann-Brauns, Abgeordnetenhaus Berlin, Ausschuss für Kulturelle Angelegenheiten, Wortprotokoll 15/58, April 25, 2005, 2.

22 Brigitte Lange, Abgeordnetenhaus Berlin, Ausschuss für Kulturelle Angelegenheiten, ibid., 5.

memory culture," which necessitates dealing with the dark past of the Berlin Wall for the sake of the next generation. Accordingly, the Berlin CDU proposal to the parliament declared that remembering "both German dictatorships ... contributes to strengthening consciousness about freedom, justice and democracy."[23] Preserving remains of the Wall and the death strip and providing information about them came to be seen as essential parts of this democratic memory culture.[24]

Tourist interest in the Berlin Wall also played an important role in the deliberations about the *Gesamtkonzept*. A strong part of the impetus for the Berlin Senate to develop a plan for approaching the history and remains of the Wall came from tourists asking, "Where is the Wall?" Again and again in the debates, public officials, historians, journalists and others spoke of tourists' desire to see and learn about the Wall, their frustration that this was harder to do than they had expected before arriving in Berlin, and the importance of satisfying the tourists' interest in the Wall. Some argued in particular that they should be able to see and learn about the Wall at the main tourist destinations, such as the Brandenburg Gate and Checkpoint Charlie.

Some German policymakers and historical experts have felt an almost a moral obligation to give tourists the information they seek. Bundestag member Eichstädt-Bohlig argued: "Berliners, Germans and people from all over the world come to the Gate to see the history of the German division, the iron curtain and the cold war."[25] "I think all people – wherever they come from – have the right to search for memory at this place. I think it's very important that this requirement is satisfied."[26] Similarly, historians Konrad Jarausch, Martin Sabrow and Hans-Hermann Hertle urged in a March 2005 memorandum: "At a time of booming *public history*, we should take account of the tourists from within Germany and beyond who look in vain for remnants of the Wall precisely in the central memory area around the Brandenburg Gate and the Reichstag."[27]

---

23 Dringlicher Antrag der Fraktion der CDU, "Gesamtkonzept zur öffentlichen Darstellung und Aufarbeitung der jüngsten Deutschen Zeitgeschichte in der Hauptstadt Berlin," Abgeordnetenhaus Berlin, 15. Wahlperiode, Drucksache 15/3378, November 11, 2004.

24 See, for example, Berlin Mayor Klaus Wowereit's later speeches in 2011 and 2013 on the anniversary of the building of the Berlin Wall on August 13.

25 Bundestag, Plenarprotokoll 15/163, March 10, 2005.

26 Bundestag Plenarprotokoll 15/184, June 30, 2005.

27 Konrad H. Jarausch, Martin Sabrow and Hans-Hermann Hertle, "Die Berliner Mauer – Erinnerung ohne Ort? Memorandum zur Bewahrung der Berliner Mauer als Erinnerungsort" (hereafter ZZF memo), March 9, 2005, 4.

Other commentators emphasized what could be called a moral responsibility to the world to remember the Berlin Wall. The historian Klaus-Dietmar Henke testified to the Berlin parliament: "The Berlin Wall belongs to world cultural heritage as a historical-political symbol. The city of Berlin and the Federal Republic of Germany must fulfill their responsibility for this heritage at [a] high level."[28] Likewise, Harald Strunz, deputy chairman of the Union of Victims of Communist Tyranny (UOKG), declared: "The rise and fall of the Berlin Wall belong – also in the view of the entire cultural world – to the historical heritage of this city and one should not squander such a heritage."[29]

Less profound motivations for increased government involvement in remembering the Wall concerned the money tourists bring to Berlin and a sense of competition with Hildebrandt and skepticism about her approach and motives (the latter is discussed more in the chapter by S. Frank in this volume). Given the stress on the Berlin economy in the wake of unification, many public officials in both the city and federal governments welcomed tourists and their wallets and felt it was in the city's economic interest to satisfy tourists' desire to see more about the Wall.[30] Officials in Berlin's tourism agency began to track carefully how many tourists visited sites related to the Wall and what their responses to the sites were.[31]

---

28 Klaus-Dietmar Henke, "Gedenkkonzept Berliner Mauer," statement to Berlin Parliament, April 18, 2005, on Flierl's draft commemorative plan (*Gedenkkonzept*) on the Berlin Wall, last accessed on August 15, 2016, http://www.bundesstiftung-aufarbeitung.de/uploads/pdf/va180405henke.pdf.

29 Harald Strunz, statement to Berlin Parliament, April 18, 2005, on Flierl's *Gedenkkonzept* on the Berlin Wall, last accessed on August 15, 2016, http://www.uokg.de/Text/akt039flirlkonzept.htm.

30 maw, "Ostalgia ain't what it used to be: Tourists Want to See More Berlin Wall," *Spiegel Online*, March 4, 2008; Ruth Spitzenpfeil, Sylke Gruhnwald, "Was Touristen an Deutschland lieben," *NZZ Online*, April 30, 2012; gn, "Gedenkstätten in Berlin: Mauer in den Köpfen," *Der Tagesspiegel*, July 11, 2012; and Hanno Hochmuth, "Berlin inszeniert seine Geschichte: Die Attraktion der Schattenorte," *Der Tagesspiegel*, February 13, 2015. See also discussion in the federal government about tourists' interest in the Berlin Wall: Deutscher Bundesag, Drucksache 17/5341, "Antwort der Bundesregierung auf die Kleine Anfrage der Abgeordneten Hans-Joachim Hacker, Elvira Drobinski-Weiß, Petra Ernstberger, weiterer Abgeordneter und der Fraktion der SPD, Drucksache 17/5110 – 20 Jahre Mauerfall und 20 Jahre Deutsche Einheit – eine Bilanz aus Sicht des Tourismus," April 4, 2011.

31 Some recent examples include Florentine Anders, "Her mit den Touristen! Rekord: Mehr als eine Million Gäste im Oktober, *Die Welt*, December 11, 2013; "Fast eine halbe Millionen Besucher mehr in Berliner Gedenkstätten," Berlinonline.de, March 24, 2015; and Mechthild Küpper, "Berlins Tourismus boomt. 'Wir werden Paris einholen', *Frankfurter Allgemeine Zeitung*, August 12, 2015.

Formulating the Gesamtkonzept

In November 2004, Mayor Wowereit instructed the senator for science, research and culture, to develop a plan for remembering and commemorating the Wall and its victims. Senator Flierl formed an inter-agency task force to take stock of all of the remains of the Wall and the whole border zone and to formulate an approach for dealing with them in the future.[32] The task force was coordinated by the tireless Rainer Klemke, whose portfolio encompassed memorial sites and museums connected with contemporary history. Comprised of representatives of the Senate chancellery, its departments for culture and city planning, the federal minister for culture and media, the Berlin Forum for History and the Present, the Berlin Wall Association at Bernauer Strasse, the Federal Foundation for the Reappraisal of the SED Dictatorship, and the central Berlin districts (Mitte and Friedrichshain-Kreuzberg) which had been separated by the Wall, the task force met regularly and also consulted with members of victims groups, historians and other experts.

There were private sessions, public hearings, and a lively debate among journalists and experts on the Wall, on German history and commemoration. Drawing on these debates, Flierl submitted a draft Berlin Wall Commemorative Plan (Gedenkkonzept) to the Berlin parliament on April 18, 2005 at a session with expert commentators.[33] On May 12, 2005, the parliament voted to commission the Senate to proceed with the development of "a Master Plan for the documentation of the Berlin Wall." Flierl then presented the final "*Gesamtkonzept* for Remembering the Berlin Wall" on June 12, 2006. It laid out guidelines for an inventory of all border remains and memorial sites, suggested future steps, focused on the development of some key sites, outlined ways to highlight and connect all sites related to the Wall, and provided a budget of 40 million Euros. The deadline for the implementation of the plan was set for the 50th anniversary of the building of the Wall on August 13, 2011.

---

32 In fact, Flierl had convened an interagency task force on Checkpoint Charlie in June in the wake of a controversy between Hildebrandt and the student actors who dressed up in military uniforms of the former Allies and GDR to pose for pictures with paying tourists. "Senatorin will Mauer nur bis Silvester dulden," *Berliner Morgenpost*, October 8, 2004.

33 Thomas Flierl, "Gedenkkonzept Berliner Mauer. Bestandsaufnahme und Handlungsempfehlungen vorgestellt bei der Veranstaltung der Stiftung zur Aufarbeitung der SED-Diktatur am 18. April 2005 im Abgeordnetenhaus von Berlin," last accessed on August 15, 2016, http://www.bundesstiftung-aufarbeitung.de/gedenkkonzept-quot%3Bberliner-mauer-quot%3B-1685.html. [hereafter Flierl's *Gedenkkonzept*].

Once the Berlin authorities decided to highlight the history of the Wall, they had to answer a series of difficult questions: How should they go about this? Which Wall sites should they focus on? What description or narrative should be attached to sites connected with the Wall? Options included highlighting the victims or the perpetrators for the 1961–1989 period, focusing on the peaceful fall of the Wall in 1989, and examining the Wall in the context of European and global Cold War history.

In the wake of Hildebrandt's Wall crosses, the public focused on commemorating the victims of the Wall, particularly people who were killed trying to escape from the GDR. But some critical experts insisted that attention should also be directed to the perpetrators who at various levels were responsible for the deaths of people at the Wall. Since Flierl himself had been an SED official and now represented the successor PDS party, critics thought it was no coincidence that his *Gedenkkonzept* of 2005 did not specifically blame the SED for the deaths at the Wall.[34]

Calling for a broader focus on different groups of people involved in and affected by the Berlin Wall, the Federal Coordinator for the Stasi Files and former member of the East German opposition, Marianne Birthler, told the Bundestag in June 2005: "There is no question that Wall commemorations always mean first commemorating the victims." But she went on to insist on discussing the repressive system that had imprisoned an entire population: "We must name those who were politically responsible."[35] The victims were only victims because there had been perpetrators. Both sides needed to be explained for people to understand the history and legacy of the Wall. The 2006 *Gesamtkonzept* would entail more of an examination of the perpetrators and not just the victims than had been present in Flierl's 2005 *Gedenkkonzept*.

Another topic to convey was the peaceful fall of the Wall in November 1989 and the role of the East German civil rights movement in bringing this about. Some politicians and experts expressed their frustration that there was still no place in Berlin that commemorated and celebrated this peaceful revolution. A founding member of the East German SPD, Stefan Hilsberg, reminded the Bundestag: "People overcame the Wall with their own power. This can and should make one proud."[36] Similarly, Hubertus Knabe, the director of the memorial at

---

34 See the written statements by Manfred Wilke, Klaus-Dietmar Henke and Thomas Rogalla for the April 18, 2005 Berlin parliament hearing on Flierl's *Gedenkkonzept*, ibid.

35 Marianne Birthler, statement, Bundestag Ausschuss für Kultur und Medien, Protokoll 15/60, Wortprotokoll 60. Sitzung, June 15, 2005.

36 Stephan Hilsberg, Bundestag Plenarprotokoll 15/184, June 30, 2005.

the former Stasi prison at Hohenschönhausen-Berlin, and Manfred Wilke, a historian and member of the Berlin CDU, argued that Berlin now had "the chance to show the positive side of GDR history and to honor those who fought for freedom and democracy under great personal risk."[37] Some CDU members of the Bundestag led by Günter Nooke had been lobbying already for several years in vain for the creation of a "Freedom and Unity Monument" to celebrate the events of 1989–90 and thus agreed that Wall memory must encompass the fall of the Wall.[38]

Yet another approach stepped back from this German focus and looked at the Wall in the broader context of European and global history during the Cold War. The historian Konrad Jarausch, Dieter Vorsteher of the German Historical Museum, and the Bundestag member Markus Meckel all argued that a crucial component of the Berlin Senate's plan to commemorate the Wall needed to be international. The Wall's "rupture through Berlin expressed the struggle between two worlds,"[39] the Cold War conflict between communism and democracy. This broader context was crucial for understanding the significance of the Berlin Wall. Therefore they called for the creation of a new museum of the division of Europe in the global context. The location they had in mind for the museum was at Checkpoint Charlie.[40] Two draft plans for such a museum were drawn up by Vorsteher and by Jarausch and were included as appendices to the finalized *Gesamtkonzept* in 2006.[41]

The proposal for this museum was quite controversial. Former East German victims and many members of the CDU feared that a focus on the Cold War shifted

---

37 Hubertus Knabe and Manfred Wilke, "Die Wunden der Teilung sichtbar machen. Vorschläge für ein Konzept der Erinnerung an die untergegangene SED-Diktatur," *Horch und Guck* 49 (2004), November 23, 2004.

38 Günter Nooke, Bundestag Ausschuss für Kultur und Medien, Protokoll 15/60, Wortprotokoll 60. Sitzung, June 15, 2005.

39 ZZF memo, "Die Berliner Mauer – Erinnerung ohne Ort?" March 9, 2005, 5. See also Flierl's *Gedenkkonzept*, April 18, 2005, which quotes extensively from the ZZF memo, 16–18.

40 Markus Meckel, Bundestag Plenarprotokoll 15/163, March 10, 2005, and Bundestag Ausschuss für Kultur und Medien, Protokoll 15/60, Wortprotokoll 60. Sitzung, June 15, 2005; Flierl's "Gedenkkonzept," April 18, 2005; and Konrad Jarausch, statement, Bundestag Ausschuss für Kultur und Medien, Protokoll 15/60, Wortprotokoll 60. Sitzung, June 15, 2005.

41 Anhang, Gesamtkonzept Berliner Mauer – Texte und Materialien, "Skizzen für ein Museum des Kalten Krieges": Dieter Vorsteher, "Checkpoint Charlie – Museum des Kalten Krieges in Europa," 14–17; and Konrad Jarausch, "Die Teilung Europas und ihre Überwindung. Ein neues Museum des Kalten Krieges?" 17–20, last accessed on August 15, 2016, http://www.stadtentwicklung.berlin.de/planen/staedtebau-projekte/bernauer_str/download/20060616_gesamtkonzept_berliner_mauer.pdf.

blame for the Wall and its victims from the SED regime to the two superpowers and their global conflict. They were suspicious that such a museum would treat the two systems equally and not deal critically enough with communism and the SED's repressive rule.[42] Some of the wording of the proposals for the new museum may have contributed to these concerns by emphasizing the interactive nature of the East-West conflict.[43]

In contrast to the above mentioned approaches to the Wall, some former members of the East German leadership, army and border guards had a different perspective. They objected to a critical view of the Wall, arguing rather that it was necessary to preserve peace and that they had been fulfilling their duties in defending and maintaining it.[44] None of the main officials or experts involved in the *Gesamtkonzept* shared this perspective, nor did the most of the media. Instead, this refusal to condemn the deadly nature of the Wall served as further motivation to educate young Germans and visitors about its true brutality. Former East German officials such as Egon Krenz have also argued, contrary to what is clear in prodigious amounts of archival evidence about the essential role of the East German leaders in pushing for the Berlin Wall, that the Soviet leaders were the driving force behind the Wall, not the East German leaders who in essence were "just following orders" and were relatively powerless in "the circumstances of the Cold War" dominated by the two superpowers.[45]

The choice of aesthetics and the physical approach to remembering the Wall with the *Gesamtkonzept* were also matters of controversy. In particular, there was a tense divide between people who passionately argued that only the reconstruction of a section of the former border strip's layers could convincingly convey what it had been like and others who vehemently and often condescendingly responded that this would create a kind of Disneyland instead of an authentic site that visitors could take seriously. The deep emotions and hostility expressed in this "authenticity vs. Disneyland" debate (which is elaborated upon in S. Frank's

---

42 Interview with Rainer Wagner, chairman of the UOKG, April 30, 2010; remarks by Uwe Lehmann-Brauns and by Andreas Apelt, Inhaltsprotokoll Kult 15/79, Ausschuss für Kulturelle Angelegenheiten, Abgeordnetenhaus Berlin, 15. Wahlperiode, June 26, 2006.

43 Dieter Vorsteher, "Checkpoint Charlie – Museum des Kalten Krieges in Europa," 15–16. See note 41.

44 See for example the book by Heinz Kessler and Fritz Streletz, *Ohne die Mauer hätte es Krieg gegeben. Zeitzeugen und Dokumente geben Auskunft* (Berlin: Edition Ost, 2011).

45 Paul Geitner, "East Gemany's last communist leader convicted in border shootings," AP, August 25, 1997; "Justice at the Wall," editorial, *The Asian Wall Street Journal*, August 29, 1997; and Geir Moulson, "East Germany's last Stalinist leader, jailed for Wall deaths, wins parole," AP, December 18, 2003.

chapter in this volume) indicated that something deeper was going on than just a difference in aesthetic approach. Members of victims groups and conservative politicians and newspapers were suspicious that anything short of a reconstruction was an attempt to downplay the brutality of the Wall and the repressive nature of the SED regime.[46] The March 2005 memorandum by Jarausch, Sabrow and Hertle therefore urged a combination of authentic remains with some reconstruction of the former death strip at Bernauer Strasse.[47]

Experts in historic preservation, the mayor, and his cultural senator, in contrast, argued that there was in fact no way to recreate the fear and deadly force behind the Berlin Wall which resulted from armed guards with a shoot-to-kill order together with aggressive dogs and the other parts of the border zone.[48] Following the reigning principles of historic preservation, [49] they argued that only authentic remains still standing in their original places were appropriate to commemorate the Wall and not reconstructions, which they insisted belonged in museums or "Hollywood," not at memorials.[50] The sites must be left "as found" in order to be to be authentic. Anything else, they argued would not be convincing as a historic site.

Behind this debate was also a lack of consensus on what the Wall remains or reconstruction should convey to visitors. Those favoring reconstruction generally wanted to focus on a simple, basic narrative: the Wall and the SED regime behind it were evil, violated human rights, and killed people. They wanted a clear, emotional message that would be easily grasped when looking at the layers of obsta-

---

46 Harald Strunz of UOKG, written statement to the hearing on Flierl's "Gedenkkonzept," Berlin parliament, April 18, 2005, last accessed on August 15, 2016, http://www.uokg.de/Text/akt039flirlkonzept.htm. and open letter of May 29, 2006 reprinted in Martin Sabrow, Rainer Eckert, Monika Flacke, et.al., eds., *Wohin treibt die DDR-Erinnerung? Dokumentation einer Debatte* (Göttingen: Vandenhoeck und Ruprecht, 2007), 293.

47 ZZF memo, "Die Berliner Mauer – Erinnerung ohne Ort?" March 9, 2005. See also Jarausch's observations, Abgeordnetenhaus Berlin, Ausschuss für Kulturelle Angelegentheiten, Wortprotokoll 15/58, April 25, 2005, 11.

48 Thomas Flierl and Michael Braun, Berlin parliament hearing, April 25, 2005, ibid; and author's interviews with Thomas Flierl, Berlin, November 26, 2009, Mayor Klaus Wowereit, Berlin, February 10, 2010; and Rainer Klemke, Berlin, August 2, 2011.

49 Gabi Dolf-Bornekämper, "Denkmalschutz für die Mauer," *Die Denkmalpflege* 58 (1/2000), 33–40, especially 35 & 37.

50 See the remarks of Leo Schmidt, Gabriele Camphausen and Rainer Klemke at the meeting with experts of the "Interagency Task Force on Remembering the Berlin Wall," February 2–3, 2005, in Monica Geyler-von Bernus and Birgit Kahl, "Protokoll der Experten-Anhörung" of Febuary 11, 2005; and the remarks of Thomas Flierl, in Inhaltsprotokoll Kult 15/79, Ausschuss für Kulturelle Angelegenheiten, Abgeordnetenhaus Berlin, 15. Wahlperiode, June 26, 2006, 13.

cles to prevent people from leaving East Germany. Those advocating authenticity favored a more restrained approach – one that did not appeal to "cheap emotions" or look like a Wall "theme park" – that would educate people about the victims, the perpetrators and the whole context surrounding the Berlin Wall.[51]

The challenge was coming up with a solution that would contain elements of both approaches: something authentic that also left an emotional impression of what the Wall was like. The final *Gesamtkonzept* clearly favored authenticity over reconstruction but – in an unintended homage to Hildebrandt's crosses – understood the importance of having emotional impact.

Choosing the Bernauer Strasse Site

The *Gesamtkonzept* also settled another debate – the question of where the focus of Wall memory should be – by choosing Bernauer Strasse over the alternatives. While Hildebrandt's crosses had brought attention to Checkpoint Charlie and the Bundestag proposal had focused on the Brandenburg Gate, there was much to be said for making the central commemorative site for the Berlin Wall at the already existing Berlin Wall Memorial at Bernauer Strasse. The biggest factor which set it apart from other sites was that it was the only place in Berlin that still had a large, intact section of the border in its depth, including the forward and rear walls and the layers in between. Thus, in September 2005, the Berlin Senate had granted Bernauer Strasse historic landmark status, protecting it from construction due to its "extraordinary political significance for the city" and preserving it for use in the future expanded Berlin Wall Memorial.

Though not as centrally located as the Brandenburg Gate or Checkpoint Charlie, Bernauer Strasse was nonetheless intimately connected to the Berlin Wall.[52] The border between East and West Berlin had been on the sidewalk in front of houses on the Eastern side of the street. When the East German regime sealed off the border and began building the Berlin Wall on August 13, 1961, people jumped out of the windows of their houses into the nets held by firemen on the West Berlin sidewalk in front of their houses. Some died trying to escape.

---

51 Author's interview with Manfred Fischer, Berlin, October 6, 2009. Fischer was a strong proponent of a restrained approach.

52 Once the Berlin Wall Memorial at Bernauer Strasse became more established, however, the home page declared that it is located "in the center of the capital," last accessed on August 15, 2016, http://www.berliner-mauer-gedenkstaette.de/de/.

As a result, the East German leaders ordered the windows of houses to be bricked up and sometimes destroyed the houses to prevent East Germans from escaping. In response, people on both sides of the Wall dug tunnels under the Wall at Bernauer Strasse for East Germans to escape. Many made it successfully, but others were caught in the process and thrown in jail by the Stasi. After the fall of the Wall, a small group of activists led by Pastor Manfred Fischer of the Church of Reconciliation on Bernauer Strasse pushed for preserving parts of the Wall there, including a block-long section, so as to create a Berlin Wall memorial.

The Berlin Parliament passed a law in 1991 creating a Berlin Wall Memorial and putting the area under historic landmark protection but failed to provide funding for the site. In 1994, the Bundestag stepped in and provided financial backing for an artistic design competition for a memorial at Bernauer Strasse. The winning design consisted of two steel walls set to intersect at right angles with the existing forward and rear walls left from the Berlin Wall, forming a square around a section of the former death strip. It was dedicated on 13 August 1998. Etched on one of the new steel walls, the dedication inscription read: "In memory of the division of the city from August 13, 1961 – November 9, 1989 and in commemoration of victims of communist tyranny." This memorial had little emotional power, and the new steel walls caused much confusion among visitors about what the real Berlin Wall was.

Feeling that the history was slipping away quickly, in the building on Bernauer Strasse that housed the offices of the Church of Reconciliation, Manfred Fischer created a place to remember and commemorate the Wall, calling it a Documentation Center. A small exhibit on the Wall opened there on November 9, 1999 for the tenth anniversary of the fall of the Wall. Across the street, a newly built Chapel of Reconciliation was dedicated in 2000 where the much larger Church of Reconciliation had stood in the death strip before being blown up in 1985 by GDR authorities. In 2003, an observation tower was opened on the roof of the Documentation Center, giving an overview from the fourth story of the former border. But many visitors, members of the media and some politicians disparaged the whole ensemble at Bernauer Strasse as being cold and confusing.[53]

The largest section of the *Gesamtkonzept* was therefore devoted to a detailed description of necessary steps to be taken at Bernauer Strasse to present a more thorough and convincing remembrance of the Wall and commemoration of the victims. The two-block long existing site at Bernauer Strasse would now be expanded to encompass eight blocks of an outdoor exhibit on the land where

---

53 Philipp Gessler, "Gegen das glatte Gedenken," *taz*, November 6, 2004; and Bernhard Schultz, "Das Kreuz mit der Erinnerung," *Der Tagesspiegel*, November 9, 2004.

the former border had been. This exhibition would be open 24 hours a day, seven days a week and would be anchored at one end by the North Station train station and at the other by the Wall Park (Mauerpark). Covering over 1.3 kilometers and 4.4 hectares of the former Berlin Wall zone, this outdoor area would include remains and markings of the layers of the border zone, information about where people were killed or escaped, the location of tunnels, foundations of buildings destroyed by East German border troops, and other such detailed, specific information to make the history of the area come alive with the help of photos, videos and recordings placed around the site.

Special attention both in this outdoor area and inside the Documentation Center would be given to individual and collective commemoration of people killed at the Wall by including a photo gallery with names and biographical information. In addition, the plan provided for a new visitors' center, an exhibit inside North Station on the so-called "ghost" train stations that were closed while the city was divided, and an improved and expanded Documentation Center with a new, permanent exhibit covering the local, national and global contexts necessary to understand the history of the Berlin Wall. The entire area would be called "The Berlin Wall Memorial." The municipal and federal governments committed themselves to supporting the permanence, stability and high quality of the Berlin Wall Memorial by each funding half of the costs. Upgrading the site necessitated more space, personnel, educational outreach, and a new institutional form which was implemented with the 2008 law establishing the Berlin Wall Foundation, a body to oversee the expanded Berlin Wall Memorial at Bernauer Strasse together with site of the Marienfelde Refugee Camp which had welcomed over one million East German refugees to West Berlin after opening in 1953.[54]

With the *Gesamtkonzept*, Bernauer Strasse's Berlin Wall Memorial would become the "central site for commemorating victims of the Berlin Wall" and for explaining and evoking the history of the Wall. The plan warned that "competing sites of central commemoration must be avoided," although individuals killed at the Wall should also be commemorated at the location where they were killed and the Bundestag might find a way to commemorate victims of the Wall at the Brandenburg Gate.[55] While the *Gesamtkonzept* prioritized Bernauer Strasse, it also settled on an otherwise de-centralized approach to remembering the Wall that would take into account most of the existing remains, memorial sites and museums connected with the Wall in Berlin. This included the Brandenburg

---

54 Gesetz über die Errichtung der Stiftung Berliner Mauer (Mauerstiftungsgesetz, MAUStG), September 17, 2008, in *Gesetz und Verordnungsblatt für Berlin* 64:24 (September 27, 2008), 25–252.
55 *Gesamtkonzept*, 17 and 38.

Gate, Checkpoint Charlie, the East Side Gallery, and multiple other sites and also small memorials for people killed at the Wall. Given that the Wall had snaked its way over 43 kilometers through the inner city of Berlin, it made sense to highlight as many places along that path as possible.

Drawing on the Bundestag's views on the importance of the Brandenburg Gate and its popularity with tourists, the *Gesamtkonzept* provided for a site of information about the Berlin Wall and the Gate to be housed inside the Brandenburg Gate metro station then under construction. The Senate endeavored to use this important, central location to direct visitors to other places in Berlin connected with the Wall and to give them basic historical information by the use of large historical pictures, maps, multi-media installations and computer terminals.

At Checkpoint Charlie, the Senate favored a more professional and broader approach to Wall history than Hildebrandt had provided and sponsored the construction of billboards at street level, called Checkpoint Gallery, describing the history of Checkpoint Charlie and the Berlin Wall and informing visitors about other sites in Berlin connected with the Berlin Wall, East Germany, and the Cold War. Checkpoint Gallery opened in August 2006 and had more than 20,000 visitors the first week. The longer-term vision of the *Gesamtkonzept*, however, was to create a "Museum of the Cold War in Europe" or a "Cold War Museum" on the site as part of a building to be constructed by investors. In addition, the *Gesamtkonzept* supported the preservation of half a dozen additional sites such as the former Tränenpalast crossing point at the Friedrichstrasse train station and the East Side Gallery expanse of 1.3 kilometers of the Wall painted by artists from around the world after the opening of the Wall.

Implementing the Gesamtkonzept

The Berlin Senate estimated that the implementation of the *Gesamtkonzept* would cost 40 million Euros ($51 million). Much of it, around 18 million Euros, would be used to buy land in the former death strip on Bernauer Strasse. In outlining the budget the Senate "assume[d] that the federal government will participate in paying at least half of the costs for implementing [this] plan, since the documentation and the remembrance of the Berlin Wall as well as the commemoration of the victims are national obligations."[56] Cooperation between the Berlin authorities and the federal government has been essential for implementing the plan.

56 Ibid., 62.

The *Gesamtkonzept* has resulted in better signage and advertising so that people can more easily find sites connected with the Wall. There are more explanatory plaques and information boards at the sites (in German and English) and directions to the sites are more prominent on the street, on maps, in brochures, via the internet, audioguides with handheld GPS systems, multimedia cell phone messaging, on public transportation with a special "Wall ticket," and via tourist agencies. Smart phone apps on the Wall have been developed for use at Bernauer Strasse and elsewhere and there are multiple Wall tours (by foot, boat, bicycle, bus and Segway) on offer. The Berlin Senate has implemented a "communication plan" to use all media possible to get out the word about sites connected with the history of the Berlin Wall, including a logo and a website: www.berlin.de/mauer. Measured by numbers of visitors, information available, visibility in the public space and reviews by experts and tourists, the *Gesamtkonzept* has been a success in providing more information on the Berlin Wall.

A central focus of implementing the *Gesamtkonzept* has been on the victims, particularly people killed trying to escape. Indeed, the *Gesamtkonzept* itself was dedicated on its first page to all people who suffered from the Wall in any way, including people killed at the Wall but also many other groups of people whose lives were harmed the Wall. More specifically, the 2007 guidelines for the design competition of the outdoor exhibit at Bernauer Strasse stated: "The task of the memorial site is to name the dead by their names, show their faces and their biographies to the public, anchor them in public memory, and create a site for individual mourning as well as collective public commemoration."[57] To do this, scholars first needed to ascertain the exact number of people killed at the Berlin Wall.[58] With support from the federal government, researchers from the Berlin Wall Memorial in cooperation with a team from the Center for Contemporary History (ZZF) in Potsdam investigated the biographical details of people who had been killed at the Wall. Maria Nooke of the Berlin Wall Memorial and Hans-Hermann Hertle from the ZZF found conclusive evidence that 136 (later increased to 139) people had been killed at the Berlin Wall, publishing

---

57 Senatsverwaltung für Stadtentwicklung, "Erweiterung der Gedenkstätte Berliner Mauer, Berlin Mitte, offener Realisierungswettbewerb für Hochbau, Freiraum und Ausstellung, Auslobung," Berlin, July 2007, 94, last accessed on August 15, 2016, http://www.stadtentwicklung.berlin.de/aktuell/wettbewerbe/ergebnisse/2007/bernauer_strasse/auslobung.shtml.

58 Konrad Jarausch's testimony, Abgeordnetenhaus Berlin, 15. Wahlperiode, Wortprotokoll Kult 15/58, Ausschuss für Kulturelle Angelegenheiten, 58. Sitzung, April 25, 2005, 9; and to the Bundestag, Deutscher Bundestag, 15. Wahlperiode, Protokoll 15/60, Ausschuss für Kultur und Medien, Wortprotokoll, 60. Sitzung, June 15, 2005, 7.

their results in a book, *The Victims at the Berlin Wall, 1961–1989: A Biographical Handbook*.[59]

These findings served as the basis for the "Window of Commemoration" memorial to the victims at Bernauer Strasse located in the middle of the former death strip. The memorial features several layers of "windows" consisting of pictures of the Wall victims in the chronological order in which they were killed. Learning from the success of Hildebrandt's Wall crosses, the guidelines for the expansion of the Berlin Wall Memorial at Bernauer Strasse made clear that the exhibit must appeal to people emotionally[60] and provide them with a real sense of what the Berlin Wall meant. The emotional heart of the expanded outdoor exhibit is this Window of Commemoration. At its dedication with Mayor Wowereit on May 21, 2010, family members and friends of the victims were invited to place white roses in their loved one's "window." With funds from the federal and state governments, researchers led by Jochen Staadt of the Free University of Berlin are still investigating how many people, including border guards, were killed at the inner-German border.[61]

In implementing the *Gesamtkonzept*, there has generally been more focus on the victims than on the perpetrators. Yet it is impossible to understand how people were shot at the Berlin Wall or imprisoned for trying to escape without understanding the roles played by border guards at the Wall and their superiors in the military, the SED and the Stasi. As time passes and young people know less about the Wall, there is more need to explain the whole system that led to the killing of people trying to escape.[62] With this in mind, the 2008 guidelines for monuments and memorials drawn up under the federal minister for culture, Bernd Neumann, specified that the expansion of the Berlin Wall Memorial at

---

59 Hans-Hermann Hertle and Maria Nooke, eds., *The Victims at the Berlin Wall, 1961–1989: A Biographical Handbook* (Berlin: Ch. Links, 2011). The German version had been published by the same press in 2009: *Die Todesopfer an der Berliner Mauer, 1961–1989. Ein biographisches Handbuch*. In 2013, two more victims were identified: "Museum ermittelt 137. Berliner Todes-Opfer," *Bild*, August 13, 2013; and "138. Berliner Mauer-Opfer ermittelt," *Der Tagesspiegel*, November 15, 2013. Another victim was identified in November 2016, bringing the total to 139.

60 See 9 of the guidelines, Senatsverwaltung für Stadtentwicklung, "Erweiterung der Gedenkstätte Berliner Mauer, Berlin Mitte, offener Realisierungswettbewerb für Hochbau, Freiraum und Ausstellung, Auslobung," Berlin, July 2007. See note 57.

61 "Tote an innerdeutscher Grenze: Forschungsprojekt dauert an," *Berliner Morgenpost*, August 11, 2015.

62 Similarly, the main exhibit at Auschwitz was redesigned to devote more attention to the perpetrators than was possible and necessary initially. Michael Kimmelman, "Auschwitz Shifts From Memorializing to Teaching," *The New York Times*, February 18, 2011.

Bernauer Strasse must make clear "the horror of the border regime."[63] At the expanded outdoor Berlin Wall Memorial, there are now stations in the former border strip where visitors can see pictures, read, listen to recordings and watch videos about the border guards, their superiors, and members of the local population who volunteered to watch the border and report anything suspicious. Memorial museums at the former Stasi prison at Hohenschönhausen and Stasi headquarters at Normannenstrasse also give information on the perpetrators.

A new focus of Wall memory since 2009 has emphasized the "Peaceful Revolution" carried out by East Germans on the streets in the fall of 1989. Twenty years after the fall of the Wall, the German political elite seemed to suddenly remember, realize, or feel confident in declaring that there was something to be proud of in recent German history, namely the peaceful fall of the Wall. As discussed above, several prominent politicians of the CDU and historians had been insisting for years that not only must more information be supplied about the brutal part of the Berlin Wall's history, but there should also be more celebration of the happy part of the history: the opening of the border and the role played by East German citizens. Commemoration of the 20th anniversary of the fall of the Wall started with the opening in May of an exhibit on the Peaceful Revolution and climaxed on November 9 with celebrations at Bornholmer Strasse (the first border crossing to open on November 9, 1989) and the Brandenburg Gate. Although not ready in time for the 20th anniversary, a "9 November 1989 Square" was dedicated by the mayor at Bornholmer Strasse the following year. For both the 20th and 25th anniversaries of the fall of the Wall, large-scale festivities took place in Berlin along the path of the former Wall and featured German and other leaders at the Brandenburg Gate. The November 9 evening celebration in 2009 featured the toppling of more than 1,000 large Styrofoam Wall dominoes, and in 2014 more than 8,000 illuminated balloons were released into the night sky, both times with tens of thousands of people in attendance.

Beginning with the 20th anniversary of the fall of the Wall, German leaders from Berlin Mayor Wowereit to Chancellor Merkel have used the memory of 1989 to create a new narrative or founding myth for united Germany: the nation was born from a peaceful, democratic revolution that toppled the Wall and then pushed for unification. After largely ignoring the role of the leaders and followers of the East German opposition in 1989, public officials now celebrated them

---

63 "Unterrichtung durch den Beauftragten der Bundesregierung für Kultur und Medien. Fortschreibung der Gedenkstättenkonzeption des Bundes. Verantwortung wahrnehmen, Aufarbeitung verstärken, Gedenken vertiefen," Deutscher Bundestag, 16. Wahlperiode, Drucksache 16/9875, June 19, 2008, 8.

as courageous heroes who created the Peaceful Revolution, capital P, capital R.[64] This is meant to inspire young Germans about their country's past and about the possibilities for the future and to foster a deeper sense of unity by re-casting the toppling of the Berlin Wall into a fundamental moment in all-German history.

Another focus of Wall memory has been lessons from the history the Wall, lessons German leaders believe are important for young Germans to learn. The most important message of Mayor Wowereit and others asserts: "Freedom and democracy must be defended anew every day. Thus we must pass on to future generations the memory of the lack of freedom and dictatorship. From an understanding of the vulnerability of democracy comes the readiness to be engaged in favor of the free rule of law and against its enemies. Freedom is not to be taken for granted."[65] Many German leaders emphasize that the history of the Wall shows the difference between democracy and dictatorship. Foreign Minister Westerwelle declared in January 2011 that the "lesson of the Wall for us as convinced democrats is to fight against political extremism having a place in Germany."[66]

The implementation of the *Gesamtkonzept* has triggered several controversies, which have continued the debates that led to its formulation. First, the most heated moment of the "authenticity vs. Disneyland debate" occurred in 2007–2008 with the announcement of the winner of the competition to design the outdoor exhibit at Bernauer Strasse. As part of the winning design, the architects planned to install tall, narrow columns of rust-colored Corten steel to mark gaps in the Wall along Bernauer Strasse. Opponents, including some victims groups and the CDU, argued that using such rods instead of using original pieces of the Wall itself (still available in a government warehouse) made the Berlin Wall and the border regime seem less oppressive and deadly than they had been. These opponents accused the leaders of the Berlin Wall Memorial of being too soft on the memory of the East German regime and sought to stop the implementation

64 The CDU-SPD federal coalition treaty of November 27, 2013 pledged "to permanently secure" the exhibit and the Robert Havemann Society's Archive of the GDR Opposition. "Deutschlands Zukunft gestalten. Koalitionsvertrag zwischen CDU, CDU und SPD. 18. Legislaturperiode," 130. Last accessed on August 15, 2016, https://www.cdu.de/sites/default/files/media/dokumente/koalitionsvertrag.pdf.

65 Speech by Mayor Klaus Wowereit, August 13, 2012, last accessed on August 15, 2016, https://www.berlin.de/rbmskzl/aktuelles/pressemitteilungen/2012/pressemitteilung.53958.php.

66 Speech by Foreign Minister Guido Westerwelle at the opening of an exhibit, "Die Mauer – eine Grenze durch Deutschland," at the Foreign Ministry commemorating the 50th anniversary of the building of the Berlin Wall, January 11, 2011.

of the winning design.[67] Officials at the Berlin Wall Memorial and in the Senate insisted that preserving the authenticity of the site required not bringing back any pieces of the Wall. Their case was bolstered by the fact that the land at the part of the site in question was owned by the Sophie Church, whose leaders said they would not let the Memorial use their land if pieces of the Wall were returned. They wanted to emphasize the post-1989 porousness of the Wall. The steel rods of the winning design were eventually installed. Controversies are ongoing at other locations on Bernauer Strasse where property owners do not want to sacrifice some or all of their backyards to the Berlin Wall Memorial.[68] Since early 2013, there has also been a conflict over the Wall at the East Side Gallery where a property investor removed pieces of the (supposedly landmark protected) Wall to access his construction site.[69]

Another source of controversy in implementing the *Gesamtkonzept* has been connected with the plans for a Cold War Museum at Checkpoint Charlie.[70] Much of the prior concern about an equidistant approach to East and West in this museum was placated by the opening in 2012 of a small exhibit in the so-called "BlackBox Cold War" at Checkpoint Charlie, a one-room indoor space that joined the outdoor Checkpoint Gallery exhibit the Senate had sponsored since 2006. The BlackBox exhibit made clear the differences between communism and democracy that many feared would be papered over with a Cold War focus on the superpowers and it situated Berlin and the Wall at the front line. The other reason for criticism, namely the conviction of other institutions, such as the Allied Museum, that the future complete Cold War Museum will take visitors away from them, however, remains.[71] Most directly threatened by the location at Checkpoint Charlie is of course Alexandra Hildebrandt's Wall Museum. There is thus a certain amount of

---

67 Sven Felix Kellerhoff, "'Alles Burra, oder was?' Das falsche Gedenken der Stiftung Berliner Mauer: Eine Polemik," *Deutschland Archiv* 42 (4/2009), 589–593.

68 Barbara Junge, "50 Jahre Mauer. Von Gassen und Sackgassen," *Der Tagesspiegel*, August 7, 2011.

69 Chris Cottrell, "In Berlin, a Protest to Keep What Remains of the Wall," *New York Times*, March 4, 2013; "East Side Gallery soll in Obhut Stiftung Berliner Mauer kommen," *Berliner Zeitung*, December 3, 2013; and Robert Ide, Ralf Schönball, and Thomas Loy, "Empörung über die Geheimdienst-Verstrickungen des Investors", *Der Tagesspiegel*, December 9, 2013.

70 On the controversy, see Konrad Jarausch, "Zwischen den Blöcken," *Der Tagesspiegel*, April 19, 2012; Thomas Loy, "Gezerre um Museum des Kalten Krieges," *Der Tagesspiegel*, August 11, 2012; Wolfgang Thierse, "Das Haus für die weltgeschichtliche Dimension. Warum wir ein Museum des Kalten Krieges brauchen und dieses am Checkpoint Charlie entstehen muss," *Der Tagesspiegel*, September 19, 2012.

71 Interview with Gundula Bavendamm by Laura Berlin and Sven Felix Kellerhof, "Der Checkpoint Charlie ist völlig überwertet," *Die Welt*, September 10, 2012.

direct competition built into the plans for the Cold War Museum. Yadegar Asisi's successful Wall panorama which opened across the street at Checkpoint Charlie the day after "BlackBox Cold War" may indicate that there are enough tourists at Checkpoint Charlie to go around.[72]

Commemorating the Berlin Wall

Both the discussion of the *Gesamtkonzept* and its implementation have resulted in more attention to and information about the history of the Berlin Wall. The push that started in 2004 to make the presence and history of the Wall in Berlin more visible has largely achieved its goals, although it took longer than the six years that had been planned for in the *Gesamtkonzept*. Indeed, it was not until 2014 that the long-awaited new indoor exhibit was opened at the Berlin Wall Memorial.[73] Over 950,000 people visited the Berlin Wall Memorial in 2015. Tour busses pack the area around the Berlin Wall Memorial, as they long have at Checkpoint Charlie and the Brandenburg Gate.

Political leaders at the municipal and federal levels in Berlin have devoted more attention to the Wall and its history in their speeches and activities, particularly on major anniversaries connected with the rise and fall of the Wall, such as the 20th and 25th anniversaries of the fall of the Wall in 2009 and 2014 and the 50th anniversary of the erection of the Wall in 2011. The media has similarly kept a steady focus on the Wall.

While it is now much easier to find remnants of the Wall in Berlin and to learn about its history, there is still no consensus on the place of the Wall or the SED regime in German history.[74] Groups of former army, Stasi and party officials still gather regularly, sometimes in their military uniforms, to remember the "good old days."[75] Precisely because some former East Germans continue to defend the

---

72 Yadegar Asisi's Wall panorama was not meant to be a permanent installation. Initially it was to remain in place for a year, but it was extended and remains standing at Checkpoint Charlie as of 2016.

73 Axel Klausmeier, chief editor, *The Berlin Wall: Berlin Wall Memorial Exhibition Catalog* (Berlin: Ch. Links Verlag, 2015).

74 Thomas Grossbölting, "Die DDR im vereinten Deutschland," *Aus Politik und Zeitgeschichte* 25–26 (2010); Grossbölting, "Geschichtskonstruktion zwischen Wissenschaft und Populärkultur," *Aus Politik und Zeitgeschichte*, October 8, 2013; and Klaus Christoph, "'Aufarbeitung der SED-Diktatur' – heute so wie gestern?" *Aus Politik und Zeitgeschichte*, October 8, 2013.

75 Rainer Erices and Jan Schönfelder, "Auftritt vor DDR-Altkadern," Mitteldeutscher Rundfunk, July 30, 2013; and "DDR-Gespenster: Stasi-Offiziere wollen wieder marschieren," *B.Z.*, December

Berlin Wall, a majority in the political and cultural elite of united Germany considers it important that young Germans and foreign tourists who visit Berlin have ample opportunity to learn about the history of the Wall. The *Gesamtkonzept* of 2006 has greatly facilitated this.

Although initially upstaged by a private individual, namely Alexandra Hildebrandt, German public officials have increasingly sought to control the narrative, including via the *Gesamtkonzept*, that is told about the history of the Wall. That narrative has two focal points: one on the brutal nature of the Wall and the importance of remembering the victims; and the other on the key role of the East German citizens in peacefully bringing down the Wall. The latter provides for Germans a much happier past that they can celebrate and be proud of than has long been the case. At the start of the deliberations and the implementation of the *Gesamtkonzept*, there was more attention given to the negative side of the Wall's history (the victims and perpetrators) than to the positive side (its toppling). Since 2009 however, this has changed as the Germans have embraced the significance of the Peaceful Revolution of 1989, including the fall of the Wall, in forging the birth of a united, democratic Germany. This has enabled German leaders to assert that their country is part of the community of nations with democratic revolutions as founding moments and to thus redefine German identity from a nation of perpetrators to a nation of active democrats.[76] Nonetheless, for at least as long as there are still survivors of the Cold War division of Germany, no one narrative about the Berlin Wall will be supported by all Germans.

10, 2013. For information on the Joint Initiative to Protect the Social Rights of Former Members of the GDR Armed Forces and Customs Administration (ISOR), last accessed on August 15, 2016, http://www.isor-sozialverein.de/.

76 For a fuller investigation of this process, see Hope M. Harrison, *After the Berlin Wall: Memory and the Making of the New Germany, 1989 to the Present* (NY: Cambridge University Press, forthcoming).

Sybille Frank

Competing for the Best Wall Memorial

The Rise of a Cold War Heritage Industry in Berlin

A regular heritage boom has swept through Germany since the 1990s: cities celebrate their historical anniversaries with large parties, stage medieval markets, lavishly reconstruct their submerged historic quarters, and rebuild their destroyed palaces or famous old churches. Countless historical relicts are being elevated to the status of landmarks, and tourist visits to historic sites are reaching ever new heights. A new museum opens in Germany every second day, while the number of private museums is growing constantly. Recent history is also becoming increasingly popular: in Berlin, for example, a private museum offers a "hands-on experience" of life in the former GDR (German Democratic Republic), and if you are fed up with sitting in a *Trabant* car or spying on your neighbor, you are welcome to satisfy your appetite in a restaurant offering typical GDR dishes.

This heritage boom is an expression of various recent changes in the ways the past is dealt with.[1] The first concerns the area of the production and management of the past. In contrast to the historical cultures of the UK and the USA, which have been strongly influenced by the private sector, the commemoration of the past in divided Germany was placed primarily in political-administrative and civic hands.[2] Due to a decline in the amount of public money available and the global accessibility of historic attractions, the field of memorializing the past, which had formerly been seen as a genuinely public task, has become increasingly dominated by the market since the 1990s, and thus by a global competitiveness among public and private agents for funding and for as many visitors as possible.[3] This fact, however, has remained practically unnoticed in reunited Germany, in view of the "vehement discussion about the nationalization of German memory in the 1990s."[4] And yet historical material, understood

1 Sybille Frank, *Wall Memorials and Heritage. The Heritage Industry of Berlin's Checkpoint Charlie* (London/New York: Routledge, 2016); Hanno Hochmuth in this volume.

2 David Lowenthal, "'History' und 'Heritage': Widerstreitende und konvergente Formen der Vergangenheitsbetrachtung," in Rosemarie Beier, ed., *Geschichtskultur in der Zweiten Moderne* (Frankfurt a.M.: Campus, 2000), 71–94.

3 Claus Leggewie and Erik Meyer, "Visualisierung und Virtualisierung von Erinnerung: Geschichtspolitik in der medialen Erlebnisgesellschaft," *zeitenblicke* 3 (1, 2004).

4 Walter Prigge, "Weltkulturerbe zwischen nationalen Gedächtnissen und kosmopolitischen Erinnerungen. Zum Gedächtnisraum des 20. Jahrhunderts," in id., ed., *Bauhaus Brasilia*

DOI 10.1515/9783110496178-013

as relevant to the present and therefore worth preserving, has long been in demand.

A second change has been the transition from a "factual" to an "emotional" approach to the past. Until the 1990s Germany was dominated by a form of presenting the past that was influenced by the modern European model, which the American geographer David Lowenthal referred to as "history."[5] At the center of this specific "rout[e] to the past"[6] was the material object, the "original," protected in its display case, and a source-based, text-centered communication of historical "facts." The relationship between the past and the present was therefore characterized not only by the distance of time, but also, through the spatial separation of observer and historic object, of space and of an intellectual approach to the past.

This route to the past was challenged in the 1990s, at first by new media formats for conveying history, such as television "histotainment." This genre combined archive material, interviews with first-hand witnesses and re-enacted scenes, presenting the past through the prism of biographical stories and human experiences. In the area of exhibitions, moreover, private experiential museums promoted a tangible understanding of using things, and infused everyday scenes with a sensual experience of the themes and objects presented. The distance between the present and the past – or between the observer and the historical object – was replaced by a personalized "hands-on history" or "witnessing" by stimulating as many senses and emotions as possible. "Heritage" is what David Lowenthal called this new route to the past, in which historical material is presented as an experiential, meaningful narrative of the past, which is closely connected to the present and to everyday human existence.[7]

Auschwitz Hiroshima. Weltkulturerbe des 20. Jahrhunderts. Modernität und Barbarei (Berlin: jovis, 2003), 14.

5 David Lowenthal, "Identity, Heritage, and History," in: John R. Gillis, ed., *Commemorations. The Politics of National Identity* (Princeton, NJ: Princeton University Press, 1996), 41–57; id., *The Heritage Crusade and the Spoils of History* (Cambridge: Cambridge University Press, 1998); id., "Fabricating Heritage," *History & Memory* 10 (1, 1998): 5–24; id., "Stewardship, Sanctimony and Selfishness – A Heritage Paradox," in: John Arnold, Kate Davies and Simon Ditchfield, eds, *History and Heritage. Consuming the Past in Contemporary Culture* (Shaftesbury: Donhead, 1998), 169–179.

6 Lowenthal, *The Heritage Crusade*, 106.

7 See footnote 5.

The Heritage Industry

By now an entire, experiential "heritage industry" is spreading its tendrils to entwine certain parts of the past, not only in Germany.[8] The institutions that benefit from it are not only communal, national, and international public authorities, but increasingly also different private agents. Since the 1990s, the number and influence of private players in this arena has grown to the same extent that the state or municipalities have gradually withdrawn from the public presentation of history, while views of the past have on the one hand diversified and on the other hand become connected to a globalized leisure and tourism industry. In this light "heritage industry" can be defined as a past-based enterprise in which various public and private agents with different opportunities to assert themselves compete in a certain place for interpretative supremacy over the past, and for profits.[9] This definition implicitly follows a cultural studies-based understanding of "heritage" as it was prominently advocated by scholars such as Stuart Hall. Hall conceptualized "heritage" as a medium for the contested production and representation of (a) meaningful shared past(s).[10] From this perspective, memory turns into heritage when it is manifested in a place and thus publicly put forward for "discussion" as common heritage.[11]

In order to be able to analyze heritage as a complex system of past-based meaning production in the present, recent research has placed it in a multidimensional matrix.[12] This matrix demonstrates both the dimensions of the realms of heritage, and the dimensions of the scales of heritage. Overlapping areas of the realms of heritage include its economic aspect in generating income, its social function in creating group identities, its political dimension in manipulating the past for political purposes, and finally its scholarly aspect for public education. The dimension of the scales of heritage is separated into the four reference frames of personal, local, national, and global scope.[13] Accordingly, people can have greatly differing experiences in a place depending on whichever realm or scale of heritage is important for them. If the past is placed as "heritage" in a

---

8 Robert Hewison, *The Heritage Industry. Britain in a Climate of Decline* (London: Methuen, 1987).

9 Frank, *Wall Memorials and Heritage.*

10 Stuart Hall, "Whose Heritage? Un-settling 'The Heritage', Re-imagining the Post-nation," *Third Text* 49 (2000): 3–13.

11 See footnote 9.

12 Brian Graham, Gregory J. Ashworth and John E. Tunbridge, *A Geography of Heritage. Power, Culture and Economy* (London/New York: Hodder Arnold, 2000); Dallen J. Timothy and Stephen W. Boyd, *Heritage Tourism* (Harlow: Pearson Education, 2003).

13 Dallen J. Timothy and Stephen W. Boyd, *Heritage Tourism* (Harlow: Pearson Education, 2003).

public space, it is exposed to all of the risks of its appropriation by supporting but also conflicting social groups, each of which may favor the representation of different realms, or scales of heritage. Moreover, if heritage is considered as an industry governed by supply and demand, requiring public consensus but also inspiring conflict, it is quite incomprehensible that to this day dealing with the heritage boom still faces great hesitancy on the part of German politics and scholarship.

The importance of a constructive dialogue between the (intellectual) "history" and (experiential) "heritage" routes to the past, and of acknowledging the rise of a heritage industry, is illustrated impressively by the example of Checkpoint Charlie in Berlin. For years this historic site has been the subject of a bitter conflict. The dispute about Checkpoint Charlie is so vehement because the debates about this place also mark the moment in which the general public became aware for the first time of an increasing "market-driven structuring of commemorative culture"[14] or in other words of the emergence of a heritage industry in Germany. At the same time the topic also centered on a chapter of Berlin, national and international history that had only just ended and that was still hurting: the era of the Cold War. It is for these reasons that the internationalization, privatization, and experiential orientation of the communication of the past at Checkpoint Charlie have been discussed in such an emotional manner on a local, national and international level.

Checkpoint Charlie, Berlin

In September 1961, one month after the construction of the Berlin Wall had started, Checkpoint Charlie was inaugurated by the British, French, and US forces that had been stationed in West Berlin since the end of World War II. As one of the few inner-city border crossing points that connected the eastern and western parts of divided Berlin, Checkpoint Charlie was reserved for diplomats, members of the Allied forces, and foreign travelers. However, only tourists were fully controlled here, whereas diplomats and Allies were allowed to pass the control point unchecked, following the freedom-of-movement agreement between the Soviets and the western Allies.

By the fall of the Berlin Wall, Checkpoint Charlie had developed into the city's most famous border crossing point. In October 1961, it became notorious as

14 See footnote 3.

the place of confrontation between American and Soviet tanks after East German soldiers had refused to let an American diplomat pass the border uncontrolled.[15] Soon afterwards Checkpoint Charlie hit the headlines again when 18-year-old apprentice Peter Fechter bled to death in the death strip nearby after having been shot by East German soldiers during his attempt to escape to the West. Nevertheless, the crossing point also became renowned for more than 1,200 successful flights to the West: many GDR citizens made use of its special status by dressing up as diplomats or soldiers, thus crossing the border unmolested. Moreover, in 1963 the Berlin Wall Museum *Haus am Checkpoint Charlie* opened on its western side to document both the terror of the Wall and the escape stories. It soon became one of West Berlin's best-visited museums. Finally, Checkpoint Charlie was heavily frequented as it was the "eye of the needle" for foreign travelers wishing to enter East Berlin.

When the Wall came down in November 1989, the former control point became obsolete. Following its official dismantling in June 1990, the place soon became attractive for investment. In 1992, the Berlin Senate sold the former borderland at Checkpoint Charlie to an international investment company that wanted to build an American Business Center on the site. However, due to a lull in the Berlin property market, the project soon ground to a halt. When the investor went bankrupt in 2003, only three of the planned five blocks of the Center had been built. The empty grounds to the east of the former border, which passed into the ownership of a bankruptcy administrator, were gradually taken over by hawkers who sold GDR souvenirs to tourists. The waste land at Checkpoint Charlie and the increasing tourist demand for signs of the division of Berlin, which had largely disappeared during the course of the 1990s, inspired various agents to elevate the former border crossing to the status of a memorial at the turn of the millennium.

Checkpoint Charlie as a typical heritage industry site

In what follows I will argue that Checkpoint Charlie can be considered to be a typical heritage industry site with regard to its spatial design. This thesis is supported by comparisons with Plimoth Plantation close to where the Mayflower

15 Werner Sikorski and Rainer Laabs, *Checkpoint Charlie und die Mauer. Ein geteiltes Volk wehrt sich*, 2nd edition (Berlin: Ullstein, 2003).

landed on the East Coast of what is now the United States. It is considered as the pioneering institution of the heritage industry.[16] In Plymouth, the spot where the first pilgrim supposedly set foot on American soil was decorated with an engraving as early as in the 18th century. In 1920, this Plymouth Rock, which was hardly distinguishable from the other rocks on the shore, was overbuilt with a portico with the intention of making the rock more conspicuous. In the 1940s the exhibition area Plimoth Plantation was opened nearby in order to provide a more vivid picture of the lives of the pilgrims. It comprised a museum that displayed findings from the excavation site of an old pilgrim settlement, and Plimoth Village, a reconstruction of this sunken village, which was animated by actors dressed in historic costumes. The actors were meant to foster interaction with the site and to add a feeling of everyday life.

The American anthropologist Barbara Kirshenblatt-Gimblett has suggested that at heritage sites "the 'actual' must be exhibited alongside the 'virtual' in a show of truth." According to her, the secret of the attraction lies in a specific combination of topographically exact markings of historic locales and contemporary artistic symbols which she calls "exhibition as knowledge," with spatial reconstructions and the presentation of historic "originals" in museum settings ("exhibition as museum display"), and the staging of culture as heritage ("exhibition as performance"[17]).

Berlin's Checkpoint Charlie resembles the Plymouth case in striking ways. In both places there is a topographically exact marking of the "theme" that made the place famous: in Plymouth, it is the engraved rock. At Checkpoint Charlie, the Berlin Senate initiated the marking of the former line of the Wall in 1997 with a double row of cobblestones laid in the street asphalt, carrying the inscription "Berliner Mauer 1961–1989."

A year later, and on the orders of the Berlin Senate, the former border crossing point was also furnished with a large lighted box that displayed two portrait photographs of a Russian and an American soldier, who each looked across towards the other onetime sector. Comparable to the idea behind the portico in Plymouth, the box testifies to the Senate's wish to enhance the marking of the course of the Wall with a widely visible contemporary piece of art indicating the location of the former border crossing.

16 Barbara Kirshenblatt-Gimblett, *Destination Culture. Tourism, Museums, and Heritage* (Berkeley, CA/Los Angeles, CA/London: University of California Press, 1998).
17 Kirshenblatt-Gimblett, *Destination Culture,* 149, 195.

Fig. 1a: Plymouth Rock.
Photo: Avishai Teicher

Fig. 1b: Former course of the Wall.
Photo: Sybille Frank

Fig. 2a: Portico in Plymouth. Photo: Raime.
Licence: GNU Free Documentation License 1.2

Fig. 2b: Soldier portraits, Berlin. Photo:
Sybille Frank

Moreover, in 2000, the Berlin Wall Museum donated to Checkpoint Charlie an exact replica of the dismantled Allied border control cabin. Combined with a copy of the famous warning sign "You are leaving the American Sector," this replica serves, like the reconstructed Plimoth Village, to re-establish much of the visual and spatial structure of the former border crossing.

Finally the drama students at Checkpoint Charlie – who dress in the uniforms of the former Allied soldiers and pose, for a few Euros, in front of the reconstructed control cabin for photo-shoots with tourists, and who stamp passports with original GDR border stamps and search car trunks for "bananas" – can be interpreted as an attempt to revive some of the social aspects at the reconstructed former border crossing, which up to then had been artifact-centered.

Summing up, the initiatives of the Berlin Senate ("exhibition as knowledge"), the private Wall Museum ("exhibition as museum display"), and the drama students ("exhibition as performance") can be understood as offers that supplement each

Fig. 3a: Plimoth Village. Photo: Muns. Licence: Creative Commons Attribution-Share Alike 2.0

Fig. 3b: Copy of the border control cabin. Photo: Sybille Frank

Fig. 4a: Pilgrim woman, tourist. Photo: picasaweb.google.com, 18.10.2008

Fig. 4b: Border officer, tourist. Photo: Sybille Frank

other by invoking different traditions of exhibition. The experiential value to tourists increases from provider to provider, and their interplay is characteristic of professionally produced heritage sites worldwide.

Checkpoint Charlie, therefore, in its current spatial guise, can be seen as a paradigmatic heritage site. But at the same time it is an unusual case.

The Conflict between Two Memorials

In contrast to the Anglo-American tradition of cooperation between public authorities and private interests in exploiting heritage for economic regeneration, political power or intercultural understanding, the Berlin government responded to the opportunity of Checkpoint Charlie in a highly disorganized fashion. When the Senate sold the parcels at the border to a private investor, it did so without giving any instructions as to how the famous historical place should be represented. Following the investor's collapse, a potpourri of private actors was allowed to capitalize on the former control point – but, once more, without being subjected to any regulations as to what should be presented there, and how it should be done. Therefore, today's Checkpoint Charlie is a place that has been resurrected spontaneously by a set of *competing* – and not co-operating – actors who try to exploit the tourist demand for signs of the former border to good effect. In this constellation the private actors started to *fight* their public competitors in an attempt to maximize their profits. This situation gave rise to the transformation of Checkpoint Charlie, once famous for successful escapes to the West, as a "dark" victims' spot.

This interpretation was pushed prominently by Alexandra Hildebrandt, the director of the privatized Wall museum *Haus am Checkpoint Charlie* which presented the terror of the Wall and the flight stories. To reconstruct Checkpoint Charlie as a victims' place, Hildebrandt set out to criticize the hawkers and the drama students for capitalizing on the pain of the Wall victims. She denounced their impersonations as scandalous, "a disgrace to the Wall victims" and an "offence against history."[18] For Hildebrandt, who even resorted to veiling her control cabin replica with tarpaulin in protest against the students, it was "unbearable to witness how a memorial place was transformed into a Disneyland."[19]

In order to enhance the plausibility of commemorating the site as a victims' place, Hildebrandt eventually erected a private Wall victims' memorial at Checkpoint Charlie in 2004 to much media acclaim. It consisted of a 200 meter long reconstruction of the Berlin Wall and 1,065 huge black wooden crosses located in the former death strip, each displaying the name, dates of birth and death, and, if available, picture of a Wall victim. Although Hildebrandt had only been granted permission for a temporary *art* event, she used the well-reported inauguration of

18 Alexandra Hildebrandt, cited in Veronika Nickel, "Checkpoint Charlie: Wieder eine Baracke verhüllt," *tageszeitung*, June 4, 2004; press release of the Wall Museum, cited in Felix Müller, "Ein Gespenst geht um am Checkpoint Charlie," *Berliner Morgenpost*, June 3, 2004.

19 Alexandra Hildebrandt, cited in Felix Müller, *Berliner Morgenpost*.

her memorial to announce that it should become a permanent site for the commemoration of the Wall victims – claiming that the hitherto existing public offers were inadequate.

Fig. 5: The private Wall memorial at Checkpoint Charlie. Photo: Sybille Frank

Until then, the remembrance of the Wall victims had been safeguarded by a memorial established by the Federal Government and the Berlin Senate in the late 1990s at Bernauer Straße, a place where many had died in escape attempts to the West. It consisted of a sealed-off "artistic reconstruction" of the Wall and its death strip, comprising some remaining original segments of the Berlin Wall; a documentation center with an exhibition on the history of the building of the Wall, aiming to make the visit an instructive experience; and a chapel in which the victims could be commemorated.

Hildebrandt set out to criticize this memorial for confiding the remembrance of the Wall to *history*. In her eyes, Bernauer Straße was an overly intellectual place that offered little more than historic treatises. In contrast, she claimed, her private memorial brought history back to life as *heritage*, since it was dedicated to triggering emotions and provoking empathy with the personally named victims. Moreover, she criticized that the peripheral location of Bernauer Straße left the impression that the remembrance of the Wall victims was merely an obligatory lip service paid by the city of Berlin. In contrast, her Checkpoint Charlie memorial

Fig. 6: The public Wall memorial at Bernauer Straße. Photos: Sybille Frank, Hans Jakel

was located in the center of the city and at a place that was already heavily frequented by tourists and that was a well-known symbol of the Cold War. Therefore it seemed to her to be simply consistent to also commemorate the victims of that Cold War era there.

According to Hildebrandt, tourists should thus not be expected to travel to the city's designated sites of commemoration, established, as the public authorities claimed, at original historic places. Instead, the sites of commemoration should travel to where the tourists were already. At Checkpoint Charlie, she argued, the experiences of national and international tourists would be far more "authentic" than at Bernauer Straße, since Checkpoint Charlie was a site familiar to them through the media. Notwithstanding the touristic success of Hildebrandt's Wall memorial, this line of argument, and the staging of the Wall victims as a tourist attraction, led to a highly controversial debate on where and how the Wall and its victims should be commemorated.

The Battle over Authenticity

In this debate, "authenticity" emerged as the criterion with which the public memorial in the Bernauer Straße and the private Wall memorial at Checkpoint Charlie were distinguished from each other. A coalition of government representatives, members of the Bernauer Straße staff, and historians castigated Checkpoint Charlie as a "Disneyfied" site at which a serious period of German and world history was commodified and trivialized for the sake of tourist consumption. According to its critics, the private Wall memorial at Checkpoint Charlie was, above all, inauthentic: The location of the reconstructed Wall and death strip was slightly displaced; the Wall segments used had never stood at Checkpoint Charlie; the former border crossing had never been the site of the death of such huge numbers of people; and the form chosen did not seem adequate to impart knowledge about the place. The critics of the private memorial argued on the basis of an essentialist concept of authenticity according to which only an unchanged, complete, and documentary reconstruction of "the original" at its original historic place could claim to be authentic.[20]

This rationale, however, provoked a dilemma: Since the remains of the Berlin Wall had been torn down almost completely, the public sites of remembrance of the Wall also had to do without historic substance. Therefore, the Wall memorial at Bernauer Straße could also be criticized for a lack of authenticity itself: The remains of the Wall at Bernauer Straße had required comprehensive restoration, as the concrete had been heavily affected by the work of wallpeckers. Moreover, the public memorial also neither displayed a complete reconstruction of the former Wall and death strip, nor had Bernauer Straße been the site of the death of hundreds of people.

As a consequence, the Berlin Senate had to develop a modified concept of authenticity, stressing that a memorial had to be "located at the original site of the events." It elevated the historic site itself to the "original" and attributed a specific theme to the place, which was derived in each case from the historical events that occurred there, and which was certified by the government and scholars as "authentic." This theme was then allowed to be represented exclusively at that place. Based on this concept, Checkpoint Charlie, mindful of the confrontation between the American and Soviet tanks in 1961, was seen as predestined for the remembrance of the Cold War and the services provided to Berlin by the Western Allies – even though the most famous Wall victim, Peter Fechter, died nearby. The legitimate site to commemorate the Wall and its victims, on the other hand, was deemed to be the exclusive reserve of Bernauer Straße. The reason given, derived from "authenticated" historical events, was that Bernauer Straße had been the site of many dramatic and often fatal, escape attempts. On this basis it was then possible to classify the memorial at Checkpoint Charlie as a Disneyfied tourist site, which represented merely "a 'private view' of history."[21]

According to British geographers Tunbridge and Ashworth, different interpretations of the term "authenticity" are one of the most frequent sources of heritage conflicts. Historians and custodians generally understand "authenticity" to mean a "fixed truth," the "genuineness" of a "historical original," which "pos-

20 For different dimensions of the term "authenticity" cf. Edward M. Bruner, "Abraham Lincoln as Authentic Reproduction: A Critique of Postmodernism," *American Anthropologist* 96 (2, 1994): 397–415.

21 Sascha Lehnartz, "Das Kreuz mit der Mauer," *Frankfurter Allgemeine Zeitung*, November 7, 2004.

sesses" authenticity, and therefore has value "in itself."[22] In contrast, heritage planners, and tourist providers define authenticity in relation to the needs of the consumer. Both opinions overlap in practice, not just due to the diversity of actors active in the field of heritage presentation, but also as a result of the particular organizational structure of the heritage industry: "The materials being used, such as museums, monumental buildings, historic townscapes, and the like, are in the custodial charge of individuals and institutions with a resource-based definition of their task, while the producers of heritage use a demand-based definition."[23]

Tunbridge and Ashworth point to the fact that conflicts about competing definitions of authenticity usually take the form of reciprocal accusations of trivialization or elitism respectively. When tourist providers commodify heritage, and create "theme parks," historians and custodians usually perceive those attractions as "inauthentic," or "Disney-like."[24] In regard to Berlin, the urban planner Frank Roost confirmed this negative connotation of the catchword "Disneyfication": "Because the American theme park is a synonym for architectural kitsch, the reference to Disney ... is used and understood as an objection to a lack of authenticity."[25]

The Berlin discussions about Checkpoint Charlie therefore signal the precise moment in which the right to authentication held by those governmental officials, academics, and memorial specialists who were traditionally entrusted with the cultivation of history was challenged by a private heritage industry that was formed at Checkpoint Charlie. Because political actors had very few possibilities to exert direct influence on Checkpoint Charlie, which had been privatized at the beginning of the 1990s, they tried to reassert their authority *culturally*, with the help of the Disneyfication accusation. By this term, the private offers at Checkpoint Charlie were castigated as dubious, trivial, touristic, and inauthentic. The providers there were ostracized from the "local community" of legitimate history communicators, and the endangered social order in the field of historical preservation was meant to be restored discursively.

Thus a broad coalition of government officials, representatives of the Bernauer Straße memorial, cultural functionaries, scientists, and journalists criti-

---

22 J.E. Tunbridge and G.J. Ashworth, *Dissonant Heritage. The Management of the Past as a Resource in Conflict* (Chichester/New York/Brisbane/Toronto/Singapore: Wiley, 1996).

23 Tunbridge and Ashworth, *Dissonant Heritage*, 11.

24 Tunbridge and Ashworth, *Dissonant Heritage*, 265; Benjamin Porter and Noel B. Salazar, "Heritage Tourism, Conflict, and the Public Interest: An Introduction," *International Journal of Heritage Studies* 11 (5, 2005): 361–370.

25 Frank Roost, "Die Disneyfizierung Berlins. Stadtumbau nach den Wünschen der Entertainmentindustrie," *scheinschlag* 2 (2001).

cized Checkpoint Charlie as being a "Disneyland,"[26] characterized by "artificial components,"[27] which was "anti-historic"[28] and "historically incorrect."[29] With the advent of global tourism, the critics argued, Checkpoint Charlie had transformed into a place where local history was being commodified by private providers and commemoration had been denigrated to mere tourist entertainment. As the national newspaper *Welt am Sonntag* commented in 2004, the site conveyed little more than the "charm of a Hollywood or Disney backdrop."[30]

The direct competition of the public and the private Wall memorials in Berlin finally came to a head in 2005, when the bankruptcy administrator on whose premises Hildebrandt's private memorial had been erected filed a claim to clear its grounds. The fact that Hildebrandt's pleas to the public to stand against the forceful removal of her memorial went unheard shows that local support for her interpretation of Checkpoint Charlie as a victims place was limited. But perhaps it would have been just as small if the Bernauer Straße memorial had been threatened, since the remembrance of the Wall generally was a contested matter in those days.

The heritage approach of the private memorial, however, had a long afterlife. Only a few months after the clearing of the site, the German parliament embraced a proposal that the Brandenburg Gate be transformed into a national memorial to the Wall and its victims. The justification of the resolution argued that the Brandenburg Gate, in contrast to Bernauer Straße, was an internationally well-known media symbol of the division of Berlin, and therefore the best place to arouse "authentic emotions" in the minds of national and international tourists. This parliamentary resolution once again preferred the model of a site of international attention that favored the creation of authentic experience in places well known through the media to the competing model of the authentic original site of the events, as advocated by the Berlin Senate.

In response, the Berlin Senate sponsored the construction of a Checkpoint Gallery at Checkpoint Charlie. This is the name of a construction fence exhibit,

---

26 Maria Nooke, scientific project manager of the Berlin Wall Documentation Centre, cited in Nikolaus Bernau, "Kreuze und Stelen," *Berliner Zeitung*, January 13, 2005.

27 Gabriele Camphausen, chair of the Berlin Wall Society, cited in Werner Schima, "Die Mauer ist wieder da," *Rheinischer Merkur*, November 8, 2004.

28 Urban Development Senator Ingeborg Junge-Reyer, cited in "Topographie: 'Schuld waren viele'," *Berliner Morgenpost*, November 30, 2004.

29 Culture Senator Thomas Flierl, cited in "Entspannung am Checkpoint Charlie," *Der Tagesspiegel*, November 17, 2004.

30 Dirk Westphal, "Mauergedenkstätte Checkpoint Charlie?," *Welt am Sonntag*, November 14, 2004.

which opened at the former control point in August 2006 and which combines life-size images with explanatory text. The exhibition tells three stories:[31] First, it presents some of the local flight narratives, and some of the victims' biographies, thereby robbing the Wall Museum of its monopoly of telling the history of the Wall from a personal perspective.

Second, the Gallery promotes the Senate's interpretation of Checkpoint Charlie as an "authentic" place to commemorate the international bloc confrontation between the U.S. and Soviet tanks, which faced each other in the Cold War era. To support this interpretation, an expert initiative of politicians and scholars has made the case for erecting a permanent Cold War museum at Checkpoint Charlie. A provisional info box that was inaugurated in the summer of 2012 with the support of the Berlin Senate is intended to further promote the Cold War museum project.

Third, the Checkpoint Gallery advertises other, more remote, publicly funded local and national sites that commemorate the German separation. Thus the Berlin Senate's concept of authenticity to "commemoration of historic events at authentic places of occurrence" is finally amalgamated with Alexandra Hildebrandt's competing concept of "commemoration of historic events at places of international attention." The internationally renowned Checkpoint Charlie now acts as an informative hub that directs visitors to diverse commemorative spikes that represent different aspects of the history of the Wall, staged at authentic places of occurrence. By these means Checkpoint Charlie today also serves to promote the Berlin Senate's contested concept of authenticity.

From History to Heritage

In the "showdown" between the public and private agents, present-day Checkpoint Charlie has thus become a "showroom," not only for the current commemoration of the Wall, but also for current heritage theories. In this site all realms of heritage – the economic (i.e. the aim to generate profits), political (i.e. the possibility of using the past for political purposes), social (i.e. the chance to shape groups and identities), and scholarly dimensions (i.e. the aim to educate and the competitive search for the "right" route to the past) come together. Moreover all scales of heritage such as the personal (i.e. the victims' perspective), local (i.e.

31 Berliner Forum für Geschichte und Gegenwart e.V., ed., *Checkpoint Charlie. Berliner Mauer-Bildergalerie an der Friedrichstraße*, Berlin, 2007.

the meaning of the Wall and its heritage for Berlin), national (i.e. the process of the division of Germany into two states), and international levels (i.e. Checkpoint Charlie as a widely known “hot spot” of the Cold War era) are brought into focus as if under a magnifying glass.

The problems produced by the privatization of Checkpoint Charlie and the lack of political management of the developments there remain, however, unresolved. On the one hand, current visitors to the former border crossing are confronted by an utterly unmanageable and confusing density of information, competing interpretations, and offers. On the other hand, the accusation of Disneyfication continues to hold sway in Berlin in order to distance public remembrance from the experiential communication of history by private agents. The Master Plan for commemorating the Berlin Wall, passed by the Berlin Senate in 2006, missed a unique opportunity to bring all of the agents together at one table. The author, Culture Senator Thomas Flierl, once again castigated Hildebrandt’s “Hollywood-like reconstruction of the Wall” as a “trivialized theme park.”[32] And yet the tourists are flocking to see Checkpoint Charlie, because what is considered in Germany to be “Disney-like” is, in contrast, a quite attractive offer to American or Japanese visitors, for example.

The surprising success of the private GDR museum in Berlin mentioned at the outset of this chapter showed once again that experiential heritage offers, such as those by Alexandra Hildebrandt and the drama students dressed in historic uniforms, were a response to a real tourist demand for experiencing what life was like during the long phase of the Cold War in Germany and Berlin. “While Berlin and the Federal Government are still negotiating a succinct concept for the Wall Memorial, a resourceful entrepreneur from Freiburg has built a ‘GDR museum’,”[33] the *Frankfurter Allgemeine Zeitung* commented on the opening of the hands-on GDR museum in the summer of 2006. Because, according to the *Neue Zürcher Zeitung*, “there is still no reasonable presentation of GDR history in Berlin,”[34] private providers stepped in to fill the gap. This example suggests that if public bodies do not take up the topics demanded by heritage tourists, then private providers will.

Similarly, the example of Checkpoint Charlie illustrates that, in a globalized age that is shaped by travel, historical events of international significance must be transformed into heritage shortly after these events have occurred – irrespec-

32 Thomas Flierl, “Dokumentation: Gedenkkonzept Berliner Mauer,” *Netzzeitung*, April 18, 2005.

33 Mechthild Küpper, “Die DDR zum Anfassen,” *Frankfurter Allgemeine Zeitung*, July 17, 2006.

34 Claudia Schwartz, “Die unvergängliche Liebe zum Trabi,” *Neue Züricher Zeitung*, July 25, 2006.

tive of the sensitivity of this process, involving as it does surviving witnesses and conflicting testimonies. The redesign of *Ground Zero* in New York into a "global site of heritage" – unwelcome among many locals, but driven forward unflinchingly by tourists – is merely a further famous example of this process.[35]

Cultures have never existed in isolation, but rather were always involved in an exchange with each other.[36] They are in a constant state of flux.[37] If seen from this perspective, "Disneyfication" no longer represents a horror scenario of the "destruction" of culture. Quite on the contrary, "foreign" cultures contribute to the fact that local traditions are constantly redefined and relocated by adding a relational dimension to local practices. The fact that this negotiating process often takes the form of a dispute about places is illustrated by the example detailed here. This makes it even more important for politicians to stop denouncing the economization and globalization of historical references in the context of an expanding, internationalizing Cold War heritage industry as mere "Disneyfication." Instead of discrediting it verbally, they should accept it, regulate it to make sure that victims are not offended, and make use of it, for example in urban development policy. And it is even more important for the world of scholarship to research these processes without prejudice and to moderate them professionally.[38] One first step in this direction has already been taken in Berlin: In order to secure a fixed place in the competition to commemorate the Berlin Wall, the public Bernauer Straße memorial has in the meantime been converted into an "experience landscape."[39]

---

35 Elizabeth Greenspan, "A Global Site of Heritage. Constructing Spaces of Memory at the World Trade Center," *International Journal of Heritage Studies* 11 (2005, 5): 371–384. See also: Elizabeth Greenspan, *Battle for Ground Zero. Inside the Political Struggle to Rebuild the World Trade Center* (Basingstoke: Palgrave Macmillan, 2013).

36 Edward M. Bruner, "Tourism in Ghana. The Representation of Slavery and the Return of the Black Diaspora," *American Anthropologist* 2 (1998): 290–304.

37 Simon Coleman and Mike Crang, "Grounded Tourists, Travelling Theory," in Simon Coleman and Mike Crang, eds, *Tourism Between Place and Performance* (New York/Oxford: Berghahn Books 2002), 1–17.

38 Regina Bendix, "Kulturelles Erbe zwischen Wirtschaft und Politik: Ein Ausblick," in Dorothee Hemme, Markus Tauschek and Regina Bendix, eds, *Prädikat "Heritage". Wertschöpfungen aus kulturellen Ressourcen* (Berlin: LIT Verlag, 2007), 337–356.

39 Hope Harrison in this volume.

Hanno Hochmuth

Contested Legacies

Cold War Memory Sites in Berlin

On top of the *Teufelsberg* hill one of the most prominent remnants of the Cold War still shapes the skyline of Berlin. At a height of 377 feet, the former listening station of the American National Security Agency (NSA) literally represents an outstanding legacy of the Western Allies presence in the divided city. From 1962 until 1992 some 1,500 American and British employees worked in the strategically located facility that was run 24 hours a day. Their task was the permanent surveillance of Eastern radio traffic from all member countries of the Warsaw Pact. The NSA field station was certainly one of the most expensive espionage efforts of the Cold War in Berlin. To what extent it really helped to overcome the East-West confrontation remains unclear. With the end of the Cold War and the reunification of both Germany and Berlin, its purpose had vanished. Shortly thereafter, the NSA left the station and sold it to the German federal government.[1]

A closer look at the former listening station reveals that the building is actually a ruin today. Under the distinctive white radar cupola one can see right through the broken facade. Despite several plans to repurpose the remaining structure, all efforts have failed so far. One investor who wanted to transform the former listening station into luxury homes and a major hotel was unable to secure the funds. Hollywood director David Lynch and his Maharishi foundation planned to erect a peace university on top of the hill, but were unsuccessful and withdrew. Environmentalists have been pleading for a complete land restoration and natural preservation of the hill. For a couple of years the complex was totally abandoned and hence badly vandalized. In 2011 some Berlin students began focusing their attention on the former listening station. Under the label "BerlinSightOut" they started to offer tours through the ruined complex and to explain its history to both Berliners and tourists.[2] The former NSA field station atop the Teufelsberg is now being transformed into a memory site of the Cold War.

The listening station shares some typical characteristics with several other Cold War memory sites in Berlin. It holds multiple layers of history, since the station was erected on a mountain of man-made rubble. Consisting of one third of

---

1 Dirk Verheyen, *United City, Divided Memories?: Cold War Legacies in Contemporary Berlin* (Lanham, MD: Lexington Books, 2008), 94.

2 See their website http://www.berlinsightout.de, last accessed on December 5, 2016.

DOI 10.1515/9783110496178-014

Berlin's World War II debris and covering the ruins of a designated Nazi military technical school, the Teufelsberg relates directly to the causes of the Cold War, thus spatially combining successive periods of Berlin's history. Similar to other sites it is a non-intentional *post hoc* monument that developed from a military legacy into a public history site. However, like elsewhere the situation is not yet settled. Due to financial problems and political debates the listening station lacks a clear perspective. Like many other Cold War memory sites in Berlin, it has a multilayered past, a contested present, and an uncertain future.

The following essay will first give a brief overview of the different Cold War legacies, memory sites and monuments in Berlin. It will then focus on the three most important museums that stand for the history of the Cold War in Berlin: the *German-Russian Museum in Berlin-Karlshorst*, the *Allied Museum in Berlin-Zehlendorf*, and the *Wall Museum at Checkpoint Charlie*. By analyzing these museums, it will consider which Cold War history they convey and what place they occupy in Berlin's urban memory landscape. The essay will conclude by discussing some of the present challenges for the commemoration of the Cold War in Berlin.

Cold War Sites in Berlin

Berlin was one of the hot spots of the Cold War.[3] Divided into four sectors after the fall of the Nazi dictatorship, the German capital became the stage for a global conflict that affected the city like almost no other place in the world. The post-war superpowers faced each other within the borders of one city. By 1948 at the latest, the confrontation between the Eastern and the Western bloc determined most aspects of the political, economic, cultural and daily life in Berlin. The conflict lasted for more than 40 years and shaped the city significantly. Hence, when the former occupational powers withdrew from the city in 1994, they left numerous historical traces.[4]

One major Cold War legacy in Berlin are the former headquarters of the four Allies, who mostly chose previous Nazi military structures for their administrations. The Soviets resided in the Berlin suburb of *Karlshorst*, which also served until 1949 as the headquarters of the Soviet Military Administration (SMAD) for

---

3 See Bernd Stöver: Der Kalte Krieg, *Geschichte eines radikalen Zeitalters 1947–1991* (Munich: C.H. Beck, 2007)

4 Regarding the different Cold War traces and memory sites in Berlin see Verheyen: *United City*, 75–100; Jula Danylow, "Den Kalten Krieg ausstellen. Ein deutsch-amerikanischer Vergleich" (Master's thesis, Free University Berlin, 2011).

the entire Soviet zone in East Germany. The US headquarters were at Clayallee in the borough of *Zehlendorf*, where the U.S. Army also possessed other barracks for their troops. The British Berlin Brigade was situated in the borough of *Charlottenburg* on the 1936 Olympic Games complex, where British officers repeatedly played polo on the May field. The Gouvernement Militaire Français de Berlin resided in the Quartier Napoléon in the borough of *Reinickendorf* in the north of West Berlin. Most Allied facilities were handed over to the German government in 1994. They are now used for different purposes like German Bundeswehr garrisons or sport clubs. However, except for the German-Russian Museum in Karlshorst, most of the former Allied military facilities offer no significant public commemoration of the former occupational powers and of the Cold War.

Only minor signs remind passersby of the joint Allied administration at its former sites. Their former use as Allied Control Council at Kleistpark and as Allied Kommandatura in Dahlem is hardly visible today. This oblivion likely resulted from the early withdrawal of the Soviets from both institutions in 1948, which transformed them into decisive sites of the early Cold War. Today, the former Allied Kommandatura serves as the presidential office of the *Free University Berlin*, which is in turn an important civil legacy of the Cold War in Berlin.[5] Founded in 1948 with significant support from the United States, it represented a counterpart to Berlin's original university, which, located in the East, came under Soviet control and was renamed Humboldt University in 1949.[6] Today both universities compete for academic excellence, but the former political and ideological division is almost forgotten and no longer a distinctive part of the universities' images.

Besides the Free University there are several other Cold War "gifts" in Berlin, most of which were established by the United States to re-educate the people of West Berlin and to strengthen their morale in the confrontation with the Communists. The *Radio in the American Sector* (RIAS) played an important role during the people's uprising on the June 17, 1953.[7] The *Amerika Haus* and the *Amerika-Gedenkbibliothek* promoted liberal thought and American culture. The *Maison*

---

5 Tent, James F. "Freie Universität Berlin 1948–1988: Eine deutsche Hochschule im Zeitgeschehen" (Berlin: 1988); Jessica Hoffmann, Helena Seidel, Nils Baratella, *Geschichte der Freien Universität Berlin. Ereignisse – Orte – Personen* (Berlin: Frank & Timme, 2008).

6 Konrad H. Jarausch, Rüdiger vom Bruch, Heinz-Elmar Tenorth, eds., *Geschichte der Universität unter den Linden. Vol. 3: Sozialistisches Experiment und Erneuerung in der Demokratie – die Humboldt-Universität zu Berlin 1945–2010* (Berlin: Akademie Verlag, 2012)

7 Bernd Stöver, "Radio mit kalkuliertem Risiko: Der RIAS als US-Sender für die DDR 1946–1961" in *Zwischen Pop und Propaganda: Radio in der DDR*, eds., Klaus Arnold, Christoph Classen (Berlin: C.H. Links Verlag, 2004), 209–228.

de France stood for the French *mission civilisatrice.*[8] The former *Congress Hall* in West Berlin (today called Haus der Kulturen der Welt, but nicknamed the "Pregnant Oyster") sought to represent the Western idea of freedom even in its modernist architecture. Cold War cultures in Berlin where also popular cultures.[9] The big festivals like the *Deutsch-Amerikanisches Volksfest* or the *Deutsch-Französisches Volksfest* contributed a great deal to the acceptance of the Western Allies by the West Berliners.[10]

Despite institutions like the former *Haus der Deutsch-Sowjetischen Freundschaft* with its famous Tajik Tearoom in the Palais am Festungsgraben, the Soviet contributions to Berlin's Cold War culture differed from the efforts of the Western powers. In order to remember the tremendous losses that the Soviet Army suffered during World War II in general and the Battle for Berlin in particular, the Soviets focused their attention mainly on the past. They erected three major war memorials in Berlin: Featuring a victorious Red Army soldier, tanks and cannons, the first memorial was built immediately after the liberation of the Nazi capital right next to the Reichstag in the *Tiergarten.* In the summer of 1945 it became part of the British sector, but nonetheless it was subsequently maintained and protected by the Russians.[11] Another Soviet memorial, suggesting a cemetery with its quiet lawns, trees and obelisk, was built in the Schönholzer Heide in the Eastern borough of *Pankow.* The largest and most representative war memorial, however, was erected in 1949 in *Treptower Park,* in the center of the Soviet sector. It displays a monumental Russian soldier standing on a destroyed Nazi swastika, while wielding a large sword in one hand and carrying a small German girl in the other. The message of the monument was clear: The Soviets saved the German people from Hitler and will guide them into a new socialist future. The Treptower Park memorial is thus also an expression of the ideological confrontation and competition of the Cold War. Like all historical monuments, it connects the past with the present in order to gain legitimacy for the future.

---

8 Verheyen, *United City*, 98.

9 For popular Cold War culture see Annette Vowinckel, Marcus M. Payk, and Thomas Lindenberger, eds., *Cold War Cultures: Perspectives on Eastern and Western European Societies* (New York: Berghahn Books, 2012).

10 The Deutsch-Amerikanisches Volksfest also had a hidden military function. The big ferris wheel significantly enhanced the Eastern radio signals for the NSA listening station on Teufelsberg. When the NSA noticed this unintended effect, the ferris wheel was kept permanently on the site of the annual fest.

11 Today the Federal Government of Germany maintains the former Soviet war memorials according to the decisions of the 2+4 Treaty from 1990.

The same is true for the West. After the Western powers had withstood the Soviet Berlin blockade in 1948/49 carrying out an unparalleled airlift to the Western sectors for more than ten months, they erected a large monument right in front of the *Tempelhof Airport* that itself became an important icon of the successful Western relief operation. The so called "Hunger Claw," as the monument was nicknamed by the West Berliners, represents the three air corridors of the Western Allies to Berlin and commemorates the 83 casualties during the Berlin Airlift. Another highly political Cold War monument is the *Liberty Bell* in the town hall of Schöneberg that since 1949 was used by the West Berlin Senate and House of Representatives after the city's administration had split.[12] The massive bell was paid for by donations from American all over the United States in order to promote the Western idea of freedom in the ideological competition between the two opposing sides of the divided city. John F. Kennedy therefore chose the square in front of the Schöneberg town hall and the Liberty Bell in its tower to give his famous speech in June 1963 ("*Ich bin ein Berliner*") expressing his solidarity with the people of Berlin after the erection of the Berlin Wall in 1961.[13]

The Berlin Wall itself is another outstanding legacy of the Cold War. It cannot be understood without the historical context of the global confrontation of two competing ideological systems that opposed each other in one city. However, the commemoration of the Berlin Wall today tends to neglect this international dimension by focusing predominantly on the division of Germany. This orientation is a product of the commemoration concept which the Berlin Senate approved in 2006 after a long and heated debate.[14] According to the Senate's decentralized approach, various legacies refer to different aspects of the division. The *Wall Memorial at the Bernauer Straße* has become the central site for the commemoration of the Berlin Wall and its victims. The former refugee camp *Notaufnahmelager Marienfelde* commemorates the successful escapes from East to West. The exhibition in the so called *Tränenpalast* at the former checkpoint at the Friedrichstraße train station offers visitors the opportunity to reflect on everyday experiences of the German division. The *Wall remnants at Niederkirchner Straße* stand for the multiple layers of history in Berlin, since they are situated right next to the exhibition Topography of Terror that commemorates the crimes committed

12 Andreas W. Daum and Veronika Liebau, *Die Freiheitsglocke in Berlin – The Freedom Bell in Berlin* (Berlin: Jaron Verlag, 2000).

13 Andreas W. Daum, *Kennedy in Berlin* (New York: Cambridge University Press, 2007).

14 Rainer E. Klemke "Das Gesamtkonzept Berliner Mauer" in *Die Mauer. Errichtung, Überwindung, Erinnerung. München Henke*, ed., Klaus-Dietmar Henke (Berlin: Taschenbuch Verlag, 2011): 377–394.

by the SS and the Gestapo, at the site of their former headquarters. The longest, still remaining part of the Berlin Wall at the *East Side Gallery* on the other hand, represents the artistic modification of the Wall and thus its peaceful overcoming. Finally, the *Brandenburg Gate* has become the symbol of German unity.[15] None of the above-mentioned public memory sites, however, is dedicated exclusively to the Cold War. Although the bloc confrontation is emphasized in the *German-Russian Museum*, the *Allied Museum* and in the *Wall Museum at Checkpoint Charlie*, the global dimension of the conflict is not yet prominently represented in Berlin's current memory landscape.

The German-Russian Museum

On the night between the 8th and the 9th of May 1945, the unconditional surrender of all German troops in the East took place in Berlin-Karlshorst. It ultimately stopped the war in Europe after the capitulation of the Western Wehrmacht in Rheims/France one day before. The victorious Soviet command had chosen a remote officers' mess of the Wehrmacht Pioneer School No. 1 in Karlshorst that had remained intact after the battle for Berlin. Subsequently the building served as the headquarters of the Soviet Military Administration for all Red Army troops in Germany. It was here that the Soviets handed over the administrative power in the Soviet zone to the East-German communist regime in 1949.

The entire Karlshorst complex was a forbidden military area, until in 1967 when, on the occasion of the 50th anniversary of October Revolution, the Political Department of the Soviet Army established a Capitulation Museum there. At the same time the Soviet Army inaugurated numerous war museums and memorials all over the Soviet Union and the Eastern bloc.[16] By celebrating the costly victory in the so called "Great Patriotic War" against the German aggressors, the Brezhnev regime in Moscow sought to gain more legitimacy and acceptance from the

15 The same applies for the *Glienicker Brücke* between (West-)Berlin and the city of Potsdam, which was an allied checkpoint and opened by the Berlin and Potsdam people on November 10, 1989. Since then annual celebrations of the German unity have been held on the bridge. A private museum in the *Villa Schöningen* right on the Potsdam side of the bridge informs about its history. The modern multimedia exhibition also focuses on the famous spy exchanges between East and West that took place on the *Glienicker Brücke* in 1965, 1985, and 1986. For further information see Mathias Döpfner, Lena Maculan, *Villa Schöningen an der Glienicker Brücke*. Ein deutsch-deutsches Museum. Berlin 2009.

16 Nina Tumarkin, *The Living and the Dead. The Rise and Fall of the Cult of World War II in Russia*, (New York: Basic Books, 1994): 7.

Soviet people. Hence, the exhibition in the new Museum was mainly directed at Soviet citizens as well as soldiers stationed in the GDR and initially written in Russian only. A quite traditional mixture of busts, statues, weapons and dioramas glorified the heroism of the Soviet soldiers and people, who eventually forced the unconditional surrender of the Germans in that very same building in Berlin-Karlshorst.[17]

When the Soviet Union collapsed and the Russian Army agreed to withdraw from unified Germany by 1994, a bi-national initiative sought to preserve the Russian Museum in Karlshorst. However, it also seemed clear that the old-fashioned initial exhibition from 1967 had to be replaced, since its legitimizing message had lost its relevance. Already in 1991 a special and rather unique German-Russian commission was created that developed ideas for transforming the museum. In a rare window of opportunity both sides agreed on the formation of an association with rotating leadership and equal participation by German and Russian representatives. While the former carry the primary financial responsibility for the museum, the latter provide relevant historical objects and materials.[18] Moreover, the bilateral commission reached a broad consensus on most of the difficult issues of the German-Russian War 1941–1945.[19] Mainly based on Reinhard Rürup's widely noticed exhibition "The War against the Soviet Union," that was first shown at the Topography of Terror, the new exhibition at the restructured *German-Russian Museum* in Karlshorst opened on May 10, 1995.[20] The inauguration took place one day after the 50th anniversary of the German surrender, albeit without significant attendance by German political representatives.[21]

The new exhibition focused mainly on the unparalleled brutality of the war between Nazi Germany and Soviet Russia. The ensuing Cold War played merely a minor role in the exhibit. Only two out of the 15 rooms were dedicated to the

---

17 For the initial exhibition see Gabriele Camphausen "Das sowjetische Museum der bedingungslosen Kapitulation" in *Erinnerung an einen Krieg: Das Museum Berlin-Karlshorst*, eds., Ingrid Damerow and Peter Jahn (Berlin: Jovis Verlasburo, 1997), 48–53.

18 Verheyen *United City*, 103.

19 Peter Jahn "Gemeinsam an den Schrecken erinnern. Das deutsch-russische Museum in Berlin-Karlshorst," in *Der Krieg und seine Museen*, ed., Hans-Martin Hinz (Frankfurt/ New York: Oxford University Press, 1997), 11–24. Yet Dirk Verheyen states that claims by the German side of a relatively uncontroversial consensus did not quite reflect reality. See Verheyen *United City*, 103. Moreover, there are also tensions and different historical interpretations of the Great War between Russia, Belarus, and Ukraine up to this date.

20 The German-Russian Museum's website is: http://www.museum-karlshorst.de/en.html, last accessed on December 5, 2016.

21 Verheyen, *United City*, 104.

post-war relationships between the USSR and the two German states. Apart from changing short-term shows and public events, the German-Russian Museum in Karlshorst does not actually serve as a Cold War memory site. Instead, it tells the pre-history of the Cold War in a quite sober and non-emotional way with lots of military objects, mostly donated by the Russian side. Since the large hall of the surrender ceremony marks the climax of the exhibition, the house can be characterized as a combination of a museum and a memorial. However, the authenticity of the site has served as its most crucial problem, not to mention its comparatively small budget of about 850,000 Euros per year. The museum is located in the relatively remote suburb of Karlshorst. Only about 35,000 visitors a year, mainly individuals, school classes and Bundeswehr soldiers, find their way to the German-Russian Museum, which was closed at the end of 2011 to be replaced by a third, renewed permanent exhibition that opened in the year 2013.[22]

The Allied Museum

Unlike the German-Russian Museum, there was no comparable exhibition on the Western Allies in Berlin until the fall of the Wall. However, when the Allied power was handed over to Germany in 1990 stipulating that all American, British and French troops would leave Berlin by 1994, German officials and Allied officers started to think about establishing a new museum that would commemorate the Western presence in Berlin. The resulting *Allied Museum*[23] is a product of the euphoria experienced during the German unification process[24] and of the museum making by the administration of Helmut Kohl, who paid a new attention on Germany's national history and established both the *Haus der Geschichte* (HdG) in Bonn and the *Deutsches Historisches Museum* (DHM) in Berlin.[25]

In 1991, Helmut Trotnow, historian and staff member at the DHM, took the initiative to establish an Allied Museum. Two years later a location for the planned museum was found. On Clayallee in Berlin-Zehlendorf the former US Army *Outpost Theater* and the adjacent *Major Arthur D. Nicholson Memorial Library*

22 Interview with Jörg Morré, Director of the German-Russian Museum in Berlin-Karlshorst (June 27, 2012).

23 The Allied Museum's website is: http://www.alliiertenmuseum.de/en/home.html, last accessed on December 5, 2016.

24 Danylow, "Den Kalten Krieg ausstellen" 22.

25 See Rosmarie Beier-de Haan, *Erinnerte Geschichte – Inszenierte Geschichte*. Ausstellungen und Museen in der Zweiten Moderne (Frankfurt/Main: Suhrkamp, 2005).

were chosen to house the future collection. At the same time an international commission of experts was set up in order to conceptualize the exhibition. In 1994, a first non-permanent show opened at Clayallee representing well-known remnants of the Cold War like the original US Army control booth from Checkpoint Charlie. The exhibition, entitled after a popular German song "They'll Always Have a Suitcase in Berlin. The Western Allies and Berlin 1944–1994,"[26] coincided with the actual withdrawal of the former Allied troops from Berlin. It turned out to be an unexpected success by attracting almost 67,000 visitors within merely three months.[27]

The permanent exhibition at the Allied Museum opened on June 27, 1998 in the presence of many veterans, as well as German and Western Allied dignitaries.[28] Having chosen the 50th anniversary of the beginning of the Berlin Airlift as its opening day, the commission clearly emphasized that the Allied Museum was dedicated to the three Western powers. Christoph Stölzl, Director of the DHM and head of the non-profit association that had meanwhile been founded to support the Allied Museum, promoted a "museum of gratitude" that should show "how enemies became protectors and, ultimately, friends."[29] At an earlier stage of the planning the title "House of the Protecting Powers" was suggested, but at the end the commission preferred the multilingual name "Allied Museum," even though this would actually also refer to the Soviet Union. However, the experts rejected this as irrelevant and emphasized that since the 1960s the Berliners have used the term Allies in reference to the Western powers only.[30] This understanding has clearly persisted after the end of the Cold War and lasted throughout the 1990s. The former Soviet Allies have thus been continuously excluded. Consequently,

---

26 The title referred to the famous Marlene Dietrich song "Ich hab noch einen Koffer in Berlin," but it should also express the friendship to the Western Allies, that should last also after their withdrawal from Berlin.

27 For the early history of the Allied Museum see Helmut Trotnow, "They'll always have a suitcase in Berlin. The birth of the exhibition and the future Allied Museum," in *An Allied Museum for Berlin,* ed. Helmut Trotnow, Ein Alliierten-Museum für Berlin. Dokumentation zur Ausstellung "Mehr als ein Koffer bleibt. Die Westmächte und Berlin 1944–1994." (Berlin: Alliierten Museum, 1995), 5–19.

28 Note the difference to the inauguration of the German-Russian Museum in Karlshorst three years before. See Verheyen, *United City*, 104 and 108.

29 Christoph Stölzl, "The Museum will Show how Enemies Became Friends," in *An Allied Museum for Berlin,* ed. Helmut Trotnow, Ein Alliierten-Museum für Berlin. Dokumentation zur Ausstellung "Mehr als ein Koffer bleibt. Die Westmächte und Berlin 1944–1994." (Berlin: Alliierten Museum, 1995), 20.

30 See Trotnow, *They'll Always Have a Suitcase in Berlin*, 16.

only the three Western powers are represented in the museum's association and also in the exhibition.

The exhibit is split between the two buildings of the museum that cover two different time periods of the American, British and French presence in Berlin. The former Outpost Theater, which is a protected monument, informs visitors about the time from 1945 to 1950, strongly emphasizing the Berlin Airlift. The section in the Nicholson Library focuses on the later years between 1951 and 1994, paying attention also to the everyday life of the Allied Troops and their positive encounters with the people of West Berlin. The exhibition was actually planned to be displayed for one year only, but it has since become permanent. Beside numerous public events the Allied Museum regularly offers special exhibitions that are also meant to fill the gaps of the somewhat impressionistic permanent exhibition. Most of the museum's objects were donated by the departing Allied Military. Hence, about 70 percent of the exhibits are military objects. Highlights of the collection are an original French dining car that commuted between France and Berlin and a massive Royal Air Force Hastings TG 503 that was used during the Airlift. Ironically, the latter was transported to the museum by a Russian helicopter. Several objects commemorate the severe ideological conflict between the two blocks in Berlin. The museum displays a large fragment of an American espionage tunnel that was dug into the Eastern zone in Berlin-Rudow in 1955.[31] There are also some typical Berlin Wall elements from Potsdamer Platz. Moreover, both the authentic control booth from Checkpoint Charlie and the original border tower from Bernauer Straße can be found at the Allied Museum.[32]

The big number of large scale objects also poses problems for the museum. A plan to build a hangar for the planes and trains did not succeed. This is one of the reasons why the Allied Museum has been trying to move to the former airport of Tempelhof. In fact, relocating the Allied Museum to Tempelhof has been discussed for many years, because the airport itself is recognized as the very symbol of the Berlin Airlift. Since the closing of the airfield in 2008 the former hangars offer a vast potential space to house the museum with its large scale objects. However, the City of Berlin had rented the massive building to the *Bread and Butter* fashion fair and transformed it temporarily into a refugee camp in the

31 In 2013 two more large fragments of the tunnel pipes have been discovered in a Brandenburg forest. See: http://www.berliner-zeitung.de/home/berliner-spionagetunnel-ein-puzzlestueck-des-kalten-krieges,10808950,21104526,view,printVersion.html, last accessed on March 7, 2013.

32 The first has been replaced by a replica on Checkpoint Charlie, whereas the Berlin Wall Memorial on Bernauer Straße reassembled and erected an original tower from a former GDR border control training camp that was found and purchased on eBay.

summer of 2015. The Federal Government of Germany, which is funding the Allied Museum with 1.3 million Euros annually, supports the Tempelhof plans of the museum, because the famous airport would be a far more prominent and central site than the current location in the remote suburb of Berlin-Zehlendorf. Today only about 65,000 visitors a year find their way to Clayallee. Most of them are school classes and organized groups like American cruise ship tourists in the summer. In Tempelhof, the Allied Museum would presumably attract far more visitors, which is the major aim of the museum's administration.[33] This is obviously also the reason why there is a certain reluctance to renew the permanent exhibition at the current location. While the federal coalition agreement between CDU and SPD from the fall of 2013 supports the move, the current refugee crisis might alter this plan.

The Wall Museum at Checkpoint Charlie

The *Wall Museum at Checkpoint Charlie* is located in a very central spot in the middle of Berlin.[34] It was initially founded by Rainer Hildebrandt in a small apartment on Bernauer Straße right after the erection of the Berlin Wall in 1961. Two years later the museum moved to its current location on Friedrichstraße right next to Checkpoint Charlie. The checkpoint had become a widely known hotspot and iconic site of the Cold War, since the American and Soviet tank confrontation in October 1961. Hildebrandt chose this location to gain attention for his struggle for human rights. A surviving resistance fighter against Hitler, he now opposed the Communist regime in the East. It was this anti-totalitarian equation between Nazism and Stalinism that shaped his museum. To be sure, this understanding was very common in West Berlin at that time. Hildebrandt received a lot of support by notable people like the publisher Axel Springer. The museum collected escape vehicles, samizdat prints, political posters and many other devotional objects from the opposition in the GDR. From the beginning, it also served as a contact point for Eastern refugees and escape helpers as well as a charitable association for wall victims.[35]

---

33 Interview with Gundula Bavendamm, then Director of the Allied Museum in Berlin-Zehlendorf (May 3, 2012).

34 The Wall Museum's website is: http://www.mauermuseum.de/index.php/en, last accessed on December 5, 2016.

35 For the Wall Museum at Checkpoint Charlie and the related debates see especially Sybille Frank, *Der Mauer um die Wette gedenken. Die Formation einer Heritage-Industrie am Berliner Checkpoint Charlie* (Frankfurt: Oxford University Press, 2009), and her chapter in this volume.

After a conflict with the Berlin Senate on funding and ideology, the Wall Museum's association transformed the exhibition into a private enterprise. For several years it has been the most successful private museum in Berlin. Moreover, it is the fourth most visited museum in the city.[36] The museum has close ties to several travel agencies that bring numerous busses full of tourists to Checkpoint Charlie. According to the museum's own numbers, 850,000 visitors come every year.[37] They gather to see wall art and fragments, to touch escape vehicles and to take a deep breath of the Cold War. The heterogeneous exhibition tries to emotionalize the visitors. It has no transparent structure and fails to meet current museological and academic standards by any means. Many different objects crowd each other and hardly fit into the space despite several extensions having been made to the museum. The message of the museum, however, has remained notably unchanged. It still accuses the vanished Communist regime and keeps the Cold War alive. It glorifies the victims of Communism and honors those who resisted against it and fought for human rights. The museum enshrines the death mask of Andrei Sakharov and cultivates the memory of its founder Rainer Hildebrand, who died in 2004.[38]

His widow Alexandra Hildebrandt succeeded him as the controversial head of the Wall Museum and became a remarkable player in Berlin's public history and heritage industry.[39] She added a rather large museum shop that sells countless wall souvenirs to the tourists. In order to meet the visitors' expectations she erected a replica of the old checkpoint booth on the Friedrichstraße next to her museum.[40] When soon afterwards students in historic uniforms began to pose in front of this booth to make some money by posing for photos, Alexandra Hildebrand objected strongly. She argued that the students disregarded the wall victims and "disneyfied" a sacred place. Hence, she hid her checkpoint booth temporarily behind a big cover in order to deny the students in Allied uniforms their background for the photos.[41] Even though Hildebrand expressed mainly political

---

36 See the official visitation numbers of Berlin's museums, issued by the City of Berlin: http://www.berlin.de/sen/kultur/presse/archiv/20111227.1015.364702.html, last accessed on March 7, 2013.

37 Ibid.

38 Danylow, *Den Kalten Krieg ausstellen*, 36–40.

39 It seems, however, difficult to cooperate with Alexandra Hildebrandt. Neither the German-Russian Museum nor the Allied Museum refer to collaborative projects with the Wall Museum that ignored any requests for an interview.

40 Both the original of the replicated old checkpoint booth of the 1960s and the later checkpoint barrack are shown in the Allied Museum.

41 See Sybille Frank "Der Mauer um die Wette gedenken," *Aus Politik und Zeitgeschichte 61, 31–34.* (2011): 47–54, especially 51.

and moral arguments, she obviously had a strong economic motive. The tourists might save the steep admission to the museum by listening to the explanations of the students concerning the history of Checkpoint Charlie. The conflict was therefore mainly about the monopoly to sell history at this famous site to an ever growing number of international visitors. Most tourists did probably not even realize the conflict. They continuously come in large numbers to see an exciting ensemble of Cold War iconography.

In October 2004 Alexandra Hildebrandt created her own private wall memorial. Right opposite her museum she rented a vacant lot on the very site of the former Checkpoint Charlie. There she erected a 600-foot long replica of the Berlin Wall as well as 1,065 wooden crosses that were meant to symbolize the victims of the deadly GDR border regime. Her emotional installation attracted many people, but several historians and politicians harshly criticized the private memorial– mostly for its missing authenticity.[42] In the end Alexandra Hildebrandt had to give up the memorial, although she had refused to withdraw from the estate that she had rented only temporarily. The crosses were dismantled under extensive media coverage. However, her initiative sparked increased attention to the city's responsibility for commemorating the Berlin Wall. It served as a catalyst for the Berlin Senate's new commemoration concept.[43] Since Hildebrandt's number of wall victims proved to be highly exaggerated,[44] the city appointed an expert commission to investigate the actual number of people who died at the Berlin Wall. This resulted in a widely appreciated handbook that reconstructs and commemorates the biographies of 136 wall victims.[45]

Plans for a Cold War Museum

Cold War memory in Berlin is part of the general memory boom that has shaped most Western societies since the 1970s and 1980s.[46] In a period of limited eco-

42 Ibid.

43 For Berlin's official commemoration concept (Gedenkstättenkonzept) regarding the Berlin Wall see Klemke, *Das Gesamtkonzept Berliner Mauer*, 377–394.

44 See Arbeitsgemeinschaft 13. August (ed.): Neue Zahl der Todesopfer des DDR-Grenzregimes – keine Endbilanz. Berlin 2004.

45 See the English translation of the book: Hans-Hermann Hertle and Maria Nooke, *The Victims at the Berlin Wall 1961–1989: A Biographical Handbook* (Berlin: Christoph Links Verlag, 2011).

46 See Paul Nolte, Öffentliche Geschichte. Die neue Nähe von Fachwissenschaft, Massenmedien und Publikum: Ursachen, Chancen und Grenzen, in: Michele Barricelli and Julia Hornig (eds.),

nomic growth and fading believe in the future,[47] people developed a new interest in history. New museums, television programs and historical magazines started to offer a wide scope of public history. This did not only serve a new, albeit traditional source of identity and legitimacy "after the boom,[48] but it also developed a new awareness regarding the difficult past and its victims. In West Germany the Nazi past and the Holocaust earned an unprecedented attention in the public sphere. Memory and coming to terms with the past (Aufarbeitung) became two key concepts that subsequently led to many history projects and new memorial sites in Berlin and elsewhere in Germany.[49]

While the memory regarding the Nazi past ultimately developed a broad consensus in Germany, the memory of the GDR after its demise in 1989/90 is still heavily debated.[50] Neo-totalitarian approaches that emphasize the repressive character of the Communist dictatorship compete with a widespread nostalgia of the everyday life in the GDR.[51] Western notions of Eastern history clash with East German memories of their own past, which are highly disputed among Easterners as well. This multifaceted conflict of memories also affects the understanding of the Cold War, since the history of postwar Germany is part of the larger context determined by the global confrontation between East and West. To be sure, Cold War memories are also subject to debate in other countries.[52] But the memory of divided Germany and its divided capital is a peculiar case.

Aufklärung, Bildung, "Histotainment"? Zeitgeschichte in Unterricht und Gesellschaft heute (Frankfurt am Main: Peter Lang, 2008) 131–146.

47 See Konrad H. Jarausch (ed.), *Das Ende der Zuversicht? Die siebziger Jahre als Geschichte* (Göttingen: Vandenhoeck & Ruprecht, 2008).

48 Anselm Doering-Manteuffel/Lutz Raphael, *Nach dem Boom. Perspektiven auf die Zeitgeschichte seit 1970* (Göttingen: Vandenhoeck & Ruprecht, 2008).

49 See Martin Sabrow, The Post-heroic Memory Society. Models of Historical Narration in the Present, in: Muriel Blaive, Christian Gerbel and Thomas Lindenberger (eds.), *Clashes in European Memory. The Case of Communist Repression and the Holocaust* (Innsbruck: StudienVerlag, 2011), 88–98.

50 See Martin Sabrow, Das Unbehagen an der Aufarbeitung. Zur Engführung von Wissenschaft, Moral und Politik in der Zeitgeschichte, in: Thomas Schaarschmidt (ed.), *Historisches Erinnern und Gedenken im Übergang vom 20. zum 21. Jahrhundert* (Frankfurt am Main: Peter Lang, 2008) 11–20.

51 For the East German memory phenomenon of the so called "Ostalgie" (that leaves out the first letter "N" from the word "Nostalgie" so that it refers to the German word "Ost" for East) see Thomas Ahbe, "Ostalgie" als eine Laien-Praxis in Ostdeutschland: Ursachen, psychische und politische Dimensionen, in: Heiner Timmermann (ed.), *Die DDR in Deutschland: Ein Rückblick auf 50 Jahre* (Berlin: Duncker & Humblot Verlag, 2001), 781–802.

52 For a number of case studies regarding the Cold War memory in the former Eastern block see Muriel Blaive, Christian Gerbel and Thomas Lindenberger (eds.), *Clashes in European Memory. The Case of Communist Repression and the Holocaust* (Innsbruck: StudienVerlag, 2011).

Cold War memory in Berlin therefore remains fragmented and incomplete: The German-Russian Museum reflects on the causes of the Cold War, but pays very little attention to the time after 1945. The Allied Museum, on the other hand, focuses on the postwar era, but leaves the Russians out of the story. "Rather than being balanced counterparts, the Museums in Zehlendorf and Karlshorst are instead dramatic symbols of contrasting and divided memory," argues Dirk Verheyen.[53] He stresses an unmistakable tendency towards a split legacy and memory regarding the Cold War in contemporary Berlin.[54] While both institutions have to follow their specific founding charters that limit their scope to one side only, they have nevertheless advanced a lot since then. In both cases a new management has already broadened the perspectives on the Cold War. Funded by the Bundesbeaufragte für Kultur und Medien (BKM) of the Federal Government both the German-Russian Museum and the Allied Museum are of national importance and play a central role in the commemoration of contemporary German history. However, they do so on the periphery of the city: The German-Russian Museum is firmly bound to the authentic site of the German surrender in Karlshorst; and even if the Allied Museum moves closer to the center to Tempelhof Airport, it will only be able to tell one part of the story.

The most problematic aspect of Cold War memorialization in Berlin is the chaotic heritage display at Checkpoint Charlie and the partisanship of the Wall Museum. In spite of its sausage stands and uniform vendors, the former border crossing point remains one of the prime tourist sites of the German capital, attracting several million visitors a year, many of whom do not care that most of what they can see there is fake. They consider authentic what meets their expectations. Hence, many tourists take the replica of the Checkpoint Charlie control booth for real. It matches their pre-existing assumptions about the famous site, which are shaped by historical pictures of the checkpoint.[55] Moreover, local, national and international visitors can hardly begin to understand the dynamics of Cold War confrontation at Checkpoint Charlie. The Wall Museum is fiercely dedicated to the Cold War, but it is still stuck in fighting the past conflict. The information one can find in the museum is out-dated and incomplete.

The realization of this deficit has inspired public and academic discussion regarding the need for improvements of the Checkpoint Charlie site. Aided by the

---

53 Verheyen, *United City*, 108.

54 Ibid., 105.

55 See Hanno Hochmuth, "His Tourismus, Public History und Berlin-Tourismus," in *Vergangenheitsbewirtschaftung. Public History zwischen Wirtschaft und Wissenschaft*, eds. Christoph Kühberger and Andreas Pudlat (Innsbruck: StudienVerlag, 2012), 173–182.

Zentrum für Zeithistorische Forschung Potsdam (ZZF), a commission of historians has designed a series of billboards on a construction fence that surrounds the vacant lots of the historic site and presents more reliable information and archival images about the history of Checkpoint Charlie. This Checkpoint Gallery displays graphic pictures from Cold War crises as well as a commentary that seeks to connect the local events with the global East-West confrontation between communism and democracy, spearheaded by the Soviet and American superpowers. Since it is out in the open and free of charge, this exhibition has attracted much attention from visitors, with international tourists connecting their own experiences to the Berlin crises and grandparents explaining to their grandchildren what it felt like to live in a divided city or country and to fear nuclear war.[56]

The Checkpoint Gallery was the first visible step in a plan to establish a new public museum right across from the private Wall Museum.[57] The proposal originated in discussions between the SPD politician Markus Meckel, the historian Konrad H. Jarausch and the deputy director of Germany's national history museum (DHM) Dieter Vorsteher during the public hearings for the Master Plan to commemorate the Wall in 2006. It was carried forward by a group of interested scholars and laymen under the aegis of Rainer Klemke, the Berlin official in charge of museums. International experts such as the director of the Cold War International History Project Christian Ostermann and decision makers like the former US Secretary of State James Baker have endorsed this idea. As discussed in several conferences, the new Cold War Museum intends to explain the conflict by telling an entangled, interactive history. The commission responsible for the project favors a 'glocal' approach that both reflects on Berlin as an outstanding center of the Cold War and on the European and global dimension of the conflict.[58] This wider international scope finds only little attention in the existing memory sites and museums in Berlin. Hence, the planned museum can also be interpreted as a reaction to the deficits in Berlin's current memory landscape in general.

Though the implementation of this plan has proven difficult for financial and political reasons, a temporal exhibition opened on the site of the planned Cold

---

56 See the essay by Hope Harrison in this volume.

57 The location of the planned museum has been sold to a new investor. The museum will presumingly occupy one floor of the planned building. To this day, however, it remains unclear when it will be completed.

58 See Konrad H. Jarausch, "Die Teilung Europas und ihre Überwindung. Überlegungen zu einem Ausstellungskonzept für Berlin," in *Zeithistorische Forschungen/Studies in Contemporary History, Online Edition, 5* (2008) H. 2, URL: http://www.zeithistorische-forschungen.de/16126041-Jarausch-2-2008.

War Museum to promote the idea in the summer of 2012. This so-called *Black-Box Cold War*[59] illustrates how a new institution could complement and connect the German-Russian Museum and the Allied Museum.[60] The planned Cold War Museum's focus on the global dimension of the Cold War could help to contextualize the conflict and decenter the ideological hostilities connected to it. This universalizing approach, however, is exactly what has evoked opposition. Christian-conservative politicians fear equidistance and object to an exhibition that would represent the Western and the Eastern side in a less emotional and more balanced way. The supporters of the new museum have to overcome a deeply rooted anti-Communist mentality in the former *Frontstadt* West Berlin.

The memory politics of the Cold War must therefore take into account that Berlin's existing landscape of memory is a patchwork of multiple historical layers and contested legacies. Most of the described memory sites and museums in Berlin reach back to the Cold War era themselves. It seems inevitable that they still carry some of its emotion as well as ideological bias. In terms of its commemoration, the Cold War is thus not over yet in Berlin.

---

59 See the exhibition's website: http://www.bfgg.de/en/centre-of-cold-war/blackbox-cold-war.html, last accessed on December 5, 2016.

60 See Jula Danylow, BlackBox Kalter Krieg. Ein Werkstattbesuch am Checkpoint Charlie, in: *Zeithistorische Forschungen/Studies in Contemporary History, Online Edition*, 11 (2014) H. 2, URL: http://www.zeithistorische-forschungen.de/2-2014/id=5110.

Select Bibliography

"A Round Table Discussion on the State of Cold War Studies," in: *Amerikanskii Ezhegodnik (The American Yearbook)* (Moscow: Nauka Publishing House, 2014)

Ammert, Niklas and Heather Sharp. "Working with the Cold War: Types of Knowledge in Swedish and Australian History Textbook Activities," in: *Journal of Educational Media, Memory, and Society,* 8.2 (2016), 58–82

Ashley, Susan and Sybille Frank eds. "Heritage-Outside-In." *Special Issue of the International Journal of Heritage Studies,* 22.7 (2016)

Blaive, Muriel, and Berthold Molden, *Grenzfälle: Österreichische und tschechische Erfahrungen am Eisernen Vorhang* (Weitra: Bibliothek der Provinz, 2009)

Bleton, Paul. *La Cristallisation de l'ombre. Les origines oubliées du roman d'espionnage sous la IIIe République* (PULIM: Limoges, 2011)

Bleton, Paul. *Les Anges de Machiavel. Essai sur l'espionnage* (Québec: Nuit blanche éditeur, 1994)

Classen, Christoph. "Captive Audience? GDR Radio in the Mirror of Listeners' Mail," in: *Cold War History* 13.2 (2013), 239–254

Classen, Christoph and Wulf Kansteiner eds. "Historical Representation and Historical Truth." *Special Issue of History & Theory* 47 (2009)

Classen, Christoph ed. "Transnational Broadcasting in Europe 1945–1990." *Spiel, Neue Folge. Eine Zeitschrift für Medienkultur* 2.1 (2016)

Cocroft, Wayne D. and Roger J.C. Thomas. *Cold War Building for Nuclear Confrontation 1946–1989* (Swindon: English Heritage, 2003)

Corner, Paul ed. *Popular Opinion in Totalitarian Regimes: Fascism, Nazism, Communism* (Oxford: Oxford University Press, 2009)

Egorova, Natalya and Alexander Chubaryan eds. *Kholodnaya Voina, 1945–1963: Istoricheskaya Perspektiva* (Moscow: Olma Press, 2003)

Frank, Sybille. *Wall Memorials and Heritage: The Heritage Industry of Berlin's Checkpoint Charlie* (London/New York: Routledge, 2016)

Frank, Sybille and Lars Meier eds. "(Im)Mobilities of Dwelling. Places and Practices." *Special Issue of Cultural Studies* 30.3 (2016)

Goedde, Petra and Richard Immerman eds. *The Oxford Handbook of the Cold War* (Oxford: Oxford University Press, 2013)

Hagopian, Patrick. *The Vietnam War in American Memory: Veterans, Memorials, and the Politics of Healing* (Amherst: University of Massachusetts Press, 2011)

Harrison, Hope M. *Driving the Soviets Up the Wall: Soviet-East German Relations, 1953–1961* (Princeton, NJ: Princeton University Press, 2003)

Hass, Kristin Ann. *Sacrificing Soldiers on the National Mall* (Berkeley: University of California Press, 2013)

Hertle, Hans-Hermann and Maria Nooke, eds. *The Victims at the Berlin Wall, 1961–1989: A Biographical Handbook* (Berlin: Ch. Links, 2011)

Hochmuth, Hanno. HisTourismus, "Public History und Berlin-Tourismus," in: *Vergangenheits-bewirtschaftung: Public History zwischen Wirtschaft und Wissenschaft*, edited by Christoph Kühberger and Andreas Pudlat (Innsbruck, 2012), 173–182

Hochmuth, Hanno, Stefanie Eisenhuth und Martin Sabrow, "West Berlin," *Special Issue of Zeithistorische Forschungen/Studies in Contemporary History* 11.2 (2014).

DOI 10.1515/9783110496178-015

Hue-Tam Ho Tai. *The Country of Memory: Remaking the Past in Late Socialist Vietnam* (Berkeley: University of California Press, 2001)

Jacobmeyer, Wolfgang ed. *Deutschlandbild und deutsche Frage in den historischen, geographischen und sozialwissenschaftlichen Unterrichtswerken der Bundesrepublik Deutschland und der Deutschen Demokratischen Republik von 1949 bis in die 80er Jahre* (Braunschweig: Georg Eckert Institut für internationale Schulbuchforschung, 1986)

Laderman, Scott. *Tours of Vietnam: War, Travel Guides, and Memory* (Durham: Duke University Press, 2009)

Laderman, Scott and Edwin A. Martini. *Four Decades On: Vietnam, the United States, and the Legacies of the Second Indochina War* (Durham: Duke University Press, 2013)

Leffer, Melvyn P. and Odd Arne Westad, eds. *The Cambridge History of the Cold War*, 3 vols. (Cambridge: Cambridge University Press, 2010)

Lowe, David and Tony Joel. *Remembering the Cold War: Global Contest and National Stories* (London: Routledge, 2013)

Mackenzie, Angus. *Secrets: The CIA's War at Home* (Berkeley: The University of California Press, 1997)

Major, Patrick and Rana Mitter eds. *Across the Blocs: Cold War Cultural and Social History*, (London: Frank Cass, 2004)

Prados, John. *The Lost Crusader: The Secret Wars of CIA Director William Colby* (New York: Oxford University Press, 2003)

Reynolds, David ed. *The Origins of the Cold War in Europe: International Perspectives* (New Haven: Yale University Press, 1994)

Schwenkel, Christina. *The American War in Contemporary Vietnam: Transnational Remembrance and Representation* (Bloomington: Indiana University Press, 2009)

Schofield, John A. and Wayne D. Cocroft. *A Fearsome Heritage: Diverse Legacies of the Cold War* (California: Left Coast Press, 2007)

Snepp, Frank. *Irreparable Harm: A Firsthand Account of How One Agent Took on the CIA in an Epic Battle over Free Speech* (Lawrence: University Press of Kansas, 1999)

Stenak, Morten, Thomas Tram Pedersen, Peer Henrik Hansen, and Martin Jespersen. *Kold Krig* (Denmark: Copenhagen: 2013)

Weichlein, Siegfried. "Katholizismus und Antikommunismus," in: *Der Antikommunismus in seiner Epoche. Weltanschauung, Bewegung, regierende Partei*, edited by Dominik Rigoll (Jena, 2016)

Weichlein, Siegfried. "Forum on Surveillance in German History," in: *German History* 34.2 (2016), 293–314

Zubok, Vladislav and Vladimir Pechatnov. "Otechestvennaya Istoriographia Kholodnoi Voiny: Nekotorye Itogy Pervogo Desyatiletya," in: *Otechestvennaya Istoria*, no. 4–5 (2003)

Name Index

About the Authors

Muriel Blaive is currently Advisor to the Director for Research and Methodology at the Institute for the Study of Totalitarian Regimes in Prague. She is a socio-political historian of postwar, communist, and post-communist Central Europe, in particular of Czechoslovakia and the Czech Republic. She graduated from the Institut d'études politiques in Paris and wrote her Ph.D. in history at EHESS in Paris. Among her publications are "Komárno, the Flagship of Symbolic Politics at the Slovak-Hungarian Border," *Revue d'études comparatives Est-Ouest*, 44.4 (2013) (with Libora Oates-Indruchová), and "Discussing the Merits of Microhistory as a Comparative Tool: The Cases of České Velenice and Komárno," *East Central Europe* 40.1-2 (2013). She also co-edited the volume *Clashes in European Memory: The Case of the Communist Repression and the Holocaust* (2011), with Christian Gerbel and Thomas Lindenberger.

Paul Bleton has been professor at TELUQ University (Montréal) for more than 30 years. He published around 20 handbooks and has been conceiving courses in e-learning. He authored essays on reading, on French conception of the American Wild West, and many articles on French pop lit. He co-authored essays, on African war fictions, and on Louis Hémon.

Christoph Classen studied history, German Studies and media studies at Hamburg University and holds a Ph.D. in contemporary history from Freie Universität Berlin. Currently he is a senior researcher at the "Department for the History of the Modern Media and Information Society" at the Centre for Contemporary History Potsdam. He is an editor for media history and contemporary history of "H-Soz-Kult," as well as "Zeitgeschichte-online," and a member of the editorial board of "VIEW – Journal of European Television History and Culture." His main areas of research are the history of media, cultures of remembrance, and political cultures.

Wayne Cocroft is an archaeologist and Manager of Historic England's Investigation East team. For over 20 years he has specialized in the archaeological recording and assessment of redundant military sites. He is co-author of *Cold War Building for Nuclear Confrontation 1946-1989* (2003) and recently *Der Teufelsberg in Berlin: Eine archäologische Bestandsaufnahme des westlichen Horchpostens im Kalten Krieg* (2016). He is a Fellow of the Society of Antiquaries of London.

Jennifer Dickey is an associate professor and the coordinator of the Public History Program at Kennesaw State University in Kennesaw, Georgia. She has a master's degree in heritage preservation and a Ph.D. in public history from Georgia State University. She is the author of *A Tough Little Patch of History: Gone with the Wind and the Politics of Memory*, co-editor of *Museums in a Global Context: National Identity, International Understanding*, and co-author of *Memories of the Mansion: The Story of Georgia's Governor's Mansion*.

Andreas Etges is senior lecturer in American history at the Amerika-Institut of the University of Munich with a special focus on American foreign relations and the history of the Cold War. He has curated several historical exhibits on John F. Kennedy and is involved in setting up an international museum of the Cold War at Checkpoint Charlie in Berlin. Among his publications are "Western Europe," in: *Oxford Handbook of the Cold War* (2013), and "Krieg in Europa im amerikanischen Film," in: *Geschichte ohne Grenzen? Europäische Dimensionen der Militärgeschichte vom 19. Jahrhundert bis heute* (2016), edited by Jörg Echternkamp and Hans-Hubertus

Mack. He is a member of both the steering committee of the International Federation for Public History and the German working group on public history.

Sybille Frank is Professor for Urban Sociology and the Sociology of Space at the Department of Sociology, Technical University Darmstadt. She holds a Ph.D. in sociology from the same university. She was a Visiting Scholar at the Berlin Social Science Center (WZB), the Priority Research Area Critical Heritage Studies at Göteborg's Universitet, the Alfred Deakin Institute for Citizenship and Globalisation in Melbourne, and the Centre for African Studies at the University of Cape Town. In 2016, she was La Sapienza Visiting Professor for Research Activities at Università di Roma La Sapienza as well as City of Vienna Visiting Professor for Urban Culture and Public Space at Technical University Vienna. Her work focuses on urban sociology, on the sociology of space and place, and on tourism and heritage studies.

Hope M. Harrison is Associate Professor of History and International Affairs at the Elliott School at George Washington University. She has published on the Cold War, the Berlin Wall, and German historical memory. Her prize-winning first book, *Driving the Soviets Up the Wall,* made extensive use of German and Russian archives to tell the story of the decision to build the Berlin Wall. Her next book, forthcoming with Cambridge University Press, examines German historical memory of the Berlin Wall since 1989. She has held research fellowships in Germany, Russia, the US and Norway.

Hanno Hochmuth is research fellow and executive manager at the Zentrum für Zeithistorische Forschung/Centre for Contemporary History (ZZF) in Potsdam. He studied history, theater studies, and communications at Freie Universität Berlin, Humboldt-Universität zu Berlin and at the University of Minnesota. From 2005 to 2011 he was a research fellow at Freie Universität Berlin, where he implemented and managed Germany's first Public History Master's program and completed his Ph.D. on public and private spheres in East and West Berlin in 2016.

Konrad H. Jarausch is Lurcy Professor of European Civilization at the University of North Carolina in Chapel Hill and Senior Fellow of the Zentrum für Zeithistorische Forschung in Potsdam. He founded the Center for European Studies at UNC and was director of the ZZF. He has written or edited about forty books on German and European history of the 19th and 20th century. His last publication was *Out of Ashes: A New History of Europe in the Twentieth Century* (2015), which was awarded the Bronislaw Geremek prize.

Christopher Moran is an Associate Professor of US National Security in the Department of Politics and International Studies at the University of Warwick. He is the author of *Classified: Secrecy and the State in Modern Britain (*2013), which won the 2014 St. Ermin's Hotel Intelligence Book of the Year Award, and more recently *Company Confessions: Secrets, Memoirs and the CIA* (2016). He is a Fellow of the Royal Historical Society and has held fellowships from the British Academy, the Library of Congress, and the Rothermere American Institute at the University of Oxford.

Christian F. Ostermann is Director of the History and Public Policy Program at the Woodrow Wilson International Center for Scholars in Washington, D.C., and in that capacity oversees the work of the Cold War International History Project (CWIHP) and the North Korea International Documentation Project. He also co-directs (with Leopoldo Nuti) the Nuclear Proliferation International History Project (NPIHP) and is co-editor of Cold War History. His most recent publications include *"Trust, but Verify." The Politics of Uncertainty & the Transformation of the Cold War Order, 1969-1991*, ed. with Martin Klimke and Reinhild Kreis (2016); "The Global Cold War: Using the Resources of the Cold War International History Project," in: Understanding and Teaching the Cold War (2016), ed. by Matt Masur; "Extended Deterrence in Europe and East Asia during the Cold War - A Reappraisal," Special Issue of the *Journal of Strategic Studies* 39:4 (2016), ed. with Leopoldo Nuti; *Sino-European Relations during the Cold War and the Rise of the Multipolar World: A Critical Oral History* (2015), ed. with Enrico Fardella and Charles Kraus.

Vladimir O. Pechatnov is Professor and Chair of European and American Studies at the Moscow State Institute of International Relations (MGIMO). His numerous publications include *Stalin, Roosevelt, Truman: The Soviet Union and the United States in the 1940s"(in Russian* (2006), "Soviet-American Relations through the Cold War," in: Oxford Handbook of the Cold War (2013), and *Stalin's Correspondence with Roosevelt and Churchill during the Great Patriotic War. A Documentary Investigation* (vol. 1-2, in Russian, 2015).

Falk Pingel is Associated Research Fellow of the Georg Eckert Institute for International Textbook Research in Braunschweig/Germany. For many years he was the institute's deputy director. Since his retirement in 2009, he has been a consultant on issues of textbook and curriculum research and revision to governmental and academic institutions as well as to international organizations.

David Reynolds is Professor of International History at Cambridge University and a Fellow of the British Academy. He is the author of eleven books on aspects of 20th-century history and has written and presented thirteen documentaries for BBC TV. His most recent works include *The Long Shadow: The Great War and the 20th Century* (2013) and, as co-editor, *Transcending the Cold War: Summits: Statecraft, and the Dissolution of Bipolarity in Europe, 1970-1990* (2016).

Siegfried Weichlein is Professor for Contemporary European History at the University of Fribourg (Switzerland). He directs a project on *The Cold War as Political Imagination* funded by the Swiss National Science Foundation (SNF). The project is interdisciplinary and includes history, literary studies, media studies and cultural analysis.